THE
SELECT WORKS
OF
THOMAS
CASE
(1598-1682)

**SOMETIME STUDENT OF
CHRIST CHURCH, OXFORD,
PREACHER OF THE GOSPEL,
AND A MEMBER OF
THE WESTMINSTER ASSEMBLY**

Soli Deo Gloria Publications
...for instruction in righteousness...

Soli Deo Gloria Publications
213 W. Vincent Street, Ligonier, PA 15658-1139
(412) 238-7741/FAX (412) 238-3002

*

The Select Works of Thomas Case
is comprised of two of Case's works:

"Correction, Instruction, or
A Treatise of Afflictions,"

and

"Mount Pisgah, or
A Prospect of Heaven, being
an Exposition of 1 Thess. IV.13-18"

Both reprinted by
the Religious Tract Society,
London, 1836.

This Soli Deo Gloria reprint is 1993.

*

ISBN 1-877611-58-1

CONTENTS OF
A TREATISE OF AFFLICTIONS

CONTENTS OF
A PROSPECT OF HEAVEN

CORRECTION, INSTRUCTION;

or

A TREATISE OF AFFLICTIONS

FIRST CONCEIVED

BY WAY OF PRIVATE MEDITATIONS;

AFTERWARD

DIGESTED INTO CERTAIN SERMONS, AND NOW PUBLISHED FOR THE HELP AND COMFORT OF HUMBLE SUFFERING CHRISTIANS.

BY THOMAS CASE, M.A.

SOMETIME STUDENT OF CHRIST CHURCH, OXFORD. PREACHER OF THE GOSPEL IN LONDON, A.D. 1652

Though He slay me, yet will I trust in Him, **Job 13:15**

MY REVEREND FRIEND,

MR. THOMAS CASE,

MINISTER OF THE GOSPEL, &c.

SIR,

I THANK you for the favour you did me in affording me a sight of your papers; I had heard much of your notions concerning afflictions, and therefore was very thirsty till you were pleased to give me to drink of the fountain: I can now say as that queen, "The half was not told me," 1 Kings x. 7. fame came much short of taste: we are perfect in no lessons so much as those into which God whippeth us; and cannot speak of any argument so warmly and feelingly, as when we speak out of present experience. To treat of afflictions when we ourselves flourish and abound in ease and plenty, savoureth more of the orator than the preacher, the brain than the heart: certainly guess and imagination cannot so well introduce such conceptions as sense and feeling.

It seemeth when you went into prison the Spirit of God went into prison with you; and when you were shut up to others, you still lay open to the visits and free breathings of his grace: the restraints and enclosures of a prison cannot prejudice the freedom of his operations. He is a close prisoner indeed that is shut up not only from the society of men, but converse with the Holy Ghost. I begin to see there is somewhat more than a strain and reach of wit in Tertullian's consolatory discourse to

A 2

the Martyrs : " You went out of prison," saith he, " when you went into it, and were but sequestered from the world, that you might converse with God ; the greatest prisoners and the most guilty are those that are at large, darkened with ignorance, chained with lusts, committed not by the proconsul, but God," &c. The Lord often manifested himself to his prophets in a wilderness, and to you in your secession and retirement.

Sir, I could even envy your prison comforts, and the sweet opportunities of a religious privacy. We that are abroad are harassed and worn out with constant public labours, and can seldom retire from the distraction of business for such free converse with God and our own souls : but we are not to choose our own portion ; crosses will come soon enough without wishing for them ; and if we were wise we might make an advantage of every condition.

Good sir, be persuaded to publish those discourses ; the subject is useful, and your manner of handling it warm and affectionate ; do not deprive the world of the comfort of your experiences. Certainly my heart is none of the tenderest; yet if heart answereth heart, I can easily foresee much success, and that you will not repent of the publication. The Lord bless your endeavours in the gospel of his dear Son.

I am, sir,

Yours in all christian observance,

THOMAS MANTON.

EXTRACT

FROM THE

EPISTLE TO THE READER.

PUBLISHED WITH THE SECOND EDITION.

A. D. 1671.

READER,—This brief discourse before thee is an epistle in itself, not mine but God's, containing matter of counsel and comfort, to the generation of his sufferers. It was written not many years ago, and yet it wanteth a new impression, the chief account whereof may be that which the apostle giveth in a like case, "You have forgotten the exhortation which speaketh unto you as unto children," &c. Heb. xii. 5. Truly there is the reason of all our non-proficiency under Divine teaching. We forget the doctrine before we come to the use: by means whereof, we are as great strangers to the cross, when we come to suffer, as if we had never heard of it; and thereby it cometh to pass that we do either despise the chastisement of the Lord, or else faint when we are rebuked of him. If the affliction be in measure, as the scripture phrase is, Isa. xxvii. 8. we are apt to despise it, as not worth taking notice of: but if the rod fetch blood, presently it is intolerable, and we begin to faint, crying out in our passion, Was ever sorrow like my sorrow? as if we could have borne any burden but that upon the back.

It is very sad to observe, suffering, persecution especially, hath got an ill name in the world. The devil and a reprobate world have brought up a scandal upon the cross, whilst sufferings immediately from God are interpreted as the fruits and evidences of God's hatred; to obviate which discouragement the apostle spends the twelve first verses of Heb. xii. by many irrefragable arguments, the main whereof is the instance of all instances, the unparalleled sufferings of the Son of God, to establish this conclusion, as a cordial to keep the hearts of all the suffering saints of God from fainting; namely, that God's rod and God's love may stand together.

Sufferings likewise from men, persecution, as for the gospel's sake, are accounted no better than the stigmata of malefactors, marks of sedition and rebellion against civil government: upon which the ignorant malicious multitude begin to cry out against them, as the heathen of old, Away with these christians, cast them into the lion's den;

Providence having so ordered it, that whosoever with Caleb, will follow the Lord fully, Num. xiv. 24. shall be exposed to the world's hatred; and not their persons only but their sufferings, be laden with the basest obloquies that the wit of malice can invent. They are reputed as:

The troublers of Israel,

The pests of human societies,

Persons not fit to live in the world, &c.

And verily the world speak as truly of them as they speak vilely; their censures did not exceed the bounds of justice; but the *cause* makes the martyr, not the *punishment.*

This duty considered, it is, not less than to wonder, observable with what titles of honour the Spirit of God in holy scriptures is pleased to dignify the sufferings of the saints, when, I say, they suffer, as christians, that is to say—

For righteousness' sake, Matt. v. 10. 1 Pet. iii. 14.

For the name of Christ, 1 Pet. iv. 14.

Not because they have sinned, but because they will not sin, Psa. xliv. 22. 1 Pet. iv. 4, 5.

When for the kingdom of God, 2 Thess. i. 5.

When they suffer that the truth of the gospel may not suffer, Gal. ii. 5.

In these cases and the like, the sufferings of the saints, however they may be ignominiously traduced, 1 Pet. iv. 14. by men that are not competent judges either of the saints or of the sufferings, 1 Cor. ii. 15.

yet they are most honourably attested by the un-
erring witness of the Holy Ghost ; they are called:
  Christians' letters testimonial for heaven, Matt.v.10.

  The gift of God, Phil. i. 29.   Answerable to that
account which our Lord had of his own sufferings,
John xviii. 11.   "The cup which my Father hath
given me, shall I not drink it?"

  The appearance of the glorious Spirit resting
upon them, 1 Pet. iv. 14.

  Their baptism for, and consecration to their
heavenly inheritance, Mark x. 38, 39.

  The after sufferings of Jesus Christ, without
which Christ's sufferings, as a body, are not complete; though, as a Mediator, they were perfect
upon the cross at what time he cried out, "It is
finished."

  Their evangelical perfection, James i. 4 ; and no
wonder, for sufferings were Christ's perfection, Heb.
ii. 10.

  A refining pot for their faith, 1 Pet. i. 7.

  The improvement of their graces, 1 Pet. i. 6, 7.

  The enhancement of their glory, 2 Cor. iv. 17.

  Their conformity to Christ their Head, 2 Tim. ii.
11, 12.

  In a word, glorious things are spoken of sufferers
and their sufferings, for the testimony of Jesus.

  For the reviving whereof upon the heads and
hearts of all Christ's confessors and martyrs, it hath
been earnestly begged by some that wish well to

the interest of the gospel, that these prison notions might be reprinted.

The Lord give them, indeed, a new impression, that they may be known to be "the epistle of Christ ministered by us, written not with ink, but with the Spirit of the living God ; not in tables of stone, but in fleshy tables of the heart," 2 Cor. iii. 3.

Surely discourses of affliction can never be unseasonable. The scripture tells us, that " many are the sufferings of the righteous," Psa. xxxiv. 19 ; and daily experience verifieth it : God chasteneth them, because they are no better, the devil and the reprobate world hate them, because they are so good. The evil spirit stirreth up his instruments to vex and molest the saints, that he may make an advantage of their troubles, one way or other, to hinder the course of the gospel. Most of his assaults are conveyed to us by afflictions : therefore when we are bidden to resist the devil, stedfast in the faith, we are told immediately, that the "same afflictions are accomplished in our brethren that are in the world," 1 Pet. v. 9.

Possibly an hour of temptation may be nearer to us than we are willing to believe.

Let us not begin to flatter ourselves with the vain confidence that God will not punish his people by those that are worse than themselves, Hab. i. 13. England hath sinned at that rate, that God may justify himself in the severe execution of that bitter reproach once threatened against a people, altogether as good as ourselves; "I will bring the worst of the heathen, and they shall possess your houses," Ezek. vii. 24.

For the preventing of so shameful a destruction, (if yet by Divine prerogative it may be prevented,) let us take the course of God's own prescribing, by sound repentance and solemn reconciliation, to prepare to meet our God, and lay hold of his strength that we make peace with him, Isa. xxvii. 5. Let us do this; and then, if judgment come, judgment itself can do us no harm: but otherwise, if mercy come, even mercy itself can do us no good. The Lord teach us, in this our day, to know the things of our peace, before they be hid from our eyes.

TO THE READER.

READER, thou hast here in these following leaves some prison-thoughts—I wish I could say experiences. If I have not written herein what I have found, I bless God, I have written what I have sought. I must humbly confess with holy Paul, "I count not myself to have apprehended;" yet through grace I can add with that blessed saint, ".but this one thing I do, forgetting those things which are behind, and reaching forth unto those things which are before, I press towards the mark," Phil. iii. 13, 14. God hath taught me somewhat of the doctrine, if he would please to teach me the use; God hath in some measure showed me what is to be gained by afflictions, if he would also teach me how to gain it, I should with Moses, account my sufferings " greater riches than the treasures of Egypt," Heb. xi. 26. The discovery is sweet; if my heart deceive me not, I would not exchange it for the wealth of both the Indies; the possession infinitely precious. For thy advantage I have been persuaded to print. My prayers shall accompany my papers, that that God, who quickeneth the dead, and calleth things that are not as though they were, would please to make these broken expressions answer the aim; and for the aim's sake despise them not, but pray thou also : and when thou prayest, remember the chiefest of sinners, the poor and unworthy author, who, whilst yet in the land of the living, will be thine, to serve thee, iu the gospel of Christ,

THOMAS CASE.

CORRECTION, INSTRUCTION.

THE ROD AND THE WORD.

PSALM XCIV. 12.

BLESSED IS THE MAN WHOM THOU CHASTENEST, O LORD, AND TEACHEST HIM OUT OF THY LAW.

THIS psalm being without a title, it is not so easily determined when, or by whom it was penned: probably by David, when himself, and the rest of the godly party, were under a sore and bitter persecution by Saul, and others of that bloody and hypocritical faction that bare sway under him.

Briefly, in the psalm the prophet doth these three things.

First. He doth appeal to God for vengeance on the persecutors; describing them by their pride, ver. 2. profaneness, ver. 3, 4. their intemperate virulency of speech, ver. 4. cruelty and bloody practices, ver. 5, 6. and, lastly, by their atheistical security, ver. 7.

Second. He turns to address the enemies, endeavouring to convince them of the brutishness and folly of their atheism, the mother and nurse of the other impieties charged on them, ver. 8. and that by a threefold argument.

1. The power and skill of God in creating the hearing and seeing organ in man, ver. 9.

B

2. The sovereignty of God, and the righteousness of his judgments, which he executes in the world, ver. 10. the former part.

3. His wisdom and knowledge, in enduing man with such an excellent intellectual faculty, whereby even the creature itself is able to attain to admirable degrees of knowledge, ver. 10, 11.

4. He labours to comfort the godly against all the pressures and persecutions under which they did groan and languish.

The first argument which the psalmist useth to this purpose is in the text, namely, the sweet fruit which is to be gathered from the bitter root of affliction ; the root indeed is bitter but the fruit is sweet, even Divine instruction, which therefore is no longer to be esteemed a punishment, but a blessing.

" Blessed is the man whom thou chastenest, O Lord, and teachest him out of thy law."

This being the subject I intend to insist upon, I shall without any more ado contract it into this doctrinal point of observation.

THAT MAN IS A BLESSED MAN, WHOSE CHAS-
TISEMENTS ARE JOINED WITH DIVINE TEACH-
INGS ; OR,

IT IS A BLESSED THING WHEN CORRECTION AND
INSTRUCTION GO TOGETHER.   THE ROD AND
THE WORD MAKE UP A COMPLETE BLESSING.

I shall take chastisements here in the utmost latitude, for all kinds and degrees of sufferings, whether from God, or man, or Satan ; whether sufferings for sin, or sufferings for righteousness' sake.   And for the doctrinal part of the point, I shall endeavour these four things.

I. To show you what those lessons are which God doth teach his people by his chastisements.

II. What the nature and properties of Divine teachings are.

III. In what tendency correction lieth in order unto these teachings; or, what use God doth make of affliction for the carrying on of the work of instruction in the hearts of his people.

IV. I shall lay down the grounds and demonstrations of the point; or, considerations to evince the happiness of that man whom God is pleased to teach by his corrections.

I begin with the lessons which God doth usually teach his people in a suffering condition. Amongst many which may fall within the experience of the suffering saints of God, I shall observe unto you twenty several lessons, which when I have presented at large, I shall then contract into three summary and comprehensive instructions, which will contain the substance of all.

1. The first lesson which God teacheth by affliction, is, compassion towards them which are in a suffering condition. Truly we are very prone to be insensible of our brethren's sufferings, when we ourselves are at ease in Zion: partly by reason of that sensuality which is in our natures, reigning in carnal men, and dwelling even in the regenerate themselves, whereby we let out our hearts so inordinately to the creature comforts which we possess, as to quench the tenderness and sense which we ought to have of the miseries and hardships of other men: partly out of the delicacy of self-love, which makes us unwilling to sour the relish of our own sweet fruitions with the bitter taste of strangers' afflictions: partly through sluggishness and torpor of spirit, which makes us unwilling to rise up from the bed of ease and pleasure to travail in the

inquiry of the state of our brethren either abroad or at home; so that, as the apostle saith in another case, we are willingly ignorant, and are not only strangers, but are content to be strangers to their miseries and calamities.

One way or other, even christians themselves, and such as are truly so called, are more or less guilty of the sin of the Gentiles; " without natural affection, unmerciful," Rom. i. 31. without bowels, without compassion.

Hence you may find, that it was one of the errands upon which God sent Israel into Egypt, that in the brick-kilns there their hard hearts might be softened and melted into compassion towards strangers and captives. Therefore when God had turned their captivity, that was one of the first lessons of which he puts them in mind, "Thou shalt not oppress a stranger;" there is the duty, which, though negatively expressed, yet, according to the rule of interpreting the commandments, doth include all the affirmative duties of mercy and compassion; and the motive follows, "for ye know the heart of a stranger." How came they to know it? " seeing ye were strangers in the land of Egypt." As if God had said, I knew thou hadst a heart of iron and bowels of brass within thee, incompassionate and cruel, and therefore, I sent you into Egypt, on purpose that by the cruelty of the Egyptians I might intender your hearts, and that by the experience of your own sufferings and miseries you might learn as long as you live to lay to heart the anguish and agonies of strangers and captives; that whensoever you see a stranger in your habitations, you may say, O here is a poor sojourner, an exile, I will surely have mercy upon him, and show him kindness, for

I myself have been a stranger and a bond-slave in Egypt; I know by experience what a fearful, trembling, bleeding heart he carrieth in his bosom, &c.

And upon this very account God still brings variety of afflictions and sorrows upon his own children; he suffereth them to be plundered, banished, imprisoned, reduced to great extremities, that by their own experience they may learn to draw out their souls to the hungry, and mercies towards such objects of pity; that they might say within themselves, I know the heart of this afflicted soul; I know what it is to be plundered, to be rich one day, and the very next day to be stript naked of all one's comforts and accommodations. I know what it is to hear poor hunger-starved children cry for bread, and there is none to give them. I know what it is to be banished from dearest relations, to be like arms and legs torn out of the body, and to lie bleeding in their separation. I know what it is to be cast into prison, to be locked up alone in the dark, with no other company but one's own fears and sorrows. I know what it is to receive the sentence of death in ourselves, &c. Shall not I pity, and pray, and pour out my soul over such as are bleeding and languishing under the like miseries? And this argument yet makes deeper impression, when a christian compares and measures his lighter burden of affliction with another's more grievous yoke, and reasons thus within himself; Imprisonment was grievous to me, and yet I enjoyed many comforts and accommodations, which others have not; I had a sweet chamber, and a soft bed, when some poor members of Jesus Christ, in the Spanish Inquisition, and the Turkish slavery, are cast into the dungeon, and sink, with Jeremiah, into the mire; their feet are hurt in the stocks, and the irons do enter into their soul; others lie bleeding and gasping upon the cold ground with their undressed wounds, exposed to all the injuries of hunger and nakedness in the open air. I saw the face of my christian friends, sometimes enjoyed refreshment in converse with dearest relations, while some of God's precious people are cast into dark and stinking prisons, and do not see the face of a christian, not of a man possibly in five, ten, or twenty years together, unless it be of their tormenters. I had fresh diet every day, not only for necessity but for delight, while other precious servants of God want their necessary bread, lie starving in the doleful places of their sorrowful restraint, and would be glad to eat the worst of food, even that which would be most loathsome to me. Oh shall not my bowels yearn, and my compassions be rolled within me, towards such objects of misery and compassion?

Truly, brethren, we see it daily in case of the stone, toothache, gout, and the like evils, how experience doth melt the heart into tears of sympathy and fellow-feeling, while strangers to such sufferings stand wondering at, and almost deriding the heart-breaking laments of poor wretches. Brethren, that you may not wonder at this, consider I beseech you what the apostle speaks of Christ himself; "It behoved him in all things to be made like unto his brethren, that he might be a merciful and faithful High Priest in things pertaining to God," Heb. ii. 17. And again, "We have not a High Priest which cannot be touched with the feeling of our infirmities, but was in all points tempted like as we are, yet without sin," Heb. iv. 15.

A man would say within himself, Why what need had the Lord Jesus to invest himself with a body of flesh that he might know the infirmities of our nature, since he was God, and knew all things? Nay, but, my brethren, it seems the knowledge which Christ had as God, was different from that knowledge which he had as man ; that which he had as God, was intuitive ; that which he had as man, was experimental : experimental knowledge of misery is the heart-affecting knowledge; and therefore Christ himself would intender his own heart, as Mediator, by his own sense and feeling. And if the Lord Jesus, who was mercy itself, would put himself into a suffering condition, that he might the more sweetly and affectionately act those mercies towards his suffering members, how much more do we, that by nature are incompassionate and cruel, need such practical teachings to work upon our own hearts ! Certainly we cannot gain so much sense of the saints' sufferings by the most artificial and skilful relation that the tongue of men or angels is able to express, no nor by all our scripture knowledge, yea though sanctified, as we do by one day's experience in the school of affliction, when God is pleased to be the school-master.

This is one end why God sends us thither, and the first lesson we learn by affliction—sympathy with, and compassion to our suffering brethren.

2. I come to the second lesson, and that is, by chastisements God doth teach us how to prize our outward mercies and comforts more, and yet to dote upon them less; to be more thankful for them, and yet less ensnared by them. This is a mystery

indeed to nature, a paradox to the world; for naturally we are very prone either to slight, or to surfeit. And yet, it is sad to consider, we can make a shift to do both at once; we can undervalue our mercies even while we glut ourselves with them, and despise them even when we are surfeiting upon them. Witness that caution inculcated by Moses and Joshua, " When thou hast eaten and art full, take heed thou forget not the Lord thy God," Deut. viii. 10—12. vi. 11, 12. Behold, while men fill themselves with the mercies of God, they can neglect the God of their mercies. When God is most liberal in remembering us, we are most ungrateful to forget God. Now therefore that we may know how to put a due estimate upon mercies, God often cuts us short, that we may learn to prize that by want, which our foolish unthankful hearts slighted in the enjoyment. Thus the prodigal, who, while yet at home, could despise the rich and well-furnished table of his father, when God sent him to school to the swine-trough, could value the bread that the servants did eat; " How many of my father's hired servants have bread enough, and to spare!" Luke xv. 17. He would have been glad of the reversion of broken meat that was cast into the common basket.

I do not believe David ever slighted the ordinances, yet certainly he never knew so well how to estimate them, as when he was banished from them; then a porter's place, the sparrow's nest, and the swallow's neighbourhood to the altar of God, were matters of envy to him, Psa. lxxxiv. The remembrance of the company of saints, the beauty of the ordinances, Psa. xlii. 4. cx. 3. and the presence of God, Psa. lxiii. 2. fetcheth tears from his eyes, and groans from his heart, in his sorrowful exile : " When I remember these things, I pour out my soul in me, &c. My tears are my meat day and night," Psa. xlii. 3, 4. Oh how amiable are the assemblies of the saints, and the ordinances of the sabbath, when we are deprived of them ! " In those days the word of the Lord was precious," 1 Sam. iii. 1. *Obj.* When was it not precious ? *Ans.* It was always precious in the worth of it : but now it was precious for the want of it : prophets and prophecy were precious because rare ; so it followeth, " There was no open vision." Want will teach us the worth of mercies. Our liberties and dearest relations how cheap and common things are they while we possess them without any check or restraint ! While we have the keeping of our mercies in our own hands, we make but small reckoning of them. Oh, but let God threaten a divorce by death or banishment, let task-masters be set over us and our comforts, who shall measure out unto us at their own pleasure ; let us be locked up awhile under close imprisonment, and there be kept fasting from our dearest enjoyments, then the sight of a friend though but through an iron grate, the exchange of a few common civilities with a yoke-fellow under the correction and control of a keeper, how sweet and precious ! Whereas months and years of arbitrary enjoyments are past through, and we scarcely sit down to reflect one serious view upon our mercies ; seldom spread them before the Lord in prayer, or send up one thankful ejaculation to God by night upon our beds, in this or the like manner ; Lord, what mercy is this which I enjoy in my yoke-fellow, children, friends, liberty, estate, comforts, and accommodations of all sorts, not for necessity only, but for delight, while others, better than I, languish under an unequal yoke, have great rebukes in their children, are separated from friends, despoiled of their estates, imprisoned, banished, afflicted, deserted, tormented! How comes it to pass that so much mercy falls to my share? that I want nothing, while others have nothing? &c. Oh how rarely do we entertain such discourses with our own hearts, but pass by mercies as common things, scarcely worth the owning, whereas in the house of bondage, in a land of captivity, the lees and dregs of those mercies will be precious, which while the vessel ran full and fresh we could hardly relish. In famine the very gleanings of our comforts are better than the whole vintage in the years of plenty.

And then also, as God teacheth us to prize our mercies, so by affliction also he doth teach us moderation in the use of them; while we value, not to surfeit. And indeed it is the inordinate use of outward comforts which renders us unfit to prize them; we lose our esteem of mercies in excess. Surfeits do usually render those things nauseous, which formerly have been our delicacies. By our excesses in creature enjoyments, reason is drowned in sense, judgment extinguished in appetite, and the affections being blunted by commonness of exercise, even pleasures themselves become a burden. Surely the excessive letting out of ourselves to sensual fruitions, is both a sin and a punishment, while thereby we lose both the creature, and God, and ourselves at once.

Now this distemper God doth many times cure by the sharp corrosive of affliction, and by hardship teacheth us moderation: partly by inuring us to abatements and wants, whereby that which at first was necessity, afterwards grows to be our choice. Hence saith the apostle, " I have learned to want," Phil. iv. 12. How? why God had taught him to live on a little. By feeding us sparingly, God abates and slackens the inordinacy of the appetite. Partly and especially, God takes off our hearts from inordinate indulgences in a suffering condition, by discovering richer and purer satisfactions in Jesus Christ. It is God's design by withdrawing the creature, to invite, and fix the soul upon himself. The voice of the rod is, O taste, and see how good the Lord is! which when the soul hath once perceived, thrusting the creature away with contempt and indignation, it opens itself to God, saying, " Whom have I in heaven but thee? and there is none upon earth that I desire in comparison of thee," Psa. lxxiii. 25. Surely it was in the school of affliction that David learned that lesson, even when the wicked prospered, and himself, with the rest of the godly, were plagued all the day long, and chastened every morning, Psa. lxxiii. 14.

This is the second, and a happy lesson, to prize comforts more, and yet dote upon our comforts less.

3. A third lesson, which God teacheth by his chastisements, is, self-denial and obediential submission to the will of God.

In our prosperity we are full of our own wills, and usually we give God counsel when God looks for obedience, as if we could tell God how it might have been better; and so we dispute our cross when we should take it up; but now by bearing a little we learn to bear more; the trial of our faith worketh patience: the more we suffer, the more God fits us for suffering, James i. 3. partly

by working us off from our own wills: folly is
bound up in the heart of God's children, as well as
our own ; "but the rod of correction driveth it far
from them," Prov. xxii. 15.   God fetcheth out the
stubbornness and perverseness of our spirits by the
discipline of the rod.   So that before he hath done
with us, we have not a will to lift up against his
will.   And surely as we say to our children, Oh, it
is a good rod, which breaks us of our obstinacy.
Partly by inuring us to the cross.   The bullock
unaccustomed to the yoke, is very impatient under
the hand of the husbandman ; but after he is
inured to labour, he willingly puts his neck under
the yoke : and so it is with christians, after a while
the yoke of affliction begins to be well settled, and
by much bearing we learn to bear with quietness.
A new cart maketh a great noise and squeaking,
but when once used, it goeth silently under the
greatest load.   None murmur so much at sufferings
as they who have suffered least : whereas on the
contrary, we see many times that they are most patient who have the heaviest burden upon their backs.
" He sitteth alone, and keepeth silence, because he
hath borne it upon him," Lam. iii. 28. which means,
he is patient because he is acquainted with sorrows.
When people cry out, " Oh, never such sufferings
as mine," it is an argument they are strangers to
afflictions.   Partly also because by chastisements
God works out by degrees the delicacy of spirit
which we contract in our prosperity ; mercy makes
us tender.   They who are always kept in the warm
house, dare not put their head out of doors in a
storm : none so unfit for sufferings as they that
have been always dandled upon the knee of Providence : the most delicate constitutions are most

unfit for hardship. But lastly and chiefly, this comes to pass because by suffering we come to taste the fruit of sufferings. "No chastening for the present seems joyous, but grievous," Heb. xii. 11. At first, chastisement seems very bitter, but afterwards it yieldeth the peaceable fruits of righteousness unto them that are exercised thereby. The fruit of patience is not found at the first brunt, but after we are well exercised and acquainted with a suffering condition : affliction is the true moly ;* though the root be bitter, yet the fruit is sweet; there is meat in the eater, out of the strong comes sweetness ; and then when the soul begins to taste the sweet fruit which grows upon the bitter root, it says with the church in the Lamentations, "It is good that a man should both hope and quietly wait for the salvation of the Lord ; it is good that a man should bear the yoke in his youth," Lam. iii. 26, 27. That is, I shall not be a loser by my sufferings, I see the fruit will abundantly compensate the smart of a suffering condition.

Thus, I say, one way or other, God works his children into a sweet obediential frame by their sufferings. Even of Christ himself, the Son of God by nature, it is said, "He learned obedience by the things which he suffered," Heb. v. 8. He came experimentally to know what it was to be subject to the will of his Father. It is most properly true of the adopted children, they learn obedience by the things which they suffer, and that not only in a passive but in an active sense. By *suffering* God's will we learn to *do* God's will. God hath no such obedient children as those whom he nurtures in the school of affliction. At length

* A herb.

God brings all his scholars to subscribe, *What God will, when God will, how God will: thy will be done on earth, as it is in heaven.* A blessed lesson!

4. A fourth lesson is, humility and meekness of spirit.

It is one of God's designs in affliction, to " hide pride from man," Job xxxiii. 17. to spread sackcloth upon all his glory, that so man may see no excellency in all the creature wherein to pride himself. God led Israel forty years in the wilderness to humble them. By the thorns of the wilderness God pricked the bladder of pride, and let out the windiness of self-opinion that was in their hearts. Prosperity usually makes men surly and supercilious towards their poor brethren ; " The rich answers roughly :" even while " the poor useth entreaties," (Prov. xviii. 23.) maketh his addresses to him with all humility and observance, he holds up his head, or turns his back upon him with scorn and contempt, and thinks himself too good to give his poor neighbour a soft and peaceable answer. They speak hard things ; these rough-cast Nabals, a man cannot tell how to speak to them. Pride is a humour which naturally runs in our veins, and it is nourished by ease and prosperity. And therefore to tame this pride of spirit that is in man, God takes him into the house of correction, puts his feet in the stocks, and there teacheth him to know himself: " He humbled thee, and suffered thee to hunger," Deut. viii. 3. Hunger brought down Israel's stomach, and did eat out that proud flesh which began to rankle. Hence it is that if you take the children of God either yet in, or newly come out of the furnace of affliction, you shall observe them to be the tamest, meekest creatures upon the earth; as it is said of the new convert, "A little child may lead them," Isa. xi. 6. Whereas before it may be they were so stiff and high in the instep, that an angel of God could not tell how to deal with them; now the meanest of God's ministers or servants may reprove and counsel, &c. "a little child may lead them." That David whom sin made so fierce that he put his poor Ammonitish prisoners and captives to death in cold blood, 2 Sam. xii. 31.* yea tormented them to death with saws, and harrows, and axes of iron; and burnt them alive in fiery brick-kilns; him did banishment and persecution make so tame, that not only the righteous might reprove him, but even the wicked might reproach him, Psa. cxli. 5. and he holds his peace, or if he speak, they be words of patience and submission: "So let him curse, because the Lord hath said, Curse David," 2 Sam. xvi. 10. A man by trouble comes to know his own heart, which in prosperity he was a stranger to; he seeth the weakness of his grace, and the strength of his corruption; how nothing is weak but grace, nothing strong but sin; and this lays him in the dust. Oh wretch that I am! And truly when a man hath learned this lesson, he is not far from deliverance. "Seek the Lord all ye meek of the earth, seek righteousness, seek meekness, it may be ye shall be hid in the day of the Lord's anger," Zeph. ii. 3. This is God's design, first, to meeken his people by affliction, and then to save them from affliction, Psa. cxlix. 4. For the Lord taketh pleasure in his people, he will beautify the meek with salvation.

* The Hebrew word means put them *to* saws, &c. and means no more than to employ them as slaves in the most menial occupation. *T. H. Horne.* ED.

5. God by affliction discovers unknown corruption in the hearts of his people, " He led thee throug ⟂ the wilderness these forty years to humble thee, and to prove thee, to know what was in thy heart," Deut. viii. 2. that is, to make thee know what was in thy heart ; what pride, what impatience, what unbelief, what idolatry, what distrust of God, what murmuring, what unthankfulness was in thy heart; and thou never tookest notice of it. I tell you christians, sin lieth very close and deep, and is not easily discerned till the fire of affliction comes and makes a separation of the precious from the vile. The furnace discovers the dross which lay hid before. " What shall I do," saith God, " for the daughter of my people ?" Jer. ix. 7. They are exceeding bad, and they know it not. " What shall I do with them ? I will melt them, and try them." Into the furnace they shall go, and there I will discover themselves to themselves, and show them what is in their hearts. In the furnace we see more corruption and more of corruption, than ever appeared or was suspected. Oh, saith the poor soul whom God hath taught in the school of affliction, I never thought my heart so bad as now I see it is, I could not have believed the world had had so much interest in my heart, and Christ so little ; I did not think my faith had been so weak, and my fears so strong. I find that faith weak in danger, which I had thought had been strong out of danger. Little did I think the sight of death would have been so terrible, parting with nearest friends and dearest relations so piercing. Oh how unskilful and unwise am I to manage a suffering condition, to discern God's ends, to find out what God would have me to do ; to moderate the violence of mine

own passions, to apply the counsels and comforts of the word for their proper ends and uses! Oh where is my patience, my love, my zeal, my rejoicing in tribulations! Ah! did I ever think to find my heart so discomposed, my affections so out of command, my graces so to seek when I should fall into divers temptations! What a deal of self-love, pride, distrust in God, creature-confidence, discontent, murmuring, rising of heart against the holy and righteous dispensations of God, is there boiling and fretting within me! Wo is me, what a heart have I!

And besides all this, in the hour of temptation, God brings old sins to remembrance. "We are verily guilty concerning our brother," Gen. xlii. 21. could Joseph's brethren say, twenty years after they had sold him for a slave, when they were in danger to be questioned for their lives, as they feared. And thus when the Israelites cry to God in their sore distress for rescue and deliverance, God puts them in mind of their old apostasies: " Ye have forsaken me, and served other gods, &c. go and cry to the gods whom ye have chosen," Judg. x. 13, 14. Suffering times are times of bringing sin to mind. " If they bethink themselves in the land whither they were carried captives," Heb. If they bring back to heart, 1 Kings viii. 47. Captivity is a time of turning in upon ourselves, and bringing back to heart our doings which have not been good in God's sight. Thus David under the rod could call himself to account, " I thought on my ways, and turned my feet," &c. Psa. cxix. 59.

This now is another lesson which God teacheth by affliction; and it is of great use to humble us, and to empty us out of ourselves, to make us

fly to Jesus Christ for righteousness and strength,
Isa. xlv. 24.   In a word, God lets us see what is
crooked that we may straighten it, what is weak
that we may strengthen it, what is wanting that
we may supply it; what is lame that it may not
be turned out of the way, but that it may rather
be healed.

6. In the school of affliction God doth teach us
to pray.   They that never prayed before will pray
in affliction.   " Lord in trouble they have visited
thee, they poured out a prayer when thy chastening
was upon them," Isa. xxvi. 16.   They that kept their
distance with God before, yea, that said to the
Almighty, Depart from us, in their affliction can
bestow a visit upon God; " In trouble they have
visited thee :" and they that never prayed before, or
at least did but now and then drop out a sleepy
sluggish wish, can now pour out a prayer when
chastisement is upon their loins.   Rebels, fools,
mariners, even the worst of men, can cry to God
in their trouble, Psa. cvii. 11. 17. 23.   The very
heathen mariners fall to their prayers in a storm,
and can awaken the sleepy prophet to this duty;
" What meanest thou, O sleeper? arise and call
upon thy God," Jonah i. 5, 6.   Hence we use to
say, " He that cannot pray, let him go to sea."
Thus I say affliction opens dumb lips, and untieth
the strings of the tongue to call upon God.

But whom God teacheth in affliction, they learn
to pray in another manner—more frequently, more
fervently.

They pray more frequently; God's people are
vessels full of the spirit of prayer, and affliction is
a piercer, whereby God draws it out.   " For my
love they are my adversaries, but I give myself

unto prayer," Psa. cix. 4. David was always a praying man, but now under persecution he did nothing else. "I give myself unto prayer:" as wicked men give themselves up to their wickedness, so David gave himself up to prayer, he made it his work. Hence you may observe that most of the psalms are nothing else almost but the runnings out of David's spirit in prayer under variety of afflictions and persecutions; as his troubles were multiplied, so his prayers did multiply. The holy man was never in that condition wherein he could not pray, &c. Alas, it is sad to consider that in our peace and tranquillity, we pray carelessly by fits and starts many times, we suffer every trifle to come and justle out prayer; but in affliction God keeps us upon our knees, and, as it were, tieth the sacrifice to the horns of the altar.

And as he teacheth us to pray more frequently, so also to pray more fervently. Even of Christ himself it is said, that being in an agony he prayed more earnestly; more intensively; he prayed till he sweat again; yea till he sweat great drops of blood, Luke xxii. 44. He sweltered out his soul through his body in prayer; the reason whereof was, because he had not only the pangs of death, but the sense of his Father's wrath to conflict withal: and so it is with believers many times; outward afflictions are accompanied with inward desertions. So it was with David, Psa. xxii. and cxvi. 3, 4, &c. And then he gathers up all his strength to prayer, and like a true son of Jacob wrestleth with God, and will not let him go till he gets the blessing, Psa. cxliii. 6, 7, &c.

Truly, christians, those prayers wherewith you contented yourselves in the day of your peace and prosperity, will not serve your turn in the hour of temptation. Then you will call to mind your short, slight, cold, dead, sleepy, formal devotions in your families and closets, and be ashamed of them. Then you will see need of praying over all your prayers again, and stir up yourselves to take hold upon God, Isa. lxiv. 7. Indeed for this very end God sends his people into captivity that he may draw out the spirit of prayer, which they have suffered to lie dead within them. " Oh my dove that art in the clefts of the rock, in the secret places of the stairs ; let me see thy countenance, let me hear thy voice, for sweet is thy voice, and thy countenance is comely," Sol. Song, ii. 14. Christ's dove never looks more beautiful in his eyes, than when her cheeks are bedewed with tears ; nor ever makes sweeter music in his ears, than when she mourns to him, out of the rock, and from under the stairs, in a dark and desolate condition : then saith Christ, " Thy countenance is comely, and sweet is thy voice."

7. By correction God brings the children of promise into more acquaintance with the word. He teacheth them out of his law. As here : " It is good for me that I have been afflicted, that I might learn thy statutes." God sent David into the school of affliction, there to learn the statutes of God. By correction the people of God learn, 1. To converse with the word of God more abundantly. 2. To understand it more clearly. 3. To relish it more sweetly.

(1.) By affliction they come to converse with the word more abundantly. It is their duty at all times to study the word ; to let it dwell richly in them in all wisdom, Col. iii. 16. Job esteemed the words of God's mouth more than his necessary food. And it is their happiness as well as their duty; "Blessed is the man that walketh not in the counsel of the ungodly, but his delight is in the law of the Lord and in his law doth he meditate day and night." Psa. i. 1, 2. But what through distraction without, and distemper within, the children of God many times grow strangers to their bibles, they suffer diversions to interpose between the word and their hearts, and as they pray carelessly, so they read carelessly, and suffer their bibles to lay by the walls while they are taken up with other entertainments in the world. And therefore God is forced to deal with them as we do with our children, to whip them to their books by the rod of correction. " It is good for me that I have been afflicted, that I might learn thy statutes." When they are cast out by the world, then they can run to the word. " Princes did sit and speak against me;" that is, they sat in counsel to take away his life, that they might condemn him as a traitor against Saul : and what did he in the mean time ? it follows, " but thy servant did meditate in thy statutes." And again, " Princes have persecuted me without a cause, but my heart standeth in awe of thy word," Psa. cxix. 23. 161. While the persecutors are consulting with the oracles of hell to sin against David, David is consulting with the oracles of heaven, that he might not sin against God. " My heart standeth in awe of thy word :' while they sinned and feared not, David feared and sinned not.

(2.) They learn by affliction to understand the word more clearly. As it was with the disciples in reference to Christ's resurrection ; the resurrection of Christ was a lively comment upon the prophecies

of Christ: " These things understood not his disciples at the first, but when Jesus was glorified, then
remembered they these things," John xii. 16. that
is, they remembered them understandingly, they
remembered them believingly, they knew what they
meant. So it is with the people of God many times
in reference to affliction ; the rod expounds the
word, providence sometimes interprets the promise.
The children of God had never understood some
scriptures, had not God sent them into the school
of affliction : then they can remember how it is
written, &c. they can bring God's word and God's
works together.

(3.) Affliction makes them relish the word more
sweetly. In prosperity many times we suffer the
luscious contentments of the world so to distemper
our palates that we cannot relish the word, taste no
more sweetness in it than in the white of an egg,
as Job speaks in another case. But when God
hath kept them for weeks, and months, and years
it may be, fasting from the world's dainties, when
they are thoroughly hunger-bitten in the creature ;
then, " How sweet are thy words to my taste ! yea,
sweeter than honey to my mouth," Psa. cxix. 103.
They are the words which David spoke in his affliction, witness ver. 23, with 24. " Princes did sit and
speak against me, but thy servant did meditate in
thy statutes :" and what follows ? " thy testimonies
are my delight." And ver. 161, with 162. " Princes
have persecuted me without a cause, &c. I rejoice
at thy word as one that findeth great spoil." The
rod did sweeten the word. It is my delight, my
joy, a nest of sweetnesses. " The full soul loatheth
an honey-comb," Prov. xxvii. 7. When we are
crammed with creature-comforts, we nauseate many

times the very word itself, which is sweeter than the honey or the honey-comb. "but to the hungry soul every bitter thing is sweet." Let God famish the world round about us, then how cordial is a word of scripture consolation! How precious are the promises! Oh, said a gracious woman reduced to great straits, I have made many a meal's meat upon the promises when I have wanted bread.

The word is never so sweet as when the world is most bitter; and therefore doth God lay mustard upon the teats of the world, that we might go to the breasts of the word, and there "suck and be satisfied with the milk of consolation," Isa. lxvi. 11. "This is my comfort in my affliction: for thy word hath quickened me," Psa. cxix. 50. Blessed be God for that correction which sweetens the word unto us.

8. God by bringing his people into troubles, especially if life-threatening dangers, doth show them the necessity of sound evidence for heaven and happiness. Alas, with what easy and slight evidences do we often content ourselves in the time of our prosperity, when the candle of the Almighty doth shine in our tabernacles! when all is peace and quiet round about us! The heart being taken up with other fruitions, we want either time or will to pursue the trial of our own estates. People mind only what will serve their turn for the present, and quiet their hearts, that they may follow their pleasures and profits with the less regret; and therefore to save themselves a labour, they take that for evidence which the sluggish carnal heart wisheth were so. But now in the hour of temptation, fig-leaves will cover nakedness no longer; nothing will

serve the turn but what will be able to stand before
God and endure the trial of fire in the day of Christ.
Oh then one clear and unquestionable evidence of interest in Christ, and the love of God, will be worth ten
thousand worlds. Shadows and appearances of grace
will vanish before the Searcher of hearts. It must be
perfect love that will cast our fear, 1 John iv.18. Truth
and soundness of grace only can give boldness in the
day of judgment. Ah, what idle and deceitful hearts
have we in the midst of us, that can take up with loose
conjectures, go to the word and sacrament with those
evidences, upon which we dare not venture to die?
And yet good and upright is the Lord who will teach
sinners his way, Psa. xxv.8; who, by the thunder-claps
of his righteous judgments will awaken the vain creature out of those foolish dreams in which, if they
should die, they were undone for ever. Well, let us be
urging and pressing this question upon our own souls;
Will this faith save me when I come to stand before
the throne of the Lamb? Will this love give me boldness in the day of judgment? Will this evidence serve
my turn when I come to die? Oh christians, let us be
afraid to lie down with that evidence in our beds,
wherewith we dare not lie down in our graves.

9. In the time of our trouble, God causeth us
to see what an evil and bitter thing it is to grieve the
good Spirit of God. When we are in the bitterness of
our spirits and want the comforter, then we begin
to call to mind how often we have grieved the Spirit,
which would have been a comforter to us, and have
sealed us up to the day of redemption; and say within
ourselves, in reference to the Spirit of God, as some-

times the sons of Jacob said one to another in reference to Joseph; "We are verily guilty concerning our brother, in that we saw the anguish of his soul when he besought us, and we would not hear; therefore is this distress come upon us," Gen. xliii. 21. In some such language I say will the soul in the hour of temptation bespeak itself; Ah, I am verily guilty concerning that tender Spirit of grace and comfort, which hath often besought me as it were with tears, saying, "Oh do not this abominable thing which I hate," Jer. xliv. 4. but I would not hear. Is not this He whose rebukes I have slighted, whose counsels I have despised, whose motions I have resisted, whose warnings I have neglected, whose warmings I have quenched, yea, whose comforts I have undervalued, and counted them as a small thing? Ah wretch, how just is it now that the Spirit of God should withdraw! that he should despise my sorrows, and laugh at my tears; shut out my prayers, quench my smoking flax, and break my bruised reed! How just were it that He, whom I would not suffer to be a reprover in the day of my peace, should now refuse to be a repairer of my soul in the hour of my temptation! How righteous a thing were it that I, who so often have carried myself to his counsels, should now lie down in sorrow. Well, if the Lord shall please to bring my soul out of trouble, and to revive my fainting spirit with his sweet consolation, I hope I shall carry myself, for the future, more obediently to the counsels and rebukes of Jesus Christ in my soul, and hearken to the least whisperings of the Spirit of grace.

10. By chastisements, God draws the soul into sweet and near communion with himself. Outward

prosperity is a great obstruction to our communion with God. Partly because, by letting out our affections inordinately to the creature, we suffer the world to come in between God and our hearts, and so intercept that sweet and constant traffic and intercourse which should be between God and us. God's people offend most in their lawful comforts, because there the snare being not so visible as in grosser sins, they are the more easily taken; we are soonest surpised where we are least jealous. Partly also for want of keeping up our watch against lesser sins. While our hearts are warmed with prosperity, we think many times small sins can do no great harm; but herein we wofully deceive ourselves. For besides that the least sin hath the nature of sin in it, as the least drop of poison is poison; and that in smaller sins there is the greater contempt of God, in asmuch as we stand out with God for a trifle, (as we count it) and venture his displeasure for a little sensual satisfaction. I say, besides these and many other considerations which may render our small sins great provocations this is one unspeakable mischief, that small sins intercept our communion with God as much as great sins, and sometimes more. For whereas great sins by making deep wounds upon conscience, make the soul go bleeding to the throne of grace, and there to mourn and lament, never to give God rest till he gives rest to the soul, and by a fresh sprinkling of the blood of Christ, to recover peace and communion with God. Smaller sins not impressing such horror upon the conscience, are swallowed in silence with less regret, and so do insensibly alienate and estrange the heart from

Jesus Christ. The least hair casts its shadow; a barley-corn laid upon the sight of the eye will keep out the light of the sun, as well as a mountain. The eye of the soul must be kept very clear that will see God: "Blessed are the pure in heart, for they shall see God," Matt. v. 8. Little sins, though they do not disturb reason so much as great sins, yet they defile conscience, and the conscience under defilement (unlamented) is shy of God, and God shy of it.

But now affliction sanctified, as it doth deaden the heart to the world, so it doth awaken and make conscience tender towards sin; the soul is made sensible of her departures from God, and of the bitter fruits of that departure, and now begins to lament after God in Augustine's language; Lord, thou hast made my heart for thyself, and it is restless and unquiet till it can rest in thee; "Return unto thy rest, O my soul." The soul hath many turnings and windings, but with Noah's dove, it can find no place for the sole of its foot to rest on, till it return into the ark, from whence it came. And now when the soul hath been weather-beaten abroad, if God will please to put forth his hand, and take it into himself, when dearest relations are become strangers, as David complains, Psa. lxxxviii. 8. 18. if God come and give the soul a visit; when the poor creature is in darkness, and can see no light, then for God to lift up the light of his countenance, and shine in a gracious smile upon the soul, and say unto it, "I am thy Salvation," of what sweet and unspeakable refreshment and consolation is this to the afflicted spirit! And what a gracious condescension is this in God, that when the soul by prosperity hath waxed wanton against Christ, and sported itself in unspouse-like familiarities **with** strangers, Jesus Christ should send it into **the** house of correction, and there by the discipline **of** the rod correct and work out the wantonness of **the** flesh, and when he hath made it meet for his presence, take it into sweet and social communion **with** himself again! Jer. iii. 1. This is stupendous mercy, goodness that cannot be paralleled in the whole creation !

11. God maketh affliction the exercise and improvement of grace. In prosperity grace many times lieth dead and useless in the soul, which affliction awakens and draweth forth into exercise: the winter of our outward comforts proves not seldom the spring of our graces. Frosts and snow do starve the weeds, and nourish the good corn. Though faith and patience be of an universal influence into the holy life, " The life I live in the flesh, I live by the faith of the Son of God," Gal. ii. 20. yet affliction giveth them their perfect work. Of the times of persecution it is said, " Here is the patience and faith of the saints," Rev. xiii. 10. that is, Now is the time for the saints of God to exert their faith and patience, and to let them have their perfect work. There is a work of patience, and there is a perfect work ; " The trial of faith worketh patience," James i. 3, 4. that is, the sufferings whereby our faith is tried, as gold is tried in the furnace, it worketh, or, as the word signifieth, it perfecteth. The cross exerciseth, and exercise perfecteth the grace of patience : as sufferings arise, so patience ariseth also ; " Be patient, brethren, till the coming of the Lord," James v. 7. Do you bear the affliction till Christ come and take it off: let your patience be of the same extent with your

THE ROD AND THE WORD.

sufferings. As patience, so faith is not acted only but perfected by temptations. Sometimes the soul finds that faith lively in a suffering condition, which before it questioned whether it were alive or not; or if affliction do not find it lively, it makes it lively. The same furnace of affliction wherein God trieth our faith he doth refine it, and purifieth it more and more from the dross of infidelity. They are the purest acts of faith, which the soul puts forth in the dark. Faith never believes more than when it cannot see, because then the soul hath nothing to stay itself upon but God, Isa. l. 10. Sense while it seems to help, makes the work of faith difficult by doubling it: a man must first believe the insufficiency of what he seeth, before he can believe the all sufficiency of him that is invisible; "We look not at the things which are seen, but at the things which are not seen," 2 Cor. iv. 18. It is harder to live by faith in abundance than in want. The soul is a step nearer living upon God, when it hath nothing to live upon but God. Yea and when God is not seen he is most believed. "My God, my God, why hast thou forsaken me?" Psa. xxii. 1. Observe, and you shall find a great deal more of precious faith in that desertion, than of complaint. For, first, faith breaks forth, "My God," before forsaken. And again you have two words of faith for one of despair; "My God, my God, why hast thou forsaken me?" Faith speaks twice before sense can speak once. And third, faith speaks confidently and positively, Thou art my God. Sense speaks dubiously, Why hast thou? as if sense durst not call it a forsaking while faith dares say, "My God." Surely faith is never so much faith as in desertion. Faith's triumphs lie

in the midst of despair, and even in this sense also;
" Having not seen, yet believing, we rejoice with
joy unspeakable and full of glory," 1 Pet. i. 8.

Godly sorrow, how is it enlarged by sanctified
affliction ! while that stream, which was wont to
run in the channel of worldly crosses, now is di-
verted into the channel of sin : " I will bear the
indignation of the Lord, because I have sinned,"
Micah vii. 9.   Any burden is light in comparison
of sin, the very indignation of God.   The soul that
God teacheth by his chastisements can stand under
the burden of God's indignation for sin, when it
cannot stand under sin, which hath kindled that
indignation.   "Ah," crieth Job upon the dunghill,
" I have sinned, what shall I do unto thee, O thou
preserver of men !"   He forgetteth his suffering in
his sin ; he saith not, I have lost all my substance ;
I am now upon the dunghill as naked as ever I
was born, save that I am clothed with wounds ; my
friends reproach me, my wife curseth me, or,
which is worse, she bids me curse God.   Satan
persecutes me, and God himself is become mine
enemy, &c. all this is befallen me ; what wilt thou
do unto me, O thou preserver of men ? but, " I have
sinned, what shall I do unto thee ?" &c.   Sufferings
lead to sin, and sense of sin swalloweth up sense of
sufferings.   And what shall I say more ? the time
would fail to instance in other graces, love, fear,
holiness, &c.   " By this shall the iniquity of Jacob
be purged, and this is all the fruit to take away his
sin," Isa. xxvii. 9.   " He for our profit, that we
might be partakers of his holiness," Heb. xii. 10.

Grace is never more grace than when besieged
with temptations.   The battle draws forth that

fortitude and prowess, which in time of peace lay chilled in the veins for want of opposition and exercise. Tribulation worketh patience.

12. A twelfth lesson, which they learn in the school of affliction, is—The necessity and excellency of the life of faith.

(1.) The necessity of living by faith : where sense endeth, faith beginneth. "The vision is for an appointed time," Hab. ii. 3, 4. But what shall we do in the mean time? why, " the just shall live by faith;" live by faith, or die in despair. When God pulls away the bulrushes of creature supports, the soul must either swim or sink. God teacheth this lesson, partly by the uncertainty of second causes, the vicissitudes that are in creature expectations ; a little hope to-day, to-morrow reduced to despair : good news to-day, Pharaoh says, Israel shall go ; bad news to-morrow, he rageth, and swears that if Moses see his face any more, he shall die, &c. Oh the ebbs and flows of sublunary hopes! One speaks a word of comfort, another speaks words of soul-wounding terror ; now a parcel of good words, anon a threatening. The sick man is in hopes of reviving to-day, to-morrow at the point of death, What a woful heart-dividing life is a life of sense. a life which is worse than death itself, to be thus bandied up and down between hopes and fears, to be baffled to and fro between the may-bes of second causes! to be like mariners upon the billows and surges of the tempestuous sea! "They mount up to heaven, they go down again to the depths; their soul is melted because of trouble : they reel to and fro, and stagger like a drunken man, and are at their wits' end," (Hebrew ; All their wisdom is swallowed up,) Psa. cvii. 26, 27. And God teacheth the necessity of a life of faith partly by the disappointment of the creature. How often doth the creature totally fail, and abuse our expectation! like the deceitful brook, to which Job most elegantly compares his brethren, Job vi. 15, 16. which mocks the traveller, and when he comes for a draught of water to quench his thirst, sends him away with confusion and shame, ver. 20. "Surely men of low degree are vanity, and men of high degree are a lie," Psa. lxii. 9. Men of low degree would help, but cannot, there is vanity : and men of high degree can help many times, but will not ; no, not when they have promised and sworn, there is a lie : both disappoint, the one by the necessity, the other by deceit ; and disappointment is one of the greatest torments that a rational creature is capable of. Trust defeated causeth sorrow of heart, and confusion of face, Isa. xx. 5. and the stronger the confidence, the more shameful is the disappointment, Jer. xiv. 3. Agag comes forth singing, "Surely the bitterness of death is past," 1 Sam. xv. 32, 33. when behold he is going to his execution : both he and his hopes are hewn in pieces before the Lord. David himself looked on his right hand, and beheld, and there was no man that would know him. Peter-like, they knew not the man ; they made as if they had never seen him before. So that churl Nabal says, "Who is David, and who is the Son of Jesse ?" 1 Sam. xxv. 10. Some runagate, some idle fellow that hath broken away from his master, &c. And it was not Nabal only that stood at this distance from him ; his nearest and dearest acquaintance cast him off: " Lover and friend hast thou put far from me, and mine acquaintance into darkness," Psa. lxxxviii. 18. " Refuge failed me, no man cared for my soul;" or, as the Hebrew hath it, No man sought after my soul, Psa. cxlii. 3, 4. St. Paul was in no better condition in the persecution which befell him at Rome; "At my first answer no man stood with me, but all men forsook me." Not a man of all them that sat under that famous apostle's ministry that would or durst appear to speak a word for him, or to him. O bitter disappointment, had not he had faith to support him under it! And truly "such is our expectation, whither we flee for help to be delivered," &c. Isa. xx. 6. Sorrow and shame is the fruit of creature-expectation. But now on the contrary, "they looked unto the Lord, and were enlightened, and their faces were not ashamed," Psa. xxxiv. 5. Faith meets with no disappointment, God is always better than our expectation; "Nevertheless the Lord stood with me, and strengthened me, &c. and I was delivered from the mouth of the lion," 2 Tim. iv. 17. By such experiences do we learn the necessity of living by faith. "I had perished in my affliction, unless thy law had been my delight;" that is, unless David had learned to live by a promise, he had been but a dead man. Surely he dieth oft whose life is bound up in the dying creature: as oft as the creature fails, his hope fails, and his heart faileth; when the creature dieth, his hope giveth up the ghost. He only lives an unchangeable life, that by faith can live in an unchangeable God.

We hear such things indeed in the word, but we believe them not till our own experience convinceth us of our infidelity. A long time do we stick totally in the creature, knowing no other life than that of sense and reason; sacrificing to our own nests, and burning incense to our own drags: and because the word tells us much of living by faith, we would fain patch up a life between faith and sense, which indeed is not a life of faith. We do not live at all by faith, if we live not all by faith ; though we may use means, we must trust God, and trust him solely : and therefore, to bring us to this, God suffers us to be tired and vexed with the mockery of second causes ; and when we have spent all upon these physicians of no value, then, and never till then, we resolve for Christ. When David had experienced sufficiently the falseness and hypocrisy of Saul and his parasites, "They delight in lies, they bless with their mouth, but they curse inwardly," Psa. lxii. 4. then he resolves never to trust creature more: "My soul, wait thou only upon God, He only is my rock and my salvation," Psa. lxii. 5, 6. Unmixed trust in God is the fruit of our experience of the creature's vanity. We never resolve exclusively for God, till with the prodigal we are whipt home stark naked to our father's house. When the church had run herself, Jer. ii. 25. barefoot in following her lovers, who answered her expectation with nothing but fear, and sent her away with shame instead of glory, Isa. xx. 6. then she can go home, and, confessing her atheism and folly, gives up herself purely to Divine protection: "Asshur shall not save us; we will not ride upon horses: neither will we say any more to the work of our hands, Ye are our gods: for in thee the fatherless findeth mercy," Hos. xiv. 3.

(2.) By the mutability and disappointment of the creature, God teacheth his people the excellency of the life of faith. David, when he learned it in the school of affliction, wrote it and publisheth it for the use and benefit of after ages ; "Happy is he

that hath the God of Jacob for his help, whose hope
is in the Lord his God," Psa. cxlvi. 5.   He had
before, ver. 3. entered a caveat against creature-
confidence, " Put not your trust in princes, nor in
the son of man :" and gives the reason of it ; " There
is no help or salvation in the best of men ; nor in
the son of man, in whom there is no help."   Alas,
he is but a little breathing clay ; and when that
breath goeth forth, he returns to his earth.   When
the breath is gone, there is nothing but a little lump
of clay remaining ; " In that very day his thoughts
perish."   When the man dieth, all his counsels and
plots and projects die with him.   And having thus
put in his caution against creature dependence, and
given in the account of the vanity thereof, he shows
the difference between trust in a dying man, and a
living God.   Trust in God is only able to make a
man happy : they may seem happy, who have the
great men of the world to trust to ; but he only is
happy, who hath the God of heaven to trust to.
" Blessed is he who hath the God of Jacob for his
help."   Why so ? Because, while they that trust in
princes shall be disappointed, he that trusts in God
shall never be disappointed : for, 1. He is Jehovah,
whose hope is in the Lord, or in Jehovah his God,
Isa. xxvi. 4.   Jehovah, a fountain of beings : He
gave a being to heaven and earth : " He made
heaven and earth, the sea, and all that therein is,"
Psa. cxlvi. 6. and he that gave being to every creature, can give being to his promise also.   Can any
thing be too hard for a creating God ? and as he
can, so he will, for He keepeth truth for ever :
" heaven and earth may pass away, but not one jot
or one tittle of his promise shall pass away till all be
fulfilled," Matt. v. 18.   Men may prove unfaithful,

but God will never prove unfaithful. He keepeth truth for ever: "Faithful is he that hath promised," Heb. x. 23. And thus the soul comes to see the sweetness and excellency of a life of faith, while others are mocked, and abused, and slain, by disappointment from the second causes : " He is kept in perfect peace, whose mind is stayed on God, because he trusteth in him," Isa. xxvi. 3. He liveth indeed, that liveth in Him to whom *always* is essential; who is The Eternal.

The excellency of a life of faith discovers itself in these four particulars :

[1.] It is a secure life. [2.] It is a sweet life. [3.] It is an easy life. [4.] It is an honourable life.

[1.] The life of faith is a secure life, the only safe life. " He shall dwell on high, his place of defence shall be in the ammunition of rocks." How securely doth he dwell, whose fortifications are impregnable, inaccessible rocks! rocks so high that none can scale them. In the Hebrew it is, He shall dwell in heights, or in high places: munition of rocks, or rocks so high that none can scale them ; rocks so thick that no breach can be made in them, rocks within rocks ; ammunition of rocks : and rocks so deep that none can undermine them. Surely a people or person rocked on every side, need not fear storming. *Objection.* But though rocks may be a good fence, they are but ill food, a man cannot feed on rocks ; rocky places are barren, though impregnable ; he may be starved, though he cannot be stormed! no, the words following relieves that fear also, " Bread shall be given him ;" he shall have bread enough, and it shall cost him nothing ; it shall be given him ; and whereas a rock is but a dry situation, without either springs or streams, and thereupon a man might be exposed to perishing for want of water, thirst will slay as well as hunger; therefore it is likewise added. " His waters shall be sure." He shall have waters which neither summer's heat nor winter's frost shall be able to dry up; never-failing waters shall fill his cisterns from day to day; " His waters shall be sure." Under such an excellent metaphor is the security of a life of faith described; and this metaphor is expounded Isa. xxvi. 1. " Salvation will God appoint for walls and bulwarks." Walls and bulwarks shall not be their salvation, but salvation their walls and bulwarks; how safely do they dwell who are walled about with salvation tself! the bulwarks are salvation, and that salvation is Jehovah; for so it follows, " Trust ye in the Lord for ever; for in the Lord Jehovah is everlasting strength;" or the Lord Jehovah is the Rock of ages. His place of defence is the munition of rocks; and the Lord Jehovah is those Rocks, a Rock of ages. Ages pass away one after another, but the Rock abides and abides for ever; " In the Lord Jehovah is everlasting strength." He that rained manna in the wilderness, will give bread; and he that fetched water out of the rock, will be " a never-failing Fountain, his waters shall be sure." Oh the security of a life of faith!

[2.] It is as sweet as it is safe. Is it not a sweet thing to fetch all our waters from the fountain, from the spring head, before they be degenerated or mudded by the miry channel? Why, " All my fresh springs are in thee," saith faith to God, Psa. lxxxvii. 7. Is it not sweet to be fixed and composed in the midst of all the mutations and

E

confusions that are under the sun? Why this is
the privilege of him that liveth by faith : " He
shall not be afraid of evil tidings, his heart is fixed,
trusting in the Lord," Psa. cxii. 7.   And again;
" Thou wilt keep him in perfect peace, whose mind
is stayed on thee, because he trusteth in thee," Is.
xxvi. 3. Heb. Peace, peace; that is, multiplied
peace ; pure unmixed peace, constant and everlasting peace is the portion of him that liveth by
faith, so far as he liveth by faith ; unless sense and
reason break in to disquiet, he liveth in a most
sweet and immutable serenity.

[3.] It is an easy life.   It is an easy life to have
all provisions brought in to a man without any
care or trouble; why, such is the privilege of a
believer ; he hath a support that supersedes all his
cares.   " In nothing be careful, but in every thing
by prayer and supplication with thanksgiving let
your requests be made known to God," Phil. iv. 6.
Faith leaveth a believer nothing to do but to pray
and give thanks ; to pray for what he wants, and
to give thanks for what he hath ; that is all he hath
to do.   It is true, believers must labour and travail
in the use of means, as well as the rest of the sons
of Adam ; but first, it is without care ; " In nothing
be careful ;" without anxious heart-dividing, soul-
distracting care.   Oh, that is the thorn, the sting,
which the sin of man and the curse of God hath
thrust into all our labours, care and distraction ;
and this faith pulls out ; so that now all the labour
of faith is an easy labour, like the labour of Adam
in Paradise.   Faith useth means, but trusteth
God ; obediently closeth with the providence of
means, but sweetly leaveth the providence of success to God.   Yea, faith can trust God, when

there are no means to use, and say, " Although
the fig-tree shall not blossom, neither shall fruit be
in the vines, the labour of the olive shall fail, and
the fields shall yield no meat, the flock shall be cut
off from the fold, and there shall be no herd in the
stalls; yet I will rejoice in the Lord, I will joy in
the God of my salvation," Hab. iii. 17, 18. Faith
can live upon God, when there is a famine upon the
whole creation. The peace of God is as a court
of guard, to fence the heart from all surprises of
fear and trouble ; " In nothing be careful, but in
every thing pray and give thanks, and the peace
of God which passeth all understanding shall keep
your hearts and minds through Christ Jesus,"
Phil. iv. 7. As faith enjoyeth God in all things in
the greatest abundance, so she can enjoy all things
in God in the deepest want.

[4.] The life of faith is an honourable life. It is
the honour of the favourite that he can go immediately to his prince when strangers must trace the
climax of court-accesses. Yea, without all peradventure, it is an honourable life to live as God
himself liveth ; and this is the glory of God, that
he liveth in himself and of himself; and truly in
their proportion such honour have all the saints.
They live in God and upon God here by faith ; and
they shall life in God and upon God hereafter by
sight, in the beatifical vision.

This is the excellency of the life of faith, and
this the people of God experience by their sufferings ; whereby God calls them out of the world,
and taking them into himself, he doth reveal to
them by degrees the mystery and privilege of living
upon God, and upon God alone.

13. By afflictions and distresses God takes us

off from self-confidence, and teacheth us to trust
him more, and ourselves less. This is the same
with the former, save only that we speak now of
trust in God, in opposition to confidence in ourselves, and not in others ; a distemper that prevails
much in our natures. Ever since we rendered
ourselves able to do nothing, nothing but sin, we
think ourselves able to do any thing : we fancy to
ourselves a kind of omnipotence, when all our
strength is to sit still. Naturally we are prone to
entertain and nourish high presumptions of our
own strength, and of our own wisdom.

(1.) Of our own strength. In our prosperity we think ourselves able to carry any cross ;
we fancy ourselves strong enough to carry away
even Samson's gates upon our shoulders, and
mettled to encounter any affliction in the world.
But when the hour of temptation comes, we find
we are but like other men, and are ready to sink
with Peter, if but one wave riseth higher than
another. Usually sufferings before they come are
like a mountain at a great distance, which seems
so small, that we think we could almost stride over
it ; but upon nearer approaches, when we come to
the foot of it, it appears insuperable, and looks so
huge, as if it would fall upon us, and crush us in
pieces. Peter is so big with love to Christ, that he
will die with him, rather than forsake him ; yea
though all the rest should betake themselves to
their heels, he will stand by him to the last drop of
blood ; and yet behold, when it comes to the trial,
a weak silly damsel is able with a single question
to fright him out of his confidence, and he doth not
only forsake, but forswear his Lord. Pendleton,
in the Book of Martyrs, says, he will fry out

a fat body in flames of martyrdom, rather than betray his religion ; but when the hour comes that Christ and religion have most need of him, he has not one drop of all that fat to spare for either.

(2.) As we are prone to presume of our own strength, so we are very apt to idolize our own wisdom ; to lean to our own understanding, and think by our policy to wind ourselves out of any labyrinth of trouble and perplexity. But we find it otherwise ; when we come into the snare, we then are forced to cry out with the church, " He hath hedged me about that I cannot get out, he hath made my chain heavy," Lam. iii. 7. Like a malefactor that hath broke prison ; he thinks to run away, but he hath a heavy chain upon his heel, that spoils his haste ; and being fenced in round about, he goeth to this corner, hoping to find some gap, but there he finds the hedge made up with thorns ; and to another corner, and there also the briers stop him. Mark ye, that is not all ; read on in the church's com-plaint, and you shall find greater obstructions : " He hath enclosed my ways with hewn stone," ver. 9. Suppose a man would venture the scratch-ing of his flesh, to break through a hedge to save his life, " skin for skin, and all that a man hath will he give for his life," yet that would not do, God had taken away the hedge, and built a wall instead of it ; a wall so high, that they could not clamber over ; a wall so thick, that they could not dig through. The meaning is, man in affliction thinks to make his way through by his own art and cunning, but upon the attempt he finds diffi-culties arising still higher and higher, so that when all is done, escape is impossible, without an immediate

E 3

rescue by the arm of omnipotence. This was Paul's
case: " Our trouble which came to us in Asia, that
we were pressed out of measure above strength, insomuch that we despaired even of life," 2 Cor. i. 8, 9.
A great strait, (what it was in particular you may
read Acts xix. from 22. so forward ; in all probability it was that uproar at Ephesus, wherein Paul
was like to have been pulled in pieces, for it was a
trouble that befell him in Asia, ver. 8.) I say, it
was a great strait, a strait wherein the apostle was
at his wits' end and bereft of all counsel how to
get out of the danger. As David complains, Psa.
xiii. 2. " How long shall I take counsel in my
soul !" that is, when he was persecuted by Saul,
and beset with innumerable dangers, he took
counsel, he thought of this means and the other
means, cast about this way and that way, how to
escape, but in vain, all his counsels left him as full
of sorrow and despair as they found him. " How
long shall I take counsel in my soul, having sorrow
in my heart ?" He had his sorrow for his pains.
Thus it was with the apostle ; all his counsel left
him in the hand of despair : " We despaired even
of life." His case was no other than the prisoner
at the bar, at what time the sentence of death is
passed upon him ; he looks upon himself, and so
do standers by, as a dead man ; he is legally dead,
dead to all intents and purposes of the law ; there
wants nothing but execution : why so it was with
Paul ; " We had the sentence of death in ourselves."
The sentence was passed in his own breast ; and
now saith Paul, I am but a dead man. This was
his strait, and it seemeth God had a plot in it, a
design upon Paul ; and what was that ? himself
will tell you ; " We had the sentence of death in

ourselves, that we should not trust in ourselves, but in God which raiseth the dead," ver. 9. See here, the design is expressed negatively and affirmatively. Negatively, that we might not trust in ourselves. God saw, even in that great apostle himself, a disposition to self-confidence, a proneness to be " exalted above measure, through the abundance of the revelations," 2 Cor. xii. 7. And therefore, as to prick the bubble of pride, God gave him a thorn in the flesh, &c. so, to work out this self-trust, God reduceth him to a state of despair, as to outward and visible probabilities ; " We had the sentence of death in ourselves, that we should not trust in ourselves ;" there is the negative branch of the design. And then the affirmative followeth, " But in God which raiseth the dead." By this desperate exigence God would teach Paul ever after where strength and counsel were to be had in the like extremities ; nowhere but in God, and in him abundantly. The God of resurrections can never be nonplussed ; he that can raise the dead, can conquer the greatest difficulty ; he that can put life into dead men, can put life into dead hopes, and raise up our expectations out of the very grave of despair : that God can put life into dead bones, is a consideration able to put life into a dead faith.

To this purpose it is very observable, that even those to whom God hath indulged the largest proportions of faith and courage, not only above other men, but above other saints ; yet even them God hath suffered not only to languish under fears, but even to despair under insuperable difficulties, before they could recover holy confidence in God. We find David, that great champion of Israel, more than once or twice surprised with

dreadful fear : " I said in my haste," Psa. xxxi. 22.
cxvi. 11.   The Hebrew signifieth, in my trembling,
in my precipitancy ; or as the septuagint translate
it, in my ecstasy, when I was almost beside myself
for fear.   Well, what did he say then ? Why he
said, " I am cut off from before thine eyes ;" that
is, God hath cast me out of his care, he looks no
more after me, I am a lost man.   And again, " I
said in my haste," in my passion, " all men are
liars ;" even Samuel himself, that told me I should
be king; he hath seen but a false vision, and a
lying divination ; God never said so to him ; no,
" I shall one day fall by the hand of Saul."

And thus the prophet Jeremiah, Lam. iii. 57.
" Thou drewest near in the day that I called upon
thee ; thou saidst, Fear not." But before God spake
a fear not to his soul, he was afraid to purpose ;
hear what he saith, ver. 53, 54.   " They have cut
off my life in the dungeon, and cast a stone upon
me ; waters flowed over mine head, then I said,
I am cut off."   Mark ye, with Paul, he had received the sentence of death in himself, he looks
upon himself as a dead man, yea as already in his
grave, and his grave-stone laid upon it ; " They
have cut off my life in the dungeon, and cast a
stone upon me ;" dead and buried, and a stone
rolled to the mouth of the sepulchre.   And thus
you may hear Jonah crying in the whale's belly,
" I am cast out of thy sight," Jon. ii. 4.   And
Zion, in the dust, tuning her lamentations.   " The
Lord hath forsaken me, and my Lord hath forgotten me," Isa. xlix. 14.   Hezekiah reporting
the sad discourses he had in his own bosom upon
the sight of death, Isa. xxxviii, 9, 10, &c.   It were
easy to multiply instances.

Why now this is continually our case, and this is still God's design. We are proud creatures, full of self-confidence; and therefore God by strange and unexpected providences doth hedge up our way with thorns, and wall up our path with hewn stones, brings to despair even of life, bereaveth us of counsel, deprives us of all our own shifts and policies, brings us under the very sentence of death; that we might not trust in ourselves, but in God which raiseth the dead. He overturns us by despair, convinces us of our impotence and folly, shows us what babes and fools we are in ourselves, that in all our future hazards and fears we might know nothing but God; "go in the strength of the Lord, and make mention of his righteousness, and of his only." And thus you see Peter, who before was so confident, that he thought all the world might forsake Christ sooner than himself, after he was convinced of his own infirmity and instability, when Christ, to put him in mind of his three-fold denial, put him upon that three fold interrogatory, " Simon Peter, lovest thou me more than these?" that is, than the rest of thy fellow-disciples, durst make no other answer but this, " Lord thou knowest;" he pleads nothing but his sincerity; and for that also he casts himself rather upon Christ's trial, than his own; " Lord, thou knowest."

14. By affliction God maketh himself known unto his people. How long do we hear of God before we know him? we get more by one practical discovery of God, than by many sermons: " I have heard of thee often by the hearing of the ear, but now mine eye seeth thee, therefore I abhor myself, and repent in dust and ashes," crieth Job upon the dunghill, Job xlii. 5, 6. In the word we do but

hear of God, in affliction we see him. Prosperity is the nurse of atheism; the understanding being clouded with the steams and vapours of those lusts which are incident to a prosperous estate, men grow brutish, and the reverence and sense of God is by little and little defaced. But now by affliction the soul being taken off from sense-pleasing objects, hath a greater disposition and liberty to retire into itself; and being freed from the attractive force of worldly allurements, the apprehensions are wont to be more serious and pregnant,* and so more capable of divine illumination. The clearer the glass is, the more fully doth it receive in the beams of the sun. When the warm breath of the world hath blown upon us, we are not so capable of the visions of God. The wicked through the pride of his heart will not know God ; " they say to the Almighty, Depart from us, for we desire not the knowledge of thy ways," Job xxi. 14. " Who is the Lord ?" saith Pharaoh. And truly the very godly themselves are exceedingly dark and low in their apprehensions of God ; our ignorance of God being never perfectly cured till we come to heaven, where we shall see him face to face, and know him as we are known. In the mean time, as by the strokes of divine vengeance God makes the wicked know him to their cost ; so by the rod of correction he makes his people to know him to their comfort. As God brought all his plagues upon Pharaoh's heart, that he might know who the Lord was in a way of wrath ; so he lays affliction upon the loins of his people, that they may know him in a way of love ; " Israel shall cry unto me, My God, we know thee." Moses never saw God so clearly, as when

* Clear, full.

he descended in a cloud, Exod. xxxiv. 5. And truly that dispensation was but a type of the method which God useth in making himself known unto his saints : He puts them into the clefts of the rock, covereth them with his hand while he passeth by, and then proclaimeth his name before them, The Lord, the Lord God, merciful and gracious, &c. The people of God have the most sensible experience of his attributes in their sufferings; his holiness, justice, faithfulness, mercy, all-sufficiency, &c.

(1.) His holiness. Affliction showeth what a sin-hating God, God is. For though his chastisements on his church be in love to their persons, they are in hatred to their corruptions ; while he saveth the sinner he destroyeth the sin. " By this shall the iniquity of Jacob be purged, and this is all the fruit to take away his sin," Isa. xxvii. 9. If the soul live, sin must die.

(2.) His justice. Afflictions are correction to the godly, punishment to the wicked ; in both God is righteous ; thus Israel knew God, " Howbeit thou art just in all that is come upon us, for thou hast done right, but we have done wickedly," Neh. ix. 33. In the severest dispensations they judge themselves, and justify God ; "Thou art just," &c. Yea when they cannot discern his meaning, they adore his righteousness ; " Righteous art thou, O Lord, when I plead with thee ; yet let me talk with thee of thy judgments ; wherefore doth the way of the wicked prosper ?" Jer. xii. 1. When the soul is unsatisfied, God is not unjustified ; " Righteous art thou, O Lord," &c.

(3.) His faithfulness. Faithfulness in the very affliction itself. " I know, O Lord, that thy judgments are right, and that thou in faithfulness hast

afflicted me," Psa. cxix. 75. Faithfulness to his
covenant ; for affliction is not so much threatened
as promised to believers ; as Psa. lxxxix. 30—32.
of which more hereafter. The more David was
afflicted, the more God's faithfulness appeared.
Oh, says the holy man, I would not have wanted
a blow of all that discipline wherewith my heavenly Father hath chastised me.

Faithfulness in hearing prayer. " This poor
man cried, and the Lord heard him, and saved him
out of all his troubles," Psa. xxxiv. 6. I never
lost a prayer by God : even when David wanted
faith, God wanted not faithfulness. " I said in my
haste, I am cut off from before thine eyes ; nevertheless thou heardest the voice of my supplications
when I cried unto thee." God was faithful notwithstanding David's unbelief : " I said in my
haste," &c. and he that believeth will not make
haste ; " nevertheless thou heardest." Unbelief itself
cannot make the faithfulness of God of none effect.
I conceive that of the apostle 2 Tim. ii. 13. to bear
this sense, " If we believe not, yet he abideth faithful, he cannot deny himself." It is not to be
understood of a *state* of unbelief, but of an *act* of
unbelief ; not of a want *of* faith, but a want *in* faith ;
neither of which can render God unfaithful ; who
is engaged not so much to our faith, as to his own
faithfulness to himself, to hear the prayer of his
troubled servants ; " Call upon me in the day of
trouble, I will deliver thee, and thou shalt glorify
me," Psa. l. 15.

This faithfulness of God believers do best experience in their sufferings : partly because then they
are most prayerful. When our elder brother Esau
is upon us, we can wrestle with our elder brother

Jesus, and not let him go till he bless us. And partly because then they are most vigilant to observe the returns of prayers: " My voice shalt thou hear in the morning, in the morning will I direct my prayer unto thee, and will look up," Psa. v. 3. In adversity we are early with God in prayer; " In the morning shalt thou hear my voice, in the morning will I direct my prayer;" it implieth double earliness, and double earnestness in prayer ; in their affliction they will seek me early. And when we have done praying, we will begin hearkening ; "I will look up." In prosperity we put up many a prayer that we never *look after;* God may deny or grant, and we hardly take notice of it. But in affliction we can press God for the returns of prayer; " Hear me speedily, O Lord, my spirit faileth, hide not thy face from me, lest I be like to them that go down into the pit;" not only denials, but delays kill us. Then we can hearken for the echo of our voice from heaven ; " I will hear what God the Lord will say, for he will speak peace to his people," Psa. lxxxv. 8. As God cannot easily deny the prayer of an afflicted soul, so if he grant, we can take notice of it, and know our prayers when we see them again ; this poor man cried, and the Lord heard him ; and this endears the heart to God and to prayer : " I love the Lord, because he hath heard my voice and my supplications ; because he hath inclined his ear unto me, therefore will I call upon him as long as I live," Psa. cxvi. 1, 2.

As faithfulness in hearing prayer, so also in making good the promise. The afflicted soul can witness unto God, "as we have heard, so have we seen," Psa. xlviii. 8. What we have heard in the promise, we have seen in the accomplishment.

F

God was never worse than his word. Affliction is a furnace, as to try the faith of God's people, so to try the faithfulness of God in his promises : and upon the trial, the church brings in her experience; " The words of the Lord are pure words, as silver tried in a furnace of earth, purified seven times," Psa. xii. 6. Let a man cast in the promise a thousand times into the furnace, it will still come out full weight : "As for God, his way is perfect, the word of the Lord is tried," Psa. xviii. 30. It is to be understood in both places of the word of the promise. A man may see heaven and earth upon a promise, and it will bear them up.

(4.) As affliction gives out the experience of God's faithfulness, so also of his mercy : mercy in the moderating of the chastisements : " In measure thou wilt debate with it," &c. Isa. xxvii. 8. In the midst of judgment he remembereth mercy, Hab. iii. 2. Even when God in his compassions saith of his afflicted church, " She hath received double of the Lord for all her sins," Isa. xl. 2. I have given her too many blows; in the sense of her own merits and his mercy she can reply, " No, Lord, thou hast punished us less than our iniquities deserve," Ezra ix. 13. Too much says God, too little saith the church. Oh blessed sight, thus to see God and the soul contending together ! " It is of the Lord's mercies that we are not consumed, because his compassions fail not," crieth the church in Babylon ; which denotes, it is banishment, it might have been destruction ; we are in Babylon, we might have been in hell ; and it is of the Lord's mercies, and his mercies alone, that we are not there. So saith the afflicted soul ; if my burning fever had been the burning lake, if my prison had been the bottomless pit; if my banishment from society with friends had been expulsion, with Cain, from the presence of God, and that for ever; God had been righteous. It is never so bad with the people of God, but it might have been worse: any thing on this side hell is pure mercy.

And as mercy in moderating, so mercy in supporting. "When I said, my foot slippeth." Now I sink, I shall never be able to stand under this affliction, I cannot bear it. "Thy mercy, O Lord, held me up," Psa. xciv. 18. When David was sinking, God put underneath him his everlasting arms, and held him up, as Christ stretched forth his hand to save Peter when he began to sink. Even when God's suffering people are not sensible of any great ecstasies, yet then they find sweet supports; "His left hand was under me, his right hand embraced me." And yet it is not supporting mercy only which they experience in their sufferings, but not seldom his refreshing, his rejoicing mercy; so it follows, "In the multitude of my thoughts within me, thy comforts delight my soul," Psa. xciv. 19. My thoughts were dark and doleful, and full of despair, and not a few of them; multitudes brake in upon me, and even swallowed me up; but thy comforts were light and life, and delight to my soul: my thoughts did not sink me so deep, but thy comforts raised me up as high: my thoughts were a hell, but thy comforts were a heaven within me. The soul hears of God's mercy in prosperity, but it tastes of God's mercy in affliction, and, as it were, oppressed with delights, can call to others, O taste and see how good the Lord is. Hence it is, that of all the days of the year, the apostle would choose, as it were, a Good Friday, a passion day, to rejoice in ; "God forbid I should rejoice in any thing **but** in the cross of Jesus Christ." Christ's sufferings for him, and his sufferings for Christ.

(5.) The all-sufficiency of God is the last attribute I mentioned, which God proclaims before his suffering people : " Now thou shalt see," saith God **to** Moses, "what I will do to Pharaoh," Exod. vi. 1. Hitherto thou hast seen what Pharaoh hath done to Israel, now thou shalt see what I can do to Pharaoh ; and so they did see. The doubling of their burdens was the dissolving of their bondage ; the extinguishing of their line was the multiplying of their seed. The same waters which were Israel's rocks were the Egyptians' grave ; " I will pursue, I will overtake, I will divide the spoil ; my lust shall be satisfied upon them : I will draw my sword, my hand shall destroy," Exod. xv. 9. so boasts the proud tyrant ; I will, I will, I will, &c. nay, not so fast Pharaoh ; let God speak the next word : "Thou didst blow with thy wind, the sea covered them, they sank as lead in the mighty waters," ver. 10. Oh sudden turn ! there lieth Pharaoh and his six " I wills," and " I shalls," drowned in the sea. Thus did God appear to his oppressed Israel in the very nick of their extremities ; " In the thing wherein they dealt proudly, God was above them," Exod. xviii. 11. "And Israel *saw* that great work which the Lord did upon the Egyptians ; and the people feared the Lord, and his servant Moses," Exod. xiv. 31. Israel *saw ;* in prosperity God works, but we see him not : affliction openeth our eyes ; when we see our dangers, then we can see God in our deliverances. God could have brought Israel to the land of promise a shorter cut, in forty days ; but he leads them about in a howling wilderness forty years, not a like place in all the world to have starved them and their flocks: and why but to proclaim to Israel, and all succeeding generations, that "man liveth not by bread alone, but by every word that proceedeth out of the mouth of the Lord doth man live?" Deut. viii. 3. Israel learned more of God's all-sufficiency in a land of drought, than they could have learned in the land flowing with milk and honey, namely, that God can feed without bread, and satisfy thirst without streams of waters: that he can make the clouds rain food, and the rock give out rivers: that the creature can do nothing without God, but God can do what he pleases without the creature.

Instances are endless: in a word, the suffering time is the time wherein God makes his attributes visible. "The Lord will be a refuge for the oppressed, a refuge in time of trouble," Psa. ix. 9. and what follows? "And they that know thy name, will put their trust in thee," ver.10. In the school of affliction God reads lectures upon his attributes, visible lectures; and expounds himself unto his people: so that many times they come to know more of God, or more experimentally by half a year's sufferings, than by many years' sermons.

15. God teacheth them in a suffering condition to mind the duties of a suffering condition; to study duty more than deliverance; seriously to inquire what it is which God calls for under the present dispensation. The soul crieth out with Paul, when laid for dead at Christ's feet, "Lord, what wilt thou have me to do?" Acts ix. 6. There is no condition or trial in the world, but it gives a man opportunity for the exercise of some special grace, and the doing of some special duty: and that is the work of

a christian, in every new state, and in every new trial, to mind what new duty God expects, what new grace he is to exert and exercise.

To mind deliverance only, is self-love, which is natural to man. "The captive exile hasteneth that he may be loosed, and that he should not die in the pit," &c. Man in affliction would fain be delivered, have the burden taken off, the yoke broken ; men make more haste to get their afflictions removed than sanctified : but this is not the work God looks for ; no, nor to think only what a man would do if he were delivered. Oh, thinks a man, if God would heal me of this sickness, deliver me out of this distress, I would walk more close with God, I would be more abundant in family-duties, I would be more fruitful in my converse ; I would do thus and thus, &c. Why now I say, though men should sit down in their afflictions, consider their ways, and make new resolutions for better things, if God shall give better times ; yet if this be all, it may be nothing else but a wile of the deceitful heart, a temptation and snare of the devil, to gain the time as it were of God ; a mere diversion to turn aside the heart from the present duty which God expects. And therefore when God intends good and happiness to the soul by the present chastisement, he pitcheth the soul upon the present duty, which is to "hear the rod, and who hath appointed it," Mic. vi. 9. to discern God's aim, and to find out the meaning of the present dispensation : to say to God, "I have born chastisement, I will not offend any more : that which I see not teach thou me, and if I have done iniquity, I will do no more," Job xxxiv. 31, 32. To reflect upon our ways and spirits, to complain of sin, and not of punishment ; "Wherefore doth a

living man complain? a man for the punishment
of his sin? Let us search and try our ways, and
turn again to the Lord," Lam. iii. 39. To think the
present condition the best: "I have learned in
whatsoever state I am, therewith to be content,"
Phil. iv. 11. In our patience to possess our souls,
Luke xxi. 19. to rejoice in God; yea to rejoice in
tribulation. Rom. v. 2, 3. To mind the public
calamities of the church more, and our private sufferings less: to pray for the welfare of Zion; "In
thy good pleasure do good unto Zion," Psa. li. 18.
To lift up Jesus Christ, and to make him glorious
by our afflictions; "That Christ may be magnified
in our bodies, whether it be by life, or by death,"
Phil. i. 20. Paul studied more how to adorn the
cross, than to avoid it; how to render persecution
amiable; and if he must suffer for Christ, yet that
Christ might not suffer by him; that Christ might
be exalted, and the church edified, Col. i. 24. This
God taught him; "I have learned," &c. And
lastly, to "commit the keeping of our souls to
God in well-doing, as unto a faithful Creator,"
1 Pet. iv. 19.

16. The sixteenth lesson is like unto it; and
that is, the privilege of a suffering condition. In
the school of affliction, one lecture which the Holy
Ghost readeth is, the fruits and advantages of a suffering condition. There is in every state of life a
snare and a privilege; and it is the folly and misery
of man left to himself, that he willingly runs into
the snare, and misseth of the privilege: he is only
able to add to his own misery, and to make his
condition worse than he finds it. Those whom God
loveth, he teacheth; he teacheth them to study, as
the duty of their present state, so the advantage.

When God takes away creature comforts, he doth not only necessitate, but by the secret impressions of love upon the heart, he emboldens the soul to look out for reparations, and to urge God for a recruit in some richer accommodations : " Lord," saith Abraham, " what wilt thou give me, seeing I go childless ?" Gen. xv. 2. God had denied Abraham a child, and He must make Abraham amends for it. In the like manner, Lord, what wilt thou give me, saith a suffering saint, since I go wifeless, and friendless, and landless, and houseless ? &c. yea Lord, what wilt thou give me, since I go ordinanceless, sermonless, sacramentless ? &c. So the disciples, " Behold, we have forsaken all and followed thee, what shall we have therefore ?" Matt. xix. 27. Faith may be a loser *for* Christ, but will not be a loser *by* Christ ; and accordingly Christ maketh an answer of faithfulness to this demand of faith " Verily I say unto you, there is no man that hath left house, or brethren, or sisters, or father, or mother, or children, or lands, for my sake, and the gospel's, but he shall receive a hundredfold now in this time," &c. Mark x. 29, 30. Advantage enough ; a hundred for one was the best year that ever Isaac had, Gen. xxvi. 12. But how shall this be made good ? why, with persecution ; " Houses, and brethren, and sisters, and mothers, and children, and lands, *with persecution.*" Persecution must make up the account. It is very observable, that year wherein Isaac received his hundredfold was Isaac's suffering year ; the year wherein famine had banished him from his own country to sojourn with Abimelech in Gerar, Gen. xxvi. 1. Isaac's best harvest was in a year of famine : and this was typical to all the children of promise ; they must receive Isaac's increase upon Isaac's account, a hundredfold with persecution. And I conceive our Saviour may allude to this type, in this promise: In persecution the people of God find their hundredfold; when they make a scripture inquiry, they find sufferings, especially those for Christ's sake, to be their letters testimonial for heaven, Luke xxi. 13.

The pledge of adoption, Heb. xii. 6, 7.—A purifier for corruption, Isa. xxvii. 9.—The improvement of holiness, Heb. xii. 10.—A fining pot to faith, 1 Pet. i. 7.—Communion with Christ. The presence of the Spirit of God and of glory, 1 Pet. iv. 13, 14.—The church's treasury, Col. i. 24.— Weak christian's strength. Strong christian's confidence, Phil. i. 13, 14. In both, the gospel's advantage.—And lastly, the enhancement of glory, 2 Cor. iv. 17, 18. Here is the hundredfold with advantage.

In a word, whatever the affliction be, that it shall be the soul's gain; " All things work together for good to them that love God," Rom. viii. 28. This God teacheth his people: it is the very design of the eighth chapter to the Romans, and of the twelve first verses of the twelfth chapter to the Hebrews, to show that God's rod and God's love go both together. And this is a sweet and blessed lesson indeed; for this quiets the heart, and supports the soul under its burden. "For this cause we faint not;" why? Because "though our outward man perisheth, yet the inward man is renewed day by day," 2 Cor. iv. 16. which means, what we lose in our bodies we gain in our souls : what we lose in our estates we get in grace; thus they bear up and comfort themselves in their deepest sorrows, while they that lie poring upon their afflictions, and are combining only to aggravate every circumstance of a suffering condition, sink their own spirits, vex their souls, dishonour God by slandering his dispensations ; and bring up an evil report upon the cross of Jesus Christ.   The spiritual privileges of God's suffering people, are therefore called " the peaceable fruits of righteousness," Heb. xii. 11. because the taste of this fruit brings in such peace and comfort into the soul, as makes it rejoice not in God only, but in tribulation, and in all these things to account itself " more than conqueror through him that hath loved us," Rom. viii. 37.

17. A lesson which God teacheth by his chastisements, is that which Christ taught Martha, namely, what is the one thing necessary ; affliction discovereth how much we are mistaken about our *must be's,* our *necessaries.* In our health, and strength, and liberty ; we think this thing *must be* done, and that thing *must be* done.   We think riches necessary, honours necessary, and a name in the world necessary ; we must get estates, and we must lay up large portions for our children, and we must raise our families, and call our lands after our own names, and the like, Psa. xlix. 11.   But in the day of adversity, when death looks us in the face, when God causeth the horror of the grave, the dread of the last judgment, and the terrors of eternity to pass before us, then we can put our mouths in the dust, smite upon our thigh, and sigh with the breaking of our loins, Oh how have I been mistaken ! how have I fed upon ashes, and a deceived heart turned me aside, so that I could not deliver my soul, nor say, Is there not a lie in my right hand ? Isa. xliv. 20.   Fool, how have I been deceived,

and made the *bye* the *main*, and the *main* the *bye*. Then we can see that pardon of sin, interest in Christ, evidence of that interest, sense of God's love, a life of grace, and assurance of glory, &c. are the only indispensables. In a word, that Christ alone is the one thing necessary, and that all other things, at the best, are but *may-be's*. Yea, but loss and dung in comparison of the excellency of the knowledge of Christ Jesus the Lord, and of interest in him, and in his righteousness, Phil. iii. 8, 9. without which the soul is undone to all eternity. And therefore, O that christians would be wise, that they would not "spend their money for that which is not bread, nor their labour for that which satisfieth not," Isa. lv. 2. but labour for faith which might realize and substantiate unseen and spiritual things, Heb. xi. 1. and give them a being to the soul. They that will not learn this lesson in the school of the word, shall learn it in the school of affliction, if they belong to God ; and therefore set your heart to it.

18. Time-redemption is another lesson which God teacheth those whom he corrects. In our tranquillity, how many golden hours do we throw down the stream, which we are like never to see again ; for one whereof the time may come, when we would give rivers of oil, the wealth of both the Indies, mountains of precious stones, if they were our own, and yet neither would they be found a sufficient price for the redemption of any one lost moment ! It was the complaint of the very moralist, and may be much more our complaint, Who is there among us, that knows how to value time, and prize a day at a due rate? Most men study rather how to pass away their time than to redeem it; prodigal of their

precious hours, as if they had more than they could
tell what to do withal: our season is short, and
we make it shorter. How sad a thing is it to hear
men complain, O what shall we do to drive away
the time?

Alas, even sabbath-time, the purest, the most
refined part of time, a creation out of a creation,
time consecrated by Divine sanction, how cheap and
common is it in most men's eyes, while many do
sin away, and the most do idle away those hallowed hours! Seneca was wont to jeer the Jews
for their ill husbandry, in that they lost one day in
seven, meaning their sabbath: truly it is too true
of the most of christians, they lose one day in seven,
whatever else; the sabbath for the most part is
but a lost day; while some spend it totally upon
their lusts, and the most, I had almost said the
best, do fill up the void spaces and intervals of
the sabbath from public worship, with idleness and
vanity! But oh, when trouble comes, and danger
comes, and death comes; when the sword is at the
body, the pistol at the breast, the knife at the throat,
death at the door, how precious would one of those
despised hours be! Evil days cry with a loud
voice in our ears, Redeem the time: that caution
was written from the tower in Rome. " Redeeming
the time because the days are evil," Eph. v. 16. In
life-threatening dangers, when God threatens, as it
were, that time shall be no more, Rev. x. 6. then
we can think of redeeming time for prayer, for
reading, for meditation, for studying and clearing
out our evidences for heaven, for doing and receiving good, according to opportunities presented;
yea, then we can gather up the very broken frag
ments of time, that nothing may be lost. Then God

teacheth the soul what a choice piece of wisdom it
is for christians, if it were possible, to be before
hand with time; for usually it comes to pass through
our unskilfulness and improvidence, that we are
surprised by death; and we that reckoned upon years
—many years—yet to come, have not, possibly, so
many hours to make ready our accounts. It may
be, this night is the summons, and then if our time
be done, and our work to be begun, in what a case
are we! The soul must needs be in perplexity at
the hour of death, that seeth the day spent, and its
work yet to do. A traveller that seeth the sun
setting when he is but entering on his journey, cannot but be aghast: the evening of our day, and the
morning of our task, do not well agree together;
that time which remaineth is too short to lament
the loss of by-past time. By such hazards God
doth come upon the soul as the angel upon Peter
in prison, and smites upon our sides, bids us rise
up quickly, and gird up ourselves, and bind on
our sandals, &c. Acts xii. 7. that we may redeem
lost opportunities, and do much work in a little
time; it is pity to lose any thing of that which is
so precious and so short, 1 Cor. vii. 29.

19. Another lesson is how to estimate, at least
to make some remote and imperfect guess at the
sufferings of Jesus Christ, Lam. i. 12. In our
prosperity we pass by the cross, that is, carelessly
and regardlessly: at the best we do but shake our
heads a little. The reading of the story of Christ's
passion stirs up some compassion towards him, and
passion against his persecutors; but it is quickly
gone: we forget as soon as we get into the world
again: but now let God pinch our flesh with some
sore affliction; let him fill our bones with pain, and

set us on fire with a burning fever; let our feet be
hurt in the stocks, and the irons enter into our
souls; let our souls be exceedingly filled with the
scorning of those that are at ease, and with the contempt of the proud; let us be destitute, afflicted,
tormented, &c. then happily we will sit down,
and look upon Him whom we have pierced, and
begin to say within ourselves, And are the chips
of the cross so heavy? what then was the cross itself,
which first my Redeemer did bear, and then it did
bear him! Are a few bodily pains so bitter? what
then were those agonies which the Lord of glory
sustained in his soul! Is the wrath of man so
piercing? what was the wrath of God, which
scorched his righteous soul, and sweltered his very
heart blood through his flesh in a cold winter's
night, so that his sweat was as great drops of blood,
trickling down to the ground! Are the buffetings
of men so grievous? what were the buffetings of
Satan, which our Lord sustained, when all the
brood of the serpent lay nibbling at the heel of his
passion! Is a burning fever so hot? how then did
the most searching flames scald my Saviour's spirit! Is it such a heart-piercing affliction to be
deserted of friends? what was it then for him, who
was the Son of God's love, the darling of his bosom,
to be deserted of his Father, which made him cry
out to the astonishment of heaven and earth, " My
God, my God, why hast thou forsaken me?" Is a
chain so heavy, a prison so loathsome, the sentence
and execution of death so dreadful, oh what was
it for him who made heaven and earth to be bound
with a chain, hurried up and down from one unrighteous judge to another, mocked, abused, spit
upon, buffeted, reviled, cast into prison, arraigned,

condemned, executed in a most shameful and an
accursed manner! Oh what was it for him to
endure all this contradiction of sinners, rage of the
devil, and wrath of God, in comparison of whom
the most righteous person that ever was may say
with the good thief on the cross, "And we indeed
justly, but He, what evil hath he done?" " He made
his grave with the wicked, and with the rich in his
death, because he had done no violence, neither
was any deceit in his mouth," Isa. liii. 9.   Blessed
be God, my prison is not Tophet, my burnings are
not unquenchable flames, my cup is not filled with
wrath : in a word, this is not hell.   Blessed be God
for Jesus Christ, by whom I am delivered from
wrath to come, 1 Thess. i. 10.   And thus, as the
Lord Jesus, by the sensible experience of his own
passion, came perfectly to understand what his poor
members suffer while they are in the body, so we,
by the remainders of his cross, which he hath be-
queathed us as a legacy, come in some measure to
understand the sufferings of Christ ; or at least, by
comparing things of such vast disproportion, to
guess at what we cannot understand.

20. The last lesson which God teacheth by affliction is, how to prize and long for heaven.   In our
prosperity, when the candle of God shines in our
tabernacles, when we wash our steps in butter, and
the rock poureth us out rivers of oil, Job xxix. 6.
we could sit down with the present world, and even
say with the disciples, though not upon so good
an account, " It is good for us to be here ; let us
here build us tabernacles." While life is sweet, death
is bitter ; and heaven itself is no temptation, while
the world gives us her friendly entertainments.
But when poverty and imprisonment, reproach

and persecution, sickness and sore diseases, do
not only pinch but vex our hearts with variety of
aggravations, we are not so fond of the creature,
but we can be content to entertain a parley with
death, and take heaven into our considerations.
Not that merely to desire to be in heaven, because
we are weary of the world, is an argument of grace,
or a lesson that needs Divine teaching; self-love will
prompt as much as that comes to.   But because,
like foolish travellers, we love our way though it be
troublesome, rather than our country ! God by this
discipline taketh off our hearts by degrees from this
present world, and maketh us look homeward :
being burdened we groan, 2 Cor. v. 4. and with
the dove, we return to the ark when the world is
afloat round about us? When David was driven
from his palace, then, "Wo is me that my pilgrimage
is prolonged :" so the Septuagint renders it.   We
should be contented, like the Israelites, with the
garlick and flesh-pots of Egypt, if God did not set
cruel taskmasters over us to double our burdens.
When God hath thus lessened our esteem of the
world, he discovers to us the excellency of heavenly
comforts, and draws out the desires of the soul to
a full fruition : When shall I come and appear in
thy presence ? Even so come, Lord Jesus.   Affliction puts heaven into all those notions which make
it heaven indeed.

To the weary it is rest, Isa. lvii. 2. Rev. xiv. 13.
—To the banished it is home, 2 Cor. v. 6.—To
the scorned and reproached it is glory, Rom. v.
2.—To the captive it is liberty, Rom. viii. 21.—
To the conflicting soul it is conquest, Rom. viii. 37.
—And to the conqueror it is a crown of life, Rev.
ii. 10. Righteousness, 2 Tim. iv. 8. Glory, 1 Pet.

v. 4.—To the hungry it is hidden manna, Rev. ii. 17.—To the thirsty it is the fountain and waters of life, and rivers of pleasure, Rev. xxii. 17. Psa. xxxvi. 8, 9.—To the grieved soul, whether with sin or sorrow, it is fulness of joy; and to the mourner it is pleasures for evermore, Psa. xvi. 11.—In a word, to them that have lain upon the dunghill, and kept their integrity, it is a throne, on which they shall sit and reign with Christ for ever and ever, Rev. iii. 21. xxii. 5.

Surely, beloved, heaven thus proportioned to every state of the afflicted soul cannot fail to be very precious; and will make the soul with a stronger or weaker impulse, desire to be dissolved and to be with Christ, which is best of all, Phil. i. 23. A christian indeed is comforted by faith, but not satisfied; or if satisfied, it is in point of security, not of desire: because here "we are absent from the Lord, and walk by faith, not by sight," 2 Cor. v. 6, 7. Hope, though it keep life in the soul, yet it is not able to fill it: he longs and thinks every day a year till he be at home in his Father's arms, and sit down on his Father's throne, crowned with his Father's honour and glory. They that walk by faith cannot be quiet till they be in the sight of those things which they believe. Jacob when he heard that Joseph was alive, though he did believe it, yet could not be satisfied with hearing of it; but saith he, "I will go and see him before I die:" so the believing soul, He, whom my soul loveth, was dead, but is alive, and behold he liveth for evermore, Rev. i. 18. I will die that I may go and see him: as Augustine, upon that answer of God to Moses, "Thou canst not see my face,

and live," Exod. xxxiii. 20. makes this quick and
sweet reply, " Then, Lord, let me die that I may
see thy face."

Thus I have presented you with those twenty
several lessons which Jesus Christ, the great Prophet of his church, teacheth his afflicted ones to
take out in the school of affliction.   And now, as I
told you in my entrance upon this subject, all these
lessons may be reduced to three great summary,
comprehensive instructions.

First. The sinfulness of sin.

Second. The emptiness of the creature.

Third. The fulness of Jesus Christ.

The first summary comprehensive lesson, is the
sinfulness of sin. Sin is always very sinful ; but in
our prosperity we are not so sensible of it : the
dust of the world doth so fill our eyes, that we
cannot make a clear and distinct discovery of the
evil that is in sin : but now, by the sharp and bitter
waters of affliction, God doth wash out that dust,
and clears the organ to make a perfect discovery,
and to discern sin, as it is, and not as usually it
doth appear : sin becomes exceeding sinful, Rom.
vii. 13. God hath four glasses, wherein he discovers
to the soul the evil that is in sin ; 1. The glass of
the law, James i. 23, 24.   2. The blood of Christ,
Rev. i. 5.   3. Afflictions and chastisements in this
present world, Lam. iii. 39. 42.   4. The torments
of hell, Matt. xxv. 41.

Indeed of all these glasses, the blood of Christ
is the clearest, and doth most fully and perfectly
represent the exceeding sinfulness that is in sin,
the stain and spot whereof could be washed out
with no other element but the blood of the Son of

God; for, as it was purchasing blood, so it was expiating blood. " He hath loved us, and washed us with his own blood," Rev. i. 5. But though this be the purest glass, yet God doth make frequent and great use of the third glass also—afflictions and chastisements for sin, to discover to the children of promise the greatness of that evil which is in sin. It is very notable how God brings the Israelites this glass in their affliction, and bids them, as it were, see their face in it. " Know therefore and see, that it is an evil and bitter thing that thou hast forsaken the Lord thy God, and that my fear is not in thee, saith the Lord God of hosts," Jer. ii. 19. In this glass he discovers to them a fourfold evil in sin.

(1.) As it is the cause of all other evils of punishment. " Hast thou not procured this unto thyself, in that thou hast forsaken the Lord thy God?" &c. Jer. ii. 17. He bids them read all their sins in their punishments; he bids them look upon sin as a mother-evil, that hath all other evils in it; which means, Thank thyself for all the affliction that is upon thee; thou hast procured this unto thyself. Art thou in captivity, in prison, in distress, &c. thank thy idolatry, and thy adulteries, whereby thou hast forsaken the Lord thy God. Thank thyself for all the misery that is upon thee. Every man's heart may say to him as Apollodorus's heart cried to him out of the boiling caldron : I have been the cause of all this. As lust when it hath conceived, brings forth sin, so sin when it is finished, when it is perfected, will bring forth death, James i. 15. Sin is the child of lust, and the mother of death.

(2.) In this glass God represents sin to their view, as an evil in itself: " Know therefore and see that it is an evil thing and bitter ;" that sin doth not only bring evil, but is evil; it is an evil thing: not only that it works bitterness, but is bitterness; it is a bitter thing: it hath a bitter root, as well as it brings forth bitter fruits. God leads the sinner by affliction to take notice not only what sin doth, but what sin is; it is evil. Yea,

(3.) That it is a pure, unmixed evil. It is an evil thing, the whole being of sin is evil. In the evil of affliction there is some good, for it hath God for the author. "Is there an evil in the city, and the Lord hath not done it?" Amos iii. 6. And it hath good for its end: "All things shall work together for good to them that love God," Rom. viii. 28. "It is good for me," saith David, "that I have been afflicted," Psa. cxix. 71. But now sin is a simple uncompounded evil, for it hath the devil for the author; "He that committeth sin is of the devil," 1 John iii. 8. and death for its end; "The wages of sin is death," Rom. vi. 23. death in its vastest comprehension, sin is evil all over.

(4.) The glass represents it yet worse, and that is, as it is an evil against God. It is a departure from God, "Thou hast forsaken the Lord thy God," Jer. ii. 17. and so again, ver. 19. "Thou hast forsaken the Lord thy God; my fear is not in thee." Sin, as the schools define it, is an aversion from God, and a conversion or turning to the creature. "My people have committed two evils; they have forsaken me the fountain of living waters, and hewed them out cisterns, broken cisterns that can hold no water," ver. 13. Sin is not only an unmixed evil, but a twisted multiplied evil. It is a departure from the fountain of life and glory, and a turning to a scanty, and a broken vessel, which leaks out as fast as it is poured in. Now here is the exceeding sinfulness of sin, that it is an evil against God; punishment is but an evil against the creature: thou hast procured this unto thyself, affliction is but a contradiction to the will of the creature; but sin is a contradiction to the will of God. Whence we may safely conclude, that there is more evil in the least sin, than there is in the greatest punishment, even hell itself; the hell that is *in* sin, is worse than the hell that is prepared *for* sin. Yea and behold one evil more in this glass, the aggravation of all the rest, and that is,

5. That sin is a causeless evil, a causeless departure, "Thou hast forsaken the Lord thy God, when he led thee by the way," Jer. ii. 17. when he led thee as a guide to direct thee, led thee as a stay to support thee; he put underneath thee his everlasting arms: he led thee as a convoy to guard thee, and led thee as a Father to provide for thee. Thou wantedst nothing, and yet thou hast forsaken the Lord thy God. This is the aggravation; " O generation," (generation of what? why of what you will; God leaves a space, as it were, that we may write down what we please; generation of vipers, generation of monsters, any thing, rather than the generation of his children:) " O generation, see ye the word of the Lord." Still he holds the glass before their eyes, and what are they to behold there? Why their causeless apostasy and rebellions; for so it follows, "Have I been a barren wilderness, a land of darkness? have ye wanted any thing? wherefore then say my people, We will come no more unto thee?" ver. 31. O this departure is causeless and wilful. God saith to the sinner, as Pharaoh said to Jeroboam, when he would be gone from him, " But what hast thou lacked with

me, that behold thou seekest to be gone from me ?"
1 Kings xi. 22, and the sinner seemeth to answer God
as Jeroboam there answered Pharaoh : " Nothing,
howbeit let me go in any wise." Jeroboam could
come to Pharaoh when he was in distress ; but,
when the storm was over at home, he will be gone
again, though he cannot tell why : and so deals the
treacherous heart with God ; and this causeless
departure from God is a high aggravation of sin :
God is often upon it, as Isa. i. 2, and Amos vi. 3—
5, &c. The soul sinneth only because it will sin ;
in a word, affliction is one of God's tribunals
where the sinner is arraigned, convicted, and condemned : " As many as I love, I rebuke and chasten ;"
the Greek words signify to convince and correct,
that is, by correction to convince of sin, Rev. iii. 19.
Truly, in affliction, sin is laid open before a man's
eyes in such sort as he is enforced to plead guilty.
God sits as judge ; conscience is witness, a thousand
witnesses ; sin the indictment ; affliction both evidence and execution. Hence it is, that, sooner or
later, the convinced soul sees sin a greater evil
than affliction, whatever it is ; and now, as it were,
forgetting the affliction, begins to mourn only for
sin, crying out with holy Job in the dust, " I have
sinned ; what shall I do unto thee, O thou Preserver
of men ?" Job vii. 20. He saith not, My substance is spoiled, my children destroyed, my body is
become filled with loathsome diseases, and myself
a terror to myself and standers by, what wilt thou
do unto me, O thou Preserver of men ? but, " I have
sinned ; what shall I do unto thee," &c. Affliction
led him to sin ; correction was made conviction,
and sin now lieth heavier upon him than all his
sufferings. This is the first comprehensive lesson.

Second.   The emptiness of the creature.

In our prosperity we stick in the creature, and
dote upon the creature, the things and persons in
this present world, as if there our happiness and
comfort were bound up: but in the day of adversity, God convinceth us of our mistakes, by causing
us to see the emptiness and vanity of all sublunary
contentments ; we begin to find the world to be
but gilded emptiness, a mere nothing.   Then ask
the soul what it thinks of the world and all the
elements thereof, the lusts of the flesh, the lusts of
the eyes, and the pride of life, as the apostle sorts
them, which formerly did so glitter in its eyes, and
the answer will be with the prophet, " All flesh
is grass, and all the goodliness thereof as the
flower of the field," Isa. xl. 6.   " Vanity of vanities,
all is vanity," Eccl. i. 2.   The afflicted soul saith of
all creature-excellency, " It is not," Prov. xxiii. 5. it
looks upon them as so many nonentities ; so many
nots.   *Not* that which it seems ; *not* that which it
promiseth ; *not* that which we expect, and flatter
ourselves with.   " Riches profit not in the day of
wrath," Prov. xi. 4.   Whatsoever it is that a man
makes his riches, whether friend, or wealth, or
parts, or creature-interest, they profit not, that is,
they cannot deliver out of the hands, either of
death or judgment.   And besides, the soul finds
by experience the unsuitableness and dissatisfaction
that is in all these seen things ; that there is no
proportion between an invisible soul and visible
comforts, between an immortal soul and perishing
contentments, between a spiritual being and an
earthly portion ; that the wind which a man takes
in by gaping will as soon fill an hungry belly, as
creature-comforts will satisfy the spirit.   In the

hour of temptation the soul says, " Miserable com
forters are ye all, physicians of no value ;" upon
which a man may bestow all that he hath in expectation of a cure, as the afflicted woman upon
her physicians, Mark v. 26. and find himself no
whit better, but rather worse.   Surely the world in
all its bravery is to the afflicted soul no better than
the cities which Solomon gave to Hiram, which he
called Cabul, that is to say, displeasing or dirty,
1 Kings ix. 13. The day of affliction is one of those
days, wherein men cast away their idols of silver
and their idols of gold, which they made each one
for himself to worship, to the moles and to the bats,
and saith unto them with indignation, Get ye
hence, Isa. ii. 20.

Third.   In the day of affliction, God discovers
to the soul the fulness of Jesus Christ.

There is an infinite fulness in Jesus Christ.   " It
pleased the Father that in him should all fulness
dwell," Col. i. 19.   The covenant of grace is suited
to all the exigences and indigences of a poor,
undone, convinced sinner ; it is " ordered in all
things," 2 Sam. xxiii. 5. In opposition to the power
of corruption in the heart, " I will put," saith God,
" my law in their inward parts," &c. Jer. xxxi.
33, 34.   In opposition to error and ignorance in
the understanding, " They shall all know me," &c.
In opposition to guilt, " I will forgive their iniquity,
and I will remember their sin no more."   And the
offices of Jesus Christ are suited to all the branches
of the covenant.   In order to the first branch, " I
will write my law in their hearts," &c.   Behold
Jesus Christ is a King.   In order to the second,
" They shall all know me," &c. behold Jesus Christ
is a Prophet. And in order to the third, " I will forgive

their iniquities," behold Jesus Christ is a Priest.
The offices of Christ fill and execute the covenant
of grace; and the fulness of God fills and acts the
offices of Jesus Christ; the power of God, and the
fulness of power. his kingly office. The wisdom
of God, and the fulness of wisdom, his prophetical
office. The righteousness of God, and the fulness
of righteousness, his priestly office. This is that
which the psalmist celebrateth in that song of
loves, "God hath anointed thee with the oil of
gladness above thy fellows," Psa. xlv. 7. Never
king was anointed with such power, never prophet with such wisdom, never priest with such
grace and righteousness: they had their stinted proportions; but "God gave not the Spirit by measure
unto him," John iii. 34. "In him dwelt all the
fulness of the Godhead bodily," Col. ii. 9. It is
not less than an infinite fulness which fills Jesus
Christ as Mediator, that we of his fulness might
receive grace for grace. But we are not always in
a capacity either to receive or to see that fulness.
And the reason is, because in our prosperity we *fill*
ourselves so with the world, with the pleasures and
profits of the world, that it fares with Christ now
as it did when he was born, there is no room for
him in the inn. While the world glitters in our eyes
with her painted gaudery, "he hath no form nor
comeliness, and when we see him, there is no beauty
that we should desire him," Isa. liii. 2. We are
very prone to love the world for the world, terminate
our affections in the creature, and do not use
earthly comforts in that way, and to that end, that
we might thereby be the more fitted to walk with
God; and when our desires are such, the more they
are, the less are our delights in Jesus Christ. This

is our sin and folly, that we do not fear the unlawful use of lawful things ; nor see where the
snare lieth to inveigle those affections to the creature which are only due to God himself; and a
great reproach it is to Jesus Christ. But now
when God spreads sackcloth upon all the beauty
and bravery of the creature, and so hideth pride
from man, when God by some flashes of lightning
strikes us blind to the world, then we can discover
beauty and excellency in Christ, infinitely tran-
scending all the beauty and excellency in the world ;
" Thou art fairer than the children of men, grace
is poured into thy lips," Psa. xlv. 2. when under
the stairs, and in the clifts of the rocks, then the
soul can sing, " My beloved is white and ruddy,
the chiefest among ten thousand," Sol. Song, v. 10.
When the God of heaven hath famished all our
gods on earth, when he hath hunger-starved us, as
to creature-comforts, in any way whatsoever, then
we can hunger after and taste the sweetness, the
fulness, which is in Jesus Christ ; O then, Christ, a
King to govern, a Prophet to teach, a Priest to save !
how precious ! then none but Christ, none but
Christ ; give me Christ or else I die. In a word,
my beloved, when once it is come (by what exigences and surprises soever) to an, Oh wretch that
I am, who shall deliver me ? then, " I thank God
through Jesus Christ our Lord," Rom. vii. 24, 25.
Truly God sees it absolutely necessary to exercise
us with a severe discipline, that he may endear
Jesus Christ to our hearts ; and seclude us from
the world, that we may study and improve his
fulness. As the law is our schoolmaster, so affliction
is an usher to the law ; affliction brings us to the
law, and the law brings us to Christ, Gal. iii. 24.

And thus I have despatched the first thing I undertook, for the opening of the doctrine, namely, the lessons which God teacheth those whom he chasteneth; both in their twenty particulars, and in their three summary comprehensive heads, to which all the rest may be reduced.

II. The nature or properties of Divine teaching.

My brethren, it is not every teaching that will make or evidence a man to be a blessed man under affliction. There is hardly any man that is under affliction, but he learns somewhat by it; and yet few are blessed: the reason is, because it matters not so much, what a man is taught, as who is the teacher, whether he be taught of God or not: yea that is not all neither; for we are not to inquire only, whether we be taught of God, but how? There is a twofold teaching of God. There is a common teaching, which even heathen, men out of the church, hypocrites and reprobates within the church, may have; the very philosophers have read excellent lectures upon affliction, Seneca and others; and there is a special teaching, proper and peculiar only to the children of promise. A covenant teaching; "All thy children shall be taught of God," Isa. liv. 13. it is the covenant of God with the Redeemer. A teaching without which no profit; "I am the Lord thy God which teacheth thee to profit;" to profit by chastisements and correction; so it followeth, "Which leadeth thee by the way that thou shouldest go," Isa. xlviii. 17. God's teachings are not only directing teachings, but leading teachings; not only to show the way, but to enable to go in the way.

Now this teaching hath a six-fold property.

1. It is an inward teaching. Inward in respect of the *object*, and inward in respect of the *subject*.

Inward in respect of the *object;* so our Saviour concerning the saving teaching of the Holy Ghost; " When the Spirit of truth is come, he will guide you into all truth," John xvi. 13. Man may lead you *unto* truth ; but it is the Spirit of God that only can lead you *into* truth. He ónly that hath the key of David, that openeth and no man shutteth, and shutteth and no man openeth, can open to you the door of truth, and show you the inside of truth. And great is the difference between these two teachings. He that comes to a stately house or place sees only the outward fabric and structure ; and even that may take much ; but he that comes into it, sees all the inward contrivances and conveyances ; he sees all the rich furniture and adornings of the several rooms and offices of the house, which are not only for use, but for delight and ornament. Surely, the very outside of truth is goodly ; but, like the king's daughter, it is all glorious within ; not pleasing only, but ravishing ; this they see who are led into truth ; by virtue whereof David saw wonderful things in the law, Psa. cxix. 18. Objects which filled his soul with wonder and delight.

As the teachings of the covenant are inward in respect of the object, so inward also in respect of the *subject*. " In the *hidden part* thou hast made me know wisdom," Psa. li. 6. and again, " I thank the Lord that gave me counsel, *my reins* also instruct me in the night seasons," Psa. xvi. 7. The reins are the most inward part of the body ; and the night season the most retired and private time :

both express the intimacy of Divine teaching; man may teach the brains, but God only teacheth the reins; the knowledge which man teacheth is a swimming knowledge, but the knowledge which Christ teacheth is a soaking knowledge. " God who commanded light to shine out of darkness, hath shined into our hearts, to give the light of the knowledge of the glory of God in the face of Jesus Christ," 2 Cor. iv. 6. It is a loaden expression, and holds forth the inward teachings of God on both sides; both in reference to the subject, and in reference to the object. In reference to the subject, he that commanded the light to shine out of darkness, hath shined into our hearts; man's light may shine into the head, but God's light doth shine into the heart. God hath his throne in heaven, but his chair, his pulpit, is in the heart; he " hath shined into our hearts." And then you have the inwardness of Divine teaching in respect of the object; " He hath given us the light of the knowledge of the glory of God in the face of Jesus Christ." Man may give knowledge, confused general knowledge, but God giveth the light of knowledge in the lustre and brightness of it. " In thy light we shall see light," Psa. xxxvi. 9. The soul seeth by the same light whereby God himself seeth, "thy light." And not only so; here is not only knowledge and light of knowledge, but the glory of that light; the light which God brings in to the sanctified understanding, is a glorious light, a marvellous light, 1 Pet. ii. 9. The soul that the Spirit of God taketh by the hand, and leadeth into truth, standeth wondering at the glory and excellency of that light which shines round about it. And then lastly, all this in the face of Jesus Christ; the face is the full discovery of a person. Moses could not see God's face, but only his back-parts he might see, Exod. xxxiii. 23. But now by the flesh of Jesus Christ God hath put a vail upon his face ; the vail of his flesh, Heb. x. 20. through which we may see the face of God ; for now in Christ it is God manifest in the flesh, 1 Tim. iii. 16. the human nature of Jesus Christ hath made God visible. In this face now of Jesus Christ do they whom God teacheth by a saving gospel-teaching see Divine truth, that is, they see it now not only by borrowed representations and natural resemblances, but in its own native beauty and lustre, "as the truth is in Jesus," Eph. iv. 21. " He hath shined into our hearts to give us the light of the knowledge of the glory of God in the face of Jesus Christ." This is the first property of Divine teaching. It is inward, and that both in respect of subject and object.

2. Divine covenant-teaching is a clear convincing teaching; so our Saviour of the Spirit ; " When he is come, he shall *convince* the world," &c. The word signifieth a clear demonstrative conviction ; so the apostle defines faith to be the evidence, or demonstration, the evident demonstration of things not seen. The Holy Ghost in his teachings, brings in divine truths with such a clear and convincing light that the soul sits down under it fully satisfied ; it is not only convinced to silence, but to assurance ; the soul doth sweetly and freely acquiesce in the present truths. " Now I know," saith Moses's father-in-law, " that the Lord is greater than all gods." He had heard of God before, but that bred but opinion only ; but now he is thoroughly convinced ; " I know that the Lord is greater than all gods," Exod. xviii. 11. So David concerning his afflictions,

" I know, Lord, that thy judgments are right, and that of faithfulness thou hast afflicted me," Psa. cxix. 75. He was fully satisfied both of the equity and fidelity of God's chastisements; right in respect of the merit, and faithful in respect of the end. And thus in all the lessons before presented to your view, and in all other, what God teacheth he teacheth with such a clear evidence of truth, that the soul is set beyond all peradventure; " Our gospel came unto you, not in word only, but also in power and in the Holy Ghost, and in much full assurance," 1 Thess. i. 5. the word hath a double and a treble emphasis; assurance, full assurance, and much full assurance; such are the teachings of the Holy Ghost. Common teaching may convince to silence, a man cannot tell how to gainsay or contradict, but the understanding may remain doubtful still : there is that which the schools call suspense or hesitancy in the understanding; there is not a full and clear assent in the understanding to the truths propounded : but a man remains, in the apostle's language, a double-minded man : or as the word signifieth, a double-soul man ; a man of a double, or doubtful, or divided spirit, floating between different opinions; one soul, as it were, believeth this way, and another soul believeth that way ; one while he believeth there is a God, and anon " the fool saith in his heart, There is no God :" sometimes he calls sin evil ; and anon again he thinks it good. He believeth, and he believeth not ; sometimes what he heareth from the word is truth of God ; sometimes he thinks again it is but an invention of man, there may possibly be some mistake in it. But now the teachings of God set a man beyond all those fluctuations and unsettledness in judgment : there is that which the apostle calls "the riches of the full assurance of understanding to the acknowledgment of the mystery of God," Col. ii. 2. Assurance of principles, even when the soul may possibly want the assurance of application.

3. Another property of Divine teaching is, it is an experimental teaching. The soul can speak experimentally of the truths it knows, " It is good for me," saith David, "that I have been afflicted," Psa. cxix. 71. why, but may not any man say as much as that? Yes, few men there are but have the notion in their heads, and on their lips : but mark, I pray, the psalmist speaks experimentally to the point, and doth instance the good which he had gained by affliction ; " I have learned thy statutes." He had learned more acquaintance with the word, more delight in the word, more conformity to the word. He knew it more, and loved it better, and was more transformed into the nature of it than ever, &c. So, "The Lord preserveth the simple," Psa. cxvi. 6. that is, God stands by his upright hearted ones to secure them from violence : a good notion ; but any man may have it in the proposition ; but David hath it in the *experience*, " I was brought low, and he helped me ;" my faith was brought low, and my comfort was brought low, and my resolutions were brought low, "my feet had well nigh slipped," Psa. lxxiii. 2. but God helped my faith, revived my comfort, strengthened my resolutions, and established my feet : " Thou hast holden me by my right hand," ver. 23. Thus St. Paul, " I know whom I have believed," &c. 2 Tim. i. 12. I have experienced his faithfulness and his all-sufficiency : I dare trust my all with him. I am sure he will keep it safe to that day. And thus they

that are taught of God in affliction can speak experimentally, in one degree or other, of the gains and
privileges of a suffering condition : they can speak
experimentally of communion with God, "Though
I walk through the valley of the shadow of death,
I will fear no evil ;" why ? "for thou art with me,"
Psa. xxiii. 4. I have had comfortable experience
of thy upholding, counselling, comforting presence
with me in my deepest desertion : so of other fruits
of affliction, "This I had," Psa. cxix. 56. this I have
got by my sufferings, I bless God I have learned
more patience, humility, self-denial, &c. to be more
sensible of my brethren's sufferings, to sit looser to
the world, to mind duty, and to trust safely with
God, to prepare for death, and to provide for eternity, one way or other it is good for me ; I could
not have been without this affliction, &c.

Common knowledge rests in generals, and lieth
more in propositions than in application ; but they
that are taught of God can say, As we have heard,
so have we *seen ;* they can go along with every
truth, and say, It is so, I have experienced this
word upon mine own heart ; they can set to their
seal that God is true, John iii. 33.

4. Divine covenant-teaching is a powerful teaching. After a man hath got many truths into the
understanding, the main work is yet to do, and that
is to bring down holy truths to action, to draw forth
Divine principles into practice : a natural man may
know much, he may have a heap of truths in his
understanding ; but they all lie strengthless in the
brain, he hath no power to live the truths he knows.
Covenant-teachings convey strength as well as light,
and do what they teach. "The Lord spake to me
with a strong hand, and instructed me that I should

not walk in the way of this people, saying, Say ye
not, A confederacy to them who say, A confederacy;
neither fear ye their fear, nor be afraid.   Sanctify
the Lord of hosts himself," &c. Isa. viii. 11—13. It is
a most sweet and comfortable scripture, and that in
two respects.   1. In respect of what it implieth.   2.
In respect of what it expresseth.   First, it implieth
thus much, that even the holy prophet himself had
no small combat and conflict within himself what
to do in such a juncture of time as that was, when
it was told the house of David, saying, " Syria is
confederate with Ephraim," Isa. vii. 2. that is,
that both those kingdoms had made a league together, and were now upon their march with their
combined forces, to make war against the house of
David.   It was sad news, and the text saith, " The
heart of Ahaz, and the heart of the people was
moved, as the trees of the wood are moved with
the wind," that is, they were terribly afraid, even
ready to die for fear, and in that fear abundance of
the people fell off to the enemy, and engaged with
them ; as it is intimated, " They refuse the waters
of Shiloah that go softly," Isa. viii. 6. that is, they
looked upon the forces of Jerusalem, as poor and
inconsiderable, no ways able to oppose and engage
so potent an adversary as came against them ; and
so deserted their own party, and rejoiced in Rezin
and Remaliah's son : they rejoiced in them, that is,
to cover their defection from their true sovereign
they cried up the invaders as their best friends, who
came to rescue them from the tyranny and oppression of Ahaz.   And it seems the prophet Isaiah
himself was surprised with fear too, for a time, and
began to dispute the matter within himself, whether
it were not best for him, to strike in with the

stronger side, and to engage in the confederacy with those two princes as the multitude did; there wanting not, probably, fair and specious pretences to justify that defection. It seems, I say, that the prophet had a sore temptation upon his spirit about this matter, and was even ready to determine the question in the affirmative, till God came in and instructed him, &c. And that is the second thing; the comfort expressed in these words : while the prophet was thus conflicting and fluctuating in his own thoughts, God came in, and by strength of hand rebuked his fears, silenced his objections, quieted his spirit, determined the dispute, and instructed him what course to take, which was not to comply, but to believe, to study duty, and leave safety with God; "Fear not their fear, nor be afraid, sanctify the Lord of hosts himself," &c. Power went forth with instruction, taught him what to do, and enabled him to do what it taught. Blessed be God, who hath a hand to teach his people with, as well as a mouth ; a hand of power, as well as a mouth of instruction : had it not been for this, the prophet himself had been certainly carried down the torrent of that apostasy, as well as others.

And there is caution in this instance as well as comfort in reference to ourselves and our brethren ; and that is, in case of surprise by some sudden gusts of fear and temptation, not rashly to judge ourselves, or our brethren ; but wisely and calmly to consider it is no other temptation than what is common to man, 1 Cor. x. 13. yea to the best of men : Job, and David, and Jeremiah, and Habakkuk, and Peter, and here Isaiah, were all nonplussed, and staggered for a time, and recovered only by a powerful word from Heaven; and therefore in such cases, it becomes christians to pity, rather than to insult, and to study to heal rather than to reject: "Considering themselves, lest they also be tempted," Gal. vi. 1. This is the privilege of the children of promise, strength goeth out from the covenant with instruction, "The Lord who commandeth light to shine out of darkness, hath shined into our hearts:" which means, God had taught us by such a word, as that whereby he made the world, a creating word, a word that giveth strength as well as counsel. And this teaching it is which the prophet David so frequently importuneth in his prayers: compare Psa. cxix. 33. with verse 35. "Teach me, O Lord, the way of thy statutes, make me to go in the path of thy commandments." "Teach me to do thy will," Psa. cxliii. 10. Mark that; not only teach me *the way*, but teach me *to go;* not only teach me thy will, but teach me to do thy will. Common teaching may teach a hypocrite the way, but having teaching only teacheth the soul *to go* in that way; an unregenerate man may know the will of God; but he knoweth not how to *do* that will. "The joy of the Lord is our strength," Neh. viii. 10.

5. A fifth property; the teachings of God are sweet and pleasant teachings. "Thou hast taught me;" what followeth? "How sweet are thy words unto my taste! yea sweeter than honey to my mouth." Psa. cxix. 102, 103. He rolled the word and promises as sugar under his tongue, and sucked from thence more sweetness than Samson did from his honey-comb. Luther said, he would not live in paradise, if he must live without the word; but with the word, saith he, I could live in hell itself. When Christ puts in his teaching hand by the hole of the door to teach the heart, "his fingers drop

sweet smelling myrrh upon the handles of the
lock," Sol. Song v. 5. The teachings of Christ
'eave a sweet remembrance of himself behind them;
' We will remember thy love more than wine,"
Sol. Song i. 4. As people, when they drink wine,
are apt to sing; so those that are filled with the
Spirit, cannot but triumph in the wonderful things
which they taste and see in the word. There cannot be but much spiritual joy in Divine teaching,
because the Spirit doth accompany the truths, and
so irradiate them with his own beauty and glory,
the light of the knowledge of the glory of God in
the face of Christ, that they do not only affect, but
ravish the heart : " Thy word is pure, therefore thy
servant loveth it," Psa. cxix. 140. The prophet
saw a beam of Divine excellency sitting upon the
word, and that did happily ensnare his soul. Truth is
burdensome to unsound spirits, because convincing ;
and they labour to extinguish that light which
disturbeth their quiet : " They hold the truth in un-
righteousness," Rom. i. 18. in the Septuagint, They
imprison the truth, and will not suffer it to do its
office. But saving teaching is sweet and delightful,
because it is suitable to the renewed part ; to which
it comes in with fresh succours, to relieve and fortify
it against the assaults of opposite corruption : I
say, it is always sweet in that respect, but never
more sweet than in affliction ; the bitterness of adversity giving a more delicate relish unto the word,
by healing the distempers of the spiritual palate :
and then the soul crieth out with Jeremiah in the
prison, " Thy words were found, and I did eat
them, and thy word was unto me the joy and the
rejoicing of my heart," Jer. xv. 16.

6. Divine teaching is an abiding teaching: "The

I

anointing which ye have received of him abideth in you," 1 John ii. 27. Notional knowledge, where it is no more, is flitting and inconsistent, and leaveth the soul dubious and uncertain. Observe how the apostle James expresseth it, speaking of the mere notional hearer, "He beholdeth himself, and goeth his way, and straightway forgetteth what manner of man he was," James i. 24. Observe, he doth not only forget what he heard, but he forgets what he was. The glass, whether word or affliction, discovered to him his spots, showed him his pride, his covetousness, the impurity of heart and life, &c. but he goeth away, and forgetteth what manner of man he was ; he forgets the word, he forgets the rod, and what both word and rod discovered to him, together with the resolutions and promises made to God in both. A godly man may forget the word, a gracious heart may have a bad memory ; but he will not so easily forget himself, he doth not forget his spots, and that keeps him in continual work, to wash and purge himself from all filthiness of flesh and spirit " Remembering mine affliction and my misery, the wormwood and the gall. My soul hath them still in remembrance, and is humbled in me," Lam. iii. 19, 20. "The double-minded man is unstable in all his ways," James i. 8. Human teaching begets at best but opinion, not faith ; the word implieth one that is distracted and divided in his thoughts, floating betwixt two contrary opinions. There are notions contradicting notions, and principles fighting against principles ; and such knowledge is not abiding knowledge : this unfixedness in principles produceth instability in practice. If a man be double-minded in his principles, he will be unstable in all his ways : none are so constant in the profession of any truth, as they

that are fully convinced and assured of it : none so
stable in their conversation, as they that are rooted
and established in the present truth. This is the
effect of God's teaching, it keeps the judgment
steady, and the heart stable.

" Teach me, O Lord, the way of thy statutes, and
I will keep it unto the end," Psa. cxix. 33. He
dares promise perseverance, if God will undertake
instruction : and accordingly he made good his promise, upon this very account ; "I have not departed
from thy judgments, for thou hast taught me."
Observe it ; he doth not say, I will keep thy statutes ; but he can say, and that many years after,
" I have kept thy statutes." Many will say in their
affliction, I will keep thy statutes ; promise fair, if
God will but deliver them : but how few can say
with David, "I have kept, I have not departed
from thy judgments !" "Of old time," saith God, "I
have broken thy yoke, and burst thy bonds, and
thou saidst, I *will not* transgress ; when upon
every high hill, and under every green tree thou
wanderest, playing the harlot," Jer. ii. 20. Good
words in trouble, but poor performance out of trouble : no sooner out of affliction, but they fall again
to their old trade of spiritual adultery against God :
no sooner their old hearts and their old temptations
meet, but they close, and embrace one another ; they
started aside like a broken bow. But David was
taught of God, and therefore he is as careful to make
good his vows as to make good vows; " I will pay
thee my vows, which my lips have uttered, and my
mouth hath spoken, when I was in trouble," Psa.lxvi.
13, 14. The after part of David's life was much more
severe and exact than the former : " I have not departed from thy judgments, for thou hast taught me."

I 2

These are the properties of Divine teachings: but lest I should lay a snare before the blind, and make the heart sad, which God would not have made sad; I must of necessity lay in a few brief cautions.

When we say God teacheth inwardly, clearly, experimentally, powerfully, sweetly, abidingly, our meaning is not so to be understood, as if God taught all at first; namely, either all truths, or all of any truth. God doth not teach all his lessons at the first entrance into the school of affliction; at least not usually, for we dare not limit God. The fruit of affliction is not gathered presently : " No chastening for the present seemeth to be joyous, but grievous, nevertheless afterward it yieldeth the peaceable fruits of righteousness unto them which are exercised thereby," Heb. xii. 11. Teaching is the fruit of affliction, and fruit is not gathered presently ; it must have a ripening time. And therefore, O thou discouraged soul, say not God doth not teach thee at all, if he do not teach thee all at once. " The entrance of thy word giveth light." God lets in light by degrees : usually God teacheth his children, as we teach ours, now a little, and then a little, Isa. xxviii. 10. somewhat this week, and more next week ; somewhat by this affliction, and more by the next affliction, and more by a third, &c. It is not to be despised if God discover to the soul the need of Divine teaching, and engage the heart in holy desires, and longings after it ; so that the afflicted soul can say in sincerity, " My soul breaketh for the longing that it hath unto thy judgments at all times," Psa. cxix. 20.

When we say, that God teacheth whom he chasteneth, and teacheth them thus and thus ; it is not to be understood as if he taught all alike. God hath several forms in the school of affliction, as well as in the school of the word. There are fathers for experience, young men for strength, and babes for the truth and being of grace, 1 John ii. 12. And, therefore, if God have not taught thee so much as another, say not, He hath not taught me at all. As one star differeth from another in glory, so also is the school of Christ. It is free grace thou art a star, though thou art not a star of the first or second magnitude; that God hath let in some Divine light, though not so much light as another may possibly have; that thou art in God's school, though, it may be, not in the highest form. In point of holy emulation we should look at the degrees of grace; but in point of thankfulness and comfort we should look at the truth and being of grace.

When we say that God teacheth powerfully and abidingly, it is not to be understood as if these teachings did put the soul into an immutable evenness of spirit, or freed it from all insurrections and disturbances from opposite corruption. Such a frame of soul is only the privilege of the glorified estate, wherein we shall see God face to face, and dwell in immutability itself to all eternity. Here the church hath its fulls and its wains. David had his sinkings, and Job his impatient fits; we have heard of the patience of Job, yea and of his impatience too: moved the taught of God may be, but not removed; fall they may, but not fall away; fearfully, but not finally; terribly, but not totally.

But these things are inseparable to covenant teaching.

(1.) The soul is thereby made sensible of the

i 3

least stirrings and whisperings of corruption. **I** find a law in my members warring against the law of my mind, Rom. vii. 23.　　Others have it, but they do not *find* it, they are not sensible of the law in their members, &c.

(2.) They are exceedingly displeased with the opposition they find in their natures against the teachings of God; and do rise up in indignation against all that contradiction which is in the unregenerate part, in what kind soever. "Why art thou cast down, O my soul? and why art thou so disquieted within me?" Is there cause for this despondency? is this done like a David, like a man after God's own heart? Is this the fruit of all the experiences of God's faithfulness and all-sufficiency? and so in other cases doth the soul chide down distempers, and uncomely workings of spirit: the soul is full of displicence* against itself; "So foolish was I, and ignorant: I was as a beast before thee," Psa. lxxiii. 22. it cannot find words bad enough to give itself.

(3.) And if that will not do, then they go to God in prayer, and spread their temptations before the Lord; "O my God, my soul is cast down within me," Psa. xlvi. 6.　　When they cannot lay the storm, and still the tempests by their own word, then, with the disciples in the ship, they go and awaken Christ, and desire him by his powerful word to rebuke them, that there may be a calm. They go and pray out their distempers, and pray their hearts into a better frame : as once it was said of Luther, that when he found distempers upon his spirit, he would never give over praying, till he had prayed his heart into that frame he prayed for.

* Discontent, dislike

(4) By virtue of the teachings of God they are enabled to maintain opposition against all the evil which they find in their own spirits. " As the flesh lusteth against the spirit, so the spirit lusteth against the flesh," Gal. v. 17. that is, the spiritual regenerate part doth as naturally rise up and make war against the flesh, and fleshly motions, as the flesh doth against the teachings of God in the spiritual part. Opposition is not only maintained by precept and rules, and an extrinsical policy, but naturally, and by virtue of an inward antipathy ; the spirit lusteth. The spiritual opposition is as suitable and agreeable to the new nature, as the sinful opposition is to the old nature. Hence is the life of a believer called a wrestling, a warfare, Eph. vi. 12.

(5.) Not only so, but by the help of Divine teaching the soul gets ground of that fleshly opposition, wherewith it is molested, by degrees. " In the day when I cried, thou answeredst me ; and strengthenedst me with strength in my soul," Psa. cxxxviii. 3. Prayer brought in God, and God brought in strength, whereby he got ground of his distempers ; and though all was not done at first, yet his comfort was, all should be done in God's time, " The Lord will perfect that which concerneth me," ver. 8. I am not perfect, but I shall be perfected. " He that hath begun a good work, will perform it till the day of Jesus Christ," Phil. i. 6.

(6.) Though the soul be not always the same for temper and acting, yet it is always the same for purpose and design. " Then shall I not be ashamed, when I have respect unto all thy commandments." Though he could not *keep* all, he could *respect* all the commandments of God. " My soul followeth hard after God," Psa. lxiii. 8. Clouds of opposition intercepted and disturbed his sweet and constant communion with God sometimes; but he brake through that crowd by main strength to recover God's presence again; " My soul followeth hard after thee ;" and Paul is pressing after perfection when he could not overtake it, Phil. iii. 12, 13.

(7.) The soul hath not always, possibly, the same *relish* and taste of Divine truths and ordinances, but it hath the same *estimate*, it keeps up high appreciating thoughts of spiritual things ; and when it cannot relish them, yet even then it doth *hunger* after them. " My soul breaketh for the longings it hath unto thy judgments *at all times*," Psa. cxix. 20. And the promise is made to hunger, &c. Matt. v. 6.

And yet, even in reference to these dispositions, which I call inseparable concomitants to saving teaching, I must add this one caution in close of all ; namely, that allowance be made in case of desertion. A child of God, for causes which here we cannot stand to mention, may be cast into so deep a state of desertion, for a time, that he may, as the apostle speaks, " forget that he was purged from his old sins," 2 Pet. i. 9. " A child of `light may walk in darkness," Isa. l. 10. And though there be no such swoon in the new man, wherein both habits and acts do cease, yet they may be so stupified by the impressions of the present temptation, as the poor soul shall be sensible of neither, but reduced into such a state as that there may be life, but no sense of that life.

Thus much therefore for the second thing propounded in the doctrinal part; the nature and properties of Divine teaching. I come now to,

III. The third thing propounded, namely, to inquire, How affliction lieth in order to instruction? what tendency chastisement hath to promote the teachings of God in the soul? what use God makes of correction to this end?

For it may possibly be demanded, Might not God as well teach his people by sin as by affliction? He might, and doth: whence that gloss of Augustine upon Rom. viii. 28. " All things work together for good to them that love God," even sin itself; and inasmuch as he saith "all things," it is evident he excepteth nothing, that doth not cooperate for good to the called according to God's purpose. All things *do work*, but all things do not work *alike*. Sin works for good, but it is by absolute omnipotence, by pure prerogative; for sin is properly the devil's creature, and in its own natural tendency works merely to destruction; no thanks to sin that any good comes of it; God beats Satan with his own weapons. But affliction is an evil of *God's making*, as Amos iii. 6. and he hath so tempered the nature of it, and doth so ingredient it by his Divine skill, that there is some fitness and disposition in it to serve and promote his own gracious designs in the children of promise. It is true, there is need of an arm of Omnipotence to make chastisement to have a saving influence upon the heart; and so there doth also even in the word itself, and Divine ordinances; they do not save by any intrinsical virtue, or power of their own; but yet there is a passive fitness in them to serve Omnipotence for Divine and saving ends; a fitness of instrumentality, Heb. iv. 12. as there is in a saw to cut, and in a wedge to cleave, &c. The instrument can do nothing alone, but there is a fitness in it to serve the hand of the workman. And thus it is, in a proportion, with affliction; it is true, there is not so immediate and direct a tendency in the rod, as there is in the word, to teach and instruct the children of God; yet there is in chastisement a subserviency to prepare the heart of man, and to put it into a better disposition to close with Divine teaching, than naturally it is capable of. The hot furnace is Christ's workhouse, the most excellent vessels of honour are formed therein. Manasseh, Paul, the jailer, were all chosen in this fire; as God saith, "I have chosen thee in the furnace of affliction," Isa. xlviii. 10. Grace works in a powerful, yet in a moral way. God speaks when we are most apt to hear; congruously, yet forcibly, by a fit accommodation of circumstances; which you may discover in these four particulars:

1. By correction God taketh down the pride of man's heart. There is not a greater obstruction to saving knowledge than pride and self-opinion, whereby man either thinks he knoweth enough, or, that not worth the learning which God teacheth; therefore it is proclaimed before the word, "Hear and give ear, be not proud; for the Lord hath spoken," Jer. xiii. 15. In Divine matters, as well as human, "only by pride cometh contention," Prov. xiii. 10. It is pride which raiseth objections against the word, and disputeth the commands when it should obey them. The proud men in Jeremiah, Jer. xliii. 2. when they could elude the message of God by his prophet no longer, do at length stiffen into downright rebellion: first they shift, "Thou speakest falsely," &c. ver. 2. and then

they resolve, " As for the word that thou hast spoken to us in the name of the Lord, we will not hearken unto thee," &c. Jer. xliv. 16. which means, Be it Baruch, or be it God, we will have none of it ; " but we will certainly do whatsoever goeth forth out of our own mouth," &c. Such a master-piece of obduration is the heart of man, that it stands like a mountain before the word, and cannot be moved, till *God* come with his instruments of affliction, and digging down those mountains (as it is proclaimed before the gospel, Luke iii. 5.) casteth them into a level ; and then God may stand, as it were, upon even ground, and talk with man. This pride of heart speaketh loud in the wicked, and whispereth too audibly even in the godly ; it is a folly bound up even in the hearts of God's chil-dren, till the correction driveth it out ; and the proud stomach being broken, the poor bleeding wretch cries out, " Lord, what wilt thou have me to do ?"

2. Affliction is God's forge wherein he softens the iron heart. There is no dealing with the iron while it remaineth in its own native coldness and hardness ; put it into the fire, make it red hot there, and you may stamp upon it any figure or impres-sion you please. " God maketh my heart soft." saith Job, Job xxiii. 16. Melted vessels are impres-sive to any form. So it is with the heart of man ; naturally it is colder and harder than the northern iron ; and that native induration is much increased by prosperity, and the patience of God towards sinners ; the iron sinew will rather break than bend. It is the hot furnace only which can make it operable and impressive to God's counsels : which course therefore, God resolveth on ; " I will melt them and try them," Jer. ix. 7. and sometimes God

is forced to make the furnace seven times hotter, to work out that dross which renders men so unformable to the ministry of the word, while God sends his prophets, rising up early, and sending them ; and yet they will not incline their ear, but harden their necks against Divine instruction.

When the earthly heart of a man is so dried and hardened by a long sunshine of prosperity, that the plough of the spiritual husbandman cannot enter, God doth soften it with showers of adversity, maketh it capable of the immortal seed, and blesseth the springing thereof, Psa. lxv. 10. The seed falleth upon stony ground, till God turn the stone into a heart of flesh.

3. By chastisement man is made more attentive unto God. In prosperity the world makes such a noise in a man's ears, that God cannot be heard ; he speaks indeed once and twice, again and again, very often ; " yet man perceiveth it not," Job xxxiii. 14. he is so busy in the crowd of worldly affairs, that God is not heeded. In the godly themselves there is much unsettledness and giddiness of mind ; naturally our thoughts are vain and scattered, the spirit slippery and inconsistent, which is a great impediment to our clear and full comprehensions of spiritual things. And therefore God deals with man as a father with his child playing in the market-place, and will not hear or mind his father's call; he comes and takes him out of the noise of the tumult, carries him into his house, lays him upon his knee with the rod in his hand, and then the father can be heard : so doth God, I say, with his children. " He openeth their ears," Job xxxiii. 16. Hebrew. He uncovereth their ears, which the world had stopped, and then instruction will

enter. When Joab would not come to Absalom, he sets his field on fire, 2 Sam. xiv. 30. And thus after neglects God brings us to treat with him by affliction. God saith as it were, " Come, let us reason together;" and the soul echos back again, " Speak Lord, for thy servant heareth :" and when the soul is thus silent unto God, he cometh and sealeth instruction by his Spirit.

4. Affliction is an eye-salve, whereby God openeth the eye of the soul to see the need and excellency of Divine teaching, by the discovery of its own brutish ignorance of God, and of his ways, under all Divine administrations. As Ephraim once bemoaned himself to the Lord, "I have been as a bullock, unaccustomed to the yoke." The prophet David will English it, " So foolish was I, and ignorant: I was as a beast before thee," Psa. lxxiii. 22. And by means of this discovery God draws out the heart into humble and holy supplication for Divine teaching ; " That which I see not teach thou me ; and if I have done iniquity, I will do no more," Job xxxiv. 32. When or how cometh the sinner thus to put in for instruction? why, " I have borne chastisement," ver. 31. Correction discovered the need of instruction ; " That which I see not, teach thou me." And thus Ephraim, " Thou hast chastised me, and I was chastised ;" but blows alone will not do it ; therefore it follows, " Turn thou me, and I shall be turned." Though chastisement alone could not turn Ephraim, yet it made him see an absolute necessity of Divine power to his conversion ; less than Omnipotence would not serve the turn.

And when God hath brought the heart once into this frame, to see, and be affected with the sense of

K

its own ignorance and impotency, and to lie in the dust at God's feet, humbly importuning an effectual teaching from heaven ; if God should withhold it, he should fail not in his promise only, but his own counsel and project ; in reference to which God cannot lie.   But when he hath prepared the heart to pray, he will cause his ear to hear, Psa. x. 17.   When God hath engaged the heart in holy desires of saving instruction, it is not mercy only in God, but faithfulness, to satisfy the desire of his own creation.   " Good and upright is the Lord, therefore he will teach sinners in the way," Psa. xxv. 8.

IV. The grounds and demonstrations of the point.   Of which in a few words, and then I shall come to the use and application.

It must needs be a blessed thing when correction and instruction meet, if we consider—

1. The lessons themselves which God teacheth his Ephraims in the school of affliction.   For instance, is it not a blessed thing to be taught how to compassionate them that are in a suffering condition ? yea, saith the psalmist, " Blessed is he that considereth the poor, the Lord will deliver him in time of trouble, the Lord will preserve him, and keep him alive, and he shall be blessed upon earth," Psa. xli. 1, 2. &c.   He is blessed, and he shall be blessed, not in heaven only, but upon earth also; and that with a multiplied blessing : see a troop follows ; " Thou wilt not deliver him unto the will of his enemies ; the Lord will strengthen him upon the bed of his languishing ; thou wilt make all his bed in his sickness," ver. 2, 3.   Oh the blessedness of a compassionate heart towards afflicted ones ! how easy must that bed be which God maketh !

And, is it not a blessed thing to know how to value our earthly comforts without doating upon them? to be thankful, and yet not to surfeit? " Blessed is he that feareth always," that is, who feareth a snare in all his earthly contentments.

And if it be a blessedness to be conformed to Jesus Christ, then surely self-denial is a lesson which will make one blessed. " If any man will come after me, let him deny himself, and take up his cross and follow me," saith our Saviour, Matt. xvi. 24. And, " Blessed are the poor in spirit, for theirs is the kingdom of heaven," and, " Blessed are the meek, for they shall inherit the earth," Matt. v. 3, 5.

If heaven and earth can make one blessed, then humility is a blessed lesson. And so it is, to have our hearts discovered to ourselves ; corruption is matter of humiliation, but sight and sense of corruption is matter of comfort and rejoicing. It is a miserable thing indeed to be poor and not to see one's poverty, Thou sayest thou art rich, but knowest not that thou art poor and miserable, Rev. iii. 17. But happy is that man to whom the Lord first discovers the hidden corruption of his heart, and then teacheth him to mourn over it; " Blessed are they that mourn for they shall be comforted," Matt. v. 4.

A man is never in a happier condition than when his heart is in a praying frame. It is a mercy with a note of observation ; " Behold he prayeth," Acts ix. 11. a man is never miserable but when he cannot pray.

And, what think ye of the world ? surely he is a blessed man that by affliction is brought acquainted with his bible, which is nothing else but a treasury and magazine of blessings : " Blessed is

K 2

the man whom thou chastisest, O Lord, and
teachest him out of thy law." It is your text, and
the first psalm is your comment, " His delight is
in the law of the Lord, and in his law doth he
meditate day and night," ver. 2. And blessed are
they whom the Lord teacheth to clear out their
evidences for heaven, to give all diligence to make
their calling and election sure, for so an abundant
entrance shall be administered unto them into the
everlasting kingdom of our Lord and Saviour
Jesus Christ, 2 Pet. i. 10, 11. When others shall
but creep to heaven as it were upon all-fours, they
shall ride as in a triumphant chariot into the gates
of the new Jerusalem.

Blessed are they, who weep over their grievings
of God's Spirit, for God shall wipe off those tears
from their eyes ; and he will comfort them whom
they have grieved. And what is the blessedness
of heaven itself, but communion with God! The
exercise of grace. The life of faith. Trust in
God that raises the dead, and calls things which
are not as though they were, and a clearer discovery of God's excellences. What are these but
heaven begun on this side heaven, glory antedated !
" This is life eternal to know thee," John xvii. 3.
our Saviour saith not, it shall be life eternal, but
it is ; eternal life is begun already where these
things are.

To be taught the duties and privileges of a suffering condition, is a blessed teaching, for hereby
the soul is enabled to taste and see what is good
and sweet in every affliction, and is set above all
that which is grievous and intolerable to nature ;
" For this cause we faint not," &c. The one only
thing necessary, must necessarily be a blessed

thing; ' It is," saith our Saviour, " the better part which shall not be taken away," Luke x. 42.

The art of time redemption is a blessing, not less than an evidence of soul redemption; if ye compare the first epistle of Peter, chap. i. ver. 17 and 18. together. Ask St. Paul, and he will tell you, that the knowledge of the sufferings of Jesus Christ is an excellent knowledge, in comparison of which all other things are loss and dung, Phil. iii. 8—10. And to long for heaven is the very first fruits of heaven; the evidence and seal of our conjugal contract with Jesus Christ; " The Spirit and the bride say, Come, Lord Jesus," Rev. xxii. 17. 20. Behold christians, to be taught of God when chastised by him, is a blessedness compounded of several precious ingredients; at least if ye will take in,

2. The nature and properties of Divine teaching; to be taught all these inwardly, clearly, experimentally, powerfully, sweetly, abidingly. This must needs be a blessed teaching, it being a teaching which doth possess the soul of the excellences which it discovereth. Doctrinal and notional knowledge is a blessing; " Blessed," saith Christ to his hearers, " are your eyes, for they see; and your ears, for they hear," Matt. xiii. 16. But it is but an occasional, preparatory blessedness, blessedness in the offer and opportunity; oh but to be taught these lessons with these qualifications; to be taught the truth as it is in Jesus; to be taught into the nature and image of the truth; to be taught into the possession of Divine excellences; this is blessedness indeed; blessedness in being; full, perfect, fruitional blessedness.

3. A teaching chastisement is the fruit of God's

K 3

distinguishing love. Chastisements, simply considered in themselves, lie in common to all the sons
and daughters of Adam since the fall; the fruit of
that first apostasy, as well as of actual and personal
departures from God : yea and deliverance also,
lieth in common. Providence dispenseth deliverance
to the worst of men. The 106th Psalm is a psalm of
promises, made to the church ; but the next psalm,
the 107th, is a psalm of providential dispensations to
the world ; and there, as you find affliction, so you
may find deliverance also out of those afflictions, to
be the portion of wicked men ; rebels, ver. 11. and
fools, ver. 19, 20. (that is, wicked fools, Solomon's
fools all along the Proverbs,) seamen, ver. 23. (for
the most part, not the most religious order in the
world ;) all these are delivered out of their troubles.
The worst of men, I say, share in this fruit of
God's providential goodness, deliverance ; but a
teaching sanctified affliction is the privy seal of special love, " My *loving kindness* will I not take from
him," Psa. lxxxix. 33. " Whom the Lord *loveth* he
chasteneth," Heb. xii. 6. that is to say, with a teaching chastisement. When word and rod meet together, when correction and instruction kiss each
other, they are the fruit of paternal affection, and
therefore must needs have a blessing bound up in
them. " As a man chasteneth his son, so the Lord
chasteneth thee," Deut. viii. 5.

4. A teaching correction is a branch of the covenant of grace, which God hath made in Christ for
the children of promise ; " All thy children shall be
taught of God," Isa. liv. 13. " They shall all know
me from the least of them, to the greatest," Jer. xxxi.
34. By virtue of Divine teaching affliction is
adopted a branch in the covenant of grace. That

89th Psalm is a song of the new covenant; "I will sing of the mercies of the Lord," ver. 1. What mercies? not providence mercies only, but promise mercies, covenant mercies; "I have made a covenant with my chosen," ver. 3. And amongst the rest of the branches of the covenant you shall find the *rod* and the *whip* have their place; "If his children forsake my law, and walk not in my judgments, &c. Then will I visit their transgression with the rod, and their iniquity with stripes," ver. 30—32. Behold rod and stripes standing here, not upon mount Ebal, the mount of curses, as branches of a covenant of works, but upon mount Gerizim, the mount of blessings, Deut. xi. 29. as branches of the covenant of grace. Affliction is not so much threatened as promised to Christ's seed. "My covenant will I not break." Psa. lxxxix. 34. When God seems even to break the bones and hearts of his people by sore and heavy strokes of correction, yet he doth not break his covenant, "My covenant will I not break." It is in order to the covenant when God chastiseth his children, and instructs them by his chastisements. Affliction separated from instruction is pure wrath, a blast from mount Ebal, Deut. xxviii. but by a matrimonial covenant those two scriptures, "I will visit," &c. Psa. lxxxix. 32. and "I will teach," Isa. liv. 13. are married together, and made one spirit, as in my text, and then they are pure grace. The covenant is the Magna Charta of heaven, and contains a list of whatever God the Father hath purposed, God the Son hath purchased, and God the Holy Ghost doth apply to the heirs of promise. The breasts of the covenant run nothing but the milk of spiritual blessing to the children of God.

5. A teaching affliction is the purchase of Christ's death and bloodshed. Christ died not to exempt his redeemed from suffering, but to sanctify their sufferings with his own blood : " I pray not that thou shouldst take them out of the world, but that thou shouldst keep them from the evil," John xvii. 15. Whatsoever Christ purchased, he prayed for ; and this was one main privilege, not freedom from the evil of affliction, but from the evil of sin ; " Sanctify them through thy truth," ver. 17. God's teachings are sanctifying teachings; "Sanctify them through thy truth : thy word is truth :" Christ's blood purchased nothing but blessings.

6. A teaching affliction is the result of all the offices of Jesus Christ. As a King, he chastens ; as a Prophet, he teacheth ; and as a Priest, he hath purchased this grace of his Father, that the *rod* might blossom ; that *correction* might be consecrated for *instruction* unto the redeemed. Behold, a sanctified affliction is a cup whereinto Jesus Christ hath wrung and pressed the juice and virtue of all his mediatorial offices ; surely that must be a cup of generous and royal wine, like that in the supper, a cup of blessing to the people of God.

And thus I have finished the fourth particular propounded for the clearing and confirming of the doctrine, the grounds and demonstrations of the point ; and with it the whole doctrinal part of this great and blessed truth, namely, That it is a blessed thing when correction and instruction, word and rod go together.

I come now to the use, for the improvement of the point. And it may serve,

I. For information.

II. For exhortation.

I. For information, and that in these particulars:

1. If they only be blessed whom God chasteneth and teacheth ; then affliction alone is not enough to evidence a man to be a happy man. No man is therefore blessed because he is chastened : blows alone are not enough, either to evince or to effect a state of blessedness. "Thou hast chastised me, and I was chastised," Jer. xxxi. 18. crieth repenting Ephraim ; which means, I have had blows enough, if blows would have done me good : nay, but under all the strokes and smitings of thy displeasure, I have been as a bullock unaccustomed to the yoke ; unteachable and untractable ; thou hast drawn one way, and I have drawn another ; thou hast pulled forward, and I have pulled backward ; all thy chastisements have left me as they found me, brutish and rebellious. Surely blows only may break the neck sooner than the heart. They are in themselves the fruit of Divine wrath, a branch of the curse, and therefore cannot possibly of themselves make the least argument of God's love to the soul. Bastards have blows as well as children, and fools because of their transgression are afflicted, Psa. cvii. 1. And yet it is very sad to consider that this is the best evidence that the most of men have for heaven ; because they suffer in this world, they think they shall be freed from sufferings in the world to come ; and because they have a hell here, they hope they shall escape hell hereafter, they hope they shall not have *two* hells : yes, poor deluded soul, thou mayest have two hells, and must have two hells without better evidence for heaven. Cain had two hells, and Judas had two hells, and millions of reprobate men and women have two

hells; one of this life, in torments of body, and horror of conscience; and another of the life to come, in unquenchable fire: and so I say shalt thou, unless thou dost get better evidence for heaven, than the present misery which is upon thee. The plagues and evils which are upon thee may be but the beginnings of sorrows: pain now in the body may be but a forerunner of torments hereafter in thy soul: thou mayst have a prison on earth, and a dungeon in hell; thou mayst now want a crumb of bread, and hereafter a drop of water; thou mayst now be the reproach of men, and hereafter the scorn of men and angels, and of God himself. And therefore be wise to salvation, by working it out with fear and trembling, Phil. ii. 12. and giving all diligence, "make your calling and election sure," 2 Pet. i. 10. God forbid that a man should take that for his security from hell, which may be but the prelibations of hell, the pledge and aggravation of endless misery.

Why, but doth not the scripture say, "Whom the Lord loveth he chasteneth, and scourgeth every son whom he receiveth?" Heb. xii. 6. And again, "As many as I love, I rebuke and chasten?" Rev. iii. 19.

Yes: but mark, I beseech you; though the scripture saith, "Whom the Lord loveth he chasteneth," it doth not say, Whomsoever the Lord chasteneth he loveth. Though it saith, "He scourgeth every son whom he receiveth," it doth not say, Whomsoever he scourgeth he receiveth him as a son. Christ saith, "As many as I love, I rebuke and chasten;" but he saith not, As many as I rebuke and chasten, I love. These scriptures include children, but they do not exclude bastards: they

tie chastening to sonship, but not sonship to chastening: the sons are chastened ; but all the chastened are not, *therefore*, sons: the beloved are
rebuked, but all that are rebuked are not, *consequently*, beloved.

But that place in Job v. 17. seems to say as
much, " Behold, happy is the man whom God correcteth."

It is true ; but one scripture must interpret another ; David must expound Eliphaz: " Happy is
the man whom God correcteth," that is, when instruction goeth along with correction, when chastisement and teaching accompany one another :
" Blessed is the man whom thou chastenest, O
Lord, and teachest him out of thy law." The scrip
ture doth not usually give things their names, but
when they are made up of all their integrals
" Whoso findeth a wife, findeth a good thing, and
obtaineth favour of the Lord," Prov. xviii. 22. that
is, a wife made up of scripture qualifications : otherwise a man may (and many men do) find a plague
in a wife, and hath her from the Lord in wrath,
and not in love. Every married woman is not a
wife *;* a bad woman is but the shadow of a wife
and so here in this case, &c.

Indeed chastening and affliction is an opportunity
of mercy, a may-be to happiness, but not, singly,
an evidence of happiness : lay no more upon it than
it will bear ; it is an opportunity, improve it ; it is
no more, do not trust it.

2. This doctrine informs us thus much, that as
affliction, simply considered, is not enough to make
or evidence a man to be happy, so neither is it
sufficient to conclude a man to be miserable. No
man is therefore miserable because afflicted. It

may prove a teaching affliction, and then he is happy. And yet this is another mistake among men ; both in reference to others, and in reference to ourselves. In reference to others ; people are very prone to judge them wretched whom they see afflicted : it was the miserable mistake of Job's friends to conclude him miserable because smitten, cursed because chastened. In reference to ourselves ; it is a merciless mistake, sometimes even of God's own children, to sit down under affliction, especially if sore and of long continuance, and conclude God doth not love them, because he doth correct them. It seems to be the very case of the believing Hebrews ; they judged themselves out of God's favour, because under God's frowns, Heb. xii. not at all beloved, because so greatly afflicted ; under many and sore persecutions, as you may see, chap. x. 32—34. And therefore it is that upon which the apostle (after he presented them with a large catalogue and list of the primitive martyrs before Christ, in the eleventh chapter) bestows the twelve first verses of the twelfth chapter, to prove by reasons drawn from nature, and instances taken out of scripture ; the first whereof is that unparalleled and astonishing instance of Jesus Christ, the first born, the Son of God's loves and delights. I say, to establish this as a conclusion of unquestionable verity, namely, that God's *love* and God's *rod* may stand together.

The truth is, my brethren, there is nothing can make a man miserable but sin. It is sin that poisons our afflictions : " The sting of death is sin," 1 Cor. xv. 56. and so we may say of all other evils, which militate under death, as soldiers under their general. The sting of sickness is sin ; and the sting of poverty is sin ; and the sting of imprisonment and banishment is sin : and so of the rest. Take the sting out, which is purchased by the blood of Christ, and evidenced by Divine teaching, and they cannot hurt nor destroy in all God's holy mountain, Isa. xi. 9. And therefore let no children of God be rash to conclude hard things against themselves, and to make evidences of wrath where God hath made none. Let christians on both sides look further than the affliction itself; the Holy Ghost having long since determined this controversy by a peremptory decision : "No man knoweth either love or hatred by all that is before them," Eccl. ix. 1. that is, no man can make a judgment, either of God's love or hatred towards him, by any of these outward dispensations. "He causeth his sun to shine upon the evil, and upon the good ; and sendeth rain on the just, and on the unjust," Matt. v. 45. The sun of prosperity shineth upon the dunghill, as well as upon the bed of spices ; and the rain of adversity falleth upon the fruitful garden, as well as upon the barren wilderness. He judgeth truly of his estate, that judgeth by the word, and not by providence. Evidences of grace consist in inward impressions, not in outward dispensations.

3. That deliverance out of trouble is not enough to evidence or make a man happy. It is not said, Blessed is the man whom thou chastenest, O Lord, and *deliverest* him out of trouble ; but, "Blessed is the man whom thou chastenest and teachest." A man may get rid of the affliction, and yet miss of the blessing. All the bread which men may eat without the sweat of their brows is not therefore hallowed ; abundance may flow in without

L

labour, and yet not without a curse, Gen. iii. 16. A man may leave his chains and his blessing behind him in prison ; and the fire of a fever may be extinguished, when the fire of hell is preparing for the sinner. It is good to be thankful for, but extremely dangerous to be contented with, a *bare* deliverance. I shall conclude this branch with this note, which alone might have stood for a distinct observation or corollary—That those prayers in troubles are not best heard which are answered with deliverance ; but those prayers are best heard which are answered with instruction. Even of our blessed Saviour it is said, "In the days of his flesh he offered up prayers and supplications with strong crying and tears, unto him that was able to save him from death, and *was heard* in that he feared," Heb. v. 7. How was he heard ? not in that, "Save me from this hour," John xii. 27. but in that, "Father, glorify thy name," ver. 28. not in deliverance, but in instruction ; for, for that he giveth thanks, "I will bless the Lord who hath given me counsel ; my reins also instruct me in the night seasons," Psa. xvi. 7. His Father taught him and strengthened him, ver. 8—11. in his passion, and this was the hearing of his supplications. That is the best return of prayers which works our *good*, when not our *wills ;* and when God doth not answer in the *letter*, if he answer in the *better*, we are no losers by our prayers : even devils themselves are heard to the letter, when his own Son is not : yet heard, in that he feared ; and therefore when we have prayed, let us refer it unto God to determine the answer.

4. Hence we may learn how to judge of our afflictions, and of our deliverances from them

and it may serve instead of a use of examination : by this, I say, we may know, when our sufferings come in wrath, and when in love. You need not, as the scripture speaks in another case, say, Who shall ascend up into heaven, to look into God's book of life and death ? or who shall descend into the deep of God's secret counsels, to make report hereof unto us ? But what saith the scripture ? " The word is nigh thee :" the word of resolution, to this inquiry, it is nigh thee, even in thy mouth, and in thy heart ; that is to say, if thou canst evidence this to thine own soul, that instruction hath accompanied correction, that God hath taught thee as well as chastened thee, thou art a blessed man, thou shalt be saved : thou hast the word of him who is the author of blessedness, and *blessedness itself*, " Blessed is the man whom the Lord chasteneth, and teacheth him out of his law."

And therefore peruse, I beseech you, that model of Divine instructions or lessons, presented to you in the doctrinal part of this discourse, either at large, in those twenty particulars ; or in the abridgement, the three great heads, to which they were reduced. And then, withal, set before your eyes those six properties of Divine covenant teaching, and compare your hearts and those lessons together. Ask your own souls, Hath God taught you those lessons, or any of them ? 1. Inwardly. 2. Convincingly. 3. Experimentally. 4. Powerfully. 5. Sweetly. 6. Abidingly, (for even a hypocritical Ahab can humble himself for a time, walk in sackcloth, and go softly ; a bulrush can hold down its head for a day.) And if the Spirit of God can bear witness to thy spirit, that thou art thus taught, happy art thou ; bless the Lord, for the Lord hath

blessed thee ; thou mayst sing David's song, " I
will bless the Lord who hath given me counsel ; my
reins also instruct me in the night season," Psa. xvi.
7. And again, " I know, O Lord, that thy judgments are right, and that thou in faithfulness hast
afflicted me," Psa. cxix. 75. If I have been *less
afflicted*, I had been *less blessed*.

But now on the other side, when there is no
interpreter to accompany affliction, to expound unto
man the meaning of the Almighty in his chastisements ; when there is not a Divine sentence in the
lips of correction ; when the rod is dumb, or the
creature deaf, and cannot hear the rod, and who
hath appointed it ; it is much to be feared, the
stroke is not the stroke of God's children. O my
brethren, it is sad when men come out of affliction
the same they went in ; when affliction leaves them
as it found them ; as ignorant, as unhumbled, as
insensible of sin as sinfulness towards their suffering brethren, as worldly, as proud, as impatient, as
unsavoury, as much strangers to Christ and their
own hearts, as regardless of eternity : in a word, as
fit for sin as they were before. This, I say, is exceedingly sad. And yet it is much sadder, when it
may be said of a man, as once it was said of Ahaz ;
" In the time of his distress he did trespass yet
more against the Lord," 2 Chron. xxviii. 22. It was
an aggravation of wickedness, concerning which we
may say, as our Saviour of the alabaster box poured
on his head—Wherever the scripture shall be
preached in the whole world, there shall also this
which this man did be published ; " *This is that king
Ahaz.*"   Surely it is a standing and a dreadful monument of reproach and infamy unto him to all
generations.   Christians, it is sad and dangerous

beyond all expression when affliction serveth but as
a gauge to give vent to the pride and murmur, the
atheism and enmity, which is in men's spirits,
against the Lord; when afflictions are but as oil
unto the fire to irritate corruption, and make it
blaze more fiercely; to continue in wonted sins,
against such sensible and real proclamations to
desist, is professed rebellion against God: a heavy
indictment which the prophet bringeth against Jerusalem; " Thou hast stricken them, but they have
not grieved; thou hast consumed them, but they
have refused to receive correction : they have made
their faces harder than a rock, they have refused
to return," Jer. v. 3.   In such cases it is to be
feared, the cup of affliction is a vial of wrath,
and the plagues of this life nothing else but some
previous drops of that storm of fire and brimstone,
wherein impenitent sinners shall be scorched and
tormented for ever.

That scripture speaks dreadfully to this purpose,
Jer. vi. 28—30.   " They are all grievous revolters,
walking with slanders; they are all corrupters;
the bellows are burned, the lead is consumed of the
fire; the founder melteth in vain; for the wicked
are not plucked away; reprobate silver shall men
call them, because the Lord hath rejected them."
" They are all grievous revolters," that is, as the
prophet Isaiah expounds it, " Ye revolt more and
more," Isa. i. 5.   Hebrew, They increase revolt,
walking with slanders; they do not only revolt, but
slander those that reprove their revolting; " They
hate him that reproveth in the gate," Amos v. 10.
they slander the prophets, and their words; nay,
God himself doth not escape the lash of their
tongues; they say, " The way of the Lord is not

equal," Ezek. xviii. when they should condemn
their own ways, they censure God's, " The way of
the Lord is not equal." They are brass and iron.
They would pass for silver and gold, a sincere and
holy people, while they are a degenerate and hypocritical generation. " They are all corrupters," Jer.
vi. 8. " They have deeply corrupted themselves,"
Hos. ix. 9. they have corrupted all their doings,
Zeph. iii. 7. " they have corrupted the covenant of
Levi," the worship, the ordinances, the truths of
God, Mal. ii. 8. " The bellows are burned in the
fire," that is, the lungs of the prophets, which have
preached unto them in the name of the Lord, rising
up early, and lifting up their voices like trumpets,
to tell Israel their transgressions, and the house of
Jacob their sins, and stretching forth their hands
unto them all the day long, they are spent. " The
lead is consumed," that is, all the melting judgments and chastisement, which, as lead is cast into
the furnace to make it the hotter, God added to
the ministry of the prophets, to make the word
more operative, they will do no good. All this
while, " the founder melteth in vain," whether God
the master-founder, or the prophets, God's co-
founders, or fellow-workmen, as the apostle calls
them ; they all melt in vain, 2 Cor. vi. 1. all
their labour is lost ; neither word, nor rod, neither
judgments nor ordinances, can stir them ; they refuse to receive correction, they will not be taught.
Men will give God the hearing, but are resolved
on their own courses. " The wicked are not
plucked away." They are the same that ever they
were ; the swearer is a swearer still, and the
drunkard is a drunkard still, and the unclean person is unclean still ; " The vile person will speak

villany, and his heart will work iniquity, to practise hypocrisy, and to utter error against the Lord," Isa. xxxii. 6. the unjust are unjust still, and the ignorant are ignorant still; nothing will better them, wicked they are, and wicked they will be. What follows? a formidable sentence; " Reprobate silver shall men call them." They would be counted silver, but it is reprobate silver, refuse silver, dross rather than pure metal; and their hypocrisy shall be made known to all men; " Reprobate silver shall men call them;" and happy they, if it were but the censure of mistaking men only; nay, but the Searcher of hearts hath no better thoughts of them; men do but call them so, because God called them so first; " Reprobate silver shall men call them, because the Lord hath rejected them." God hath cast them out as the founder casts out his dross to the dunghill, and they shall never stand among the vessels of honour, in whom the Lord will be glorified. A fearful sentence! the sum whereof is this—That when teaching goeth not along with correction, when men come out of the furnace, and lose nothing of their dross, it is a sad indication of a reprobate spirit, without timely and serious reflection, nigh unto cursing. " O consider this, you that forget God" and his chastisements, " lest he tear you in pieces, and there be none to deliver," Psa. l. 22.

5. A fifth branch of information may be to teach us thus much—That they may be blessed whom the world accounts miserable. The world judgeth merely by outward appearances, and therefore may easily be mistaken. They see the chastisement which is upon the flesh, and thence conclude a man miserable; but they cannot discover that Divine

teaching which is upon the spirit, which truly rendereth him incomparably blessed. The men of the world are incompetent judges of the estate and condition of God's children. The godly man's happiness or misery is not to be judged by the world's sense and feeling, but by his own; it lieth inward (save only so far as by the fruits it is discernible) and the world's faculty of judging is only outward, made up of sense and reason; therefore said the apostle, " The spiritual man judgeth all things, yet he himself is judged of no man;" that is, he is able to judge of the condition of the men of the world, but the men of the world are not able to judge of his condition, because it is above their faculty. The natural man *thinks* the spiritual man, under affliction, to be miserable; but the spiritual man *knows* the natural man, in the midst of his greatest abundance and bravery, to be miserable *indeed.* Therefore may the saints in their troubles think it, with St. Paul, a very small thing to be judged of man's judgment, 1 Cor. iv. 3. This is but man's day of judging; so the word signifieth; God's day is coming when things and persons shall be valued by another standard. Christ in his day shall judge not after the sight of the eyes, that is, not as things appear to sense and reason; nor after the hearing of the ears; that is, according to the report of the world; but with righteousness shall he judge; that is, he shall judge of things and persons as they are, and not as they appear. Moreover, this is also another comfort: " We have the mind of Christ," 1 Cor. ii. 16. the judgment of Christ, by virtue whereof we are enabled, in our measure, to judge of things and persons, as Christ himself judgeth.

6. A sixth branch of information—Is chastisement a blessing when accompanied with instruction? See then, and admire the wisdom, power, and goodness of God, who can make his people better by their sufferings. Who knows how to fetch oil out of the scorpion, to extract gold out of clay! to draw the richest wine out of gall and wormwood! that can turn the greatest evil of the body to the greatest good of the soul! the curse itself into a blessing! that can make the withered rod of affliction to bud, yea to bring forth the peaceable fruits of righteousness to them that are exercised thereby! Behold I show you a mystery: sin brought affliction *into* the world, and God makes affliction to carry sin *out* of the world. Persecution is but the pruning of Christ's vine, &c. The almond tree is said to be made fruitful by driving nails into it, letting out a noxious gum that hindereth the fruitfulness thereof. God never intendeth more good to his children than when he seems to deal most severely with them. The very heathen have observed it to us : God doth not love his children with a weak womanish affection, but with a strong masculine love, and had rather they suffer hardship than perish : " Whom the Lord loveth he chasteneth, and scourgeth *every* son whom he receiveth." God will rather fetch blood, than lose a soul ; break Ephraim's bones, than suffer him to go on in the frowardness of his heart. Destroy the flesh, that the spirit may be saved in the day of the Lord Jesus. " We are chastened of the Lord, that we should not be condemned with the world," 1 Cor. xi. 32. His discipline is made up of severity and love ; he doth chastise, but he will teach also, that so his children may inherit the blessing ;

the discipline is sharp, but the end is sweet. " Bless the Lord, O my soul, and all that is within me bless his holy name : bless the Lord, O my soul, and forget not all his benefits."

7. It shows us, that a suffering condition is not so formidable a thing as flesh and blood doth represent it. It is ignorance and unbelief which slandereth the dispensations of God, and casteth reproach upon the cross of Christ. He that heard the words of God, which saw the vision of the Almighty, having his eyes opened, could by way of holy triumph ask this question, " Wherefore should I fear in the days of evil ?" Psa. xlix. 5. which denotes, What is there in an afflicted estate so much to be dreaded ? let any man show me a reason, and I will give way to fear and despondency. And that is more observable which follows ; " When the iniquity of my heels shall compass me about ?" This is an addition of the greatest weight and wonder imaginable ; the meaning is—When my transgressions pursue me so close, that they even tread upon my heels, as it were ; when sin itself hath brought me into the snare, when God is correcting me for my iniquities ; why truly, christians, that is the thing which a child of God doth most of all tremble at, to consider that he hath *sinned himself* into a suffering condition. In sufferings purely evangelical, namely, persecution for righteousness' sake, a gracious heart can see, many times, more cause of rejoicing than of perplexity, and look upon them as a gift rather than an imposition ; but afflictions and miseries, which sin brings upon a man, seem to be judicial and penal, and carry a face of wrath rather than of love. Observe it, even in these the psalmist can see no just cause of fear ;

' Wherefore should I fear in the days of evil, when the iniquity of my heels shall compass me about?" See, when sin and sorrows besiege him on every side he is fearless, and knows no reason to the contrary, unless any one can tell him what it is: How so? surely upon the same account in my text, because David had a God that could teach as well as chastise; and therefore, though sin were as poison in his cup of affliction, yet Divine teaching could antidote that poison, and turn it into a cup of blessing unto him: "Thy rod and thy staff comfort me," Psa. xxiii. 4.

O that the children of God in affliction, or entering upon sufferings, would sit down and dwell upon this consideration, the fruit and advantage which God knoweth how to bring out of all their sorrows, even the peaceable fruits of righteousness. This would keep them from uncomely despondencies and dejections of spirit; " For this cause we faint not," saith the apostle, 2 Cor. iv. 16. 18. For what cause? " while we look not at the things which are seen, but at the things which are not seen;" that is to say, not at the visible sufferings, but at the invisible fruit and advantage of our sufferings. This holds up head, and keeps up heart; and maketh the soul not only to be patient, but to glory in tribulation; " Knowing that tribulation worketh patience, and patience experience, and experience hope; and hope maketh not ashamed; because the love of God is shed abroad in our hearts by the Holy Ghost which is given to us," Rom. v. 3—5. This is the way to counterpoise the temptation; and in the conflict between the flesh and the spirit, to come in to the succour of the better part.

8. It shows us the reason why God doth keep

some of his people so long under the discipline of
the rod. Truly God doth not only bring his children into the school of affliction, but many times
keeps them long there: " The rod of the wicked
indeed shall not *always* rest on the back of the
righteous," Psa. cxxv. 3. But it may lie long, for
months, for years, for many years together; seventy
years were the Jews in the house of correction at
Babylon ; four hundred years in the brick-kilns of
Egypt. History and experience will serve in instances without number. Hence you have the
people of God so often at their *how-longs* in their
sufferings, " But thou, O Lord, *how long* ?" Psa.
vi. 3. " *How long* wilt thou forget me, O Lord ?
for ever ? *How long* wilt thou hide thy face from
me? *How long* shall I take counsel in my soul ?
How long shall mine enemy be exalted over me ?"
Psa. xiii. 1, 2. In this psalm where my text is,
" *How long* shall the wicked, *how long* shall the
wicked triumph ?" twice *how long,* before he can
vent his complaint ; and yet again the third time,
" *How long* shall they utter and speak hard
things ?" " *How long,*" cries Jeremiah, " shall I
see the standard, and hear the sound of the trumpet ?" Jer. iv. 21. And Zechariah, " O Lord of
hosts, *how long* wilt thou not have mercy on
Jerusalem, and on the cities of Judah ?" Zech. i. 12.
The souls under the altar, Rev. vi. 10. cry with
a loud voice, " *How long,* O Lord, holy and
true, dost thou not avenge our blood on them that
dwell on the earth ?" Verily God doth keep his
people, sometimes, so long under their pressures,
that they begin at length even to give themselves
up to despair, and to conclude they shall never see
deliverance. Thus you find not only the common

multitude of the Jews in the Babylonian captivity, concluding desperately, " Our bones are dried, our hope is lost, we are cut off for our parts," dry bones may as well live, as our captivity have an end; but even the prophet Jeremiah himself, (whether in his own person, or in the name of the whole church, I know not, possibly both,) " They have cut off my life in the dungeon, and cast a stone upon me," Lam. iii. 53. He seems to himself to be in the condition of a man that is dead and buried, and the grave-stone rolled to the mouth of the sepulchre: a metaphor expressing a hopeless and desperate condition: yea hence it is, that when deliverance is nigh, they cannot believe it, though a prophet of God, or an angel from heaven, should report it. " Thou shalt arise, and have mercy upon Zion; for the time to favour her, yea the *set time* is come," sings the prophet Daniel, or some other that lived near the expiration of the seventy years' captivity; and yet in the mean time the Jews reply as before, " Our bones are dried, our hope is lost, we are cut off for our parts;" which means, Tell not us of God's arising, &c. we shall never see Zion again, we are but dead men. Observe it by the way, they that would not believe the captivity while it was in the *threatening*, Hab. i. 5. would not believe deliverance when it was in the *promise;* a just judgment upon them, that those who *would* not believe God threatening *should* not believe God promising. But that is not all; deliverance was so incredible after so long a captivity, that they could not believe it when they saw it. " When the Lord turned again the captivity of Zion, we were like them that dream," Psa. cxxvi. 1. They knew not, as it fared with Peter, half awake and half asleep, Acts xii. 9.

M

whether it was true, or whether they saw a vision only; is this a real deliverance? or are we in a dream only? Our Saviour tells us, that when the Son of man shall come, (that is with particular deliverances to his church,) he shall not find faith on the earth, Luke xviii. 8. there will not be faith enough in the people of God to believe it, by reason of the long pressures and persecutions that have been upon them.

Now, I say, what is the reason that God suffers affliction to lie so long upon the backs of his children? Truly one reason is, because they have lived long in sin; they have been long sinning, and therefore God is long correcting. God puts them to *their how-longs*, because they have put God to *his how-longs*. "*How long* refuse ye to keep my commandments, and my laws? *How long* will this people provoke me? and *how long* will it be ere they believe?" Exod. vi. 28. "*How long* shall thy vain thoughts lodge within thee?" Jer. iv. 14. "*How long* will it be ere they attain to innocency," &c. Hosea viii. 5. And truly if they have made God complain of *their how-longs*, no wonder if God make them complain of *his how-longs*. But then again, another and the main reason is, because the work is not yet done; they do not receive instruction by their correction, else affliction would quickly cease. God giveth not a blow, he draws not a drop of blood, more than *needs;* "For a season, if *need* be, ye are in heaviness," 1 Pet. i. 6. If there be *heaviness*, there is *need* of it; and if heaviness *continue long*, there is *need* of it. It is not to gratify their enemies that God keeps them so long under their lash, but to teach them; not that God afflicts willingly, &c. Lam. iii. 33. but that he may do them good in their latter end; that by the rod of correction he may drive out that folly which is in their hearts. And when that is done, then they shall stay no longer for their deliverance; then God opens the prison doors, and throws the rod into the fire; and infinite mercy it is, that they are *not delivered* till they are *bettered;* that God will not cease *chastening* till they are willing to cease *sinning;* saying, " I have borne affliction, I will offend no more; that which I see not, teach thou me; and if I have done wickedly, I will do so no more."

9. Take notice from hence, what unteachable creatures we are by nature, who will not set our hearts to receive instruction till we are whipped to it by the rod of correction, and hardly then. Unless God multiply stripes, it is not multiplying of precepts that will do us good; there must be stripe upon stripe, and affliction upon affliction, as well as line upon line, and precept upon precept, or else it is in vain. We are so brutish, with Ephraim, that we make God spend his rods upon us; and when all is done, God must turn us by main strength, or else our folly will not depart from us. This is a lamentation, and should be for a lamentation. We would say, that were a very bad child that will be taught no longer than the rod is upon his back! such are we; we are so indocile that we put God to it, as it were, to study what methods and courses to take with us; " How shall I do for the daughter of my people? I will melt them, and try them," &c. Jer. ix. 7. Well, let us judge ourselves, and justify God.

10. It showeth us, on the contrary, how much gracious hearts are in love with the word, for the

improvement of their spiritual knowledge wherein, they can put such an estimate upon their sufferings; and account that their blessing which other men call their misery. "Blessed is the man whom thou chastenest and teachest." The psalmist in another place speaketh very warmly to this purpose; " It is good for me that I have been afflicted," Psa. cxix. 71. Why? that I might learn thy statutes. He loveth the word so dearly, that for the word's sake, he is in love with affliction. The whip, the rod, the prison, the wilderness, any thing, is precious that brings instruction with it. Carnal people can be content to die in their ignorance, so they may die in their nest; whereas gracious hearts think not much to go to school to a prison; and even while the blood is running down the back can say, It is good, because they are taught by it. O the different account that grace and nature make of the same dispensation! it is proud disdain to scorn to be taught by the lowest of God's ushers. The treasure is precious, though in an earthen vessel: there is none too old, none too wise, none too high, to be put into the meanest school on this side heaven.

I have done with the use of information: I come now, in the second place, to the

II. Use of exhortation.

And it is to four sorts of people: 1. Such as are yet free from sufferings; 2. Such as are under sufferings; 3. Such as are come out of a suffering condition; 4. Parents, in reference to their children.

1. The first branch of exhortation is to such as through the patience and forbearance of God are yet free from chastisement and affliction; the

candle of the Almighty doth shine in their tabernacle, and they wash their steps in butter, &c.
Why now, would ye prevent chastisement, and keep
off the strokes of Divine displeasure from yourselves
or families? Let me commend unto you a twofold
caution from this doctrine :

(1.) Study these lessons well while ye are in the
school of the word.

(2.) Labour to be instructed by the chastisements
and afflictions which you see upon other men.

(1.) If you would prevent chastisement, study
these and the like lessons well, while ye are under
the teachings of the word. Therefore doth God
send us into the school of affliction, because we
have been non-proficients in the school of the
gospel : because we will not hear the word, we
force God to turn us over to a severer discipline,
and to have our ears bored with affliction ; and then
saith God, "Now hear the rod, and who hath appointed it." O my beloved, labour, I beseech you,
to profit much by the teachings of Jesus Christ in
the gospel : set your hearts to all the truths and
counsels of God revealed to you therein. The
gospel is the model or platform of sound words,
able to make you sound christians, wise to salvation, 2 Tim. i. 13. O let your profiting be made
known to all men. In special, set your hearts to
those instructions or lessons propounded in the
doctrinal part of this subject ; for the neglect
whereof God is forced to send his people into captivity, that there he may teach them with the briers
and thorns of the wilderness. In particular—

Learn, in the time of your peace and tranquillity,
to lay to heart the sufferings of the rest of your
brethren that are in the world. "Remember them

that are in bonds, as bound with them," Heb. xiii.
3. Think of them that are in prison, whose feet
are hurt in the stocks, and the irons do enter into
their soul, with the very same affection and afflic·
tion of spirit, as if you yourselves lay bound in
chains by them in the same dungeon ; put your
souls in their souls' steads : and content not yourselves with those loose, and fruitless, and transient
glances, which those that are at ease in Zion do
usually cast upon men in misery ; a cold " Lord
have mercy on them," and there is an end. " Remember them that are in bonds, *as bound with
them ;*" and that you may know you are not to
confine your compassion to prisoners only, it follows, "and them that suffer adversity," &c. Learn
to sympathize with all the people of God under any
adversity whatsoever ; hide not your eyes, and shut
not up your bowels of compassion from any that
are in a suffering condition ; and that upon this
account, "As being yourselves in the body." If the
duty respect thy brother, the motive respects thyself ; thou are yet in the body: and while you
remain in the flesh, you cannot promise yourselves
one hour's exemption from troubles ; but are exposed to the same common calamities which attend
a state of mortality ; as it is an argument of comfort to them that are in affliction, that their temptations and trials are common to men, 1 Cor. x. 13.
God doth not single them out to encounter with
unparalleled affliction : so on the other side it is an
incentive to compassion to them that are free, to
consider that they are liable to the same temptations ; and therefore should measure out the same
compassions to their suffering brethren, that they
would expect in the same trials ; not knowing how

soon the cup of tren bling may be put into their own hand. Be sure, insensibleness of other men's miseries will hasten it: "They put far away the evil day; they lie upon beds of ivory, &c. eat lambs out of the flock, and calves out of the stall, &c. drink wine in bowls," &c. Amos vi. 3—6. that is, they give themselves up to all manner of sensuality, and thereby drown the sense of their brethren's miseries; they are not grieved for the afflictions of Joseph: they lay not the affliction of the church to heart, it never cost them an hour's sleep, they abated nothing of all their sensual excesses; they never turn aside to shed one tear over bleeding Zion in secret: what follows; "Why," saith God, "therefore now shall they go captive with the first that go captive, and the banquet of them that stretched themselves shall be removed," ver. 7. As if God should have said; As I live, because you have not pitied your brethren in captivity, you yourselves shall be led away captive, and the next turn shall be yours; and there you shall learn by experience, what it is to be plundered, and what it is to lie in chains, what it is to have cruel taskmasters set over you, what it is to want bread. You shall banquet it no more: you shall feel by sense what you would not feel by sympathy. And therefore, christians, set your hearts to the afflictions of the church and people of God; it is the great duty which the times call for; and I am afraid God is now visiting England and London for the neglect of this duty. We are verily guilty concerning our brethren, in Germany, in Ireland, in England, and Scotland, &c. in that we saw the anguish of their souls, when they besought us, and we would not hear; therefore is this distress come upon us. We have not grieved their sorrows, nor wept their tears, nor sighed their groans, nor bled their blood; and therefore may fear, lest God should say unto us also, even unto us, "With the next that go into captivity, they shall go into captivity:" with the next that are plundered and spoiled, London shall be plundered and spoiled; with the next that shall be imprisoned, you shall be taken prisoners; with the next that shall be slain with the sword, you shall be slain with the sword; your wives shall be made widows, and your children shall be made fatherless, and your dwellings shall cast you out, and be left desolate. And therefore let us look to it, and know in this our day the things of our peace, before they be hid from our eyes. Show compassion, that you may not need compassion, or, if you need it, you may find it.

In like manner set your hearts to the other lessons which God teacheth by his chastisements.

Prize creature comforts more, and surfeit upon them less: be more thankful, and less sensual. Especially prize a gospel while ye have a gospel; prize it by its worth, that you may not prize it by the want, Amos viii. 11. prize it that you may keep it, lest you prize it one day when you cannot recover it. That is a dreadful word, "They shall go with their flocks and with their herds to seek the Lord, but they shall not find him," Hosea v. 6. "And I will send a famine, not a famine of bread, nor a thirst for water, but of hearing the words of the Lord," Amos viii. 11. "And they shall run to and fro, to seek the word of the Lord, and shall not find it," ver. 12.

Study self-denial, meekness of spirit; labour to discover the hidden corruptions of your own hearts;

be still digging into that dunghill, you will find it a bottomless pit. "The heart is deceitful above all things, and desperately wicked : who can know it ? I the Lord search the heart," Jer. xvii. 9, 10. O, entreat the Lord to discover your hearts to you.

Study scripture evidence for your interest in Christ: rest not in any evidence, which you will not venture your souls upon, if you were to die this moment.

Labour to maintain sweet communion with God; to be able to say with the apostle, and to say truly, " Our fellowship is with the Father, and with his Son Jesus Christ," 1 John i. 3. Make God your choice, and not your necessity; and labour to maintain such constant converse with him, that when you die, you may change your place only, but not your company.

Live up in the exercise of your graces : " Add to your faith virtue, to virtue knowledge, and to knowledge temperance, and to temperance godliness, and to godliness brotherly kindness, and to brotherly kindness charity," 2 Pet. i. 5—7. Be adding one grace to another, and one degree of grace to another, and one exercise of grace to another exercise of grace, that you may not put God to add affliction to affliction, and sorrow to sorrow : while others are adding sin to sin, drunkenness to thirst, do you add grace to grace : " Be stedfast and unmovable, always abounding in the work of the Lord," &c.

Acquaint yourselves with God, and good shall come thereby, Job xxii. 21. Study to know God more, and love him better : " This is life eternal," &c. John xvii. 3. "Then shall we know, if we follow on to know the Lord," Hos. vi. 3.

Mind, I beseech you, while you are in your strength and peace, that one thing necessary : there is but one thing necessary ; there are many *maybe's*, but one *must-be.* O take heed of industrious folly, and dispirit not yourselves in the pursuit of trifles ; mind your work.

Redeem the time, the days are evil. O that christians would study the worth of time ; value a day : say of every hour, yea of every moment, This is time. Redeem time while you have it : redeem time while time may do you good. Evil days are coming, wherein you will say, I have no pleasure in them. Yea, the days are evil ; evil with sin, evil with sorrow : redeem the time to do good, to receive good, that neither you may be the worse for the times, nor the times for you. Happy shall that man be called, who contributeth not to the heap of the God-provoking abominations, nor receiveth impressions from the hypocrisy and prevarication of the present generation !

Study the sufferings of Jesus Christ. Resolve, with Paul, to know nothing but Jesus Christ, and him crucified. A due contemplation of the cross will heighten Christ's love, and lessen your own sufferings.

And labour to get your conversation in heaven : looking for, and hasting to, or, as the word signifies, hasting, the coming of Christ, 2 Pet. iii. 12. Say, Come, Lord Jesus Christ, come quickly.

In a word, brethren, study, and study thoroughly, the sinfulness of sin, the emptiness of the creature, the fulness of Christ. And in all these, and the like lessons, labour for an inward, convincing, experimental, powerful, sweet, abiding teaching.

Content not yourselves, christians, with a gene

ral, slight, superficial, unsavoury, powerless, flitting knowledge. Rest not in notions; be not satisfied with expressions without impressions; nor with impressions, that are not abiding impressions, that are like figures written in the sand: this is the ruin of professors. Those professors, their names shall be written in the dust, who write Divine instructions in the dust: at least, if God have a mind to do you good, expect that he should send you into the house of correction, and there teach you with scourges, and write his instructions in your blood.

And therefore if you would prevent so severe a discipline, O improve your time well in the school of the word; "While you have the light, walk in the light, lest darkness come upon you," John xii. 36. While you sit under the teachings of the gospel, labour to get knowledge answerable to the means, and grace answerable to your knowledge. Thus much for the first caution.

(2.) If you would prevent affliction, labour to be instructed by the chastisements which you see upon other men. God deals with his children as tutors do with the children of princes, whip them upon strangers' backs. Thus God scourged Israel upon the back of the nations round about: "I have cut off the nations, their towers are desolate, I made their streets waste that none passeth by, their cities are destroyed, so that there is no man, that there is none inhabitant," Zeph. iii. 6. Short work! but their punishment was Israel's caution; "I said, Surely thou wilt fear me, thou wilt receive instruction." The world's judgments are the church's instructions, and God looked that his people should have made that use of this practical

doctrine; " I said, Surely thou wilt fear me,
thou wilt receive instructions." God had gracious
ends in this dispensation ; his severity to strangers
was his tender mercy towards Israel ; he spared
not the nations, that he might spare them,
so their dwellings should not be cut off, ver. 7.
God cut off the nations, ver. 6. that he might not
cut off Israel. Behold (as the apostle saith in
another case, Rom. xi. 22.) the goodness and severity of God ; severity to the nations, but goodness
towards Israel if they had continued in his goodness, and received instruction by their neighbour's destruction. And as God punished Israel
upon the nations' backs, so God punished Judah
upon Israel's back ; " Go ye now to my place in
Shiloh, and see what I did to it, for the wickedness
of my people Israel," Jer. vii. 12. Israel's chastisements should have been Jerusalem's teachings,
and by their stripes she should have been healed ;
for the neglect whereof God is highly displeased,
and speaks concerning this in a very angry dialect :
" And I saw when for all the causes whereby backsliding Israel had committed adultery, I had put
her away, and given her a bill of divorce ; yet her
treacherous sister Judah feared not, but went and
played the harlot also," Jer. iii. 8. God took it ill,
that Jerusalem should slight the kindness of such a
caution, and despise the counsel which was written
to her in her sister's blood, which denotes—I would
have made Jerusalem wise by Samaria's harms,
and taught her by a rod which she only saw ; but
she feared not ; she hardened her heart through
unbelief, and either would not understand the
caution, or dared me to my face to do my worst,
while by her shameless whoredoms she went on to

provoke me to jealousy. This hasteneth that judgment upon herself which she despised on others : Judah must feel Israel's rod, because she would not hear it. As Israel must suffer those judgments on the nations which she would not improve; by those very nations by whom she would not be instructed, she must be destroyed, Zeph. iii. 8. So Judah must feel what she feared not at a distance ; she that would not tremble at her sister's divorce must suffer divorce herself, and be judged as women that break wedlock, &c. Ezek. xvi. 38. " And bear her own shame for her sins that she had committed more abominable than they," ver. 52.

Beloved christians, if we would prevent the like severity, let us take heed of the like security. God hath been a long time scourging England upon Germany's back, and upon Ireland's back, and upon Scotland's back ; God hath for these many years scourged London on the back of all the cities and counties round about ; and God doth daily scourge every one of us in particular upon the back of our suffering brethren, in divers kinds : his design is, that we should fear him, that we should receive instruction. If we altogether fail his expectation, we may fear that the same rods are preparing for our backs wherewith they have bled, yea that their rods shall be turned into scorpions to us , we sin worse than others, when we sin those very sins for which others have been punished before our faces, and add contempt to their transgressions ; and how just will it be with God, if as we aggravate their sins, so he aggravate upon us their plagues ; that we that would not be bettered by God's warning pieces, should be destroyed by God's murdering pieces ; that we that would not see and learn, should feel and perish. Even particular judgments should be our documents; " Remember Lot's wife ;" her pillar of salt should season our hearts, that when the judgments of God are abroad in the earth, we that are the inhabitants, not of the earth only, but of Zion also, may learn righteousness. Even those judgments which the magistrate doth execute by God's appointment, are chiefly for caution to standers by, that others may " hear and fear, and do no more any such wickedness," &c. Deut. xiii. 11. How much more those judgments which the Lord himself doth execute! See Psa. lxiv. 7—9. 2 Pet. ii. 6. When the father is correcting one child, the whole family should fear and tremble. " Go to my place in Shiloh," saith God to the Jews, " and see what I did to it for the wickedness of my people Israel," Jer. vii. 12. If we would learn by other men's sufferings, we should prevent our own ; this is the way to prevent sufferings.

The Lord make us wise to salvation.

2. I come to the second branch of exhortation. To such as yet lie under affliction, and the chastisements of the Almighty.

Take notice, O thou afflicted soul, what God's design is in afflicting thee, and make it thy design, namely, that thou mayst be taught, that correction may be turned into instruction ; " Hear the rod, and who hath appointed it." It is the great mistake and folly of men, that they make more haste to get their afflictions removed than sanctified. " The captive exile hasteneth that he may be loosed, and that he should not die in the pit," &c. Isa. li.14. which denotes that men would fain break prison, or leap out at the window, before God open the door ; but this their

way is their folly ; so the following words imply :
" But I am the Lord thy God that divided the sea,
whose waves roared; the Lord of hosts is his
name," ver. 15. which means, Men would fain
be delivered, but they take not the right course:
deliverance belongs unto me, " I am the Lord thy
God that divided the sea," and made it a way for
my ransomed to pass over, and that when it was
most tempestuous, when the waves thereof roared.
When I will deliver, no obstruction can stand in
the way; and yet Israel now in captivity will not
look to me : I am the Lord of hosts, that have all
the armies in heaven and earth at my command;
and yet when they are besieged with troubles and
dangers, I cannot hear from them, they run to the
creature and neglect God ; or if they cry to me in
their distresses, it is for deliverance only, but not for
teaching, though " I have put my words in thy
mouth," ver. 16. that is, I have given them my laws
and statutes, wherein I have made known my
design in affliction, why I send them into captivity,
namely, that there I might *teach them ;* that I
might humble them, and prove them, and make
them know what is in their heart. This is the
shortest way to deliverance, and in this path if they
had trod, " I would have planted the heavens, and
laid the foundations of the earth," ver. 16. even the
new heavens and the new earth of Jerusalem's
restoration, and have said to Zion, " Thou art my
people," in the same verse. This is God's method
wherein he will own his people, and wherein if
they meet him, they shall not stay long for their
deliverance.

And therefore be wise, " O thou afflicted, tossed
with tempest, and not comforted," Isa. liv. 11. be

instructed, lest God's soul depart from thee ; make
more haste to be taught, than to be delivered ; and
choose rather to have thy affliction sanctified than
removed.   That is observable in Elihu's speech,
Job xxxvi. 13. " Hypocrites in heart heap up
wrath," that is, add to their own calamities ; why ?
" They cry not when he bindeth them," Why as
it is, Job xxxiv. 32. " That which I see not teach
thou me : if I have done iniquity, I will do no
more."

(1.) Consider, that this is God's design, that he
might teach thee by his chastisements, and if thou
crossest God's design, it is just with God to cross
thy design ; if thou wilt not let God have his end
in instruction, he will not let thee have thy end in
enlargement.   The only way to retard deliverance,
is to make too much haste to be delivered ; and he
that believeth will not make haste.

(2.) Consider, that bare deliverance is not the
blessing.   I told you before, that deliverance alone
is but the fruit of common bounty ; I will tell you
more now : deliverance alone may be the fruit of
the curse ; a man may be delivered in wrath, and
not in love ; deliverance from one affliction may
but make way for another, for a greater.   Affliction
may return, like the unclean spirit, with seven more
worse than itself. So God threatens an unteachable
people ; " If by these things ye will not be reformed, but will walk contrary to me," cross my
design in my chastisements, " then will I walk contrary to you."   I will cross your design, and instead of deliverance, " I will punish you yet seven
times for your sins," Lev. xxvi. 23, 24.   The
blessing of correction is instruction : O let not God
go till he bless thee.   It is a sad thing to have

affliction, but not the *blessing* of affliction ; to feel
the *wood* of the cross, but not the *good* of the cross;
to taste the *bitter root*, but not the *sweet fruit* of a
suffering condition ; the *curse*, but not the *cordial.*
Truly in such a case one affliction may not only
make way for another, for more, for greater ; but
affliction here may make way for damnation hereafter; and as one saith, By all the fire of affliction
in this world, a man may be but parboiled for hell.
And therefore mind instruction, study the lessons
of a suffering condition, and be importunate for
nothing so much as to be taught of God ; and to
be taught not with a common teaching, but that
special, covenant, saving teaching, which changeth
the soul into the nature of the truth, and makes the
soul holy as it is holy, and pure as it is pure, and
heavenly as it is heavenly. He chastens us "for
our profit, that we might be partakers of his holiness," Heb. xii. 10.

3. The third branch of exhortation is, to them
that are come out of affliction and fiery trials. Sit
down, christian, and reflect upon thyself, turn in
upon thine own heart, examine thyself—Have
teachings accompanied chastisements ? hath the rod
budded ? cast up thy accounts. What hast thou
learned in the school of affliction ? not to go over
the larger catechism of those twenty lessons again.
View the abbreviate ; hath God discovered to thee
the sinfulness of sin, the emptiness of the creature, the
fulness of Christ ? Is no evil like to the evil of sin ?
no good like to Jesus Christ ? Is the world become
an empty vanity, a mockery, a nothing in thine
eyes ? Canst thou say, " It is good I have been
afflicted ?" and canst thou point out that good, and
say, Thus I had, this I have got by my sufferings ;

I know Divine truth more inwardly, more clearly, more experimentally, more powerfully, more sweetly than ever; it hath a more abiding impression upon my heart? I would speak a word,

(1.) To them that can evidence these teachings to their own souls.

(2.) To them that cannot.

(1) To those who through grace do find the fruit of affliction in the savory and saving teachings of God upon their hearts; let me by way of exhortation commend a threefold duty to you.

[1.] Study to be thankful.

[2.] Labour to preserve the teachings of God upon thy spirit.

[3.] Learn to pray for them that are afflicted, and what to pray.

[1.] Study to be thankful. Hath God taught thee as well as chastised thee? O say with David, " What shall I render to the Lord?" For consider how great things God hath done for thy soul.

God hath done more for thee, than if he had never brought thee into affliction and trouble, or than if he had brought thee out the same day on which he sent thee in: if he had delivered thee upon the first prayer that ever thou madest in thine affliction, it had not been a comparable mercy to his teachings of thee by affliction. Prevention and deliverance may be in wrath, but God never teacheth the soul but it is in love.

God hath doubled his mercy and loving kindness to thee, he hath commanded deliverance and instruction too: a twisted mercy; yea, as deliverance and instruction were the return of prayer, a treble, a multiplied mercy: which should greatly endear the heart to God, and make it sing with David, " I

will love the Lord, because he hath heard the voice
of my supplication," Psa. cxvi. 1. Upon the return
of prayer in a single deliverance, God expects the
return of praise, " Call upon me in the day of
trouble, I will deliver thee, and thou shalt glorify
me," Psa. l. 15. how much more when he wreaths
and twists his mercies one in another ! double, and
treble, and multiplied mercy, calls for double, and
treble, and multiplied thankfulness. When God
loads us with mercy we should load him with our
praises.

Instruction is the seal of God, which set upon
correction doth seal up adoption and son-ship, to
them that are exercised thereby · the children of
affliction are, by Divine teaching, sealed up the children of promise : " If his children forsake my law,"
speaking of Christ's spiritual seed, " I will visit their
transgression with a rod, &c. but my loving-kind-
ness will I not take away," Psa. lxxxix. 31—33.
I will visit them with the rod, that is, I will teach
them with the rod, it shall be a rod of instruction
to them, that is the children's portion ; " If his children forsake me," &c. Heb. xii. 7. God deals with
you as with sons. Behold, O thou christian soul,
God hath done that for thee in thy sufferings, which
possibly he denied thee in thy prosperity, given
thee an evidence of thy son-ship ; he hath made thy
suffering time thy sealing time ; and hath allured
thee, and brought thee into the wilderness, and there
hath spoken comfortably to thy heart," Hos. ii. 14.
Thy Patmos hath been thy paradise wherein he hath
given thee his loves.

God hath consecrated thy sufferings by his teachings : afflictions have taken orders, as it were, and
stand no longer in the rank of ordinary providences,

but serve now in the order of gospel-ordinances, officiating in the holy garment of Divine promises, and to the same uses. What is the great end and design of the promises? the apostle tells us, "There are given to us exceeding great and precious promises, that by them we should be partakers of the Divine nature," 2 Pet. i. 4. that is, of gracious dispositions and qualities, which make the soul resemble God, holy as he is holy, &c. this is the end of Divine promises and ordinances; and mark, what the apostle Peter affirms of the promises, the very same doth the apostle Paul affirm of God's chastisements, "He for our profit, that we might be partakers of his holiness," Heb. xii. 10. See, by virtue of Divine teaching afflictions advanced to the same degree and office with gospel ordinances and promises; so that what hinders, why we may not give those titles of honour to afflictions, which the apostle here gives to the promises, and say, There are given unto us exceeding great and precious afflictions, that by them we might be partakers of the Divine nature, that is, made partakers of his holiness, Phil. i. 29. See, O thou afflicted soul, by teaching God hath changed the very nature of affliction; he hath turned thy water into wine; a prison, a bed of sickness, into a school, into a temple, wherein he hath taught thee into his own likeness.

As God hath consecrated thy sufferings, so he hath consecrated thee also by thy sufferings. As it is said of Christ, " He made the Captain of our salvation perfect through sufferings," Heb. ii. 10. as the Greek means, he consummated, or perfected; Christ became a perfect Mediator by his passion; the cross was the complement and absolution of his mediatorial office: hence you hear him cry upon the cross, "It is finished." John xix. 30. And thus also may it be said of the members of Christ; they are perfected by sufferings. Chastisement being coupled with teaching, is the consecration and consummation of the saints: "I fill up," saith Paul, "that which is behind of the afflictions of Christ in my flesh," Col. i. 24. the after sufferings of Christ. As Christ as a Mediator, so Christ as one body, with his members, is completed by sufferings: "I fill up that which is behind:" Christ is not full till all his members have had their measure of sufferings: you have need of patience, that when you have done the will of God, you may inherit the promises, Heb. x. 36. When we have done God's will, all is not done; there is somewhat to be suffered, without which the christian is not in a capacity to receive his inheritance; you have need of patience, to carry you through the suffering part of your work, as well as the doing, that so being perfect, you may inherit the promises.

By adding instruction to correction, God hath crowned thee with the blessing: " Blessed is the man whom thou chastenest and teachest." God hath turned the crown of thorns into a crown of gold, and set it on thy head, and now brings thee forth wearing this crown, and shows thee, as it were, to the world as a monument of free grace, proclaiming before thee, " Thus shall it be done to the man whom God will honour."

Well then, christian, sit down, and consult with thine own soul, what to render for so rich a mercy; and behold, it is resolved to thy hand: " I will deliver thee, and thou shalt glorify me," Psa. l. 15.

Behold God hath not only delivered, but taught thee, now therefore he expecteth glory from thee.

Glorify God with *thy lips;* "I cried to him with my lips, and he was glorified with my tongue." Let the lips of prayer be turned into the tongue of praise; make your tongues your glory, by proclaiming God's glory; be telling what great things God hath done for you; say with David, " Come and hear all ye that fear God, and I will tell you what he hath done for my soul," Psa. lxvi. 16. abundantly utter the memory of his great goodness, make his praise glorious.   Extol him in psalms of thanksgiving: " Sing unto the Lord, O ye saints of his, give thanks at the remembrance of his holiness," Psa. xxx. 4.   " He that offereth me praise, glorifieth me," Psa. l. 23.

Glorify God with *thy life,* live his praise; hath God taught thee?   If thou wouldst glorify God, go and put all the lessons which thou hast learned into print; " Show forth the praises of him that hath called thee out of darkness into his marvellous light," 1 Pet. ii. 9. print them in such a legible character, that whoso runs may read: *lip praise* is good, but *life praise* is better; " He that offers me praise glorifieth me, and to him that ordereth his conversation aright will I show the salvation of God," Psa. l. 23.   It is good to speak so, that men may see; that standers-by may be God's witnesses and yours, that you are taught of God; and say, Lo, what hath God wrought! how holily, and humbly, and fruitfully, and self-denyingly do these servants of God walk since they came out of tribulation!   Live so, that you may take off the scandal of the cross of Christ, and bring men into love with a suffering condition : " Let your light so shine before men, that they may see your good works, and glorify your Father which is in heaven," Matt. v. 16. that you may be a little heaven sparkling with bright stars of Divine graces, as it was said of Joseph.

Now God hath taught thee, be thou ready to teach others. It is a debt which thou owest to all thou conversest with ; when thou art converted, strengthen thy brethren. Communicate what God hath taught thee to thy yoke-fellow, children, servants, friends, upon all seasonable opportunities. Sanctified knowledge is communicative; freely thou hast received, freely give. God never lighted this candle, that it should be put under the bed, or under the bushel, Mark iv. 21. the bed of pleasure, or the bushel of profit ; but that it may be put into the candlestick of thy conversation, and so shine before men, that they may see, and glorify thy Father which is in heaven. This is indeed to glorify God.

[2.] Labour to preserve the teachings of God upon thy spirit. Study how to maintain that sweet gracious frame of heart into which God hath taught thee by affliction. It is the duty which christians should practise, as oft as they come from the word, or any other Divine ordinance. When we come out of a sabbath, we should sit down, and observe with what frame of spirit God sends us away from the ordinance ; if the ordinance hath left no savoury gracious impression upon the heart, to lie in the dust, and mourn, and commune with our own hearts, and lament after God. If there be an ordinance frame, we should rejoice in it, bless God for it, and labour to keep up such a frame upon the heart till the next solemn approach to God. Christians, how much more should this be our care and study when we come out of God's furnace, that solemn ordinance of affliction, to labour to maintain that melting frame of heart, that warmth and heat, that life and vigour which we have brought with us out of affliction. Look to yourselves, that ye lose not those things which God hath wrought in you, 2 John 8. To that end take a few means or helps.

First. Be often reading over the lessons which God hath taught you; frequently revive the remembrance of them in your heads, and work the impressions of them upon your hearts: labour not only to say them without book, but indeed to get them by heart. I tell you, christians, you have need to take much pains with yourselves, to keep the teachings of God alive upon your spirits. For be sure of this, that you will find a great difference between your hearts yet under affliction, and when the affliction is taken off; and without infinite watchfulness your hearts will be too hard for you: " The heart is deceitful above all things, and desperately wicked," Jer. xvii. 9. There is much of a Pharaoh-like disposition in every man, very prone to harden when the storm is over. It is sad and wonderful to consider, how a corruption will lie as if it were quite dead, while danger and death are before us, and how suddenly and powerfully it will revive; and without special take-heed, betray the soul, when the danger is over. That caution which God by Moses gave the Israelites in the wilderness, may make every wise christian to tremble: " I know their imaginations, which they go about, even now, before I have brought them into the land, which

I sware," Deut. xxxi. 21. Their hearts were secretly projecting for their lusts, even while they were yet smarting under the rod : and in the howling wilderness they are forecasting how to satisfy sense, and serve their carnal interests, when they should come into the land that flowed with milk and honey. Possibly, these were not downright resolves ; but said the Lord, " I know their imaginations." O my brethren, we should hearken to the whisperings of lust in our own bosoms, and labour to suppress them ; to crush the serpent while it is in the shell ; for if there be such floatings of sin in the imagination, while yet in durance, what projecting and contrivements will there be in the heart when liberty and enlargement shall present temptations and opportunities ? And therefore " keep we our hearts with all diligence," Prov. iv. 23. or as the Hebrew phraseth it, Of all keepings keep our hearts, for out of them come the issues of life : and when the days of affliction and trouble are gone, work truths, and counsels received, frequently and fixedly upon your consciences ; that you may, like good scribes, instructed to the kingdom of God, bring out of your treasures things new and old, Matt. xiii. 52. and have always in a readiness wherewith to oppose and check temptation, and may practise every lesson which God hath taught you, in the season thereof.

Secondly. Renew, also, often upon your souls, the remembrance of the sharpness and bitterness of the affliction : it will be a notable corrective to sensuality, and give check to sinful excesses. The flesh will quickly grow wanton when it findeth ease ; Jeshurun, when the neck was got from under the yoke, quickly " waxed fat, and kicked," Deut.xxxii.15.

o

"They soon forgat his works, they waited not for
his counsel, but lusted exceedingly," Psa. cvi. 13,
15.   Works and counsel, chastisements and teachings were quickly forgotten, when once the affliction
was over.   They quickly forgot a barren wilderness,
in a land that flowed with milk and honey.   "They
waited not for his counsel:" they grew weary of
counsel, when once free from correction ; and chose
rather to walk by the dictate of their own lusts,
than of God's laws, till at length God grew as
weary (if I may so say) of counselling, as they were
of being counselled ; and "gave them up to their
own hearts' lusts, to walk in their own counsels,"
Psa. lxxxi. 12.   That they who would not live by
God's counsels, should perish by their own.   And
therefore, you that are come out of the house of
bondage, remember the sorrows of a suffering condition ; set not your heart so much upon the
pleasure of your present enlargement, as upon the
bitterness of your former captivity.   The church
found great advantage in it, when returned from
Babylon : " Remembering mine affliction and my
misery, the wormwood and the gall, my soul hath
them continually in remembrance :" and what was
the fruit of it ? it follows, "and is humbled in me,"
Lam. iii. 19, 20.   The meaning is this ; The people
of God among the Jews, that desired to keep close
to God after their great deliverance, experienced a
serious and constant remembrance of those seventy
years' sufferings, to be an excellent preservative to
that humble and gracious frame of heart, which
God wrought them into, in their captivity.   And
yet that is not all ; as remembrance of affliction
preserved humility, so humility strengthened faith :
"This I recall to mind, therefore have I hope :"

tribulation wrought patience, and patience experience, and experience hope, &c. Rom. v. 3. By the kindly operation of the remembrance of former dispensations, she began to conceive good hope through grace, that God had not chastened her in wrath, but in love ; and that all her tribulations were the fruit of the promise, not of the threatening ; a blessing, not a curse. Go you, and do likewise.

Third. Call often to mind the sad discourses and reasonings, the fears and tremblings, which you have had in your bosoms in the times of trouble and distress. Thus the church, " I forgat prosperity," Lam. iii. 17. She had been so long in a suffering condition, that now she can scarcely remember that ever she saw a good day in all her life : and at length she sits down, and gives herself up to despair ; " And *I said*, My strength and my hope is perished from the Lord." She remembereth what unbelieving conclusions she made in her affliction ; "*I said*," &c. And so the prophet Jeremiah, ver. 54. " Waters flowed over mine head ; then *I said*, I am cut off:" when he began to sink in the mire, he remembereth how his heart began to sink with fear ; he calleth to mind, what faithless language his heart spake ; "*I said*, I am cut off."

Thus David, " *I said* in my passion," &c. Psa. xxxi. 22. and cxvi. 11. and " Then *I said*, I am cast out of thy sight," Jonah ii. 4. Hezekiah makes a large narrative of what discourses he had in his own soul, what time he had received the sentence of death ; and leaveth it in writing to all posterity, " The *writing* of Hezekiah king of Judah, when he had been sick ; *I said* in the cutting off of my days," Isa. xxxviii. 9, 10. what did he say ? truly he uttered very strange complaints for such an eminent saint as he was : " I shall go to the gates of the grave ; I am deprived of the residue of my years : I shall behold man no more with the inhabitants of the world ; mine age is departed :" and a great deal more to that purpose. The sum whereof is this ; I shall die, I shall die ; I must take my leave of this world, and worms must eat my flesh in the grave, &c. Such uncomely words he uttered ; but he remembereth them afterward, and is contented to shame himself for them to all the world : he puts his fleshly complaints in writing, that he may humble himself, and caution, yea and comfort others.

And thus, christians, should we do ; we should call to mind our *saids ;* that is, we should sit down and recount the impatiences and short-spiritednesses, the murmur and unbelief, the love of a present world, the fear of death, the hard thoughts of God ; all the irregularities and distempers of our own spirits, in the time of tribulation ; " *I said, I said,*" &c. Doubtless it would be of singular use, as, to humble our souls, and to check corruption ; so to endear and preserve the teachings of God upon your souls ; while you might tune David's thanksgiving, conceived upon some such like occasion, " Good and upright is the Lord : therefore will he teach sinners in the way," Psa. xxv. 8. which means, I sinned against the Lord in my affliction, by my impatience, unbelief, unhumbledness, &c. yet he was pleased, not altogether to leave me without the teachings of his Spirit ; not because I was good, but because he was good ; not because I pleased him, but because mercy pleased him : not because I was upright before him, but because he was upright, true and faithful to his own promise, hath he done it ; good and upright is the Lord, and therefore he hath taught me, though I was a sinner, in the way.

Fourth. Remember your vows. When God, by the fire of affliction, showed you your folly, discovered to you the hidden corruption of your hearts, and brought your ways and doings to remembrance, which were not good ; you were ashamed, yea, even confounded, and said, as it is in Job, " Lord, wherein I have done wickedly, I will do so no more." But take heed it be not so with you, as it was with backsliding Israel, of whom God thus complaineth ; " Of old time I have broken thy yoke, and burst thy bands, and thou saidst, I will not transgress," Jer. ii. 20. which means, I brought thee, hundreds of years since, out of the land of Egypt, out of the house of bondage, and then thou madest me fair promises, I remember the kindness of thy youth, the love of thine espousals, ver. 2. Thou saidst, I will do so no more. Lord, I will be covetous no more, and idolatrous no more, adulterous no more ; I will murmur no more, I will no more depart from thee, thou art the guide of my youth. Good words, had she been as good as her word : but O read what followeth, and tremble ; " When upon every high hill and under every green tree thou wanderest, playing the harlot ;" that is, no sooner her old heart and her old temptations met, but presently they fell into mutual embraces. And this is the temper of our hearts, for all the world : we are very good while we are in affliction, and promise fair ; but no sooner is the trial over, but we forget God's teachings and our own vows, and return into

the same course and fashion of conversation as
before. Now therefore, if you would preserve the
teachings of God upon your spirits, sit down, remember your vows ; and, spreading them before
the Lord, say with David, " I will pay thee my
vows, which my lips have uttered, and my mouth
hath spoken, when I was in trouble," Psa. lxvi.
13, 14. Lord, through grace assisting, I will be
as ready to pay my vows, now I am well, as I was
to make vows when I was sick, &c. " Thy vows
are upon me, I will render praises unto thee," Psa.
lvi. 12. When you have made good vows, be as
careful to make good your vows unto the Lord :
" Vow, and pay unto the Lord your God," Psa.
lxxvi. 11.

Fifth. If you would preserve the teaching of
God upon thy heart, attend constantly and con-
scionably upon the ministry of the word. The
truth is, the word and the rod teach the same
lessons. The rod many times is but the word's
remembrancer : and therefore as the rod quickens
the word, so the word back again will revive and
sanctify the teachings of the rod. They mutually
help to set one another with deeper impressions.
And therefore hear wisdom, " watching daily at her
gates, waiting at the posts of her doors," Prov. viii.
34. if thou wouldst be blessed. It will be of a
twofold advantage. 1. It will help your memories : as the rod repeateth the word, so the
word will repeat the instructions of the rod ; the
gospel will bring to remembrance what you have
learned in the school of affliction. 2. It will
quicken affection. To hear that repeated by the
still sweet voice of the gospel, which before God
taught you in the voice of thunder, this cannot but

affect, and make you bespeak the gospel, as once the Israelites did Moses, " Speak thou unto us all that the Lord our God shall speak unto thee, and we will hear it, and do it," Deut. v. 25—27. but let us not hear the voice of God any more, that terrible voice of judgment, lest we die. And certainly God will take it as well at your hands as he did at Israel's, and will answer in some such language, I have heard the voice of this people, they have well said all that they have spoken : O that there were such a heart in them, that they would fear me and keep my commandments, that it might be well with them, ver. 28, 29. and that I might not bring upon them such evils as I have done, any more.

Sixth. Be often feeding that frame of heart which God hath taught thee into. Do by it, as thou daily beggest God would do by thee ; give it day by day its daily bread ; meditations suitable to the nature of that grace which thou wouldst maintain ; threatenings, promises, truths, scripture considerations, agreeable to the lesson. Take heed of feeding corruption with thoughts of the sweetness that is in sin ; take heed of starving grace by withdrawing from it suitable aliment. You will re- quire at the nurse's hands the blood of your infants that are starved. Will not God be much more jealous over the births and issues of his own Spirit ? meditate much upon the sinfulness of sin, the emptiness of the creature, the fulness of Christ, the exquisiteness of his sufferings, the severity of the last judgment, the torments of hell, the joys of heaven, the infinite perfections of the Divine nature, and the horror of eternity. Rich in meditation, and rich in grace.

Seventh. Be much in prayer. As it was not enough for God to make the first creation, but he must uphold it by the word of his power, Heb. i. 3. or else it would quickly have returned into its first nothing; so it is with the second creation, Heb. xii. 3. Christ is the finisher as well as the author of grace. He that hath begun a good work in you, must perfect it, Phil. i. 6. Stability only comes from the unchangeable God; and therefore pray, that God would put of his unchangeableness upon you. Pray as Luther was wont to pray, Confirm, O Lord, in us what thou hast wrought, and perfect the work thou hast begun in us to thy glory, so be it; which he seems to have taken out of Psalm lxviii. 28. " Strengthen, O God, that which thou hast wrought in us." Pray that prayer which David prayed over that liberal frame of heart which God had formed in his people for the service of the temple. " O Lord God of Abraham, and Isaac, and Jacob our fathers, keep this for ever in the imagination of the thoughts of the heart of thy people, and prepare their heart unto thee," 1 Chron. xxix. 18. or stablish their heart. O be earnest with God for stability of heart, that thy goodness may not be as the morning cloud, and as the early dew, Hos. vi. 4. but that it may in some proportion resemble the Author of it, and be yesterday, and to-day, and for ever the same, Heb. xiii. 8.

In a word, by all these means and helps, and what other God hath sanctified for this gracious end, labour, christians, to be such *out* of your afflictions, as you promised God and yourselves to be when you were *in;* that neither God nor your own souls may have cause to repent of your sufferings ; that the fruit of chastening may be repentance never to be repented of, that is, never to fall back again. Having in your troubles repented of your sins, take heed when you are delivered, that you repent not of your repentance ; and he that doth not repent *of* his repentance now, shall never have cause to repent *for* his repentance hereafter.

And thus I have done with the second duty of those who through grace do find they have been taught by affliction.

I come now to the third duty.

[3.] Pray for the afflicted ; and when you pray, say, Lord, teach them, as well as correct them, that they may be blessed. O pray thus for England ; she hath been a long time sorely chastised of the Lord, and yet hath been all this while like a bullock unaccustomed to the yoke ; O pray, " Turn us, Lord, and we shall be turned: thou art the Lord our God." Pray, that God would teach England in this day of her visitation the things of her peace before they be hid from her eyes, Luke xix. 42. O pray that we may be instructed, lest God's soul depart from us. If correction go not forth into instruction ; if England be not at length reformed by all the judgments of God upon her, she hath seen her best days, and may expect to be made desolate, a land not inhabited, Jer. vi. 8. there is no balm for our pain, neither any physician that can heal our malady.

Pray thus for all your friends, who are or have been in the furnace of affliction ; pray that they may come forth as gold purified seven times in the fire, that they may lose nothing there but their rust or dross. Pray, Lord, what they see not, teach them, and if they have done wickedly, let them do so no more. One great use which christians should make of reading the scripture, is to learn from thence the language of prayer. And, O, that the professors of this age would in this particular learn what to pray, and how to pray for their brethren in tribulation. O that they would censure less, and pray more, and instead of speaking one of another, speak more one to another, and one for another; that was the good old way; " Then they that feared the Lord spake often one to another," Mal. iii. 16. But O the tender, praying, healing, restoring spirit is departed; and if christians stir not up themselves to call it back again, it is a sad presage that God is departing too; and wo unto us when God departeth from us, Hos. ix. 12. We are like water spilt upon the ground, that cannot be gathered up again. We judge before we inquire, and reject before we admonish. Our brethren, upon vain surmises, are to us as heathens and publicans, before we have been to them as christians and fellow members. And this we think becometh us, and we take a kind of pride and contentment in it. But O to inform, to convince, to exhort, to pray, to put the bone in joint again if out; this were done like the disciples of Christ; to show ourselves christians indeed, professors not of the letter, but of the spirit, and would gain our brethren instead of blasting them. Consider what I say, and the Lord give you a right understanding in all things.

And, thus much for such as are come out of affliction, and find that it hath been through free grace a teaching affliction.

(2.) But now secondly, to such as cannot evidence to their own souls that chastening hath been

accompanied with Divine teaching in any gospel proportion, or at least are not deeply sensible of the
want of it; here is a word of exhortation for them,
suffer it I beseech you; roll yourselves in the dust
before the Lord; smite upon your thigh, sigh
with the breaking of your loins, and cry out with
Ephraim, " Thou hast chastised me, and I was
chastised, as a bullock unaccustomed to the yoke,"
Jer. xxxi. 18. I have felt the blows of God, but
that is all; I have received no more instruction by
all my correction than a brute beast; or if I had, I
have quickly lost it; it is fled " like a bird, from
the birth, &c. Hos. ix. 11. Truly thou hast cause to
sit down and even wish for thy affliction again. God
had put himself into thy hands, as it were, and thou
hast let him go without the blessing, the blessing
of saving instruction. How mayst thou even wish,
I say, O that I were in prison again, in my sick bed
again, in banishment again, and so as to other
things. However, humble thyself greatly before
the Lord, and wrestle mightily for the after teachings of God upon thy heart; pray, " Turn me Lord,
and I shall be turned : for thou art the Lord my
God ;" what affliction hath not done, Lord do thou ;
set omnipotency on work, and it shall be done ;
" turn me, and I *shall be* turned ;" that so thy soul
may yet speak to the praise of free grace. " After
that I was turned, I repented ; and after that I was
instructed, I smote upon my thigh : I was ashamed,
yea, even confounded, because I did bear the reproach of my youth," Jer. xxxi. 19. Urge the
Lord, as Samson did after his victory ; " Thou hast
given this great deliverance into the hand of thy
servant, and shall I now die for thirst, and fall into
the hand of the uncircumcised ?" Judg. xv. 18.

Say thou, Lord, thou hast given thy servant this great deliverance from danger and death, and shall I now perish for want of teaching, and go down to hell among the uncircumcised? " Teach me thy way, O Lord, I will walk in thy truth: unite my heart to fear thy name," Psa. lxxxvi. 11. " Teach me to do thy will; for thou art my God: thy spirit is good ; lead me into the land of uprightness," Psa. cxliii. 10. In a word, desire the Lord that he would do all the work, and then take all the glory. Say, Lord, teach me as well as deliver me, and I shall be blessed.

4. The fourth and last branch of exhortation is to parents and governors; to exhort them in the education of their children to imitate God ; and that in two things.

(1.) In affording their children due correction.

(2.) To correction to add instruction.

(1.) Afford your children due correction. It is the counsel of the Holy Ghost, " Chasten thy son while there is hope, and let not thy soul spare for his crying," Prov. xix. 18. Behold, God coun-selleth you that are parents, or instead of parents, to do with your children as he doth with his ; wisely to use the discipline of the rod, before vicious dispositions grow into habits, and folly be so deeply rooted, that the rod of correction will not drive it out, Prov. xxii. 15. Error and folly, saith one very well, are the knots of Satan, wherewith he ties children to the stake to be burnt in hell ; and these knots are most easily cut betimes ; or if you should make the child bleed in cutting them, let it not cause you to withdraw your hand ; for so it followeth, " Chasten thy son, &c. and let not thy soul spare for his crying." It is not only foolish, but cruel pity to forbear correction for a few childish tears, to suffer the child to howl in hell for sin, rather than to shed a few tears for the preventing of it. Foolish fathers and mothers call this love, but the Father of spirits calls it hatred; " He that spareth the rod, hateth his son," Prov. xiii. 24. Surely there is nothing so ill-spared, as that whereby the child is bettered, such sparing is hatred; and because you *hate* your children *in* not correcting them, they come afterward to hate you *by* not correcting them. But that is not all; the parent's lenity in this case makes way for God's severity. Pity to the flesh is cruelty to the soul; so the Hebrew may be rendered, Spare not to his destruction, or to cause him to die, that is, to occasion his destruction. The foolish indulgence of the parent may be, and often is the death of the child, eternal death. Parents spare their children in their folly to the destruction both of body and soul. And this may help us to expound that other parallel text, " Withhold not correction from the child : for if thou beatest him with the rod, he shall not die," Prov. xxiii. 13. The meaning may be, either that correction will not kill him ; the rod will break no bones ; so preventing and reproving at once the silly and sinful tenderness of fond parents, who think if they should correct their children, they would presently die of it ; they are as afraid to use the rod, as if it were a sword. Abraham feared not so much to sacrifice his son, as such parents fear to chasten him. Nay, but saith the Holy Ghost, fear not correction, for behold, the strokes of the rod are not the strokes of death ; it is but a rod it is not a serpent, take it into thy hand ; it may smart, it will not sting. To obviate the fear of parents in

P

this case, God himself giveth them his word for it, " He shall not die." This, I say, may be the meaning, By correcting thy child thou shalt not murder him.   Or else, which I rather conceive, the words may be a motive drawn from the fruit of correction ; " Withhold not correction from the child ;" why? " He shall not die," that is, it may be, and, through Divine blessing accompanying it, is often a means to prevent death : it may prevent the first and second death, to which the child is exposed by the sinful indulgence of the parent.   The word used in this place, saith one, seems to note an immortality ; so that " He shall not die," is all one as if the Holy Ghost had said, He shall live for ever ; the rod on the flesh shall be a means to save the soul in the day of the Lord Jesus : " We are chastened, that we should not be condemned with the world," 1 Cor. xi. 32.   Such smitings, as David saith in another case, " shall be a kindness," Psa. cxli. 5. and such rebukes are so far from breaking the head, that they shall be an excellent oil which shall cure and give life.   The very philosopher could say, Correction is a kind of physic or medicine.   Alas, our children are sick, and cruel is that mercy which will suffer them to die, yea eternally, rather than disgust their palates with a little bitter physic.   Apes and monkeys they be in the forms of men and women who thus hug their little ones to death ; parricides rather than parents ; of whom we may say, as sometime the Roman emperor said of Herod, when he heard that he had murdered his own son amongst the rest of the infants in Bethlehem, that so he might be sure (as he supposed) to destroy the King of the Jews, Surely it were better to be such people's swine than their sons.   O hateful indulgence.

merciless pity ! to lose a child for want of correction !
such parents throw both the rod and the child into
the fire at once ; the rod into the fire of the chimney,
and the child into the fire of hell. This is not
done like God, for, " Whom the Lord loveth he
chasteneth, and scourgeth every son whom he receiveth," Heb. xii. 6. And so doth every wisely
loving parent ; " He that spareth the rod hateth
his son, but he that loveth him chasteneth him betimes," Prov. xiii. 24. As moths are beaten out of a
garment with a rod, so must vices out of children's
hearts.

And for want of this disciplinary love, how
have some children accused their parents, on their
death-bed, yea at the gallows ! and how many do
and will curse them in hell, in some such language
as Cyprian supposeth : The treacherous fondness
of our parents hath brought us into these torments,
our fathers and mothers have been our murderers ;
they that gave us our natural life, have deprived us
of a better ; and they that would not correct us
with the rod, have occasioned us now to be tormented with scorpions. O it would grieve the heart
of the most unnatural parent in the world to hear
the doleful complaints, and those hideous yellings
of poor children in hell fire, whom their fondness
hath sent thither. And O that they would listen
to them, before they themselves come into that
place of torment, and *there* find *no mercy*, because
here they have showed their children *so much*. The
child goeth to hell for his wickedness, and the
parent many times for his mercy. Yea even in this
life, how do many godly parents smart for their fondness, because they will not make their children smart
for their folly. Eli and David would not so much as

rebuke their sons, and God gave them both great rebukes in their sons. It is said of Elⁱ, " His sons made themselves vile, and he restrained them not," 1 Sam. iii. 13. the Hebrew signifieth, He frowned not upon them. Oh sad ! for want of a frown to destroy a soul ! the soul of a child ! to smile a child to hell ! Consider of it ; I am much afraid this unchristian, yea, unnatural indulgence of parents, is the fountain of all that confusion, under which England at this time reels and staggers like a drunken man : and for this very sin, at least for this among others, yea, and for this above others, God is visiting all the families of the land, from the throne to the poorest cottage. Parents have laid the foundation of their own sorrows, their children's ruin, and the desolation of the nation, in the looseness and delicacy of their education ; and yet are not sensible of it to this day. We have not corrected our children, and therefore God is correcting us in our children. We have not crossed them in their unlawful desires,* and therefore God doth cross us in our righteous desires. We have walked (even in this point, exceedingly) contrary to God, and to his discipline ; and therefore God is walking contrary to us, and is punishing us seven times more for this iniquity. And therefore, O that parents would at length awaken themselves, to follow both the pattern and precept of their heavenly Father ; who, as he correcteth whom he loveth, so he commands them to correct, if they love their children. " Withhold not correction from the child ; for if thou correct him with the rod, he shall not die." If if be needful that

---

* God makes our children our rods, because we have withheld the rod from them. We gave them too much rest, and therefore they give us none, Prov. xxix. 17. Lev. xxvi.

the rod draw blood, it is for their safety ; it is as the physician deals with them to prevent a fever ; a fever of boiling passions here, and of boiling fire and brimstone hereafter: it is to cure, not to kill ; yea, thou killest, if thou dost not wound : and therefore again I say, withhold it not. Give the rod unto thy child, and he will one day give thee thanks for it. Yea, it is worth observation, that the same word in the original, which is translated withhold, signifieth also to forbid; meeting with another distemper in parents, who as they will not correct their children themselves, so also they forbid others to correct them, under whose tuition they put them. As if they were afraid their children would not have sin enough here, nor hell enough hereafter, they lay in caveats against the means which God hath sanctified for their reclaiming. What tears of blood are sufficient to bewail this folly? You that are godly-wise, and wisely-loving, take heed of it; and when you commit your children to others' hands, do not in the mean while hold their hands. If thou judgest them not wise, why dost thou choose them? if thou choose them, why dost thou not trust them? Well then, if the rod be in thine own hand, withhold it not; if in thy friend's hand, forbid it not. Certainly there is great need of this duty, which the Spirit of God doth frequently inculcate all along the Proverbs. I will conclude this branch of the exhortation with inverting the counsel of our Saviour in this particular sense; Be ye not merciful, that you may be the children of your heavenly Father, Matt. v. 44, 45. for "whom he loveth he correcteth, and scourgeth every son whom he receiveth." Go, thou, and do likewise ; and this shall be your mercy and love to

your children: " He that spareth the rod, hateth
his son ; but he that loveth him, chasteneth him
betimes," Prov. xiii. 24.

(2) You that are parents, or instead of parents,
if you would have your children happy, add instruction to correction. Imitate God in this part of
paternal discipline also ; let chastisement and instruction go together. It is that which the Holy
Ghost urgeth upon you ; " Bring them up in the
nurture and admonition of the Lord," Eph. vi. 4.
There are two words relating to both these parental
duties ; in the chastisement or correction ; and it is
added of the Lord : that is, either in the chastisement, wherewith the Lord exerciseth his children ;
or in the chastisement which the Lord commandeth
earthly parents to exercise towards their children:
this is the first duty, of which already. And then
there is another word, which holdeth forth the end
and design of parental correction, and that is, in
the admonition and instruction of the Lord : that
is, in counsels and instructions taken out of the
word of God, or such as are approved of by God.
The sum is this, that while we chasten the flesh,
we should labour to inform and form the mind and
spirit, by infusing right principles, pressing and
urging upon their tender hearts counsel, reproof,
and instruction, as the matter requireth. This is
the duty of parents, to imitate God, to let instruction expound correction ; and with a rod in the
hand, and a word in the mouth, to train up their
children to life eternal. A dumb rod is but a
brutish discipline, and will certainly leave them
more brutish than it found them. Chastisement
without teaching may sooner break the bones
than the heart ; it may mortify the flesh, but not

corruption; extinguish nature, but never beget grace.
" But the rod and *reproof* give wisdom," Prov.
xxix. 15. Instruction added to correction, as it
makes excellent christians, so it makes good children. There are parents that are severe enough
to their children ; they spare for no blows :
instead of breaking them of their wills, by a wise
and moderate correction, they are ready to break
their bones, and their necks too sometimes, in
their moods and passions. But they never mind
the other branches of paternal discipline, instruction and admonition: of such parents I suppose the
apostle speaketh ; " We have had fathers of our
flesh, who corrected and chastened us after *their
own pleasure*," Heb. xii. 9, 10. He speaketh not
of *all* parents; but his meaning is, There are such
men and women in the world, who are most unlike to God ; and in smiting their children rather
please themselves than profit their children. He
for our profit, but they after their own pleasure,
to give vent to their passion, and satisfy their
vindictive rage and fury : and when is that?
truly when the rod and reproof do not go together ; it is an argument there is more passion than
judgment, more lust than love, in such chastisements. Such parents do rather betray their own
folly, than take a course to make their children
wise. The rod and reproof give wisdom : neither alone will do it : the rod without reproof will
harden the heart, and teach the children sooner to
hate the parent, than to hate sin ; and reproof without the rod will leave no impression. " Reproofs
of instruction are the way of life," Prov. vi. 23 or
corrections of instruction : a lesson set on with correction is best remembered. It is Divine truth that

must be the instrument of working saving grace
in the heart : " Sanctify them through thy truth, thy
word is truth," John xvii. 17. It is the commendation of Timothy's mother, that from his very
infancy she instructed him in the " scriptures, which
were able to make him wise to salvation," 2 Tim.
iii. 15. When there is a Divine sentence in the
mouth of the rod, it brings wisdom and life with it.

And therefore, O that parents would imitate the
Father of spirits in this blessed art of paternal
discipline : join the word of instruction to the rod
of correction ; teach as well as chastise : " Reprove,
rebuke, exhort with all long suffering and doctrine,"
2 Tim. iv. 2. It is true, it is enjoined Timothy as
a pastoral duty ; but it is as true, that every parent
is a king, a prophet, and a priest : a king to govern
and chastise ; a prophet, to teach and instruct ; and
a priest, to offer up spiritual sacrifice to God,
prayer and praise with and for the family. O that
every child might have cause to give their parents
that commendation, which once Augustin gave his
mother. My mother, saith he, made it her
business to make God my Father, because she
travailed with my everlasting salvation, with more
tenderness and sorrow, than ever she did with my
first birth. O that natural parents could bespeak
the fruit of their loins, as St. Paul bespeaks his
Galatians, " My little children, of whom I travail
in birth again, until Christ be formed in you,"
Gal. iv. 19. that so they might rejoice in the
second, more than ever they did in the first birth.
Why, this is done by the word and the rod, " Correct thy son, and he shall give thee rest ; yea, he
shall give delight unto thy soul," Prov. xxix. 17.
Correct ! how ? the 15th verse answers ; the **rod**

and reproof give wisdom ; thus give your children correction, and they shall give you rest and delight. Though correction for the present do not give them rest, for no chastening for the present seemeth to be joyous, but grievous; yet it will make them give you rest; and though correction doth not delight them, yet it shall make them give delight to you. What greater delight than to see your children walking in the truth ! 3 John 4. and to think thus with yourselves, (not as Cassiodor expresseth it, that so many sons, so many counsellors to the state, but) that, so many children God hath given you, so many children you have brought up for God, and so many heirs for the kingdom of heaven. Well; chastise and teach them out of the law of God, and thy children shall be blessed. Which that they may, indeed, take one short caution more ; and that is—

Add prayer to instruction. As teaching should accompany chastisement, so prayer should accompany teaching. God need use only the rod and the word ; because the blessing is in his own hand, he can command a blessing. It is not so with us ; as Paul may plant, and Apollos may water, but God must give the increase; so the Father may correct, the mother may instruct, both may do both, but God must give the blessing : and therefore christian parents, while they add instruction to correction, should add prayer to instruction. Means are ours, success is God's ; and therefore let us put the rod into the hand of instruction, instruction into the hand of prayer, and *all* into the hand of God. I knew a worthy gracious lady living in the city, who would never use the rod but as with much pious instruction before, so after, would cause the child, if of capacity, or ever it stirred from the place, solemnly to kneel down and beg a blessing of God upon it. Go you and do likewise. Pray, and teach your children to pray, that God would so bless correction and instruction, that both may make you and your children blessed. Amen.

Mount Pisgah;

or

A Prospect of Heaven.

being

An Exposition on 1 Thess. 4:13-18

---

by Thomas Case

Sometime Student of Christ Church, Oxford;
Minister of the Gospel, and a member of
the Westminster Assembly of Divines

TO

THE HONOURABLE,

AND HIS MUCH HONOURED SON-IN-LAW,

Sir ROBERT BOOTH, Knt.,

Lord Chief Justice of the Common-Pleas in Ireland,

GRACE, MERCY, AND PEACE.

Dear Sir,

These meditations presented to you, were first in tended for a diversion to your and my sorrow, conceived by the death of that excellent child, your first-born, your Ben-jamin;* but his precious mother's Ben-oni,† for she brought him forth, not with the hazard only, but with the loss of her own life; his birth was her death : from which very moment of time you were pleased to intrust his education to his tender grandmother, your pious mother, and

---

* The son of the right hand.   † Son of my grief.

a 2

myself ; a deposit, than which there could nothing
have been more sacred to us in the world : I am
sure we were as tender of it, as of our own lives;
yea, verily, our lives were bound up in the child's
life.   He was indeed a delectable child, in whom
nature and grace seemed to be at a strife, which
should excel in her workmanship : and as he
grew in age, so he grew in sweetness of disposition, and in all natural and moral endowments, of which his age was capable : yea, he
outgrew his age, and was always beforehand with
his education ; imbibing instruction faster than
we durst rationally infuse it, for fear of hurting
the tender vessel ; so that he seemed to be a
man before his childhood was expired.   As many
loved him as knew him ; and were in dispute
with themselves, whether such maturity did pro-
phesy an eminent life, or an immature death.
I must confess, whether my infirmity or no, I
know not, I was often offended at the mention
of the latter, as too boldly entrenching upon
God's prerogative ; but such, it seems, was the
Divine decree; so it proved.   His work was done
betimes, and ours about him before we thought
of it ; and while we said of him in our hearts,
as once Lamech said of his son Noah, This
child shall comfort us, Gen. v. 29; he shall live

with us; God said, Nay, he shall leave you, and shall live with me: for before he was eleven years old, God snatched him out of our tuition, and removed him into a higher form; where he should learn no more by the sight of the eye, and hearing of the ear, which are subject to mistake, but by clear and perfect vision; where he knows more than we could teach him; yea, is able to teach us what we are not capable of understanding: while we see but in a glass darkly, he is seeing face to face. Oh could I but write what he is able to dictate concerning the facial vision,* which I am now, with fear and trembling, but peeping into; what a rare exposition should I publish to the world, upon the present context before us! Such as eye never read, and ear never heard, nor can ever enter into the heart of man, until we enter into that light where he is; where his intellectual eye is married to the Sun of righteousness, and his naked will is swimming and bathing itself in rivers of pleasures for ever. This may be indeed, what these papers wished to be, and that is all, a perfumed handkerchief to wipe off tears from your eyes, and fill your soul with joy. Your loss is his infinite gain.

It was a satisfaction good enough for a heathen,

* The sight of Christ face to face.

a 3

who, when one brought him the tidings of his
eldest son's death, was able to reply, " I knew my
son was mortal." Your comfort may express itself
in a higher strain, I know my son is immortal ;
for though nature did not make him immortal
by his generation, grace hath made him immortal
by his regeneration : so that all that you and I
have to do, is but to breathe after that perfection, of which, through grace, I am humbly confident he is already possessed : " Let us so run that
we may obtain." As for myself, so many deaths
have been rushing in upon me, " deep calling unto
deep," as have not only retarded this work, but
threatened its destruction. But since it hath
pleased the living God to let me live to publish
this work, such as it is, dear son, I dedicate it
to your name, to be as an Absalom's pillar, until
God may raise up a living monument in the room
of that which he hath removed : and because this
may be too weak and obscure, let me provoke
you, sir, to erect to yourself a monument that
may be worthy of you; let your own life be a
name to you when you are dead ; a name better
than of sons and daughters ; by filling that
honourable station wherein God hath fixed you,
and all your other relations, with such fruitfulness, wisdom, and fidelity, that all who know you,
may rise up and call you blessed; yea, that your

name may be as a sweet perfume to posterity. Live your own life and your son's too.

As for me, I cannot long survive, having so often received in myself the sentence of death, 2 Cor. i. 9; I have lived already one full age of man, and am now in the third year* of my labour and sorrow, Psa. xc. 10, and it is little I can do for God. I must decrease, but may you increase; yet pray for me, that I may live much in a little time; and that myself and your aged mother may, like those trees of God, Psa. xcii. 14, 15, bring forth more fruit in old age than in the beginning, to show that the Lord is upright, &c.

Farewell, honoured son, and God Almighty make you amends for the loan which you have lent to God, if not in the stream, yet in the fountain. May He bless you, and make you a blessing. So prayeth

Your faithful, and most

affectionate Father-in-law,

THOMAS CASE.

* Aged 73 years.

TO MY WORTHY SON-IN-LAW,

WILLIAM HAWES,

DOCTOR IN PHYSIC;

AND TO MRS. ELIZABETH HAWES

HIS VIRTUOUS CONSORT,

GRACE, MERCY, AND PEACE.

DEAR SON AND DAUGHTER,

It is not, certainly, without some special design
of Providence, that these meditations, which were
conceived upon the death of your hopeful nephew,
the only son of your elder brother, Sir Robert
Booth, now in Ireland; should not, by reason of
those distempers which have ever since pursued
me incessantly, as you, to your trouble, know;
be published until this time, when our sorrows
are doubled in the death of your precious child,
Martin Hawes, your first-born : possibly, as we
may rationally conjecture, that we should not too
soon forget the affliction and the misery, the

wormwood and the gall; but that our souls having them continually in remembrace, might be humbled in us, Lam. iii. 19, 20. Possibly, that the children being every way alike, both in person and in disposition, one and the same plaster might give ease and cure to the wound; and one and the same monument perpetuate their memorial unto posterity.

Truly they were a pair of lovely babes; babes in age, though men in knowledge and understanding; of whom we may, in their capacity, sing, as David once in his funeral elegies of Saul and Jonathan, "They were pleasant in their lives, in their death they were not divided."

Their lives indeed were short; so it seemed good to the Divine wisdom, after he had showed two such excellent pieces in the light for a while, timely to lay them up amongst his jewels, lest they should receive hurt or stain from a present evil world. But although their lives were short, yet verily they were precious, such, as allowing them this abatement, that they were children; neither parents nor standers-by could rationally have wished they had been otherwise than they were. And though there were some distance of years, yet the rewas the greatest parity of persons observed between them, that though they were but the brother's and sister's sons, you could not, had they been together, have distinguished them from brethren, or twins.

For elegance of person, loveliness of countenance, solidness of judgment, acuteness of wit, tenaciousness of memory, sweetness of disposition, universal innocence, and modesty in behaviour; obedience to parents, next or remote, submission to governors, observance to superiors, love to equals, condescension to inferiors, and candour to all.

And, that which deservedly is of higher value with God, reverend attention to his word read or preached, together with some suitable ability to give a methodical repetition of both; studious in learning catechisms, of which they were able to give such a rational account, as if they had been candidates for the university; as many, both of the nobility and others in the parish of Giles'-in-the-Fields can, at this day, witness; love to the best things, and a due respect to the best men; with a more than a childish dislike of, and adverseness to what they understood to be evil. &c.

These desirablenesses, according to, yea, and above the rate of children, rendered them so like one another, as if one soul had animated two bodies.

And as they were alike in their lives, so in their death they were not divided; or if a little in time, not at all in the manner and circumstances.

They both lived with us, but died with you; they lived with the divine, but died with the physician, to show that neither religion doth kill, nor physic can keep alive.

Nevertheless, though they died with you, they came not to die, any further than the hidden decree of the Divine will had before determined.

They died alive, as it were, death gave them so little warning. Neither parents nor children understood wherefore they came; until within a very few days, death showed his commission, and as soon executed it.

They died, both of them, in the absence of their trustees, who, though one step higher in the parental line, were not, I am sure, half a step lower in parental affection, which the Divine eye saw and pitied; and, therefore, out of com-

passion, hiding from us what he was about to do;
as he snatched us from the elder, by sending us
abroad; so he snatched the younger from us by
sending him home to his father's house : so pity-
ing our infirmity, who otherwise, possibly, might
not have parted with them so willingly, nor have
borne their loss so patiently. The loss of two
such choice patterns of Divine workmanship, could
not but have been a heart-breaking object to us,
as it was to you, but that their constant absence
from you was a preparative, whereby the terror of
death was something abated : their very absence so
long before was a little death.

That which sweeteneth it to us all, is, (that
God hath not left us to mourn as men without
hope,) that in the context before us, the children
are not dead, but sleep, they sleep in Jesus.

If any stander-by shall judge, possibly, that
my affection hath transported my charity into
excess, my apology is this, that I had rather be
guilty of an excess in charity, than a defect in
thankfulness. I know we cannot expect such
rational accounts of grace in children, as may be
found in adult saints; but that that doxology, " Out
of the mouths of babes and sucklings hast thou
ordained strength," Psa. viii. 2, doth not exclude

b

children, though not confine the meaning of the
words so narrow, is the judgment of old St.
Ignatius; who from those scripture instances of
Samuel, Josiah, and others, denieth not but that
the Spirit of God working in young ones, doth
many times give out early discoveries of the grace
of the covenant, when elder persons do only carry
their gray hairs as a badge of their ingratitude
to God.

As for your dear children, God hath not left
himself without further witness in their death,
of an interest in them; those heavenly whispers
which the tender aunt, laying her ear to the pale
lips of her dying nephew, as he lay upon his back,
with eyes fixed heavenward, when he wanted
strength to make his heart audible,—" God —
Christ—Grace," &c.

And her own dear child's delight in that little
book, " A Guide to Heaven;" a book little in
bulk, but great in excellency; which, as it caused
him to make it his vade-mecum while he lived;
his golden cup, out of which he drank his morning's draught every morning in his bed: so it
caused him to take it with him as his viaticum to
heaven, when he came to die; for it was found with
him when dead. These, I say, are overplusses of

Divine grace, and witnesses of Divine love, to those dying babes from their heavenly Father.

Wherefore, dear children, let not the consolations of God seem small unto you, but improve them for your own comfort and quickening, in the holy education of the surviving treasures of your blood; that if they live, you may have comfort in their lives; or if they die, you may have hope in their deaths.

" Be ye stedfast, unmovable, always abounding in the work of the Lord, forasmuch as ye know that your labour is not in vain in the Lord."

And accept of this imperfect monument, set up for your continual inspection, and the blessed children's memorial: by

Your faithful and most affectionate

Father-in-law,

THOMAS CASE.

TO THE READER.

THE AUTHOR WISHETH GRACE AND PEACE FROM GOD OUR FATHER, AND FROM THE LORD JESUS CHRIST.

———————

READER,—To help the weaker sort of christians in the understanding of this more dark and difficult context, which containeth the description of our Lord's last coming; and to quicken the more slow and drowsy spirits, to a greater vigour in the pursuit of the glory which is to be revealed at that coming; have I, not without the importunity of divers friends, sensible of their need of the meanest helps, put myself upon the publishing of these more private essays calculated only for the use of my own family.

Yet since they may, by the blessing of God, be of a larger influence; and knowing that good is so much the more good, by how much it is a more diffusive good, I chose rather to adventure my name, than be guilty of sacrilege, in not casting in my mite into the public treasury of the church's service.

Being, by the good providence of God, hitherto spared and kept alive, I have looked upon it as my duty, (the death-watch every night, in my bed, sounding in my ears,) to leave some watch-word behind me, to awaken this sleepy and secure generation; wherein the most, I would it might not be said the better part, of christians have lost the sight of heaven, and are digging hard into the earth, to search whether, possibly, they might not meet with a chief good between this and the centre!

But oh, that before they go off the superfices, they would look back, to see from whence they are fallen, and repent, and do their first works, Rev. ii. 5.

Behold, I am here showing you the thing which you are so eagerly pursuing; it is risen, it is not here. Oh that you would, with Moses, get up into the mount, from whence you might take the prospect of that good land, where only blessedness dwelleth.

I must confess the vision is much darkened by the dimness of the eye, and the feebleness of the hand, which drew this imperfect landscape; but this I dare be bold to say, that by the optic glass of faith, upon the knee of prayer, a man may make such a discovery of glory here, as, when he cometh down from this mount, may serve quite to extinguish all the glory of this nether world, and to fix the eye, with that proto-martyr, stedfastly looking up into heaven, to see the glory of God, and Jesus standing on the right hand of God, Acts vii. 55. Which, if it may be in any measure the fruit of these poor labours; let them take the praise of men, whose portion it is ; while I shall, with more alacrity, leave these tents of Kedar, where my pilgrimage hath been thus far prolonged, and mount up to that full-eyed vision, where blessedness and eternity are of one length, ever with the Lord. Ambitious of that epitaph, by a learned hand, set upon the monument of that incomparable Culverwell :

What this to know, as we are known should be,
The author could not tell, but's gone to see.

And who, for that little moment, is thine, christian reader, in tears and prayers.

THOMAS CASE

MOUNT PISGAH;

OR,

WORDS OF COMFORT ON THE DEATH OF OUR GRACIOUS RELATIONS.

1 THESSALONIANS IV. 18.

WHEREFORE, COMFORT ONE ANOTHER WITH THESE WORDS.

THESE words! What words are these? Scripture words in their general nature; more particularly the words of comfort contained in this context from ver. 13, " I would not have you to be ignorant, brethren," &c., down to my text.

For therein doth the apostle, by the dictate of the Holy Ghost, lay down a model or platform of consolatory arguments, as so many sovereign antidotes against immoderate sorrow for our godly relations which are departed : and with these words the apostle would have christians to comfort themselves, and one another. Comfort one another with these words. I will improve these words, First, for comfort; Secondly, for counsel.

The words of comfort laid down by the apostle in this model may be reduced unto ten heads, some of them very comprehensive, and all of them exceedingly cordial and restorative.

B

I. The first word of comfort is this, namely, that our gracious relations, over whose departure we stand mourning and weeping, are but fallen asleep; " I would not have you ignorant, brethren, concerning them which are asleep." We may say of departed saints, as our Saviour said concerning the damsel, Matt. ix. 24, they are not dead, but sleep: the same phrase he also used to his disciples concerning Lazarus; " Our friend Lazarus sleepeth," John xi. 11. That which we call death is not death indeed to the saints of God; it is but the image of death, the shadow and metaphor of death, death's younger brother, a mere sleep, and no more. There are two main properties of death which do carry in them a lively resemblance of sleep. The first is, that sleep is nothing else but the binding up of the senses for a little time; a locking up of the doors, and shutting of the windows of the body for a season, that so nature may take the sweeter rest and repose, being freed from all disturbance and distractions: sleep is but a mere parenthesis to the labours and travails of this present life. Secondly, sleep is but a partial privation, a privation of the act only, not of the habit of reason. They that sleep in the night, do awake again in the morning; then the soul returneth to the discharge of all her offices again: in the internal faculties, to the act of judging, and discourse in the intellect; to recalling things for the present, and recording things for future use in the memory; to its empire and command in the will, to its judicature in the conscience: so likewise the soul returns again to the execution of all her functions in the external senses; to seeing in the eye, to hearing in the ear, to tasting in the palate; as also to working in the hands, to walking in the feet, and so as to the rest. In a word, the whole man is restored again to itself, as it were by a new creation; that which lay as senseless and useless all the night, is raised again more fresh and active in the morning than it lay down at night.

Such as this is what we commonly call death, but with this considerable advantage, that in the interim of death the soul acts more vigorously than before, as being released from the weights and entanglements of the body.

First, it is but a longer and closer binding up of the senses; nature's long vacation. The grave is a bed, wherein the body is laid to rest, with its curtains drawn close about it, that it may not be disturbed in its repose; so the Holy Ghost pleaseth to phrase it: " He shall enter into peace, they shall rest in their beds, each one walking in his uprightness," Isa. lvii. 2. Death is nothing else but a writ of ease to the poor weary servants of Christ, a total cessation from all their labour of nature, sin, and affliction. " Blessed are the dead that die in the Lord, that they may rest from their labours," &c. Rev. xiv. 13. While the souls of the saints do rest in Abraham's bosom, their bodies do sweetly sleep in their beds of dust, as in a safe and consecrated dormitory. Thus death is but a sleep.

Secondly, and then again, as they that sleep in the night do awake in the morning, so shall the saints of God do: this heaviness may endure for a night, (this night of mortality,) but joy cometh in the morning: in the morning of the resurrection they shall awake again, Ps. xvii. 15. It will not be an everlasting night, an endless sleep, but as surely as we awake in the morning, when we have slept comfortably all night, so surely shall the saints then awake, and shall stand upon their feet, and we shall behold them again with exceeding joy.

Oh, blessed morning! How should we long and wait for that morning, more than they that watch for the dawning of the day?

Let this teach us to moderate our sorrow over departed christian friends; for, do we sigh and lament when any of the family are gone to bed before us, in the evening? Do we cry out, Woe and alas, my father is fallen asleep, my mother is laid to rest; my sweet child, the delight of mine eyes, the joy of my heart, his eyes have closed, and the curtains drawn close about him? Do we, I say, thus take on, and afflict ourselves in this case? no surely; why then do we so here? the case is the same; only if the night be a little longer, the morning will be infinitely more joyous, and make us more abundant compensation for our patience and expectation. We call also the absence of our friends by a wrong name. We say, My father is dead, my mother is dead, my Isaac is dead. Dead! the letter killeth. Death is the most terrible of all terrible things; the very name of it strikes a chilness and coldness into our hearts. Let us then call things as God calls them; let us make use of the notions which God hath suggested to us; let us say, My parent is at rest, my beloved babe is fallen asleep, and, behold the terror of death will cease.

If God hath clothed this horrid thing, death, with softer notions for our comfort, let not the consolations of the Almighty be a small thing with us. Oh, how comfortable lives might we live, had we but the right notions of things, and faith to realize them! Our friends are not dead but sleep. Comfort one another with this word.

II. The next consolatory argument is, the hopeful condition of these our sleeping relations; blessed be God, we are not without hope of their happiness, even while they thus sleep.

There be indeed those that die, and neither carry away any hope with them, nor leave any hope behind them, to their surviving relations : " but the righteous hath hope in his death," Prov. xiv. 32. When our gracious relations die, we must use the word sometimes, that we may be understood, there is hope; they are infinite gainers by their death. Sometimes they die full of hope, Job xix. 25—27. Thus holy Paul, " We know that if the earthly house of this tabernacle were dissolved, we have a building of God, an house not made with hands, eternal in the heavens," 2 Cor. v. 1. Glorious triumph! And thus again, we may find him in his own name, and in the name of other of his brethren and companions in tribulation, and in the kingdom and patience of Jesus Christ, marching out of the field of this world in a victorious manner, with colours flying, and drums beating; and thus insulting over death as a conqueror; " O death, where is thy sting? O grave, where is thy victory? The sting of death is sin, the strength of sin is the law; but thanks be to God, which giveth us the victory, through our Lord Jesus Christ!" 1 Cor. xv. 56, 57. Oh, the superabundant consolation of the heirs of promise! And if the departure of any of the saints of God is under a cloud, so that they are not able to express their own hopes, yet they leave behind them solid scripture evidences of their interest in God's everlasting electing love, and of their effectual vocation out of the world into the kingdom and fellowship of his dear Son Jesus Christ our Lord,

Gal. v. 22, 23. Such evidences as their poverty of
spirit; their holy mourning for their own and other
men's sins, Matt. v. 3; their hungering and thirst-
ing after righteousness, ver. 6; their purity of heart,
visible in the holiness of their lives, ver. 8; their
peaceable and peace-making dispositions, ver. 9;
their patient bearing of the cross, ver. 10—12; their
keeping of the word of God in the precepts of it, and
keeping close to it in the truth of it, ch. vii. 24;
their superlative love to Christ, Matt. x. 37; their
cordial love to the saints, 1 John iii. 14; their contempt of the world, 1 John ii. 15; their desire of
Christ's appearance, 2 Tim. iv. 8; in a word, their
conformity to Christ their head, Rom. viii. 29.

The remembrance of these graces of the Spirit
may well administer abundant matter of hope and
rejoicing to surviving friends, that those relations
which are fallen asleep, were a people whom G˄d
hath set apart for himself, precious in his sight,
honourable and beloved of him; a people formed
for himself, to show forth his praise, and made meet
to be partakers of the inheritance of the saints in
light, Col. i. 12.

They who bury their relations and their hopes
together in one grave, have just cause for mourning,
yea, for excessive mourning; but with you that
(upon these scripture evidences) have good hope
through grace, concerning your deceased friends, it
is otherwise; you know that while you are mourning on earth, they are rejoicing in heaven; that
while you are clothed with black, they are clothed in
white, even in the long, white robe of Christ's righteousness; that while you are rolling yourselves in
the dust, they are sitting with Christ upon his
throne. Do not then, I beseech you, profane your

scriptural hope with an unscriptural mourning;
give not the world occasion to judge either yourselves to be living without faith, or your relations to
have died without hope; but let your christian
moderation be known to all men, that it may be a
visible testimony to all the world, of God's grace in
them, and of your hopes of their glory with God.
Therefore comfort one another with this word also.

III. Another word of comfort is, that our gracious
relations are not alone in their death. The captain
of their salvation marched before them through
those black regions of death and the grave, Jesus
died; this is implied in the following words, " If
we believe that Jesus died." This is an argument
that carrieth in it strong consolation. Our christian
relations in dying run no greater hazard than
Abraham, Isaac, and Jacob did; no greater hazard
than all the patriarchs, and prophets, and apostles
did, for they all in their generations died. Yea,
what shall I say? they run no other hazard than
the Lord of all the patriarchs, prophets, and apostles
did, for Jesus died; this is wonderful indeed; the
Lord of life yielded up the ghost; the eternal Son
of God was laid in the grave!

We indeed die justly: death is but our wages;
wages as truly earned as ever was a penny by the
poor hireling for his day's labour. We have forfeited
our lives over and over again, by continual reiterated
treasons against the supreme Majesty of heaven and
earth; yea, the best blood which runs in our veins
is traitor's blood by succession from our first rebellious parents.

But he! what evil had he done? He was " holy,
harmless, undefiled, separate from sinners," Heb. vii.
26. He did no sin, neither was there guile found

in his mouth; he fulfilled all righteousness; and
yet Jesus died! And why so? Surely " he was
wounded for our transgressions, he was bruised for
our iniquities, the chastisement of our peace was
upon him, and by his stripes we are healed," Isa.
liii. 5. Behold! God the Father so loved us, that
he spared not his own Son, but delivered him up to
the death for us all, Rom. viii. 32; and shall we
think much to give up the dearest treasures of our
blood, in death to him ?

Behold ! God the Son so loved us, that he died
for love of us; he died the first death, that we
might not die the second death; he died for us,
that we might live with him ; and shall we count
our lives, or the lives of our dearest relations too
dear for him? especially when neither we nor ours
are in any capacity to reap the fruit and advantage
of his death until we die also ! and the sooner we
die the sooner shall we reap those fruits. Behold !
God's first-born was laid in the sepulchre ; and
shall we think God deals hardly with us, if we follow our first-born to the grave, and leave them there,
till our Lord himself come to awaken them?
Jesus died, and was buried, that he might sanctify
death to us by his death, and by his being buried
might perfume the grave, and make it a sweet
dormitory, or bed of spices for his members to rest
in, until the morning of the resurrection. O christians, let us comfort ourselves, and one another,
with these words also, Jesus died.

IV. The fourth word is yet more full of consolation, and that is, although Jesus died, yet he " rose
again." He died indeed, but he rose again from the
dead. God suffered his dear Son to be laid in the
sepulchre, but he did not leave him there nor suffer

any taint of corruption to seize upon his precious body. And to that end Christ made haste to rise again out of the grave; he rose the third day, and that very early in the morning, as soon as ever it could be called day. The alarm no sooner went off, as it were, but the Lord Jesus did lift up his royal head, and put on his glorious apparel, and came forth out of his grave, as a bridegroom out of his chamber, in state and triumph.

And this was the cordial which our Lord himself took before his passion. " Thou wilt not leave my soul in hell, neither wilt thou suffer thine holy one to see corruption : therefo e my heart is glad, and my glory rejoiceth," &c. Ps. xvi. 9, 10. This was his triumphant song: and it may be ours, as well as his, whether in reference to ourselves or to our gracious relations. For wherefore was not Christ left in hell, that is, in hades, or in the state of the dead? It was that he might lift up us also out of the pit. And wherefore did his body see no corruption, no, not for the least particle of time? It was that our mortal bodies might not inherit rottenness and oblivion in the dust for ever. Indeed, in this phrase, " Jesus arose again," there are three things implied, which interest every believer in this triumph of Christ's resurrection,—power,—right,— office.

1. Jesus rose again, it implieth Christ's power, namely, that Jesus Christ rose by his own power. It is not merely said, Jesus was raised, which might have spoken him passive only in his resurrection; but Jesus rose, which speaketh him active in the matter. Yes, he rose as a conqueror by his own strength; as he himself professeth, " I have power to lay down my life, and I have power to take it up

again," John x. 18.   It is true, it is elsewhere said
that " Christ was raised from the dead by the glory
of the Father," Rom. vi. 4 ; and likewise, that he was
quickened by the Spirit, 1 Pet. iii. 18, to show that
neither the Father nor the Holy Ghost were excluded from a joint share and concurrence in his
resurrection; but here, as elsewhere, it is said also,
that Christ rose, to show that he was not merely
passive in his resurrection, as the children of the
resurrection are, but that he rose also by the mighty
power that was seated in his own royal person.

Death and the grave had swallowed a morsel
which they could not keep: but as the whale, when
it had swallowed Jonah, in this the type of Christ,
was forced to cast him up again, it being impossible
Christ should be holden by death. The power of the
Word incarnate loosed or dissolved the bonds of
death, as a thread of tow is broken when it is
touched with the fire.   Yea, Samson like, Jesus
Christ did break in sunder the bars of the grave,
and carried away the gates of death upon his
shoulders, making a show of them openly.

Thus Jesus rose again as a conqueror by his own
power, and this is our triumph and rejoicing : for
surely he that thus raised up himself, can raise up
us also, and will indeed raise us up by the same
power, whereby he is able to subdue even all things
unto himself, Phil. iii. 21.

2. Jesus rose again ; it implieth his office ; he
rose as a Jesus, a Saviour, the Mediator of our peace ;
who having finished the work he came about, namely,
to satisfy Divine justice, and to bring in everlasting
righteousness, so making peace by the blood of his
cross,—God the Father sent a public officer from
heaven, to open the prison doors ; an angel to roll

away the stone from the mouth of the sepulchre, Matt. xxviii. 2; thereby proclaiming to all the world that the debt was paid, and that God had received full satisfaction for the sins of the elect, saying, as it were, Deliver him, for I have received a ransom.

This is another ground of our triumph, that Jesus rose; that is, he rose as our Jesus, our Saviour, and so by dying, hath delivered us from death, and from him "that had the power of death, which is the devil," Heb. ii. 14. "Jesus who delivered us from the wrath to come." 1 Thess. i. 10.

3. Jesus rose again; it implieth his right to us, and interest in us. He rose as our Jesus, that is, as a public head, in whom all believers are considered. Jesus Christ as he died not in a private capacity, for he had no sin of his own, for which death might have any dominion over him, so neither did he rise again in a private capacity, but in a public capacity. He rose as he was our *Goel*, that is, our next of kin, unto whom the right of redemption did belong: he rose as our Surety; he rose as the heavenly Bridegroom, having espoused the church himself on the cross; he rose as the Captain of our salvation, as the public head and representative of all the elect of God.

And this consideration layeth another foundation for our triumph in Christ's resurrection; namely, that there is an inseparable connexion between the resurrection of Christ and the resurrection of the saints, and it is fourfold; a connexion of—1. Merit; 2. Influence; 3. Design; 4. Union.

(1.) A connexion of merit. "To this end Christ both died, and rose again, that he might be the Lord both of the dead and the living,"

Rom. xiv. 9. Intimating that by his death he merited
of the Father, that both in death and in life, both
dying and rising again, he might dispose of the saints
to his own advantage. Why, now the Lord Jesus
having bought his saints at so dear a rate, if they
should not rise again, he should lose his purchase;
there were no more merit in the death of Christ
than in the death of any of the sons of Adam; and
even in this respect Christ had died in vain, and
risen in vain.

(2.) A connexion of influence. There is power
in the resurrection of Christ, for the quickening of
the dead. Hence it is that our Lord calls himself
the resurrection and the life; namely, to intimate to
us, that by the same spirit of holiness whereby he
raised himself from the dead, he will also quicken
our mortal bodies. This inseparably links the
resurrection of the saints with the resurrection of
Christ: for surely were it not so, the resurrection of
Jesus Christ would signify no more than the resurrection of Lazarus, or any other of the saints mentioned, Matt xxvii. 52, 53. Yea, the resurrection
of Christ would not be of so great virtue and influence as the dry bones of the prophet, the very touch
whereof raised the dead man which was cast into his
grave, 2 Kings xiii. 21.

(3.) A connexion of design. The Lord Jesus
had a design upon the saints in his rising again from
the dead: and what that was he tells us in the last
affectionate prayer before his passion, John xvii. 24,
" Father, I will that they also whom thou hast given
me be with me where I am, that they may behold my
glory." Therefore Christ arose and ascended, that
he might come again and awake them out of their
graves, and take them home to himself into mansions

of glory: so he comforted his disciples before his departure, " If I go and prepare a place for you, I will come again, and receive you unto myself; that where I am, there ye may be also," John xiv. 3.

This is then a third inseparable connexion between Jesus rising again from the dead and the saints rising again; because without this, Christ should lose the very plan and object of his own resurrection. This must not be, it cannot be.

(4.) A connexion of union. Christ is the head, and the saints are the members of his mystical body; and if the head be risen, the members cannot be long behind; for, can the head live, and the members remain dead? yea, can the life of the saints live, and they themselves continue in a state of death? This is a happy contradiction, a blessed impossibility! Oh write this comfortable word upon your hearts, christians, Christ is our life. Christ is your life, and the life of your christian relations; and as surely as Christ is risen, they shall rise; and because he lives, those members of his, for whom you weep and bleed, as dead, shall live also with him. Surely if the devil and all the powers of darkness were not able to keep Christ in the grave, neither shall they be able to hold one of his members there for ever! Hence you shall find the holy apostle arguing from the resurrection of Christ to the resurrection of christians; " If Christ rose from the dead, how say some that there is no resurrection of the dead?" 1 Cor. xv. 12; and back again from the resurrection of christians to the resurrection of Christ, " If there be no resurrection of the dead, then is Christ not risen," ver. 13. Indeed the form of words is negative, but the sense is affirmative; and for the greater assurance it is repeated over and over

c

in the following verses; backward and forward as
convertibles; grant one, and ye grant the other;
deny one, and ye deny the other.   And the result is
this, " But now is Christ risen from the dead, and
become the first-fruits of them that slept," ver. 20;
Christ is risen, and risen as our first-fruits, as a
pledge and part of the whole harvest; for if the first-
fruits be holy, the lump is also holy : if the first-
fruits be laid up safe in God's barns, the whole
harvest shall, in due time, be safely brought in
thither also, only it must stay its time appointed by
the great Husbandman, whose method is this, first,
" Christ the first-fruits, afterward, they that are
Christ's at his coming," ver. 23.

Be of good cheer, christians, weep not, it is the
Father's good pleasure, that not a sheaf, not an ear,
not one grain be lost; so witnesseth the truth and
the life ; the truth to testify it, and the life to make
it good ; " This is the Father's will which hath sent
me, that of all which he hath given me, I should
lose nothing, but should raise it up again at the last
day," John vi. 39.   Nothing of all that, &c.; that
is, not the least person, nor the least member of the
least person, how mean and contemptible soever.

Will this content thee, christian ?   Thy sweet
relation is not lost but sown, and that which is sown
is not quickened unless it die.   At the harvest time
thou shalt have thy seed again ; when that which
thou callest perishing shall be thy improvement ;
thy treasure is not cast away, but put to use ; and
thy loss shall be thy gain.

Thus we see that the resurrection of the saints
stands upon a surer foundation than our faith; it
stands upon a four-fold foundation, as you have
heard — the Merit — Influence —Design —Union—

which is between Christ and his saints ; a foundation which stands surer than heaven and earth. Heaven and earth may pass away, but not one of these foundations shall ever pass away, or fail; " the foundation of the Lord standeth sure," 2 Tim. ii. 19. So then, not their resurrection, but our comfort in their resurrection, is that which depends upon our faith. Sense stands weeping and crying out, My parent is dead, my yoke-fellow is lost, my dear child is perished : No, saith faith, they are alive, they are safe, they are happy. And all this, faith inferreth upon Christ's resurrection : so that whosoever hath faith enough to put Christ's resurrection into the premises, may, by the same act of faith, put the saints' resurrection into the conclusion. He that by an eye of faith, can look upon Christ's resurrection as past, may, by the same eye of faith, see the resurrection of the saints as to come : he that by faith can say, Christ is risen ; may, with the same breath of faith, say also, The saints shall rise: "Because I live, you shall live also:" as a pledge and instance whereof, when Christ arose, many of the saints which slept, were enlarged out of the prison of the grave, the heart strings whereof were now broken, to attend the solemnity of their Lord's resurrection, Matt. xxvii. 52, 53 ; and were as another kind of first-fruits of the last resurrection of all believers.

By all these evidences and demonstrations, Jesus Christ, now in heaven, speaks to his mourners, as once he did, in the days of his flesh, to Martha, "Thy brother shall rise again ;" so he speaks to us, Man, woman, thy yoke-fellow shall rise again; thine Isaac, whom thou lovedst, shall rise again. And oh, that we had but faith enough to answer with Martha ! " I know that he shall rise again in the resurrection at the last day " This would be a sovereign cordial to keep our hearts from fainting under our sorrows. If indeed we have not faith to realize this comfortable truth, our dear relations, if they could speak, would cry to us out of their graves in some such language as that in which our Saviour rebuked the women which followed him to his cross, " Daughters of Jerusalem weep not for me," &c. So ours; Son, daughter, husband, wife, father, mother, (and whatever other dear relations,) weep not for us, but weep for yourselves, and for the unbelief of your own hearts.

Christians, there is the spring-head of all our misery, our unbelief; it is unbelief which robs us first of our sweet relations, and afterwards of our comforts in their gains : and, if we look not to it the better, it will keep us and them asunder to all eternity : we cannot enter in to their rest, if we continue in our unbelief : cry we then with the father of the child, " Lord, I believe ; help thou my unbelief," Mark ix. 24. If we believe that Jesus rose again, even so them also which sleep in Jesus will God bring with him.

V. The next word of comfort is, that saints sleep in Jesus. The first word of comfort in this model was, that our christian relations departed this life, are not dead, but fallen asleep. Here followeth a word of comfort, of a richer import, which tells us, that as they do but sleep, so they sleep in Jesus.

This expression noteth to us, that blessed and admirable union, 1 Cor. xv. 18, which is between Jesus Christ, and his saints, a union frequently set out to us in scripture under a twofold notion :—
1. Christ in the believer ; 2. The believer in Christ.

1. Christ in the believer; " If Christ be in you,

the body is dead," &c. Rom. viii. 10. " Christ in you the hope of glory," Col. i. 27 ; and here in the text, they are said to be in Jesus.

2. The believer in Christ; "Of him are ye in Christ Jesus; who of God is made," &c. 1 Cor. i. 30. " If any man be in Christ, he is a new creature," 2 Cor. v. 17. " The saints in Christ," Col. i. 2. See both together, " You in me, and I in you," John xiv. 20. " Abide in me, and I in you." xv. 4, " He that abideth in me, and I in him," ver. 5.

These expressions are the same for substance, both setting forth to us the union itself; a mutual, intimate in-dwelling, or in-being, between Christ and his saints; He in them, and they in him, so making one.

They differ somewhat in the notion and import of the phrase, hinting to us a different mode and fruit of this mutual in-being, namely, Christ is in the believer, by his Spirit, 1 John iv. 13, and 1 Cor. xii. 13. The believer in Christ, by faith, John i. 12. Christ in the believer, by inhabitation, Eph. iii. 17. The believer in Christ, by implantation, John xv. 2 ; Rom. vi. 3, 5. Christ in the believer, as the head in the body, Col. i. 18 ; as the root in the branches, John xv. 5. Believers are in Christ, as the members are in the head, Eph. i. 23 ; as the branches in the root, John xv. 1, 7. Christ in the believer, implieth life and influence from Christ, Col. 3, 4 ; 1 Pet. ii. 5. The believer in Christ, implieth communion and fellowship with Christ. When Christ is said to be in the believer, we are to understand it in reference to sanctification. When the believer is said to be in Christ, it is in order to justification, 1 Cor. i. 30. It is Christ without us, that justifieth; it is Christ within us, that sanctifieth. Grace in the apostle's phrase, is Christ formed in the heart, Gal. iv. 19.

These and the like expressions, hold forth that transcendent and mysterious union which is between Christ and the believing soul, whereby they are not only joined together; but in a sober gospel-sense united, made one as it were; Christ becomes one with them, and they one with Christ.

This union with Christ, for the clearer and safer understanding of so great and precious a mystery, I shall endeavour more fully to open in these six distinguishing properties: it is a union, 1. Spiritual— 2. Real—3. Operative—4. Enriching—5. Intimate —6 Indissoluble.

(1.) It is a spiritual union. When we speak of this union, we must abstract it from all that is gross and fleshy; there is nothing in it obvious to sense, perceptible by the eye, or by the ear, or by the touch, or taste; it is not effected by any corporeal contact; Christ and the believer are not tied together by any material bonds, and fleshy sinews, but their union is a pure, immaterial, sublime union, altogether spiritual.

It is so partly, inasmuch as by this union Christ and the believer are made one spirit; "He that is joined unto the Lord, is one spirit," 1 Cor. vi. 17; not only one spiritually, but one spirit: not as exclusive to the body itself, "For we are members of his body, of his flesh, and of his bones," Eph. v. 30; but expressing to us the top and perfection of this union. He that is joined to an harlot is one flesh, in an impure and carnal sense. Man and wife, though their conjunction be more honourable, yet are but one flesh also in a conjugal sense : "For two, saith he, shall be one flesh; and he that is joined to the Lord, is one spirit," 1 Cor. vi. 16, 17; a union infinitely more honourable than that of marriage. The believer is joined to Christ, into one and the same spirit; he is animated, and acted by one and the same spirit with Christ, though in a different degree and measure, "For God giveth not the Spirit by measure unto him," John iii. 34. Christ as mediator, for in that capacity believers are united unto him, received the Spirit without measure.

Believers have but their stinted measure and proportion, and yet, notwithstanding, the Spirit of God dwelling as truly in them, as it did in Christ himself, though not essentially, they thereby become one spirit with Christ.

Also, it is a spiritual union, partly, because the bonds and ligaments of this union are not carnal, but spiritual; the bond of this union, on the part of Christ, is the Spirit, whereby he unites himself to the believer. The presence of the Spirit maketh this union, by virtue of which God communicates with us, as with his sons, and we communicate with God, as with our heavenly Father. And the bond of this union, on the part of the believer, is faith, whereby the believer is united to Christ. As the scion is engrafted into the stock, and thereby grows up to be one with the stock, so is the believer implanted into Christ by faith, Eph. iii. 17; grows up in him, receiveth life and nourishment from him, and is preserved in him to life eternal; "Kept by the power of God, through faith, unto salvation," 1 Pet. i. 5.

(2.) It is a real union, and that in a tenfold distinction

[1.] In opposition to an imaginary union; it is

no metaphysical notion, or like those things which logicians call intellectual beings; or your mathematical lines, which have their existence only in the understanding and fancy.

[2.] Nor is it a relative union only; as father and child, master and servant are united : such a union there is between Christ and believers ; but that is not all.

[3] Neither is it a legal union only. Christ and the believer are not one only, as the debtor and the surety are one in law, in a forensical sense ; that is, in the interpretation and judgment of the court.   In this sense they are one indeed, namely, in the judgment of God, as a judge, but not only so.

[4.] Nor is it a union only of assent in point of doctrine and judgment, though so much it is, for saith the apostle, in the name of all believers, " We have the mind of Christ," 1 Cor. ii. 16.   The believer, so far as he is a believer, is of the same mind, judgment, and opinion with Jesus Christ in all things.   And this truly gives them a kind of oneness ; hence a firm and stedfast continuance in the faith, that is in the doctrine of Jesus Christ, is called an in-being in Christ, John xv. 4, 6; and an abiding in Christ, 1 John ii. 24, 28 ; as a professional or doctrinal union with Christ.   This the saints of God have, but neither is this all.

[5.] Nor yet is it merely a union of consent ; the believer is not one with Christ, only by consent of wills.   The Arians, whilst they blasphemously deny the deity of the Son, betray a double ignorance ; and if but ignorance, their sin is the less ; the one in the doctrine, or assertion itself; the other in the ground which they allege for it, which is Christ's own words, praying to his Father for believers ;

"That they may be one, even as we are one," John xvii. 22; whence they, supposing believers to be one with the Father and the Son only by consent of wills, do infer, neither are the Father and the Son one in any other sense. But say we, they err in the very foundation: we acknowledge indeed believers to be so far one with Christ, and that is a very sweet and precious union: to will and nill the same things, is a high degree of love and oneness; but to say no more of the union betwixt Christ and his saints, is to say too little.

[6.] Neither is this union barely a sacramental union; whereby christians, in either of the sacraments, or any other evangelical institution, are in an elemental, professional way joined to Christ, and Christ to them. Thus all, good and bad, elect and reprobate, Simon Magus as well as any of the believing Samaritans, Acts viii. 12, 13, Judas as well as Peter: all, I say, are made one with Christ in an external professional use of those gospel-institutions; while in the mean time a real believer, in a true, living, spiritual, saving way, is made partaker of Christ, and of all his benefits in all gospel ordinances.

[7.] In contradistinction to the union which we have with Christ, by virtue of his assuming our human nature. Christ was incarnate in the womb of the virgin, and thereby was personally united to our flesh; which is the highest advancement of the human nature that can be conceived, " For verily he took not on him the nature of angels, but he took on him the seed of Abraham," Heb. ii. 16. Christ assumed man's nature, being God from all eternity; he took on him the one, to the other; and so made of those two natures one person: by this we have a kind of union with Jesus Christ. This is a near and an honourable conjunction; for by this means Jesus Christ is become our Immanuel, God with us, bone of our bone, and flesh of our flesh; but this is not all that is meant by this union.

[8.] It is real, in contradistinction to that contemplative union which the saints have with Christ in their holy meditations. Meditation doth bring the object and the faculty together, and makes them one: and thus the saints are often united to Jesus Christ in holy contemplation, whereby they let in Christ into their souls, and their souls into Christ, and become, as it were, one spirit, or one in spirit, with him: but neither is this all.

[9.] It is a real union, in contradistinction to reconciliatory union. Falling out separates between person and person; reconciliation makes them one again; reconciliation is the atonement of enemies: and thus indeed, God and sinners are reconciled by Christ; by him we have received the atonement; those whom sin made two, Christ makes one, Rom. v. 11. This is a choice fruit of Christ's death, a concomitant of our union with Christ, yet not the very union itself, or not the whole of this union.

[10.] This union is real, in contradistinction to affectionate union. Love is as a uniting affection, it makes the lover and the beloved one; as if two persons had but one soul between them: thus Christ loves the saints, Rev. i. 5; and the saints love Christ again, 1 Pet. i. 8. Christ's love to them is the cause; their love to Christ, is the effect, 1 John iv. 19. Yet this union is rather a fruit of that union we are now speaking of, than the union itself; as in marriage, the conjugal bond and conjugal love are distinct things.

None of all these reach the nature of this union. The scripture describes it to be a real and a solid union ; as real as that between head and members, root and branches ; for, although it be a spiritual union, yet doth it not therefore cease to be real ; things are not therefore less real, because spiritual, yea therefore more real. God, who is the most absolute and real being, a being who gives being to every thing which hath a being, is most spiritual ; "God is a spirit," John iv. 24. and the nearer any being or excellency approximates unto God, the more real it is, the more itself ; as we see in angels, and the souls of men.

Thus is it with this union, it is spiritual, but yet so true and real, that in comparison with it, all unions and conjunctions in nature are nothing else but so many figures and shadows. It is as real as the believer himself, as real as Christ himself ; Christ and the believer are not more really one in themselves, than they are in, and with one another spiritually, 1 Cor. vi. 16. Yea our Lord carrieth us one step higher ; it is a union as real as that essential union between the Father and the Son. "As thou Father art in me, and I in thee, that they also may be one in us," John xvii. 21 ; that is, as truly, as verily, though not substantially ; it denotes, I say, the reality of the union, though not the kind and manner of it.

(3.) This union is an operative union. Christ is in the believer, as the soul is in the body, a principle of life and operation. "I live," saith the apostle ; but as if he had said too much, he recalls what he had said, " yet not I ; but, Christ liveth in me," Gal. ii. 20. Col. iii. 4. It is not so much I that live, as Christ in me. Christ is my life, it is he that

animates me.   It is he that doth all his work in me
and my works for me.   Though the act be mine, the
strength is his; " I can do all things through Christ
that strengtheneth me," Phil. iv. 13.   I am but the
instrument only, which his hand manageth; it is his
finger that toucheth me, his skill that makes the music.
It is such a union as from whence the believer, by
faith, draws life and virtue from Jesus Christ to all
spiritual and saving intents and purposes; yea, whereby all the offices of the holy life become sweet, easy,
and delightful ; those duties and employments,which
unto the unregenerate man are hard and grievous,
and even so many impossibles, by faith, improving
its union with Christ, are made light and easy,
even as the operations of another nature, 1 John
v. 4.   All this the apostle would have us to understand, when he saith, " His commandments are not
grievous," ver. 3.

(4.) This union is a soul-enriching union.   By
virtue of this blessed union the saints are invested
into all the unsearchable riches of Jesus Christ ; as
by virtue of the marriage-knot the wife is instated
into all the revenues and privileges of her husband,
" Of him are ye in Christ Jesus, who of God is made
unto us wisdom, righteousness, sanctification, and
redemption," 1 Cor. i. 30.   Observe christians ! in
Christ Jesus : there is the union, and thence flows
communion and fellowship with him in all his privileges, wisdom, righteousness, sanctification, and
redemption.   Here you have the very epitome and
sum total of the gospel; the whole Christ in four
words ; the benefit and fruit of all his offices, suitable and sufficient to supply all the defects and
indigences of the creature.   For behold ! here is
wisdom for our folly ; righteousness for our guilt;

sanctification for our impure natures, and redemp·
tion for our every way lost and undone condition.
Wisdom to make us wise to salvation, there is the
fruit of his prophetical office. Righteousness for our
justification; "Christ is the end," or complement,
" of the law for righteousness to every one that believeth," Rom. x. 4, there is the fruit of his priestly
office. Sanctification, to begin holiness where it is
wanting, and to increase it where it is begun;
Christ is a fountain of holiness, as well as a fountain of happiness, there is the fruit of his kingly
office. Redemption, fully and finally to deliver us
from the power of darkness, from wrath to come,
from all the remainders of sin and misery, and to
translate us into the kingdom of grace and glory;
there is the joint-fruit of all his offices.

Behold christians! This is the rich and precious
fruit which grows upon the offices of Jesus Christ,
and all made ours by means of this glorious union.
First, in Christ, then follows wisdom, righteousness,
sanctification, and redemption.

Yea, one step higher yet: by virtue of this
union with Christ, believers are not only made
partakers of the fruits of Christ's offices, but are
in a subordinate sense invested into the very offices
themselves. Was he anointed to be a King? so
are they: " He hath made us kings," &c. Rev. i. 6.
Was Christ anointed to be a Prophet? Believers
also partake of the same unction; " Ye have an
unction from the Holy One, and ye know all things,"
1 John ii. 20. Was Christ anointed to be a Priest?
so are they; "Ye are a chosen generation, a royal
priesthood," 1 Pet. ii. 9. Here are two offices twisted
together—royal, there is their kingly office; priesthood, there is their sacerdotal; a kingdom of priests,

D

Exod. xix. 6, as Moses phraseth it; priests, as they stand in relation to God, " to offer up spiritual sacrifices acceptable to God, by Jesus Christ," 1 Pet. ii. 5; and kings in respect of men, to rule over others, and themselves too. This is much, and yet this is not all; by virtue of this union, believers share with Christ in all his communicable titles and dignities. Is he a Son? so are they; Christ, the Son of God by nature; they the sons of God by adoption, Gal. iv. 5. Was Christ the Heir of all things? Heb. i. 2. Believers are heirs also in him, and with him: " If children, then heirs; heirs of God, and joint-heirs with Jesus Christ," Rom. viii. 17. Though they are not joint-purchasers by their good works, as the papist would make them; yet they are joint-heirs by grace, as God hath made them, by virtue of their union with Jesus Christ.

Doth Christ call God his Father and his God? behold! he, being not ashamed to call them brethren, lets them know that he is their God and Father, Heb. ii. 11. " Go to my brethren, and say to them, I ascend to my Father, and your Father; and to my God, and your God," John xx. 17.

Once more: hath the Father appointed him a kingdom? so doth he appoint unto them a kingdom, Luke xxii. 29. Hath the Father assigned him a throne? so doth Christ assign unto his saints a throne also. " To him that overcometh, will I grant to sit with me in my throne, even as I also overcame, and am set down with my Father in his throne," Rev. iii. 21.

My brethren! what a soul-enriching, beatifical union is this! There are unions in nature which convey nothing, communicate nothing, but empty and insignificant titles; which make the person admitted into them not a whit the richer, the better, not a jot the more noble or happy: but this union introduces the believer into the full enjoyment of Christ, with all his riches, and all his glory; insomuch, as the spouse gives in the whole account in this vast and invaluable sum, "My beloved is mine, and I am his," Cant ii. 16. He is mine; the whole Christ is mine in his natures, offices, excellences, prerogatives, and inheritance; in all he is, and in all he hath, it is all mine, for my good, and for my glory. This is the voice of her faith, and then this is the voice of her love, " I am his;" in all I am, in all I have, in all I can make by my interest in the world; and if it were a thousand times more, he should have it all, and all too little for Him who hath loved me, and washed me in his own blood, and hath taken me into so rich and glorious an union with his own self. To him be glory for ever, Amen.

(5.) It is a near, inward, intimate union. To hint the intimateness of this union, the Holy Ghost in scripture, carries us through the climax of all unions under heaven, and shows how they all fall short of this blessed union in respect of closeness and intimacy. It tells you to look how the house and foundation are one, so are Christ and believers, 1 Pet. ii. 4—6; yea higher.

It tells you to look how husband and wife are one, so is Christ and his saints, Hos. ii. 19; Eph. v. 30; only with this incomparable difference, husband and wife make but one flesh, but Christ and the believer make one spirit, 1 Cor. vi. 16, 17.

It tells us, yet higher, to look how the head and members are one, so is Christ and his church, 1 Cor. xii. 12; how root and branches are one, John xv.

1, 6, so Christ and believers; and closer yet, the scripture tells us to look how food and the body are one, so also is Christ and the believer one; hence we hear of eating his flesh, and drinking his blood, John vi. 51, 53—56; and nearer yet, if nearer can be It tells us, that look how the soul and body are one, how life and the subject wherein it resides are one, so is Christ and the believer; " When Christ, who is our life, shall appear," &c. Col. iii. 4.

Behold here, christians, is a union which amounts well nigh to an identity; say only, with Cyprian, it is not such a union as is between the two natures in Christ, which makes them but one person; not such a union as is between the three glorious persons in the blessed Trinity, who, notwithstanding the distinction of their personality, are but one nature and essence; and you cannot say or think too highly of this union; yea whatsoever you can say or think, will be short of the intimacy and excellency of this union.

I must add this to what I have said, that because no union under heaven was close enough to express the oneness which is betwixt Christ and the believer; therefore our Lord Jesus himself carries us up to heaven, there to contemplate the essential union which is between the Father and the Son, and puts them into the same parallel, " As thou Father art in me, and I in thee, that they also may be one in us," John xvii. 21. Yet still we must be careful to understand the words of Christ in a sober sense, lest, whilst our Lord doth honour our union with himself, by comparing it to Divine union in the Trinity, we do in the least dishonour that union by levelling it with ours; we must duly remember, that this comparative particle *as*, doth not here intend equality, but likeness only; the truth of the intimacy, and not the nature or the degree of it; to lift up this mystical union above all other unions in nature; but we must still keep the Divine union in its own place.

(6.) This union is an indissoluble union. This union between Christ and the believer, is not capable of any separation. They are so one, that all the violence of the world, or all the powers of darkness, can never be able to make them two again.

Hence the apostle's triumphant challenge, "Who shall separate us from the love of Christ?" Rom. viii. 35. If the question did not imply a strong negation, the apostle himself doth give us a negation in words at length, "Neither death, nor life, nor angels, nor principalities, nor powers, nor things present, nor things to come, nor height, nor depth, nor any other creature, shall be able to separate us," &c. ver. 38, 39.

A long catalogue, consisting of a large induction of various particulars; but in all these it is observable; he only instanceth in the creature, nor any other creature—he leaveth out God, and why? because God himself is the author of this union; " Of him are ye in Christ Jesus," 1 Cor. i. 30.

Here is the foundation then upon which the apostle erecteth this triumph : God, who only can dissolve this union, will not; the creature, which only would dissolve this union, cannot; so it stands on a surer foundation than heaven and earth, our life is hid with Christ in God. The believer is in Christ, as Christ is in God, hence the inseparableness of this union : there is no more possibility of pulling the believer out of the bosom of Christ, than there is of removing Christ out of the bosom of his Father, John x. 28, 29.

This is the transcendent excellency of this union above all others, it is eternal. Indeed it had a beginning, but it shall never have an end. All other unions may suffer a dissolution; a whirlwind may throw the house from off its foundation, as we see in the case of Job's children, Job i. 18, 19. A bill of divorce may dissolve the union betwixt man and wife, Matt. v. 31, 32. An axe may dissolve the union between the head and members. Death dissolves the union between the soul and body, &c. But nothing can dissolve the union between Christ and the believers; " Nothing shall be able to separate us," &c.

My text gives us a further instance of this; the saints sleep in Jesus; the union ceaseth not, no not in the grave. Observe the progress of it, it began in their regeneration; then they received their first implantation into Christ, Rom. vi. 3—5; hence the apostle makes regeneration and being in Christ synonymous, ver. 3, 4. Next, they are said to live in Christ, and Christ in them, Gal. ii. 20. Then to show there is no in and out in this union, as some fondly dream, we read of their abiding in Christ, not only by way of precept as John xv. 4, 5, but by way of promise also, as 1 John ii 27. " Ye shall abide in him ;" which certainly doth express assurance and establishment for ever, Rom. iv. 16. Therefore they are said in the next place, to die in Christ; " Blessed are the dead that die in the Lord :" so verse 16, after the text, makes mention of the dead in Christ; so that, what dissolves all other unions dissolves not this.

Yea, see one strain higher yet ; not only in death, but even after death this union holds ; the saints are said to sleep in Jesus, ver. 14 ; that part of the saints which is capable of sleep, is not capable of separation from Christ ; while their more noble part is united to Christ in heaven, amongst the spirits of just men made perfect, Heb. xii. 23, Christ is united to their more ignoble part in the grave, their very dust ; they sleep in Jesus.

Thus I have opened unto you the blessed and admirable union which is between Christ and his saints, and its most excellent and transcendent properties.

Opened, did I say ? Alas it is impossible ! This union is a mystery, a great mystery, Eph. v. 32 ; next to that union between the three glorious persons in the Trinity, and that other, like unto it, between the two natures in Christ, profound and ineffable ! The heart of man is not able to conceive it, nor the tongue of an angel to express it : the natural man knows it not at all, no more of it than a brute knows what the union is between the soul and body in man ; it is above his principle, 1 Cor. ii. 14. The spiritual man understandeth it very imperfectly ; all we know is rather, that so it is, than what it is ; the full and perfect knowledge of it is reserved for the future state ; so our Lord hath told us : " At that day ye shall know, that I am in my Father, and ye in me, and I in you," John xiv. 20 ; then, and not till then : we shall never perfectly understand this union until we come fully to enjoy it. In the mean time, if a short improvement of such a rich point might not be judged improper in such a contemplative discourse as this is, a few things might be hinted from hence, by way of use.

Use 1. Here we may discover the main foundation and reason of the saints' perseverance. Surely it consists not in the nature of grace infused in their regeneration; this differs not specifically from the grace which Adam received in his first creation; that was the image of God, Gen. i. 26, 27; and so is this, Col. iii. 10, and therefore of itself cannot produce any higher or more noble effects under the one covenant, than it did under the other. Nor doth it consist in the liberty and rectitude of their own wills, though regenerate. But here is the ground and foundation of the saints' perseverance; they are not only fixed stars in Christ's right hand, Rev. iii. 1; if no more, it would be hard pulling them thence, but their lives are bound up in the same bundle with Christ's own life; " Our life is hid with Christ in God," Col. iii. 3. Christ and his saints have, as it were, but one life between them, and that life is Christ's; whence Christ himself makes the inference, " Because I live, you shall live also," John xiv. 19. Until I hear that Christ is dead the second time, which I am sure I shall never do, for " Christ being raised from the dead, dieth no more, death hath no more dominion over him," &c. Rom. vi. 9, I dare not believe the possibility of the saints' total and final apostasy.

Only, because Satan can transform himself into an angel of light, and the heart is deceitful above all things, and desperately wicked, my earnest advice to all such as do pretend to this blessed union, as to mine own soul, is, to give all diligence, upon solid scripture evidence; that is to say, by the precious and powerful influences of this union upon their souls, and by the gracious reciprocations of faith and love, and sweet holy communion with the

Father and the Son, &c.; by these, I say, and the like, to secure the assumption, I am thus united to Christ; and the conclusion, need not fear the gates of Rome, or hell; but the believer may boldly send forth St. Paul's challenge, "Who shall condemn? What shall separate? Thanks be to God, who hath given us the victory through our Lord Jesus Christ," Rom. viii. 34, 35; 1 Cor. xv. 57.

Use 2. Hence we may take notice of the honour and dignity of the saints, how meanly and basely soever reputed, in and by a reprobate world, even as the filth of the world, and the offscouring of all things, 1 Cor. iv. 13. I say, though the saints of God are thus base and contemptible in the opinion of the ignorant world, yet they have another rate and value set upon them in heaven. God is not ashamed to be called their God, nor Christ ashamed to call them brethren, Heb. xi. 16; ii. 11. Yea, he dignifies them with the style of his spouse, the bride, the Lamb's wife, Cant. iv. 8, 11; Rev. xxi. 9; and all this upon the account of that admirable and inconceivable union which is between Christ and them, by virtue whereof they are in Christ, and Christ in them, as to their more divine part, their souls, 1 Cor. vi. 17; and even as to their earthly and corruptible part, their bodies, members of Christ, and temples for the Holy Ghost to dwell in; yea, saith my text, their very dust is united to Christ: they "sleep in Jesus." Such honour have all his saints.

Use 3. How should the sense of it engage them to honour Christ, who hath put such great honour upon them! yea, to honour themselves whom Christ hath so highly honoured! to stand upon their advancement, and not to profane themselves by any

thing that is common or unclean, or upon the least
account unsuitable to their glorious union with Jesus
Christ; but to possess their vessels in sanctification
and honour, 1 Thess. iv. 4, as under an holy awe of
that tremendous sentence, " If any man defile the
temple of God, him will God destroy," 1 Cor. iii. 17.
Surely the thought of so near and intimate a union
with the Son of God, should make sin become an impossibility; and upon all the adulterous solicitations
of the flesh, world, or Satan, to make holy Joseph's
quick reply, How can I do this great wickedness,
and sin against my union with Jesus Christ !

Use 4.   And oh that such as have for many
years together sat under the ministry of the gospel
of Christ, and to this day are altogether strangers to
this blessed union with Christ, would now, with
all seriousness, apply themselves to know it, and to
know it experimentally; oh that they would, with
holy Paul, " account all things loss and dung for the
excellency of the knowledge of Jesus Christ," Phil.
iii. 8, even this, that they may " be found in him,"
ver. 9, to know him with interest, to know him in
this mysterious and beatifical union, Christ in them,
and they in Christ. Alas ! this is the undoing mistake
of thousands who are called christians; they know
somewhat of the history of Christ ; they have some
notions of a Christ in their heads, but this is the
precipice upon which they ruin themselves, they
think to be saved by a Christ without them ; they
hang upon the outside of the ark, they live upon
bare notions : the Son of God took our nature upon
him, died for sins, rose again, and is gone up into
heaven, and sits at God's right hand : and therefore
conclude they shall be saved. Oh but what a fallacy
do they put upon their own souls, James i. 22.

Christ is the hope of salvation, it is true, but it is not simply Christ in our nature, not simply Christ on the cross, not Christ in the grave, no, not alone Christ on the throne, but, saith the apostle, "Christ in you, the hope of glory," Col. i. 27. It were an easy thing to be saved, if a Christ without us were all; and I know no reason why reprobate men and devils might not get to heaven on such terms.

Christ must be in us by his Spirit, and we must be in Christ by faith, or else our persons and our hope are both reprobate, 2 Cor. xiii. 5. Appear before God's tribunal in the great day without this union, and plead what you will, your answer will be, " I never knew you; depart from me," &c. Matt. vii. 21—23; Luke xiii. 26, 27.

Believe this, oh all you carnal, Christless christians, and tremble ; and swim no longer down the stream of security, lest it empty you forth into the lake of perdition ; but work out your salvation with fear and trembling, and give all diligence to make this conjunction with Christ sure to your own souls ; that when he shall appear you may also appear with him in glory, Phil. ii. 12 ; Col. iii. 4.

Remember, all your true and solid comfort and rejoicing in life, in death, and at the day of judgment, is all bound up in your union with Jesus Christ; Christ in you, the hope of glory.

Use 5. The doctrine of this glorious union with Christ, is not more for the honour of the living, than for the comfort of the dying saints, and of their surviving mourners.

Why do ye tremble at the thoughts of death, O ye saints of God? and why do you indeed, what the Jews supposed Mary did, go so often to the sepulchre to weep there? John xi. 31. Behold, your beloved

Lazarus is not dead, but sleepeth; yea, that which
is of an infinitely higher consideration, he sleeps in
Jesus. Did he live in Christ? behold he died in
Christ also; did he die in Christ? behold he sleeps
in Christ; Christ is nearly related to the saints'
dust; their ashes are not laid up in the grave so
much as in Christ; yea, though they should pass
through ever so many changes and revolutions, and
should be scattered at length into all quarters and
corners of the world, he that calls the stars by their
own names, knows every dust of their precious
bodies, keeps them in his hand, and is as really
united to them as to his own human nature in
heaven.

This may be as Jonathan's honey upon the top
of the rod: taste of it, O ye mourners of hope, and
your eyes will be enlightened: look not on your
precious relations, so much as they lie rotting in the
grave, or resolved into dust, as upon their dust as it
is laid up in a sacred urn, in the hand and bosom,
as it were, of Jesus Christ; for which he himself will
be responsible, and bring it forth safely and entirely
in the morning of the resurrection; for so it followeth,
" them which sleep in Jesus will God bring with
him."

VI. The next word of comfort is, God will bring
his sleeping saints with him, that is, with his Son
Jesus Christ the Lord. For so it follows, " The
Lord himself shall descend," &c.; and when he
cometh, he will bring them with him that sleep in
him. The propriety of the work is ascribed to Jesus
Christ, God-man, the Mediator between God and
man; he shall bring them with him when he de-
scendeth from heaven.

1. When the Lord shall descend, he will bring

the spirits of just men made perfect with him from heaven. The souls of all his glorified saints, whose bodies to this moment have slept in the grave, shall follow Christ out of the gates of the New Jerusalem to attend that glorious solemnity: so it is prophesied, " Behold the Lord cometh with ten thousand of his saints," Jude ver. 14. When Christ cometh to judge the world, there shall not be a saint left in heaven, saith Chrysostom. Heaven shall, as it were, be left empty, to attend the King of glory going forth out of his royal palace, to finish the work of the great and last judgment of the world; he shall come attended with all his saints, they shall fill up his train.

2. As Christ will bring their souls with him from neaven, so he will bring their bodies from the grave. Christ at his coming to judgment, will first go to the graves of the saints, and cry to them aloud in some such language as once he did to their souls in the days of their unregeneracy, when dead in sins and trespasses, in the gospel call, " Awake thou that sleepest, and stand up from the dead, and I will give thee life." Or, as in the days of his flesh he did to Lazarus, when he had lain four days rotting in the grave, (a lively emblem and type of the general resurrection,) " Lazarus come forth," John xi. 43 ; and they that are dead shall come forth. It was the tenour of his own prediction, while yet in the world, " The hour is coming in the which all that are in the graves shall hear the voice of the Son of man, and shall come forth," &e.

When that hour has come, Christ by his mighty power shall command the bodies of his saints to come forth, shall unite dust to dust, every dust in its own proper place, and form it into the same body

E

it was when it was dissolved and laid down in the grave: and thus made up into a beautiful structure, more beautiful than ever it was in its first creation: Christ will put each soul into its own body again, and unite them together into the same sweet conjugal society and fellowship they possessed before their separation: this friendly espoused pair shall now be solemnly married together, before God, and men, and angels, never to suffer divorce any more, and they shall become one entire person, as they were in the days of their first contract.

O christians! think with yourselves what a joyful meeting that will be; when two such ancient friends, that have been parted so long, shall meet, and embrace, and kiss one another, never to suffer any more divorce, or fear of divorce, to eternity! How will the soul bless God, when it shall receive its own body again, its true yoke-fellow and fellow-labourer, which laboured with it much in the Lord, and which was wont to be its oratory and temple, wherein the soul performed all its *sacra*, its holy devotions, in season and out of season?

And how will the body rejoice to see the soul again, to whom it was espoused, which was the guide of its youth, that, in its capacity, which Christ is to the soul, its king, priest, and prophet, and by virtue of whose conjunction with it, the very body, as poor and mean as it was in its original extraction, was preferred and admitted into fellowship and communion with the Son of God; and, upon that account, not forgotten all the while it slept in the land of forgetfulness, and thought not of itself: I say, solace yourselves with the anticipation of that triumph and exultation that will fill this blessed new-married couple! especially when they shall receive one another so much more excellent than themselves at their last parting; that the body shall seem to be transformed into a soul, and the soul transformed into an angel of light; rejoice, O christian soul, to think how these two morning stars will sing for joy, in this their new and for ever blessed conjunction.

3. He will bring soul and body thus united. Christ shall bring with him unto the place where the great assize of the quick and dead shall be solemnly kept, which the 17th verse tells us will be in the air; thither Christ will bring with him all his elect, when he hath awakened them; and that upon a twofold account.

(1.) For the greater solemnity of that last and tremendous judgment. The saints shall be brought out of their graves to attend the judge, for his greater state and grandeur, and to strike the greater terror into the hearts of reprobate men an dangels; who then shall be brought forth in chains to the tribunal of Christ, to see and suffer the severity and impartiality of that last trial. The glory of a king consists in the multitude of his nobles and royal attendants; the judge of assize is brought in with the *posse comitatus*, the power and gallantry of the country, for the striking of the greater terror and awe into the hearts of offenders. Angels and saints shall be Christ's life-guard, as it were; or as his troops and legions, which shall conduct him in state and triumph to the judgment seat.

(2.) That they may accompany him, and be with him throughout the whole carriage and conduct of the last judicial process, to hear and applaud his righteous proceedings. This is that which the apostle calls, the saints judging the world, and judging

E 2

angels, 1 Cor. vi. 2, 3; yea, it seems that is not all;
our Saviour tells his apostles, that in that day, they
shall sit on twelve thrones, judging the twelve tribes,
&c. Matt. xix. 28. Judging or condemning, how?
certainly not as bare spectators only, but as assessors,
to sit with him on the bench, to justify and consent
to the judgment of Christ, the great and supreme
Judge; giving in their full and free suffrages to the
final sentence which he shall pass upon the reprobate world, of Jews and gentiles, of men and devils;
probably in some such language as we hear from
the saints upon the downfal of antichrist; " Great
and marvellous are thy works, Lord God Almighty;
just and true are thy ways, thou King of saints: for
thy judgments are made manife t," Rev. xv. 3, 4.

Here the apostles and ministers of the gospel
judged the wicked of the world by their doctrine;
and both ministers and others of God's faithful servants judged them by their holy lives, and patient
bearing of the cross.

But now the preachers of the gospel, with the
rest of the saints, shall judge the world judicially;
and, probably, by an audible vote too, and with the
judgment of Jesus Christ; " Thou art righteous, O
Lord, which art, and wast, and shalt be, because
thou hast judged thus," Rev. xvi. 5; this honour
shall all the saints have at that day: thus Christ
shall bring the raised saints with him to the place of
judgment.

4. God shall bring them with him; that is, that
last and solemn judgment being finished, Christ
shall carry all his saints back with him, from the
place of judgment, the nether heavens, into the
upper, the supreme heavens, where the throne of
God is, and the seat of glorified angels and saints.

All the saints of God shall follow the Judge in a triumphant manner into the streets of the New Jerusalem, the gates whereof shall be set wide open to receive them; an abundant entrance shall be administered unto them into the everlasting kingdom of the Lord and Saviour Jesus Christ, where they shall be welcomed home with loud acclamations of joy; heaven will ring again with triumphant shoutings. Thus also God shall bring them with him that sleep in Jesus; he will bring them into the glory of his Father.

This is another word of comfort, and there is great need of it, upon a twofold account :

(1.) In reference to the saints of God yet living. You are now scorned and persecuted; the ungodly world doth now judge you, and condemn you: the Psalmist observed it in his time; " They gather themselves together against the souls of the righteous, and condemn the innocent blood," Psa. xciv. 21. Innocence is no security against cruelty and oppression; yea, it seems no wine so sweet to wicked men as innocent blood: " Ye have condemned and killed the just," James v. 6 : and yet, that open violence may not want a pretence of justice, they act in the form of a legal process; before they kill, they condemn: but, alas! those fig-leaves will not cover their nakedness. It is the just, whom they unjustly condemn and murder; so it was in David's time, and so it was in St. James's time, and so it is now: the reprobate world holds on its course to this day; and so it will be to the end of the world. God's righteous Abels must expect no better justice at the tribunals of these unrighteous Cains.

But " be patient, brethren, unto the coming of the Lord; and stablish your hearts, for the coming of the

E 3

Lord draweth nigh,"James v.7, 8; and then the scene shall be altered; you shall have the law, as it were, in your own hands; your turn shall be to sit upon the bench, and your enemies shall stand at the bar. They judge and condemn you now, but there is a day coming when you shall judge and condemn them; and they indeed unrighteously, but you shall condemn them righteously, because your judgment shall be according to the judgment of that righteous Judge of heaven and earth, the Searcher of the hearts; who will judge men by those two impartial books, the book of his own remembrance, and the book of their consciences.

(2.) It is a word of comfort in reference to the saints departed, our gracious relations; the sense of whose loss and absence we are not able to bear, while we think of them as smothered and extinguished in their own ashes, silent in the land of forgetfulness; in whose sweet converse we were wont to solace ourselves with much delight, their souls having left the habitation of their bodies, and their bodies resolved into dust, and that dust, possibly, mixed with the dust of wicked men, or of the brute creatures; it may be, dispersed into the remotest parts of the world. Ah, these be some of the heart-dividing thoughts wherewith we do afflict our souls! But give check to your passions, O ye mourners of hope, and make use of the cordials which your heavenly Physician hath prescribed to keep you from fainting.

Think not so much on your gracious relations, as lying in the grave, their beauty turned into rottenness and deformity; think not of them as, possibly, by a premature death, as you may think, snatched from an earthly inheritance before their time: but think on them as co-heirs with Jesus Christ, riding now in triumph with him, and with the whole gene-ral assembly and church of the first-born, whose names are written in heaven, to take possession of their inheritance with the saints in light. Thus behold them, not as they are in the night of the shadow of death, but as they shall be in the morning of the resurrection, when God will bring them with him, and, I had almost said, mourn if you can.

VII. The next word of comfort in this model is, the obviating or removing an objection or discouragement which, probably, might possess the spirits of God's dying saints; and that is, lest the saints which shall be found alive at the last day, might possibly be happier, or, at least, sooner happy, than the saints which are fallen asleep before that day.

Now for the rolling of this stumbling block and stone of offence out of the way.

The apostle acquaints believers with the order and method of that great and solemn transaction at Christ's coming; and this he doth two ways,— 1. Negatively.—2. Affirmatively.

1. Negatively. He peremptorily denieth that the living saints, at Christ's coming in glory, shall have any the least advantage, above the sleeping saints, by their being found alive at that day: "We which are alive and remain, shall not prevent them which are asleep," ver. 15; that is, the living saints shall not prevent the dead saints in any privilege of the resurrection, or of the appearance of the Lord Jesus. It might probably be a temptation upon the Thessalonians, or other christians; either that the saints only which should be found alive at the last day, should have the happiness of seeing the Lord Jesus coming in his glory, with all his

mighty angels, to judge the world, and they only should enjoy the privilege of his glorious appearance; that all the saints that died before that day, even from the beginning of the world, were a lost generation, that should never come forth again to the light, or to behold the glory of that day, or to enjoy the blessed fruits and consequences of it.

Or, at least, that they should be the first in that happiness to see his glory, and have the first share in the felicities and triumph of that day, or ever the sleeping saints should be awakened or got out of their beds of dust.

The apostle doth therefore, I say, peremptorily and positively remove this scruple and fear out of the minds of christians; he assures us that it is an utter mistake, it is neither so, nor so; he tells us that all believers who had died from the first Adam downward, until the coming of the second Adam, shall have as good a share in the privileges and glory of that day, as they who stand upon their feet, and are found among the living at Christ's coming.

Secondly, and as soon; the living shall not prevent, or go before, or get the start of the dead, in any one of the beatitudes and honours of the resurrection of Jesus Christ. They shall neither go forth to meet this glorious Bridegroom one moment sooner than their brethren that are in their graves, nor shall they see him coming in his glory, one moment sooner; nor, consequently, be owned by Christ, or received by him, or taken up to him, or be placed upon thrones with him, or receive their absolution and justification from him, or their glorification with him, one moment before their fellow-saints that are yet in their dormitories.

But then how much stronger consolation doth

the affirmative part afford! which, although it lie in the close of the next verse, yet it being the main branch of the apostle's account, whereby he satisfieth the doubt of the dying servants of God, we must of necessity speak of it here.

2. Affirmatively. The dead in Christ shall rise first. He doth exactly state the method of Christ's procedure at the last judgment, namely, that the first business which shall be then transacted, shall be the awakening and raising all the saints of God out of their graves, which from Adam, until that moment, have slept in the dust: " the dead in Christ shall rise first;" nothing shall be done till that be done. The very first work Christ will do at his coming, will be to send forth his angels with a great sound of a trumpet, first to awaken the elect out of their sleep; Awake you that sleep in the dust; and then to gather them from the four winds, from the one end of heaven to the other, Matt. xxiv. 31 ; and when they shall have put on their wedding garments, to conduct them in state and triumph to meet with their royal Bridegroom, now come forth more than half way to meet them, and to consummate the marriage which was long since contracted in the day of their espousals.

It were easy to enlarge here, but, in a word, the sum of this affirmative account is this, that the saints who sleep in the grave at Christ's coming, shall be so far from being made less happy, or later happy in the coming of Christ than the saints who then shall be found alive, that they shall be first remembered ; the first care Christ will take when he comes in the clouds, shall be not about the living, but the dead saints ; the dead in Christ shall rise first. They shall be the first fruits of the resurrection. They that have slept so long in the`r beds of dust shall be first awakened, before any thing be done about them that never slept; they that were unclothed, and saw corruption in the grave, must first have their bodies clothed upon with incorruption; and then the surviving saints, at Christ's coming, shall be joined to them that have for so many years and ages slept in Jesus. The dead in Christ shall rise first, and both be presented together before the Judge.

It were too little to say, This may much alleviate the bitterness of death, our own, or our godly relations'; surely it may greatly augment our joy. They and we shall be so far from being losers, by laying down our earthly tabernacles in the dust, before we see Christ coming in his glory, that it shall be our advantage. If there be any privilege, any joy, any glory, any triumph at that day, it shall be theirs who sleep in Jesus; and theirs as soon as their surviving brethren's. The first dawnings of the Sun of righteousness, coming in his majesty, shall shine upon their faces; the first fruits of that jubilee shall be reserved for a recompense of their long sleep in the grave, they shall begin the health in this cup of salvation; the primacy of all that blessed solemnity belongs to the departed saints. " The dead in Christ shall rise first." O christians, comfort one another with this word. And the rather, because this is not an uncertain conjecture which the apostle lays down here, but an assertion of infallible certainty, which he had from the Divine oracle, the word of the Lord ; which brings me to the authority which the apostle brings for this doctrine ; " This I say unto you by the word of the Lord," ver. 15. He quotes Divine authority for what he delivereth. It being a doctrine of so much encouragement and satisfaction unto dying saints ; a doctrine above human capacity, and it seemeth not commonly understood by the churches and saints of God at that time ; he doth not pass it in his own name, or upon his own authority, but tells us from whence he had it. What I deliver now unto you, I speak not of myself, but from the mouth of him that is the Truth itself, the mouth of Jesus Christ ; this we say unto you in the word of the Lord.

VIII. The next word of comfort is, "The Lord himself shall descend." Here the apostle describes unto us the last coming of Christ to judgment. In which description we have three considerable particulars. 1. The person that shall come; "The Lord himself." 2. The certainty of his coming; "He shall come." 3. The manner of his coming; "With a shout."

1. The person that shall come :

"The Lord himself;" that is, Jesus Christ; God-man, the Mediator between God and man ; he that came at first to purchase and redeem the elect of God ; the same person will now come to raise them out of their graves, to gather them together, and to bring them with him unto glory. He will not send a deputy angel about the solemn work of that day ; but will descend himself in person to finish that last and grand trust of his mediatorial office.

The Lord himself will descend in his own person, because the judgment must be visible ; and therefore, the judge must be so too. There is a dispute whether Christ shall sit on a visible throne ; and it is very probable he will : sure we are from the scripture, that he shall appear in the clouds of heaven, that he may be heard and seen of all. "Behold, he cometh with clouds, and every eye shall see him," Rev. i. 7. Clouds are visible things; and these clouds shall not obscure him, but rather render him more conspicuous; " every eye shall see him." He shall so come with clouds, that they shall be a throne to exalt and lift him up to the view of all the world; therefore is the posture noted as well as the throne: " Ye shall see the Son of man sitting on the right hand of power, and coming in the clouds of heaven," Matt. xxvi. 64. Clouds shall be his throne, and sitting will be the posture; the posture of a judge.

The Lord himself shall appear for a recompense to his abasement. It is requisite that he who was judged by the world, should now come to judge the world. He came at first humble, lowly, despised, sitting upon an ass, spit upon, crucified: but he shall come again in power and great glory.

It is good sometimes to compare the two comings of Christ together. At first he came into the flesh; he showed himself in the nature of man, to be judged. But at his second coming, he shall come in the flesh. He shall come from heaven, in the same human nature which he carried up with him into heaven: there to be the Judge both of the quick and the dead.

His forerunner then was John the Baptist; the voice of one crying in the wilderness: at his second coming his forerunner shall be an archangel. " With the voice of the archangel, and with the trump of God;" as in the text. Then his companions were poor fishermen; now his attendants shall be the mighty angels of heaven, 2 Thess. i. 7. Then he came riding on an ass, a colt, the foal of an ass; now, he shall come riding on the clouds, sitting on a throne. At his first coming, he appeared in the form of a Servant; now, he shall come as a Lord, in the glory of his Father. Then he drank of the brook in the way; but now shall he lift up his head. This, for the recompense of his humiliation.

Also, our Lord Jesus Christ must come himself at the last day to perfect and finish his mediatorial office.

At his first coming, his mediatorial work was to pay a price to Divine justice, and so to purchase us of his Father. At his second coming, his mediatorial work will be, to gather all his redeemed ones together, and to present them a glorious church to his Father, not having spot or wrinkle, or any such thing: but holy and without blemish: in some such language as was long before prophesied : " Behold, here am I, and the children whom thou hast given me," Isa. viii. 18.

At his first coming, his mediatorial work was to fight with the devil, and all the powers of darkness, and to rescue what he had bought of the Father, out of the power of Satan, that strong man armed, who kept his goods in peace. At his second coming, his mediatorial work will be to vanquish all those enemies, out of whose dominion he hath freed his elect; to bind them with chains, to cast them into everlasting darkness, and to seal the bottomless pit upon them for ever.

And when he hath done this, the Lord Jesus shall deliver up the kingdom to his Father: his office is not completed till this be done. God's oath is passed upon it, and cannot be reversed, Isa. xlv. 23, &c. The text is applied to Christ, presently upon his exaltation, to this very purpose, Phil. ii. 10.

Use 1. This subject serves for infinite terror to the wicked. That the judgment now should be put

F

into the hand of Him, whom, of all the world, they counted their enemy: at least, if they did not call him so, they used him so. Oh, what a dreadful sight will his appearance be! If Ahab cried out with so much discomposure of spirit, at the sudden appearance of Elijah the prophet of God, " Hast thou found me, O mine enemy ?" with what horror and affrightment will reprobate sinners cry out, when they shall be dragged from before the tribunal of the Lord Jesus, the Lord of the prophets, Hast thou found us, O our enemy! If Joseph's brethren were so astonished at the presence of Joseph, when he said unto them, " I am Joseph, whom you sold into Egypt!" how will all the world of ungodly men be confounded at the presence of the Lord, now coming in the glory of his Father, to judge them ; when he shall say unto them, I am Jesus. I am Jesus, whom ye sold for less than ever Judas sold me, even for the price of a base lust. I am Jesus, whom ye crucified over and over again to yourselves; and put me to an open shame! I am Jesus, whose person you have slighted; whose government you have spurned at; crying in the pride and rebellion of your obstinate spirits, " We will not have this man to reign over us." I am Jesus, whose counsel you have rejected; whose threatenings you have laughed to scorn; whose promises you have derided and set at nought. I am Jesus, whose blood you have trampled under your feet as an unholy thing, even doing despite to the Spirit of grace, &c.

Now will the reprobate world be confounded at the presence of their Judge! Behold, in the days of his flesh, when he appeared in the form of a Servant, and was even led away as a sheep to the slaughter, and as a lamb before the shearer, not opening his mouth, by way of murmur against his Father, or reviling against his enemies, yet how did that lamb-like word, " I am he," fill the hearts of those sturdy soldiers, who came to apprehend him, with horror, and strike them to the ground, like a blast of thunder and lightning!

Oh, how will that word, when he shall come clothed with majesty and terror, with all the glorious host of heaven attending his person, " I am he," fill reprobate souls with astonishment and distraction, and even strike them backward into hell before their time! How will it cause them to woo the mountains and rocks, now as hard and inexorable as their hearts once were in the day of God's patience, crying out to them, to the amazement of heaven and earth, " Mountains, fall on us; rocks, cover us, and hide us from the face of him that sitteth on the throne, and from the wrath of the Lamb; for the great day of his wrath is come, and who shall be able to stand?" Rev. vi. 16, 17.

But all in vain! As the Lord Jesus once, in the day of his grace, cried unto them, and they would not answer, &c.; so they shall now cry to heaven and earth, to rocks and mountains, and they shall not answer; yea, the Judge shall " laugh at their calamity, and mock when their fear cometh," Prov. i. 26. " Oh consider this, ye that forget God, lest he tear you in pieces, and there be none to deliver," Psalm l. 22.

Use 2. This doctrine of Christ's personal appearance, speaks great consolation to the godly; the sheep of Christ, which have heard his voice speaking to them in the gospel of peace, and have obeyed it.

Behold, he that in the days of his flesh came to be their Redeemer, now in the day of his power

shall come to be their Judge. He that so often
pleaded for them to his Father, and for whom they
so often pleaded and contended, with a disobedient
and gainsaying generation; he shall now be their
Judge, and pass sentence upon them : their Friend,
their Brother, their Head, their Husband. What
need they fear that tribunal, where not their enemies, who were wont falsely to accuse and condemn
them; no, not their prejudiced and imprudent
friends, who sometimes have rashly and causelessly
misjudged them ; much less the accuser of the
brethren, " who accused them before their God,
day and night," Rev. xii. 10 ; none of these, I say,
shall sit in judgment ; but their dear Redeemer,
who for their sake came down from heaven : who
loved them so dearly, that he died for love of them,
that he might redeem them, and wash them in his
own blood. He that regenerated, sanctified, justified, preserved, and perfected them : he to whom,
both in life and death, they were so nearly and inseparably united ; and by virtue of which conjunction, they are now awakened, and set upon their feet
again, in a most beautiful and perfect state ; I say,
where he, and none but he, who long since became
their Advocate, shall now (by the appointment of
the Father) be their Judge. Oh, what matter of joy
and triumph will this administer unto the saints at
that day ! How may they lift up their heads with
joy, because their redemption and Redeemer shall
then draw nigh !

Again, the doctrine of Christ's personal appearance at the last day affords no less consolation in
reference to the saints departed ; and to this very
end, doth the Holy Ghost mention it in this place,
" the Lord himself shall descend from heaven."

Christ bought them at too dear a rate to leave any one of them in the grave; and therefore, to make all sure, he will come in person, and finish his work himself. As sure as he ascended up into heaven after his own resurrection, so surely shall he descend from heaven to perfect that resurrection in his saints, which brings me to the second particular.

2. The certainty of his coming is couched in the verb here, he shall descend from heaven. He shall; that is, most certainly and infallibly.

And so all the scriptures which mention the coming of the Lord, speak of it as a most unalterable decree and statute of heaven; thus the apostle to the Athenians, " God hath appointed a day, wherein he will judge the world in righteousness, by that Man whom he hath ordained, whereof he hath given us assurance," &c. Acts xvii. 31.

See how many words are here heaped one upon another, to assure our faith of the infallible certainty of Christ's coming.

First, he hath appointed a day: there is the Divine appointment and decree, passed upon it in God's eternal purpose and counsel. It is a statute enacted in heaven, that there shall be a future judgment; a statute more sure than ever the laws of the Medes and Persians; for heaven and earth may pass away, but God's decree shall stand, &c. And then there is a certain day appointed for it, a stated time by the same power; a day which can neither be adjourned nor accelerated. The time is fixed. He hath appointed a day, and it cannot be altered. And then the work is determined as well as the day, and that is judgment; " wherein he will judge." The judgment is not left arbitrary or contingent;

but God is resolved on it.   He will judge ; not, per-adventure, he may judge ; but as sure as he is God, he will judge.   The persons to be judged are also specified ; not less than the whole world.   He will judge the world, not a single person shall escape that judgment ; " we must all appear before the judgment-seat of Christ," 2 Cor. v. 10.   As the persons to be judged, so likewise the person that is to judge, is named, and designed to it already ; that Man, that special, that peculiar Man, the Man Christ Jesus.   And to make all sure, he hath his commission already.   That man whom he hath ordained the judge, is elected and commissioned under the broad seal of heaven, is passed, John vi. 27.   And if all this be not enough, there is yet further assurance and evidence given of it already to the world, open and evident demonstration, if men will not shut their eyes—of which he hath given assurance unto all men : what that assurance is, I shall show anon.   In the mean time see how the Holy Ghost useth all the words and expressions which may create a firm assent to the doctrine of Christ's coming to judgment ; that there may be no room for doubting left, no hesitancy in the minds of men.

The personal coming of Christ to judgment is established on a four-fold foundation.

(1.) His purchase : would Christ buy a people at so dear a rate, and then go away and come no more at them ?

(2.) Also his promise.   " And if I go, I will come again," John xiv. 3 ; he will, especially con-sidering the design of his leaving them for a time, it was but to go and prepare a place for them, and he hath done it ; the place is prepared ; mansions

in his Father's house are made ready for them,
ver. 2.   Why now, Christ being gone to this very
end, and all things prepared for their entertainment,
if he should not come again, he should certainly
fail, not his promise only, but his project too; this
cannot be.   He that never yet failed his own promise, nor his people's expectations, will not now do
it · no, I will come and receive you.

(3.) Witness the sacrament of his last supper;
which is nothing else but a pledge and seal to keep
alive the memorial of his second coming.   " As oft
as ye eat of this bread, and drink of this cup, ye do
show the Lord's death till he come," 1 Cor. xi. 26.
Now when the Lord Jesus Christ hath engaged the
expectation of his people, by so solemn a covenant,
if he should fail their expectation, this grand institution had been in vain.   Nay surely, he never said
to the seed of Jacob, " Seek ye my face in vain,"
Isa. xlv. 19 : he speaketh righteousness.

(4.) His resurrection; that is, the assurance
given in Acts xvii. 31, He will judge the world
by that Man whom he hath appointed.   How
may we be sure of that ? why he hath given the
world assurance of it; what assurance ? in that
he hath raised Christ from the dead. He hath given
assurance, he hath offered faith; the meaning is,
God could not have confirmed his purpose and promise of sending Christ to judge the world at the
last day, by a more firm and solemn argument, than
by raising him from the dead, after he had paid the
debt, made satisfaction to Divine justice upon the
cross.

Now, therefore, O ye saints of God, cast not away
your confidences, either in respect of yourselves, or
of your sweet relations which have outrun you to

the sepulchre.   He that shall come, will come, and will not tarry.   In the mean time, let the just live by their faith : keep up your faith, and your faith will keep up your hearts from sinking; " for this cause we faint not," &c. 2 Cor. iv. 16.

3. The manner of Christ's coming.

In the description whereof we find a three-fold summons or citation to all the world, to make their appearance at this great assize.

(1.) The first solemn summons is a shout : the Lord shall descend from heaven with a shout.   The word in the Greek signifies such a shout as is to be heard amongst mariners and seamen, when, after a long and dangerous voyage, they begin to descry the haven, crying with loud and united voices, a shore, a shore ! as the poet describes the Italians, when they saw their native country ; lifting up their voices, and making the heavens ring again with Italy, Italy ! Or, as armies when they join battle, rend the air with their loud acclamations.   In like manner shall the mighty angels of God, with united clamour, proclaim the advent of their Lord, crying aloud with a voice that shall be heard from one end of the heavens to another ; the earth and sea, and hell itself, shall hear and tremble.   " Behold, the Lord cometh," Jude, ver. 14.   " Behold, the Bridegroom cometh," Matt. xxv. 6.

(2.) The second summons is the voice of the archangel.   This clause some take to be exegetical to the former, expounding that hortatory clamour or shout mentioned before ; with a shout, that is, with the voice of the archangel.   Others conceive it to be added by way of eminency ; all the angels shall shout for joy, but the voice of the archangel shall be heard above all the rest : louder and shriller than all the other angels, as captain-general to them all.

(3.) The third summons is the trump of God; it may signify a mighty trump; after the manner of the Hebrew phrase, which useth to call works and wonders of unusual proportion, works of God, and wonders of God; so the trump of God, that is, a mighty trump; a voice of more dreadful horror than all that went before. But, whether it be to be understood metaphorically or properly, is questioned amongst expositors. Some understand it only metaphorically, and in an analogical sense, signifying no more than the virtue and power of Christ's voice and proclamation, summoning both the living and the dead to appear at his tribunal.

But why we may not take it literally and in propriety of speech, for the voice of an audible trump, which shall be louder than all the former, I see no reason. And it may well be the same with that which the apostle calls " the last trump," 1 Cor. xv. 52; this sounding last of all, or continuing longer than the former; our Lord calls it, " the great sound of a trumpet," Matt. xxiv. 31.

Thus are these three summonses distinct, and each of them louder and shriller than the former. And it may allude to the manner of the calling together of the Jews to their public worship, and that (possibly) typical to this; signifying thus much to the world, that like as their assemblies were summoned by the sound of trumpets, so the last and solemn day of judgment, that great general assembly of the living and the dead, shall be summoned together by the sound of trumpets from heaven; the vastest and most universal assembly that ever was beheld by the eye of creature.

But a clearer type and prophecy hereof seems to be that at the giving of the law, when God came down on mount Sinai, to give the law, it was in a very glorious manner, " with thunder and lightnings, and a thick cloud upon the mount, and the voice of the trumpet exceeding loud," &c. Exod. xix. 16.

This did typify unto us, Christ's second coming at the end of the world to require the law; which surely ought to excel in glory.

When Christ came into the flesh, his herald was John the Baptist, a man of a mean and contemptible presence, a preacher of repentance, " Repent ye, for the kingdom of heaven is at hand," Matt. iii. 2. Now his forerunners and heralds shall be, the mighty angels of God.

Then he came in a still, soft voice; " The voice of one crying in the wilderness, Prepare ye the way of the Lord, make his paths straight," Matt. iii. 3. Now, he shall come with a loud and terrible voice. Voice upon voice, trump upon trump, alarm upon alarm; each louder and more dreadful than other, in comparison whereof, the loudest thunder which was ever heard from the clouds of God, shall be but as the blowing of a ram's horn; a dreadful shout, which shall even shake the heavens and the earth, and hell itself, Heb. xii. 26.

Oh to the wicked, surely this will be a tremendous blast, which shall not so much raise as affright them out of their graves, with horror and amazement. Behold the judge cometh, arise ye dead, and come to judgment. This will be the dreadful meaning of that ministerial excitation, in the consciences of the reprobate world: Appear in court, there to answer for all the contempt to the calls and counsels of Jesus Christ in his blessed gospel!

The three-fold alarm—shout, and voice, and trump, shall be no more terror or amazement to the saints of Christ, than the roaring of cannons, when armies of friends approach a besieged city for the relief of them that are within. These sounds and rattlings, how terrible a sense soever they may impress upon the hearts and consciences of the wicked, will be to them that sleep in Jesus as the sweetest melody that ever sounded in their ears, as the voice of harpers harping with their harps, to awaken them out of their sweet sleep, with the sweetest music and harmony that ever sounded in their ears; and these shall be their heavenly ditties. "Awake and sing, O ye that dwell in the dust," &c. Or, (as in the gospel-call, a little varied,) " Arise, shine, for thy light is come, and the glory of the Lord is risen upon thee; for, behold, the darkness shall cover the earth;" even (everlasting) darkness, all the wicked of the world; but the Lord shall " rise upon thee, and his glory shall be seen upon thee" to all eternity, Isa. lx. 1, 2.

O ye saints and servants of God, " Lift up your heads with joy, for your redemption draweth nigh," Luke xxi. 28, and comfort one another with this word also, concerning your gracious relations which are gone to rest.

The Lord Jesus himself shall come to awaken them; and those triumphant summons and alarms which shall usher in his coming, as they shall add to the glory and majesty of their Lord, in whose bosom they have slept all this while, so they shall, on the one side, bid war and battle to the reprobate world, and on the other side, call together the assemblies of the saints, who have made a " covenant with him by sacrifice," Psa. l. 5, and it shall be for their honour and exaltation in that day of his triumph.

The sum is this : your dear ones, whose immature departure you so much lament, that are asleep in the dust, shall arise ; Christ himself shall come for them, and that in a most triumphant manner, for their glory and their enemies' shame, Isa. lxvi. 5.

IX. I now come to consider the blessed consequences of Christ's coming, which are three :

1. The resurrection of the saints which are fallen asleep. " The dead in Christ shall rise first."

2. The triumphant ascent of both (the living and sleeping saints together) into the clouds; " we which are alive, shall be caught up together with them into the clouds."

3. The blessed meeting of all the saints together with Jesus Christ, their Lord and Bridegroom; who comes from the seat of the blessed, the third heaven, to meet them above half way, even to the lowest region of the air. " To meet the Lord in the air."

The first consequence is, the resurrection of the saints. " The dead in Christ shall rise first."

The apostle supposeth the query, " some man will say, How are the dead raised ? and with what body do they come ?" 1 Cor. xv. 35. A query neither frivolous nor impertinent ; and therefore himself (by the Spirit) thinks it worth the solving.

He gives us to understand, that the saints shall rise with the very same bodies they lay down with in the graves; it is expressed under the metaphor of seed ; God giveth it a body, &c. and to every seed his own body : his own body, not specifically only, but numerically its own proper body, no ways alienated or transformed into another. And holy Job,

even in the depths of distress, believed and preached
the very same doctrine long before. " Though
after my skin, worms destroy this body," that is,
after worms have digged through my skin to consume my flesh; " yet in my flesh I shall see God;
whom I shall see for myself, and mine eyes shall
behold, and not another," &c. Job xix. 26, 27.

To this if it be objected, that in the 37th verse
of 1 Cor. xv. under the metaphor of seed, he
tells the incredulous fool that cannot believe this
article of faith, the resurrection, " Thou sowest
not that body which shall be." Not that body
which shall be. It seems then the body shall be
another thing, from that which is now sown.

Yea, and indeed so it shall be, in respect of
quality, though not of kind. There is diversity in
one and the self-same body; as it is in the me-
taphorical, so it shall be with the natural; the grain
is sown mean and bare, but it springeth up after
another manner, beautiful and green; yet the same
grain : the body likewise is the same, when it riseth as
it was sown, for substance, parts, members, and
organs, but not the same for beauty and excellent
properties.

The infant shall rise a man of perfect age, the
lame shall rise sound, the blind shall rise seeing, the
deaf shall hear, the dumb shall be able to speak,
the resurrection shall take away all defects and
excesses of nature, the deformities of the saints
shall not be raised together with their bodies; yea,
deformities shall be turned into comelinesses and
beauties; and yet all these alterations do no more
change or destroy the individuality of person, than
youth doth make the person numerically different
from what it was in infancy, or old age from what it

G

was in youth ; or as it was in the persons of all sorts, which Christ healed in the day of his flesh ; they were the same individuals after cure, as they were before ; cure makes not another individual man of a cripple nor health of the sick ; so shall it be in the resurrection, the bodies of the saints, (for of them only I speak, not at all of the wicked,) shall be the same for substance and matter ; but wonderfully changed for form and supernatural endowments and qualities : which brings me to the particular description of the resurrection in respect of admirable and transcendent properties ; of which our apostle hath instanced four.

First, it is sown in corruption ; it is raised in incorruption. It is sown in corruption. Behold, the body is corruptible, while it liveth ; a nursery of such seeds and principles, as will inevitably destroy itself ; an hospital of all manner of diseases : but when it is dead, it is corruption itself ; the fondest relation who laid it in the bosom, cannot now endure it in the sight · " Give me a burying place," said Abraham of his beloved Sarah, " that I may bury my dead out of my sight," Gen. xxiii. 4. It is now the picture of all ghastly loathsomeness. But oh, how unlike itself shall it be in the resurrection ! It is raised in incorruption ; when Christ hath fetched the body out of the grave, and set it upon its feet again, there shall not be the least savour of mortality upon it ; as there was no smell of the fire upon the raiment of the three children, when they came out of the fiery furnace, Dan. iii. 27. All the principles of corruption and mortality shall be put off, and left, together with the grave-clothes, in the sepulchre. It shall be an angelified body, flesh immortalized ; subject to no more corruption than the soul itself. There shall be no more death nor fear of death, nor possibility of death for ever.

" It is sown in dishonour." As soon as the soul is enlarged from its imprisonment, the body is presently stripped naked of all its robes and honourable attire, and wrapped up in a poor shroud of no other use than to hide deformity; and, as a mean contemptible thing, it is buried under ground. But, be the burial never so ignoble, the resurrection of it shall be glorious, Psa. lxxix. 2.

" It is raised in glory." We may truly say, Solomon in all his glory was not arrayed like one of these children of the resurrection ; there shall be a glory put upon the body which shall outshine the sun in its brightest refulgency.

The soul, which is the candle of the Lord, is here for a time put into a dark lantern of the body ; but then the glorified soul being returned into its ancient habitation, and become a vessel replenished with immortal and unmixed light, will transmit such beams of glory into the refined body that it shall shine like an angel of light ; the body of the poorest Lazarus that ever lay on the dunghill, shall be clothed with such rays of beauty, as will transcend the most absolute beauty that ever mortal eye beheld.

The soul shall possess an external irradiation :— as Jesus Christ is the brightness of the Father's glory, so shall the saints at his coming (in their proportion) be, the brightness of Christ's glory ; the beams of that glory, which shall shine forth from the glorified person of their Redeemer, shall reflect such a glittering splendour upon the saints in the resurrection, that they shall be glorious even to admiration ; they shall be admired by the very angels, by one **another,** and even by themselves also; they shall wonder to behold this strange change wrought upon themselves.

" It is sown in weakness;" weakness indeed! What more impotent than man while yet alive, vanity itself, Psa. xxxix. 5. Yea, hear that text out, and you will say he is vanity indeed ; for first it is every man, kings as well as beggars ; every man, take where ye will ; and as it is every man, so it is every vanity, or, altogether vanity ; every man is the centre of every vanity, he is not only mixed vanity, partly something and partly nothing, some solidity and some froth, but vanity throughout ; vanity and nothing else ! And then again it is every man in his best estate; or, according to the Hebrew, standing. Ye need not stay till he is down, when he is languishing, suppose, in his sick bed ; but, take him standing in his most erect posture, when he is most himself in his bravery ; or, as it is Isa. xl. 6, take him in his goodliness, gallantry, in his freshest colours and excellences; and yet then, even then, he is vanity ; every man is every vanity ; and that you may not doubt of it, the Holy Ghost hath set a double seal to it, one in the front, Verily, and another at the end of the text, Selah; " Verily, every man in his best estate is altogether vanity, Selah ;" such a piece of vanity, that he is not able at his best to free himself of, or fence himself against the injuries of the most contemptible creature that ever God made.

Thus weak he is in his strength, what is he in his weakness? So feeble he is when he stands, how feeble when he is fallen, in sickness, in his old decrepit age, his second infancy, in death.

But now behold this feeble thing shall be raised in power ; the body even of the weakest infant, shall be invested with an angelical power; a monument whereof, the formidable host of Sennacherib king of Assyria hath erected for all posterity; wherein one angel went out and smote one hundred four score and five thousand, 2 Kings xix. 35, who over night, like so many Goliaths, defied the armies of the living God; but in the morning lay upon the ground so many blasted, lifeless corpses, and all by the ministry of one angel.   Such vessels of strength and activity shall the bodies of the saints be in the resurrection; they shall be clothed with mighty power; Gideon, Samson, Jephthah, David, and all his famous worthies are but as babes to the children of the resurrection : he that is weak among them shall be as David, and he that is as David shall be as the angel of God.   Again,

"It is sown a natural body;" such a body as is animated, sustained, by the soul; yet in so low a way, that it is subject to corruption, and is no sooner deserted by the soul, but it resolves into dust or natural; such a body as stands in need of natural helps, of meat, drink, rest, sleep, to shore up the feeble tabernacle of dust for a while : and all will not do; but down it will come—roof, and walls, and props, and all.   Or again, natural, that is, such as hath natural motions, operations, and affections, such as are proper only to the fallen nature of man; feeble, slow, limited, and temporary.

But now behold, in opposition to all these acceptations, "it is raised a spiritual body;" not in regard of the substance of it, as if it were turned into a spirit; but, because animated and acted by the soul now in its glorified capacity, made perfect with all heavenly qualifications, and so spiritualized in all its faculties and operations, that it is called no more by the name

G 3

of a soul, but of a spirit, Heb. xii. 23. To the conduct and motions whereof, the body now shall yield absolute and immutable obedience and conformity. Here the soul depends, as it were, upon the body : because, though the body be acted by the soul, yet the soul acts according to the temperament of the body, and the disposition of the organs.

But in the resurrection, it shall not be so; the body then shall depend wholly upon the soul, and be actuated properly and undisturbedly by the soul. Here the soul seems to be flesh itself, because actuated by the flesh, and is oft subservient to the flesh ; but then the very body shall seem to be a spirit, because actuated by the spirit, and shall be universally and uniformly serviceable to the spirit ; the soul shall immediately be actuated by God, and the body shall immediately be actuated by the soul ; thus it shall be a spiritual body.

It is raised a spiritual body, because it shall subsist as a spirit; it shall stand in no need of those gross material aliments of meat, and drink, and sleep, by which it is now underpropt; but it shall be sustained merely by virtue of its union with the soul, as the soul by virtue of its union with Jesus Christ ; this is to be a spiritual body, when the body shall subsist as a spirit, or as an angel doth subsist.

Likewise the operations of the body shall then be all spiritual operations ; it shall then be abased no more to any of the servile drudgeries of this present state ; it shall work no more, toil no more, sin no more ; the offices of the body shall be as far above its present functions, as the work of a king transcends the employment of a swineherd ; they shall for ever be freed from all those uses which do imply a state of infirmity, and shall be taken up wholly in heavenly and angelical services, as to stand before the throne of God, and of the Lamb, and to praise him for ever and ever.

And lastly, the body shall then be spiritual, because it shall be endued with spiritual affections; it shall not be liable to weariness, sickness, pain, or external injuries, any more than a spirit is. In the resurrection, the bodies of the saints shall not cease to be flesh and blood, but they shall be divested of all the defects and infirmities of flesh and blood, ver. 50, 51. This is the mystery of it, " We shall be changed." The fire of the last judgment, that only purgatory of the saints that we dull protestants know, shall not consume the bodies of the saints, but their corruption only; it shall not destroy the substances, but refine their qualities; as the goldsmith maketh a new vessel of old plate, not by altering the metal, but by changing the form and fashion. The furnace of the resurrection shall purge out all the slime, and dross, and filth, and imperfection out of the bodies of the saints, and refine them into a body that shall exceed the celestial bodies of the sun, moon, and stars, in splendour and purity.

Behold, these are now the beatifical properties wherewith the very bodies of the saints shall be arrayed and beautified in the resurrection! A change which we are not in a capacity to understand till we shall possess it. And all these admirable properties the blessed apostle hath cast up into one word, a word of a most incomprehensible signification, the vast comprehensive estimate of all the rest; ' Our vile bodies shall be fashioned like to Christ's glorious body," Phil. iii. 21.

Oh who can tell how glorious the glorified body of Christ is! Behold, if such was the brightness of

Moses' face, at the giving of the law, that the Israelites were not able to bear it ; "They were afraid,"
saith the text, "to come nigh him," Exod. xxxiv. 30 ;
if St. Stephen's countenance did shine as the face of
an angel, when he stood holding up his hand at the
bar of his unrighteous judges, in the posture of a
malefactor, Acts vi. 15 ; what think we is the
lustre and brightness which shines forth from the
glorified body of the Lord Jesus, who is the blessed
and only potentate, the King of kings, and Lord of
lords, who only hath immortality, dwelling in the
light which no man can approach unto, whom no
man hath seen, nor can see, 1 Tim. vi. 15, 16. Behold
in his transfiguration, his face did shine as the sun,
and his raiment was white as snow, Matt. xvii. 2.
What glorious beams of light and glory do Moses,
and Elias, and Peter, now see sparkling from his glorified person exalted to the right hand of the Majesty
on high, that is, on the highest throne of the highest
Majesty in the court of heaven, Heb. i. 3 ; surely the
glorified body of Christ doth as far surpass the sun
in brightness, as the sun surpasseth a clod of earth ;
and yet to this exemplar of glory, must the bodies of
the saints be conformed in the resurrection ! Surely,
glorious things are spoken of the resurrection ; so
great, so glorious, that, had not the Spirit of God
spoken them before, it had been daring presumption, to have reported or believed it.

This doctrine of the glorious resurrection of the
body may serve by way of counsel.　You that would
secure unto yourselves an interest in the glory
which shall be put upon the saints' bodies in the
resurrection, labour to experience this beatifical
transfiguration, first in your souls, on this side of the
grave.　Oh labour to get your vile spirits to be

made like to Christ's glorious spirit.   Oh labour to
get his image and similitude to be deeply engraven
upon your hearts; and to scatter the beams of it
in your conversations, for the enlightening of a dark
world, Phil. ii 15

Behold this shall be the evidence and first-fruits
of your future conformity to Him in the resurrection
of the just.   The ground and reason is, because
that blessed transfiguration which shall conform the
saints to Christ, their Head and Husband in the resurrection, and from thenceforth to all eternity, hath
its beginning here in regeneration, or the new birth,
wherein they are renewed in the spirit of their minds,
Eph. iv. 23, 24.   And upon this very account, is
the resurrection styled also the regeneration, Matt.
xix. 28.   It is called the regeneration, because the
resurrection shall perfect in the saints what the
regeneration began ; conformity to Christ their Head
and Husband in holiness.   Yea, at the resurrection,
the image of Jesus Christ shall be completed ; as
on their souls, so on their bodies also : because, that
image was began upon their souls on this side the
grave in their new birth ; accordingly as they were
predestinated to both in the purpose of God from all
eternity.   The resurrection to grace here, and to
glory hereafter, is but one and the same regeneration,
Rom. viii. 29.   Whosoever, therefore, is a stranger
to this transformation of spirit, in the resurrection to
grace, shall never partake of that transfiguration of
body in the resurrection to glory.

This doctrine also may serve by way of comfort ;
and for that end it is written by the Comforter himself in this model : for comfort, I say, in reference
to our sweet relations that sleep in Jesus ; over
whom, not seldom, we spend our fruitless tears, take

we heed lest sinful also, while we compare their
once lively, sweet, amiable countenances, which
sparkled with so much beauty and delight in our
eyes, with their pale, ghastly visages in the grave ;
where they say to corruption, Thou art my father;
and to the worm, Thou art my mother, and my sister,
Job xvii. 14. We look upon them, I say, not without a kind of trembling and horror ; as if their spirits
appeared to us out of their graves; or that we ourselves were buried with them alive in the same coffin.

Ah, sirs, why stand ye not, with the men of Galilee,
gazing up into heaven? Acts i. 11 ; but, with Peter,
stooping down, and looking into the sepulchre.
Behold I bring you glad tidings of great joy ; the
day is coming, when that corruptible shall put on incorruption, and that mortal shall put on immortality ; when that poor dust, over which thou now
mournest, that vile body, shall put on its angelical
robes, and shall more surpass itself in its freshest
and liveliest colours, while yet in the land of the
living, than that beautiful pile of flesh and blood
did exceed itself, when it was resolved into rottenness and dust.

Look not, then, O ye children of God, upon yourselves or your relations, as they lie in the grave ;
but, contemplate them, as they shall be in the morning of the resurrection ; oh what a glorious change
shalt thou behold ! How unlike itself, shall this poor
vile body appear in the resurrection.

Be of good comfort, O ye mourners of hope ;
here is a perfumed handkerchief to wipe off all tears
from your eyes ; you that sow in tears, shall reap in
joy ; you that carry forth precious seed weeping, shall
come again rejoicing, and bring your sheaves with
you. The resurrection shall make amends for all'

2. I come now to the second consequence of Christ's rising—the saints' triumphant ascension. " Then we which are alive and remain, shall be caught up together with them in the clouds," &c. ver. 17.

Here, we have a further instance of the saints' conformity unto Christ in the resurrection. Christ himself, when he was risen, did ascend; he was carried up into heaven : so shall it be with the saints, when they are raised up out of their beds of dust, they shall be caught up into the clouds ; they shall ascend to meet their Lord.

And this ascension, according to the analogy of scripture, we may conceive, shall be effected by a threefold medium.

(1.) The ascension of the saints in the clouds shall be effected by the power of Christ.

By the same power whereby he raised them out of their graves, will he lift them up unto himself. This will be the continuation and perfection of the resurrection ; the proper work of him who is the Resurrection and the Life; it is the second part of the resurrection, without which the first would differ little from the state of the dead. In vain should the saints be raised out of the dust, if, being raised, Christ should leave them at a distance from him : and the resurrection of the saints themselves would look too like the resurrection of the wicked, a punishment rather than a bliss ; separation from Christ being half, yea, the worst half of hell : though even there the damned have a kind of life. Surely the children of the resurrection might have too real occasion to weep Absalom's dissembling complaint to his abused Father ; " Why am I come from Geshur, if I may not see the king's face?" Why are we brought up out of the grave, if we mav not enjoy the Lamb's presence ?

But the Amen, the faithful and true Witness, cannot be worse than his word ; he spake it at his departure to his disciples, and he will make it good at his return ; " I will come again, and receive you unto myself, that where I am, there ye may be also," John xiv. 3.

In order, therefore, to the accomplishment of this promise, the first work the Lord Jesus will do, at his coming in his kingdom, after he hath awakened his spouse out of her sleep, will be to lift her up unto himself, now sitting upon his triumphant throne to judge both the quick and dead.

This is the first receiving of them unto himself, his drawing of them up unto him, according to his own phrase in the days of his flesh ; "And I, if I be lifted up from the earth, will draw all men unto me :" all men, that is, all my redeemed ones; which promise, although the Spirit expounds it of his being lifted up upon the cross, yet we may, not without warrant, extend it also to his glorious exaltation in the great day of his judging the world : this being both the design and reward of his passion ; to the intent that whom he drew to himself by the merit of his cross, he might also actually draw unto himself by the power of his resurrection and ascension. " I will draw all men unto me ;" or, I will attract unto me ; as the loadstone draweth the metal unto itself by its magnetic virtue, or as the sun draweth up the vapours of the earth by its attractive beams. so will the Lord Jesus Christ that sun of righteousness, when his glory shall arise upon the world with healing under his wings, draw all his saints unto himself, by the sovereign attractive influence of that mysterious union between himself and his members.

(2.) A second medium is the ministry of the angels; for which, though we have not certainty of demonstration to compel belief, yet we want not more than bare probability of argument to invite assent.

For if it be in the commission of the angels to be ministering spirits " for them who shall be heirs of salvation," Heb. i. 14, we have no reason to imagine their commission should expire until the time when the saints shall be actually and safely invested into their long-expected inheritance. And, therefore, if they were the saints' life-guard in the state of their defilement and infirmity, to bear them up in their hands, lest at any time they should dash their foot against a stone; how much more ready and active now, in the saints' virgin state of purity and perfection, will the angels be, to be their convoy to conduct them in their ascension, going now to meet the Lamb! Sure we are, the Lord Jesus, though he be the Resurrection and the Life, yet is pleased to make much use of the ministry of the angels about the resurrection of the godly; they shall sound the first trump, at the sounding whereof, the dead do rise.

They gather the elect together from the four corners of the earth, and sever the wicked from them; the tares and all things that offend, and them which work iniquity, are by them bound up in bundles, and cast into the fire. All this is the angels' office. Why should we think the service of the angels should cease, until the whole scene of the resurrection be finished?

Yea, to determine our dubious thoughts, we hear the Lord of the harvest giving charge to his reapers, which are none but angels, not only to reap the wheat, but to carry in the sheaves into his barn; I will say to the reapers, gather the wheat into my barn! Behold, this is the angels' office; their work is not done till the good corn is housed.

This, in the metaphor of the marriage of the Lamb, is nothing else but the angels' attendance on the saints, the Lamb's wife, while she is making ready; that when she is arrayed in fine linen, clean and white, they may then take her up in their winged arms, and conduct her in state to the place where her royal Bridegroom is staying for her. Rev. xix. 7, 8.

(3.) The spirituality and power wherewith the bodies of the saints are endowed in the resurrection, may well concur also to this ascension.

By virtue of that marvellous spirituality and agility, wherewith the resurrection shall, if I may so say, invest the saints' bodies, they shall be able to mount upward, and move with admirable celerity up and down, to and fro in the air; as swallows in a sun-shine day dart themselves through the sky; or as the angels themselves, who with equal facility descend and ascend with a motion as swift as their wills.

In the resurrection, indeed, the saints were purely passive, as passive as when their bodies were first formed out of the dust, and had the breath of life breathed into them. But now in their ascension they shall be active and agile. Moved, indeed, they shall be, by an extrinsic power; why else are they said to be caught up into the air? But yet not so, but that they may move themselves by an intrinsic principle; else those supernatural affections of their re-animated bodies might seem to be superfluous and insignificant, 1 Cor. xv. 42—44. Suitably to this it is related of Elijah's ascension, a prophecy and figure of this universal translation of the saints, that although a chariot of fire parted him and Elisha, yet he went up by a whirlwind into heaven : he was carried, and yet he went up; so the saints, &c.

Thus I have showed the probability, at least, of a threefold medium in the saints' ascension.

This concurrence of mediums is no other than we meet with in the ascension of our Lord in his own person. For of the Lord Jesus himself, after his resurrection, it is said, " He was taken up," or lifted up, Acts i. 9; the phrase may import the power of the Father, as formerly, in raising him up from the dead. So, now also, in lifting him up into glory, according to that, Acts v. 31, " Him hath God exalted with his right hand:" here is the power of the Father in the Son's ascension. And then you have the subserviency of second causes added ; first a cloud is prepared, as a royal chariot, to carry up this King of glory to his princely pavilion ; " A cloud received him out of their sight." And then a royal guard of mighty angels surround the chariot, if not for support, yet for the greater state and solemnity of their Lord's ascension ; he was " carried up into heaven," Luke xxiv. 51.

Yet notwithstanding all this, it is said of the Lord Jesus, he went up, while the disciples looked stedfastly towards heaven, Acts i. 10. He went onward, or he went upward; as implying that his motion was not only passive, but active: he mounted up into heaven by his own Divine power; he ascended. Behold, here we have a perfect pattern of the saints' ascension in all the mediums of it; they hold exact proportion with their Lord. The Father lifted up the Lord Jesus; the Lord Jesus, he lifts up his saints. A cloud received him; the saints also are caught up in the clouds. Angels attend upon their Lord in his ascension; nor do they refuse their attendance on the saints in their ascension. Jesus Christ, notwithstanding, ascended by the power of his own glorified person : the saints likewise ascend by virtue of those supernatural properties wherewith their bodies are adorned in the resurrection.

The Lord Jesus, from his throne, shall call them up by a powerful voice : "Come up hither." Clouds shall be their chariots and horses to carry them. And yet they shall ascend upwards by a supernatural principle, spontaneously, and of their own proper motion.

While, in the mean time, the whole world of reprobate men and angels shall be left below upon the earth, looking upward and gnashing their teeth, to see such a sudden and tremendous turn of things : the saints, whom they despised and persecuted, snatched out of their reach, and ascending in so much pomp and royalty to meet their glorious Redeemer; they themselves being left behind with a certain looking for of judgment and fiery indignation, which shall devour the adversaries. Then shall begin their weeping, and wailing, and gnashing of teeth, which shall never have an end.

Use 1. In the first place, this subject may serve as a cordial to the saints of God; whether in reference to their own dissolution, or the dissolution of their gracious relations already fallen asleep.

Behold! the descent of the saints of God into the grave, is not with so much weakness, ignominy, and abasement, as their ascent after the resurrection, to meet their Lord in the air, shall be with power, triumph, and glory. Christ shall draw them; clouds shall carry them; angels shall conduct them. Yea, they shall mount up to heaven, by virtue of those Christ-like impressions stamped upon their glorified bodies in the resurrection. Each one of these were sufficient. All these must needs be exceeding glorious! Yet such honour have all the saints!

Use 2. There is caution in it, as well as comfort; and that is, begin this ascension betimes. Labour to experience this heavenly motion on this side of the grave. " Lift up your heads, O ye gates, and be ye lift up, ye everlasting doors." Behold the resurrection and ascension in the future state of happiness, have their spring and rise in the present state of holiness; they are linked in, and joined one to another, in the eternal counsel and purpose of God; with the very same connexion wherewith harvest and seed-time are linked together. So that, look what impossibility there is in nature, that there should be a harvest where there was no seed-time; the same impossibility there is that such a person should share in the resurrection of glory, that is a stranger to the resurrection of grace, the new birth , or that a man or woman should ascend to meet Jesus Christ in the clouds, who in a supposed state of regeneration, labours not often to meet Christ in the mount of holy meditation. " If therefore ye be risen with Christ, seek those things which are above, where Christ sits at God's right hand; set your affections on things above," Col. iii. 1, 2.

Christ, after he arose from the dead, did often ascend to his Father, till, at the end of forty days, he went up to heaven in the sight of his disciples, Acts i. 9, 10. Do ye also imitate your blessed Lord, in your frequent ascensions after him; and thereby evidence to yourselves, not only that you are already risen with Christ, in the resurrection of holiness, but that ye shall also arise with him, and ascend to him at his coming in his glory.

Christians, let not that man think ever to be caught up to meet the Lord in the air, who is content with being a stranger to Christ in the Spirit, without God in the world, and without hope, Eph. ii. 12. He burieth his hope of ascending where Christ is, who burieth his heart and affections in the dunghill of worldly and sensual fruitions. Oh labour to say with the apostle, Though our abode be on earth, " our conversation is in heaven, from whence we look for the Saviour," Phil. iii. 20. Though ye walk below, yet we live above. Though ye use the world, yet labour to enjoy God, and to be able to say with holy David, " Whom have I in heaven but thee? and there is none upon earth that I desire beside thee," Psa lxxiii. 25. Though ye have your converse with men, let your communion be " with the Father and with his Son, Jesus Christ," 1 John i. 3. Labour to say with Augustine, Our bodies are on earth, our hearts in heaven: while the men of the world earthlize heavenly things, do you study how to heavenlize earthly things : labour, as he did, to eat and drink, and sleep, eternal life.

So may you, with a holy confidence, go along with

the apostle, from whence we look for the Lord Jesus. Christians can no further look for the Lord Jesus to descend from heaven, than as they themselves, in the mean time, labour to be often ascending with him into heaven. Heavenly-mindedness is the saints' evidence, and first-fruits of their heavenly blessedness.

3. The saints' joyful meeting, and it is twofold; 1. One with another; 2. With Christ their head. The one is implied, the other expressed.

(1.) The saints' meeting one with another, is implied in this adverbial particle, together, " We shall be caught up together with him ;" that is, we which shall be found alive upon the face of the earth at Christ's coming; together with them which being fallen asleep before, of elder or later time, Christ hath now raised up out of their graves; " We and they, shall all be caught up together," &c.

The scripture takes notice of the saints' meeting one with another, as distinct from their meeting with the Lord Jesus; " The elect shall be gathered together from the four winds, from one end of the heavens to another," Matt. xxiv. 31. At what distance soever they were dispersed and scattered, they shall all meet together into one distinct body, or assembly; and then co-ascend, to meet their Lord. Some of the schoolmen apply that passage of the prophet, " They shall mount up with wings as eagles," Isa. xl. 31, to this ascension of the saints after the resurrection. Whether that be so or no; we may not incongruously suppose, the elect of God to be gathered together into some one vast capacious tract or region of ground on the right hand of the judgment-seat, from thence to take their flight together to meet the Judge in the air.

Use 1. This universal gathering together of the
saints in total separation from the wicked may be improved as a threefold ground of comfort. In case of
undue mixtures of saints and sinners, whether in
church assemblies or in civil societies. How far
either of them may be lawful, is not an inquiry proper
for this place, sure I am much in both is unavoidable.
A total separation from impure society in either, may
well be the object of our wishes, but it cannot be of
our hope; while we are in the world we may separate
from church to church, we may remove from country
to country, rove up and down from the one end of the
world unto another, but, the apostle tells us, we must
go one step further, if we will avoid the society of
sinners; " then, must ye needs go out of the world."

Yea, but here is the comfort, and it is the signal
use our Lord makes of this very doctrine; the
time is coming when a thorough separation shall be
made; under that double parable of the seed and
the net, Matt. xiii. In the one the tares grow up
with the wheat, ver. 26. In the other, all kinds
of fishes are gathered, good and bad, ver. 47.
Concerning the former, the servants of the house-
holder were offended at it; it grieved them at the
heart to see the weeds growing, yea, and it may
be, overgrowing the good corn, and so hinder-
ing the maturing of it, ver. 27. They make
their addresses to him for a present separation,
and offer their faithful service for an utter eradication
of the tares : " Wilt thou that we gather them up?"
ver. 28. Nay, saith the lord, a total extirpation
of the tares, may do more hurt than ye are aware
of, ver. 29. Better, it seems it is, that some tares
should remain, than that the least grain of wheat to
perish : the distinguishing time is at hand ; in the

time of harvest I will give order to the reapers for a perfect separation.

Yes, christians, be of good cheer, the time is coming when impure mixtures will no more be a temptation to the saints of God, for ever. Saints and sinners shall no more be burdensome one to another. The seed of the serpent shall no more be an offence to the seed of the woman, but there shall be a perfect separation. The sheep shall be separated from the goats, the elect from the reprobate; there shall not be a servant of the Lord amongst the worshippers of Baal, nor a son of Belial among the sons of God; sinners and none but sinners, saints and none but saints, shall make up these two distinct congregations. Nay, so terrible will the glory which Christ will put upon his saints be, upon the faces of the reprobates, and so great the horror of their own guilty consciences, that they shall now as much dread their society, as once they hated it, and choose rather to leap alive into the burning lake, than to mix themselves unto them, or so much as to put their head within that holy assembly.

Use 2. This circumstance of the gathering together saints, and their total separation from the wicked, is improved for comfort, by our Lord Jesus Christ himself.

In case of undue exclusion from church ordinances, of such as Christ would not have excluded. Our Lord Jesus hath foretold, that the power of the keys should fall, sometimes, into such hands, as would so diametrically pervert the use of them, as that ofttimes none should be excluded, but whom Christ would have admitted; nor admitted, but such as Christ would have shut out.

" They shall put you out of their synagogues,"

John xvi. 2 ; that is, excommunicate you : you,
my disciples; you, my friends.   Hard measure!
but here is comfort ; the time is coming, wherein all
the elect shall be congregated into one universal assembly; never to suffer exclusion or ejectment any
more to all eternity. And then their unrighteous
excommunicators shall be righteously excommunicated ; yea, they shall be excommunicated with the
highest sort of excommunication, higher than any
church of Christ ever used, excommunicated for
ever ; delivered unto Satan, not for the destruction of
the flesh only, but to be punished with everlasting
destruction from the presence of the Lord, and from
the glory of his power ; " When he shall come to be
glorified in his saints," 2 Thess. i. 9,10. That is a
dreadful excommunication indeed ; the anathema
maranatha in the highest sense.

Now, the saints of God are glad to get into corners
by twos and by threes, and blessed be God, not
without a promise to seek the face of God ; but in that
glorious morning of the resurrection, they shall
meet by millions and myriads of millions, Jude 14 ;
and there shall be none to disturb or offend them ;
yea their enemies shall look on, and gnash their teeth
for anguish and vexation of spirit, to see them now
got for ever out of their power.

Use 3. And lastly, this universal gathering together of the saints may serve for comfort in case of
the saints' separation one from another, whether by
the unrighteous hand of violence, or the righteous
hand of providence.   Now, by means of dispersion,
imprisonments, exile, &c. the people of God are like
arms and legs torn out of the body, and lie bleeding in their separations.*   Yea, God himself is
* Referring to the days of persecution for conscience sake. *Ed.*

pleased to make sad breaches between them and their sweetest relations by death; under which they are many times like Rachel, weeping for her children, and refuse to be comforted, because they are not; lifting up their voices and crying, Oh! my father Abraham, and oh! my son Isaac. Oh! Absalom my son, my son Absalom, would God I had died for thee. I will go down to the grave to my son, mourning, &c. But here is comfort; the time is coming when the parent and child, husband and wife, friend and friend, with the whole family of heaven and earth, from all their dispersions, from the utmost part of the earth, to the utmost part of heaven, shall meet together, and embrace one another; everlasting joy shall be upon their heads, and sorrow and mourning shall flee away.

In a word; how may all the saints of God, in what state or condition soever for the present, solace themselves in the anticipation of the triumphant gathering together of the elect of God! What a joyful sight will it be, when all the saints and servants of the most high God, which ever saw one another's faces, or heard of one another's name; yea, and all they which never saw or heard of each other. All of every tongue, nation, kindred or family of the earth, of what age, sex, generation soever, from the day wherein God made time, to the day wherein time shall be no more, shall meet together, and stand on tip-toe, ready to take their flight, to meet their Lord and Bridegroom, coming in the clouds with his mighty angels! Yea, what a glorious sight will it be, to see all the glorious company of the apostles, the goodly fellowship of the prophets, the whole army of martyrs, with the holy church throughout all the world!

A congregation of kings and priests in all their royal robes; yea, as I may so say, a congregation or constellation of morning stars, yea of so many noon-day suns, arising from the earth, ascending together through the several regions of the air, to meet the Sun of righteousness, now descending from his own orb of supreme glory and majesty in the highest heavens, to judge both the quick and the dead! Surely such an assembly eye never saw, ear never heard of, nor can it enter into the heart of man to conceive, how immense, how august, how exceeding, it will be in glory!

(2.) The saints' meeting with Christ their Head, to meet the Lord in the air. Notice,

[1.] The persons meeting; Christ and his saints. He descends to meet them, and they ascend to meet him. Such is the love and condescension of the Lord Jesus to his saints, that he cometh out of his royal pavilion more than half way to meet them; and then sends his chariots and horsemen, a guard of angels, to carry them up in the clouds, and to con-duct them unto the place, where he stayeth for them. There shall they be brought into his royal presence, and like a royal spouse, who hath been long separated from her bridegroom by distance of place, they shall fall down before him, and with tears of joy shall wash his feet, and wipe them dry with the kisses of their lips; while, at the same time, Christ will take his bride up into his arms, and, with the father of the prodigal, fall upon her neck, and kiss her; and with all the inconceivable expressions of love and joy, receive her to himself, and bid her welcome into his presence. Oh! what soul can conceive what mutual joy and triumph there will be between Jesus Christ and his saints in this blessed interview!

Oh how welcome will the saints be to the Lord
Jesus at that day, when he shall look upon them
under a threefold relation!

1. As the Father's election : to see the whole
number of names which were given unto him by the
Father, from all eternity, as the fruit and reward of
his passion, John xvii. 6, now all gathered together, and given into his actual possession, as an
inheritance for ever, Eph. i. 18.

2. As the purchase of his own blood. If it was a
satisfaction to the Lord Jesus, when he was in
the throes and agonies of his travail with them
upon the cross, to see his seed, when they were but
in the swaddling clothes of their imperfect regeneration, Isa. liii. 11, according to their successive
generations, wherein they were to be brought into
the church ; oh what infinite satisfaction will it now
be to the Lord Jesus, to see the travail of his soul in
their perfect and consummate estate ; all the mixtures of corruption and infirmity now removed, and
they come to a perfect man, to the measure of the
stature of the fulness of Christ! to see them all
brought in ; not a soul wanting of all those whose
names he bare upon his breast, while he hung upon
the cross ! that not one drop of blood, not one prayer,
not a sigh, or groan, or tear, that ever he spent for
them, in the days of the flesh is lost or fruitless, as
to any one soul whom he purchased of the Father!
In the pastoral charge of Christ, there was one
" son of perdition," John xvii. 12 ; but in his mediatorial charge, not one soul shall miscarry ; but
all shall be presented to him safe and entire, at his
appearance. And over them shall he glory, saying,
as it were, All these are mine, the travail of my
soul, the purchase of my blood, the fruit of my

I

agonies; for these I was born, and for these I was
made under the law; for these I bled, and for these
I made myself an offering for sin. " Father, I will
that they also whom thou hast given me, be with me
where I am, that they may behold my glory, which
thou hast given me," John xvii. 24. Come near
unto me, my sons, and my daughters, that I may
kiss you. See, the smell of my redeemed is as the
" smell of a field which the Lord hath blessed,"
Gen. xxvii. 27.

3. As the charge of the Holy Ghost. Whom the
Father did elect,the Son was to purchase ; and whom
the Son purchased, the Spirit was to sanctify. Who
therefore is called the Holy Ghost, not only because,
as the third glorious person in the blessed Trinity, he
is essentially holy in himself; but because, by office,
ne is a fountain of holiness to all the elect. The
blood of Christ indeed is the fountain of merit ; but
the Spirit of Christ the fountain of operation and
efficacy ; gathering the elect out of the world, wherein
they lay, in common with the rest of the lost sons
and daughters of Adam ; planting their souls with
the habits of grace, which are therefore called the
" fruits of the Spirit," Gal, v. 22, 23, and then supporting, preserving, and ripening those habits into
perfection.

Thus will the Lord Jesus, the King of glory, rejoice to meet the saints. And surely the saints, according to their finite capacity, will not less rejoice
and triumph to meet their Lord. Oh ! to meet him
now, whom their soul loved; whom in the days of
their pilgrimage, they often sought and could not
find ; and when they could not find him, mourned
for him, lamented after him ; bedewed their cheeks
with tears ; asking solicitously of every one they

met, " Saw ye not him, whom my soul loveth ?"
I say, to meet him, now on the throne of his glory;
of whom, could they have had but a glimpse in a
glass darkly, in the evangelical ordinances, their
souls would have made them " like the chariots of
Amminadib," Can. vi. 12. To see him, whom having
not seen they loved; and in whom, though they
then saw him not, yet believing, they rejoiced with joy
unspeakable and full of glory! I say, now to see
him, and so to see him, as to have a full sight of his
unveiled face, shining more gloriously than ten thousand suns at noon-day! Once more, so to see him,
as never to lose the sight of him to all eternity. How
will this transport their souls with unspeakable ex-
tasies of joy, which will cause them to break forth
into triumphant hymns, yea, and to call to their now
fellow angels, to help them with their celestial hallelujahs!

[2.] The place of meeting, and that is, in the
air. We shall be caught up to meet the Lord in the
air; that is the place where Christ stays for his
saints. There, they meet him ; and there, this great
assize will be held. The Judge shall sit upon the
throne, and all the saints shall be placed on bright
clouds, as on seats or scaffolds round about him.

If it be demanded, Why this solemn meeting
must be in the air? it may suffice for answer, The
Lord Jesus hath made choice of this place. Surely,
it is the prerogative of this great Judge of the quick
and the dead, to appoint the place where he will
hold this last and tremendous judgment. And we
may well acquiesce in the choice, not only because
his will is the sovereign law of the creature, but as
his infinite wisdom hath judged it the place most
convenient for the design.

I 2

Ana yet, if it be lawful to make our conjectures, where scripture is silent, we may humbly suppose this twofold account of it. 1. The capacity of the place. 2. The conspicuity of the judgment.

1. The capacity of the place : vast, and, as to us, infinite will be the numberless numbers of those that shall meet in this universal assembly. " Behold, the Lord will come with ten thousands of his saints," Jude 14 ; yea " thousand thousands minister unto him, and ten thousand times ten thousand stand before him," Dan. vii. 10 ; all the saints that slept in Jesus from the creation of man, and all the saints which are found alive upon the earth at Christ's coming, must all appear before the Lord Jesus. And besides these, the Judge cometh with his royal satellites, his officers of state, myriads and legions of angels : " All his holy angels," Matt. xxv. 31. There shall not be an angel, as it were, left in heaven. Jacob met two hosts or camps of angels of God, in his travel, Gen. xxxii. 1, 2. Our Saviour mentions more than twelve legions, Matt. xxvi. 53 ; which as a commanded party, would have been, in an instant, sent out for his rescue, if there had been need. What an infinite army of angels must it needs be then, when all the angels come in Christ's train! " An innumerable company of angels!" Heb. xii. 22. And all these must not appear in confused heaps and multitudes, but in their distinct ranks and order ; and the saints are to sit in order, in their several degrees round about the throne. Now the place had need be of a vast extent and circumference, that will suffice to receive and contain such variety of multitudes. So that even in this respect, no place so fit for this august and solemn convention as the air, for its vast extensiveness and capacity.

2. Much more in respect of conspicuity, that so, the Judge and judgment, with all the assessors and attendants, might be more eminently visible from heaven above to the earth beneath, that the whole process of this general assize may be heard and seen by all, good and bad, elect and reprobate, heaven and hell. Heaven would be too high, the earth would be too low; the smoke of the bottomless pit would obscure this glorious vision. The air, where is no interposition of hills and mountains, and now, serened and brightened by the confluence of so many glorious suns, will render this last tremendous transaction visible and audible to every creature. Behold, he cometh with clouds! Clouds which will not obscure him, but bright clouds, which, filled with the beams of his glory, shall render him most visible and conspicuous. So it is prophesied, " Every eye shall see him," &c. Rev. i. 7; Matt. xxiv. 30. Thus it shall be, and this will make for the exceeding glory and majesty of the Judge.

[3.] The ends of this meeting; and the ends why the saints ascend to meet Christ in the air, we may conceive to be such as these :

1. Their public reception and owning by Christ.

2. Their full and perfect justification.

3. The consummation of their nuptial contract.

4. Their confession, or sitting together with Christ in the judgment.

5. Their complete and final benediction, or blessed sentence.

6. Their solemn and triumphant attendance on the Judge, going to take possession of the kingdom.

These, or the like, ends of the saints' meeting with the Lord in the air, are not obscurely hinted to us in scripture.

1. Their public reception and owning by Christ. The elect angels having gathered together the elect saints, according to the commission upon which they were sent forth, " Go ye and gather my saints together unto me ; those that have made a covenant with me by sacrifice," and having carried them up into the air, where the Judge stayeth for them; I say, their angels shall now present them before Him, in the rich and glorious attire of their perfected resurrection ; wherein their once vile bodies are now made like to Christ's glorious body. With gladness and rejoicing shall they be brought into the King's presence ; and the first public act which the King shall do, is solemnly to receive them, " Come ye blessed of my Father ;" and embracing them in his arms, and kissing them, as it were, as Joseph once did his brethren, in the open view of heaven and earth.

He will solemnly own them, and acknowledge them in their persons and relation unto himself ; a prerogative long before promised, " They shall be mine when I make up my jewels," Mal. iii. 17. That is the very work which Christ is now come about ; to make up his jewels, to lay them up in their heavenly cabinet. And the first word he will speak, is, " These are mine ;" he appropriates them for his own ; they are mine, my jewels, my gems, my precious treasure. As the saints have not been ashamed of Christ before men ; so neither will Christ now be ashamed of them before his Father, and all his mighty angels, Luke ix. 26. He will not be ashamed to call them brethren, Heb. ii. 11 ; yea, he will appropriate them as his children ; a seed given him of his Father, as the great reward of his passion ; saying, These be the children which God has given me, ver. 13; my sons and my daughters, who have served me; thus he owns them in their relations.

He will own and acknowledge all the holy duties, public and private, which they have done in obedience to his commands. Their hearing, praying, fasting, and afflicting their souls for their own sins, and for other men's sins; their fearing of God, and laying to heart the reproaches of religion, and blasphemies cast upon his name; their mutual holy conferences, one with another, all these were written in a book of remembrance of old, Mal. iii. 16, and laid up before him, that they might never be forgotten; and now the book shall be brought forth, and read in the audience of the world, for their greater honour: even the very secret duties which they have performed in their closets, when no eye saw them but God's; even they shall be proclaimed in the audience of this universal assembly at the last day. Thy Father which saw in secret, will now reward thee openly, Matt. vi. 6. Not a prayer, but it was filled up; not a sigh, nor groan, but it is booked; not a tear, but is bottled; not a holy ejaculation, but was upon record, and shall be now publicly produced and acknowledged, Psa. lvi. 8. " I know your works, and charity, and service, and faith, and your patience, and your works; and the last to be more than the first," Rev. ii. 19.

Jesus Christ at that day will own the fidelity of his saints, their constancy and perseverance in their holy profession, and confess them before all the world. " I know your works, and where you have dwelt, even where Satan's seat was, and you have held fast my name, and have not denied my faith, even in those days wherein Antipas (Cranmer, Ridley,

Latimer, &c.) was my faithful martyr, who was slain among you, where Satan dwelleth," Rev. ii. 13; behold! to you who have been faithful to the death, do I now give a crown of life, ver. 10. To you who have overcome, " do I grant to sit with me in my throne, as I also overcame, and am set down with my Father in his throne," ch. iii. 21.

He will own and acknowledge the saints, in their sufferings for his sake. All the reproaches, hard speeches, incivilities, abuses, scandals, persecutions, whichever they sustained in their names, persons, livelihoods, and lives, upon Christ's and the gospel's account, he will acknowledge; and bespeak them in some such language as he once encouraged his disciples in the days of his flesh; " You are they which have continued with me in my temptations, and behold, I appoint unto you a kingdom, as my Father hath appointed unto me; that you may eat and drink at my table, in my kingdom," &c. Luke xxii. 28—30.

Also, the Lord Jesus will own all the services and offices of love done to himself, or to any of his members; clothing, feeding, visiting them when sick, coming to them when in prison; he will acknowledge all before heaven and earth: yea, what they themselves have forgotten, never thought worthy of their own notice, much less of Christ's notice; " Lord, when saw we thee an hungred, and fed thee; or thirsty, and gave thee drink ? " &c.

All this shall be proclaimed in the audience of that general assembly; " Forasmuch as ye have done it to one of these little ones, ye have done it unto me," Matt. xxv. 40; yea, those very acts of charity, which have been done so secretly, that the left hand did not know what the right hand did,

Matt. vi. 3, shall be now published upon the house-top, the great house of heaven and earth. They were not so closely done, but they shall as openly be rewarded; the book of God's remembrance shall be brought forth and opened, and publicly read, that all the good which any of the saints of God ever did, may be mentioned to their everlasting praise.

Observe, as a circumstance of signal honour, that, in that large recital which shall then be read of the saints' lives, there is not the least mention made of sin; they had, sure enough, the remainders of their original corruption surviving their conversion, defiling and molesting their most holy services; which were as so many scourges in their sides, and thorns in their eyes, incessantly tempting them, and exposing them to temptation; forcing from them sad laments and outcries; "O wretched man that I am, who shall deliver me?" Rom. vii. 24. They had, and not rarely, their actual surprises and seductions, their lapses and relapses, which brought them upon their knees with holy Job's confession, "I have sinned, what shall I do unto thee, O thou Preserver of men?' Job vii. 20, but none of these things come up into remembrance against them in that day. As, here below, God saw no iniquity in Jacob, nor perverseness in Israel, to impute it to them: so, in their appearance before the Judge, God remembereth no iniquity against the saints, to charge it upon them, or to reproach them with it. In the petty sessions which Christ held with some of his saints and churches here on earth, amongst their commendations, there were some exceptions; and some faultinesses were charged upon them, an "howbeit," 2 Chron. xxxii. 31, a "nevertheless," ch. xxxiii. 17, as abatements of their excellences. "Nevertheless,

I have a few things against thee," Rev. ii. So in
the process against the church of Ephesus, ver. 4,
" nevertheless ;" a " but" against Pergamos, ver. 14,
against Thyatira, ver. 20, a " notwithstanding," &c.
But now in the judicial process of this last and universal assizes, there is not found in all those volu-
minous records, which shall be opened, so much as
one unsavoury " but" to blemish the fair characters of
the saints : as if (even before they got into heaven)
they had obtained that privilege, to be, just men
made perfect ! This is very wonderful.

Had reprobate men and angels had the drawing
up of the report of the saints' lives, what a black
bill of indictment would they have preferred against
them ! to be sure, all the evil which they ever did
in their whole lives, with all their blackest aggravations, should have been raked up, and produced
against them. Yea, if the saints themselves had
been trusted with giving in the history of their own
lives, they would not have dealt much more kindly
by themselves, than the seed of the serpent would
have done ; to be sure, if there were anything worse
than other, they would not have concealed it ; vili-
fying the good, and aggravating the bad, as some
times they were wont to do in their desertions, even
beyond truth and justice, as if Satan had hired them
to belie themselves : but now the righteous Judge of
heaven and earth is far from dealing so with them :
but, as if he himself had never known any evil by
them ; he brings in his presentment, all fair and
well, and so it is proclaimed in that high court of
justice.

Another circumstance of honour in Christ's acknowledgment of the graces in, and duties performed by his saints, is, that although their graces

were nothing else but so many drops of Christ's own fulness, and their duties so many operations of his own Spirit in them; nothing theirs, but the very act of believing, and the act of repentance, and the act of love to Christ, and the act of prayer; yet Christ is pleased to ascribe all the praise, and all the glory, both of their graces and duties, unto the saints, as if not only the act itself, but the principle also, from whence they acted, had been their own. This is truly wonderful! here is the breadth and length, depth and height of the love of Christ, which passeth knowledge, Eph. iii. 18, 19.

Oh, how will it fill the saints with amazement, while they are secretly accusing themselves, with Joseph's brethren, We are utterly guilty concerning our brother, our lord and elder brother, I say, to hear the Lord himself not charging them with the least unkindness; yea, representing them before God, men and angels, even, as it were, as immaculate as the angels themselves, who kept their first estate; yea in all this, putting the crown upon their heads, Rev. iv. 10, which they cast down at his feet, saying, Not unto us, O Lord, not unto us, but unto thy name, give the glory. Behold such honour have all the saints!

2. I come now to a second end of the saints' meeting with Christ in the air, and that is their full and final justification.

They shall receive public absolution. Pardon of sin is the privative part of justification; imputation of righteousness is the positive part. Pardon, or remission, is the sinner's justification from sin; both from the guilt of sin, and from the sentence or punishment due to sin. " By him, all that believe are justified from all things, from which they cannot

be justified by the law of Moses," Acts xiii. 39
This now must be one branch of the solemn justification of the saints at their meeting with the Lord
Jesus in the air; as a Judge, he shall fully and
finally, in open court, absolve the saints from all
their sins, both guilt and punishment, from which
there was no absolution ever to be expected by the
covenant of works.

Sin enough there was, for which God might sentence all the Jacobs in the world to condemnation;
and cast all the Israels that ever were, into the
bottomless pit; but it is gone, it is forgiven; pardon
makes such a clear riddance of sin, that it is as if it
had never been; the scarlet sinner is as " white as
snow," Isa. i. 18; snow newly fallen from the sky,
which was never sullied: the crimson sinner is " as
wool," wool which never received the least tincture
in the dye. Here is the reason why, when the iniquity of Israel is sought for, there is none; and the
sins of Judah, and they are not to be found: " For I
will pardon them," &c. Jer. l. 20. Yea, not forgiven only, but forgotten; and should they now be
remembered? Jer. xxxi. 34. The Judge had long
since cast their sins behind his back; and he will
not now surely set them before his face, Isa. xxxviii.
17; he had cast them into the depths of the seas
(bottomless depths of everlasting oblivion) that they
might be buoyed up no more for ever: yea, the
Lord Jesus nailed all their sins to his cross, Col. ii.
14, and buried them all in his grave; yea, and
crossed the debt-book with the red lines of his own
blood, Rom. iii. 25. If now he should call them to
remembrance, to charge the saints with their sins,
he should undo what he had done; he should cross
the great design of his cross, upon the matter, deny

himself to be risen again from the dead, and disown his own hand and seal! Rom. iv. 25. Upon this foundation stands the absolute impossibility that sin, the least sin, the least circumstance of sin, should be so much as once mentioned by the Judge, in the process of that judicial trial, unless it be in a way of absolution; and so sin shall be mentioned indeed, but in order to the magnifying of their pardon and absolution.

The saints shall then be fully and finally absolved in their own consciences. It is true, there are some of the saints even in this life, to whose consciences the Spirit of God doth evidence and seal up remission of sin; who are not only safe, but sure; and possess not only the blessedness of a pardoned estate, but the comfort and assurance of that blessedness: nevertheless, not all the saints, nor any at all times, nor always in the same degree. They have their dark times, their eclipses, as well as their transfigurations; and no wonder, since the Sun of righteousness himself suffered an eclipse upon the cross so dreadful, as forced the great master of astronomy in Egypt to cry out, Either the God of nature suffers, or the whole frame of nature is dissolved; and caused the Lord Jesus himself, to the just astonishment of heaven and earth, to cry out, "My God, my God, why hast thou forsaken me?" Is it any wonder then, if many of the poor saints of God, like Paul and his shipwrecked company, see neither sun-light nor star-light for many days together; and no small tempest doth often lie upon them, so that all hope of being saved is taken away? Acts xxvii. 20; yea, not a few precious deserted Hemans are there, who from their youth up are afflicted and ready to die, and while they suffer the terrors of

K

God, are distracted, Psa. lxxxviii. 15 ; yea, and that which is more tremendous, their sun, as to any observation which standers by could make, though very rarely, hath set in a cloud.

But now, at this blessed day, the Judge of the quick and the dead shall absolve the saints of God, not only at the tribunal of his own justice, but at the tribunal of their conscience ; he will proclaim that name in their bosoms, which he proclaimed before Moses, The Lord, the Lord God, merciful and gracious, long-suffering, abundant in goodness and truth ; pardoning iniquity, transgression, and sin, &c. And he will speak so audibly, that every saint shall hear the voice ; and so particularly, that every one shall know he speaketh to him ; and shall all echo back again with joy and joint acclamation, " Who is a God like unto thee, pardoning iniquity ? " &c. Micah vii. 18.

Also, the saints are then said to receive their full and final absolution ; because then their absolution shall be proclaimed in open court ; the Judge in person shall pronounce their absolution in the audience of God, and all the elect angels, and of the whole world of men and devils. What Christ, in the days of his flesh, said to one poor trembling penitent, he will now say to all, Sons and daughters, be of good cheer, your sins are forgiven you : this will be good cheer indeed. These are the times of refreshment from the presence of the Lord, when the sins of the saints shall be blotted out, Acts iii. 19. Blotted they were before out of God's book ; but now they shall be blotted out in the sight of all the world ; so that now, indeed, Who shall lay anything to the charge of God's elect ? since heaven and earth, yea, and hell itself must be witnesses to the crossing of the book, and to the cancelling of the bond; wherein they stood obliged to Divine justice! Oh, what inexpressible, inconceivable refreshment will this be to the saints of God! even the perfecting of all their former refreshments! The sense of their pardon pronounced by the Spirit, tc some of their consciences within, was wont to be exceeding sweet; yea, any scriptural hopes of pardoning mercy, though apprehended by a weak and trembling hand of faith, were a reviving to their drooping spirits; what must needs then the highest plerophory,* ratified by the most solemn proclamation of the great Judge, (before the upper and nether world, as well as to conscience,) be, but life from the dead? Surely it will be even heaven, before the saints come to heaven! Nor shall any reflection either upon sin or sorrow, ever damp that joy any more; nor shall willow-boughs mix with the palms of the saints' triumph in that blessed jubilee; but joy shall be upon their heads, and sorrow and sighing shall flee away.

The second branch of the saints' justification, is, that the Judge will pronounce them perfectly righteous.

This may seem superfluous, as supposed to be included in the sentence of absolution. Not to be a sinner, seemeth to imply a saint; to be pardoned all sin, and all the degrees of sin, and all kinds of sin, omissive as well as commissive; all defects of perfection, all want of conformity to, as well as transgression of the law of God, this seemeth to be perfection.

It doth seem so, and truly it doth but seem so; for pardon relates to what is past only; "remission

---

* Full persuasion.

K 2

of sins that are past," Rom. iii. 25; it is but a freedom from guilt, and a freedom from punishment; it doth not suppose any real and positive righteousness, which may set a man perfect before the tribunal of God's justice.

If a scholar in the university be a candidate for an office there, or a fellowship in a college, where the statutes do require such and such qualifications, and upon examination, he be found not guilty of murder, or sacrilege, or any other crime, this will not capacitate the candidate for the preferment: this is the case in hand. The saints are now candidates for heaven and glory, and absolution or pardon is not sufficient to capacitate them for this glory. Before he can be so capacitated, he must be constituted perfectly righteous.

The person under the notion of not guilty, is an absolved person, and acquitted from hell and eternal damnation. And, as under the notion of righteous, he is capacitated for heaven and life everlasting: not guilty relates to freedom from hell; righteousness relateth to heaven as the proper qualification thereof. Do this, and live; though, where the one is, there is the other, yet the one is not formally the other.

And according to these two capacities and places, there are two great works which the Redeemer did undertake for the redeemed: the one to make satisfaction for sin to Divine justice by his blood, that is, by his death; the other, to yield most absolute conformity to the law of God, both in nature and life.

By the one, we may conceive the redeemed freed from hell and everlasting burnings; by the other, we may conceive them qualified for heaven and everlasting glory.

Interested in this twofold work of Christ, we

may suppose the believing sinner appearing at the tribunal of the great God, pleading his righteousness, and pronounced righteous in the court of Divine justice. Thus the sinner is brought in, as it were, in a way of judicial process, Isa. xlv. 24, holding up his hand at the judgment seat, the Judge on the bench bespeaking him thus : Sinner, thou standest indicted for breaking the holy, and just, and good law of thy Maker, and hereof art proved guilty; sinner, what hast thou to say for thyself? &c. Rom. iii. 9. To this the sinner, upon his bended knee, confesseth guilty ; but withal, humbly craves leave to plead for himself full satisfaction made by his Surety: " It is Christ that died," Rom. viii. 34. and whereas it is further objected by the Judge : But, sinner, the law requireth an exact and perfect righteousness in thy personal fulfilling of the law ! Sinner, where is thy righteousness ? The believing sinner humbly replieth, My righteousness is upon the bench ; in the Lord have I righteousness ; Christ my Surety hath fulfilled the law on my behalf, to that I appeal, and by that I will be tried : this done, the plea is accepted as good in law. The sinner is pronounced righteous, and goeth away glorying and rejoicing ! Righteous, righteous ! " In the Lord shall all the seed of Israel be justified, and shall glory," Isa. xlv. 25.

How does the prospect of being pronounced perfectly righteous through the imputation of the positive righteousness of Christ, tend to the settling of solid peace in the conscience of the believing sinner ! That justification by faith is the aptest medium to establish solid peace in the bosom of a poor sensible sinner, may appear by comparing works and faith together. Send a poor sinner to his own righteousness, which is of the law, his own good works, holiness, fasting, prayer, or the best service that ever he did for God, they can afford him little ground of confidence; alas! hence his fears, and doubts, and diffidence do arise: his prayers need pardon, his tears need washing, his very righteousness will condemn him, Job x. Here is no place for the sole of his foot to stand upon. "If thou, Lord, shouldst mark iniquity, O Lord, who shall stand?" Psa. cxxx. 3. This was that which scared Paul from coming to the law for justification. Why, saith he, "I through the law am dead to the law," Gal. ii. 19; which denotes, I seek not to the law for justification and life; the law may thank itself; I come to the law for justification, and it convinceth me of sin; I plead my innocence, that I am not so great a sinner as others are; I plead my righteousness, my duties, and good meanings, and good desires; and it tells me, they are all too light; the best of my duties will not save me, but the least of my sins will damn me, Job ix. 20, 21. It tells me, mine own righteousnesses do, as filthy rags, defile me, and my duties themselves do witness against me. I plead repentance, and it laughs me to scorn: it tells me, my repentance needs pardon, and my tears need washing. Besides, if they were ever so good, what careth it for my repentance? It looketh for my obedience, perfect and personal, which, because I have not, it tells me, I am cursed, and pronounceth sentence; and when it hath so done, it hath no mercy at all for me, though I seek it carefully with tears. What can I expect from so severe a judge? I will come no more to that tribunal: behold, I appeal to the gospel; there repentance will pass, and tears will find pity; there imperfect obedience will find acceptance, though not to justification; there, there is a better righteousness provided for me; an exact, perfect righteousness; as perfect as that of the law; for it is, indeed, the very righteousness of the law; though not performed by me, yet by my Surety for me, the Lord my righteousness. Here is a foundation for the feet of my faith to stand upon; here I can have pardon of all my debts, though the law will not abate me one farthing; here are long white robes, though I never spun a thread of them with my own fingers. To this tribunal will I come, and here will I wait for my justification; if I perish, I perish.

Here, may an objector say, is foundation for presumption to stand on; here is a bed for security to sleep in; here is a doctrine to send men merrily to hell; while they break the law, to tell them, there is one that hath fulfilled it for them; while they sin, Christ hath righteousness enough to justify them. Surely this is a doctrine that makes God not only the justifier of sinners, but the justifier of sin too: so disputed the free-will men of former times against the apostles; and so the free-will men of our times against us: but, for answer:

First, the apostle disclaims the consequence with a vehement negation; God forbid any one should be so impudent to force such a scandalous conclusion upon such immaculate premises.

Secondly, he shows the reason of it; and the reason is taken from the new covenant, wherein God hath inseparably joined the merit of Christ's cross and the power of Christ's cross together; insomuch, that whosoever hath a share in the merit of his cross for justification, hath also an interest in the power of his cross, for mortification: he instanceth in himself, Gal. ii. 20, "I am crucified with Christ;" which denotes, while, through grace, I appeal to the merit of Christ's death for my justification; I can also, through grace, evidence my appeal to be scriptural, by the power of the cross, whereby the "world is crucified to me, and I to the world," Gal. vi. 14.

And as it is with me, so it is with all truly justified persons; for, they that are Christ's, have crucified the flesh, with the affections and lusts thereof, Gal. v. 24. They have crucified them, and they do crucify them; they are upon the cross, and, with their Lord and Redeemer, refuse to come down, till they can say with him, "It is finished;" therefore, let the scandal of the cross and of justification cease for ever.

The sinner hath an indispensable necessity of such a righteousness to his justification, as for the securing of his appearance in the day of judgment. The great apostle, who had as fair a show for a legal justification as any other in the world, protesteth he dares not think of appearing without this positive righteousness in the last and dreadful judgment; but, oh that I may be found in him, not having mine own righteousness, which is of the law, Phil. iii. 9. In him, in Christ, not in myself; in his mediatorial righteousness, not in mine own personal righteousnesses: away with them, they are but filthy rags; rotten rags in comparison with Christ's robes. Give me the righteousness which is of God by faith, of God's ordination, and of faith's application.

And then again, how does this way of justifying believing sinners before the great tribunal exalt the infinite excellency of our glorious Redeemer, set forth, Heb. vii. 26: " Such a High Priest became us," saith the apostle, " who is holy, harmless, undefiled, separate from sinners, made higher than the heavens."

And as such a High Priest became us, so, truly, such a way of justifying believing sinners became him; namely, it was becoming a person of such transcendent worth and excellence, to justify his redeemed in the most ample and glorious way, &c.; by working out for them, and then investing them with, a righteousness adequate to the law of God; a righteousness that should be every way commensurate to the miserable estate of fallen man, and to the holy design of the glorious God. It was a becoming thing, that the second Adam might restore as good a righteousness as the first Adam lost; that this should justify as fully as the other did condemn. This is the very design of that famous parallel instituted by the apostle between the two Adams, Rom. v. 15—21; namely, to signify an equality, not of number in the persons receiving, but of efficacy in the persons deriving, and communicating what was their own to either of their seeds. The first Adam to his natural seed, and the second Adam to his spiritual seed; to the end that men and angels might take notice, that Jesus Christ, the second Adam, was not less powerful to save, than the first Adam was to destroy. To which purpose it is of great use to observe how exact the apostle is, in setting the specialties of either Adam's legacy one over against the other; the wound and the cure, the damage and the reparation.

Observe the parallel, in Romans v. 15—21,

The first Adam propagates his	The second Adam obtains
Offence.	Forgiveness for many offences.
Guilt.	A gift of righteousness, 17.
Death, ver. 15.	Life, ver. 18.
Condemnation.	Justification, 18.
Bondage, slavery.	Reigning in life.
Sin, ver. 19.	Righteousness.

Every way the salve is as sovereign as the wound was mortal; the cure as vital as the sickness deadly.

Thus it became our High Priest to justify his redeemed ! The great apostle cannot pass it by without special notice; " He is able to save them to the uttermost that come unto God by him," Heb. vii. 25. To the uttermost of what? To the uttermost obligation of the law, preceptive as well as penal; to bring in perfect righteousness as well as perfect innocence : to the uttermost demand of Divine justice; perfect conformity to the Divine will, as well as perfect satisfaction to Divine justice: to the uttermost indigence and necessity of the lost creature; qualification as well as absolution : to the uttermost of our High Priest's perfection, in whom dwelt all the fulness of the Godhead bodily.

Oh, for such a one to have saved a cheap way, to drive the purchase to as low a price as might be, by pardoning their sin, and making reparation to Divine justice; to satisfy for the wrong which man had done to the Creator and his law ; this only, with reverence may we speak it, had not become so august a Redeemer as the Son of God was. But, to set him upon his legs again, to make him as good a man as he was in his created perfection, such as all the attributes of God should acquiesce in; to put him into a capacity of demanding eternal life, not by gift only, but by merit, through a Redeemer; yet so still, as it is the Redeemer's merit, not man's: not that Christ hath merited, that we might merit, (as the papists would vainly varnish that proud doctrine of merit;) no: all was done by him, and is ours only by imputation.

Such a High Priest became us; and such a glorious way of saving sinners became him, who was made higher than the heavens; that is, than all created perfections whatsoever, angels, cherubim, or seraphim, or whatever order else may be possibly conceived.

This is the righteousness wherewith our Redeemer saveth us, and we need not fear to wrap up ourselves in this fine linen, to put on these robes; we need not fear to be made too rich by Christ, who, " when he was rich, became poor, that we through his poverty might be made rich," 2 Cor. viii. 9.

And this righteousness, indeed, was made over to the saints of God by imputation, at the very first moment of their conversion. In this they lived; in this they died, as standard-bearers wrapt up and buried in their colours: and in this they shall arise and appear at that glorious appearing of the great God, and our Saviour Jesus Christ, who will then, and thus, be glorified in all them that believe, to the admiration of all the elect angels, the extreme horror of the reprobate, and the infinite joy and rapture of the saints; who shall then sing, " I will greatly rejoice in the Lord, my soul shall be joyful in my God: for he hath clothed me with the garments of salvation, he hath covered me with the robe of righteousness; as a bridegroom decketh himself with ornaments, and as a bride adorneth herself with her jewels," Isa. lxi. 10.

Oh how glorious will Christ be in his saints, when they shall all wear one and the same sparkling livery with Christ! and this shall be his name, Jehovah Tzed-kenu, "The Lord our righteousness," Jer. xxiii. 6.

3. The third end of the saints' meeting with Christ in the air, is, the solemn consummation of the saints' nuptials with Christ their bridegroom. They were contracted here on earth, when Christ and the saints gained one another's consent; Jesus Christ did then solemnly espouse the saints to himself; " I betrothed thee unto me for ever, yea, I betrothed thee unto me in righteousness, and in judgment, and in loving kindness, and in mercies; I even betrothed thee unto me in faithfulness," Hos. ii. 19, 20. Indeed, the church in herself, when Christ came to make love to her, was a very unlovely creature, whose emblem, therefore, is a poor wretched infant in the blood of its nativity. But Jesus Christ did first love her with a love of pity: " I saw thee polluted in thine own blood," Ezek. xvi. 4. 6. I saw thee, that is, I cast an eye of pity upon thee, my bowels yearned towards thee; and then, as loveless as she was, that he might have a legal right to her, he purchased her of his Father; he purchased her at a dear rate, for he gave himself for her, Eph. v. 25. Christ gave himself *for* her, and then he gave himself *to* her. They were wont to buy their wives of the father of the damsel; but never did husband buy a wife at such a rate as the Lord Jesus did the church. Shechem bid fairly for Dinah, Jacob's daughter; " Ask me never so much dowry and gift, and I will give ac-

cording as ye shall say unto me," Gen xxxiv. 12.
Jacob served seven years for Rachel, as it fell out,
twice over; yea, but the Lord Jesus gave himself for his church; he purchased it with his own
blood, Acts xx. 28. That he might love it with
a love of complacency, he doth sanctify it, and
cleanse it, by the " washing of water by the word,"
Eph. v. 26. As he doth purchase the church with
his blood; so he doth purify the church by his Spirit,
compared to water for the cleansing virtue thereof,
in the ministry of the word. Christ and his church
like one another so well, that they mutually engage
and contract themselves one to another; they do
mutually give away themselves, one for, and one to
another; " My beloved is mine, and I am his,"
Cant. ii. 16.

This was the wedding unto which John was in-
vited; " Come hither, I will show thee the bride,
the Lamb's wife," Rev. xxi. 9. He that had the
bride was the Bridegroom, the Lord Jesus, King of
kings, &c.; but John, the friend of the Bridegroom,
stood and rejoiced greatly to hear the Bridegroom's voice, John iii. 29; then indeed was his
joy fulfilled. At the consummation of this spiritual
union between Christ and his saints, what inconceivable triumph and rejoicing will there be ! The
loud music of heaven shall sound, the voice of mighty
thunderings, all the angels, cherubim, seraphim,
with all the blessed quoir of celestial spirits, who
attend this glorious King of saints, shall praise God
with the music of their hallelujahs; yea, all the
saints of God, whether patriarchs or prophets, and
apostles, all the martyrs and confessors of Jesus
Christ, with the whole number of the redeemed, who
are both guests and bride in this glorious solemnity

will make the arches of heaven to echo, when they
shall be joyful in glory, and the high praises of God
shall be in their mouths, singing one to another,
" Let us rejoice and be glad, for the marriage of the
Lamb is come, and his wife hath made herself
ready," Rev. xix. 7. The gates of hell, and the
very foundations of the kingdom of darkness, shall
tremble, and be confounded at the report of this triumphant jubilee.

4. This sacred solemnity finished, the next act in
that solemn meeting will be, that the Bridegroom
will take the queen his bride, and set her upon his
throne, at his right hand, as an assessor with himself in the following part of the judgment, which he,
as Judge, shall pass upon the reprobate world of
men and devils. They all this while stand trembling below upon the earth, beholding, to their infinite shame and horror, all this glory put upon the
saints ; and fearfully looking for their own judgment, and that fiery indignation which shall devour the adversaries, which now succeeds. For
the elect angels, who are appointed to attend the
Judge, shall now drag that miserable company of
prisoners, those reprobate caitiffs of infernal spirits,
and wicked men, before the tribunal of the great
Judge; there they shall pass under a most impartial, exact, and severe trial; the books shall be
opened, the book of God's remembrance and the
book of their own consciences, Mal. iii. 16, and out
of them they shall be judged for all the evils which
ever they committed from the time they first had a
being in the world. The reprobate angels shall then
be judged for their first apostasy ; and for all their
malice and revenge, which since that cursed defection, they ever acted against God, and against his

saints; yea, and against the precious souls of men,
which, they being damned themselves, ceased not to
draw into the same condemnation. " The angels
which kept not their first estate," or principality,
" but left their own habitation, he hath reserved in
chains under darkness, unto the judgment of the great
day," Jude 6. With these chains rattling at their
heels, shall they be dragged to the bar of Divine
judgment; and there, having received their dreadful
sentence, they shall be hanged up in chains, in the
midst of unquenchable flames to all eternity. But
first they shall have a just and a fair trial. And as
the reprobate angels, so the reprobate world of ungodly men and women, shall be judged for all the
wickedness done in the body. For the sin of their
natures, for they " were by nature children of wrath,"
Eph. ii. 3 : and for their actual sins, for as they were
children of wrath, so also they were children of disobedience; they shall be judged for their atheism,
whether secret, by which, as fools, they have said in
their hearts only, " There is no God," Psa. xiv. 1 ;
or open, whereby, as proud blasphemers, " they have
set their mouth against the heavens," Psa. lxxiii. 9,
saying, " How doth God know? and Is there knowledge in the Most High ? " ver. 11. Who through the
pride of their countenance, would not seek after
God, yea, contemning God, said concerning all this
wickedness, and that to God's face, " Tush, thou
wilt not require it," Psa. x. 4. 13. But that judgment shall fully convince the atheist; and he that
would not believe a God, shall know him by the
judgments which he executeth. Then shall the
idolater, whether pagan or romish, or of what other
impression soever; the blasphemer of God's name,
whether by prodigious oaths, or by lighter taking his

name in vain; the profaner of the sabbath, who
violateth that holy day of God, by work or sport,
either by sinning or idling out that holy time, eithei
by writing against the sabbath, or by living down
the sabbath; the disobedient to fathers or mothers,
natural or political; the murderer, the adulterer, the
thief, the false accuser, the covetous, whom God
hateth; all these, I say, in what degree of wickedness soever, even to every idle word, Matt. xii. 36,
and every vile, yea, vain thought, which, with
David, Psa. cxix. 113, they have not hated, shall
be judged out of those books.   The gospel-sinner
shall then be brought to the bar, to answer for
his unbelief, impenitency, his rejecting of Christ's
yoke, his despising the tenders and offers of free
grace; his ignorance of, and disobedience to, the
gospel, shall then be judged: the " Lord Jesus is
now revealed from heaven, with his mighty angels,
in flaming fire, to take vengeance on them that know
not God, and obey not the gospel of our Lord Jesus
Christ," 2 Thess. i 7, 8. All the persecutions, whether
by the mouth of the sword, imprisonment, banishment, martyrdom, &c.; or by the sword of the
mouth, revilings, scandals, false accusations, cruel
mockings of proud sinners; now, they shall be all
charged upon the world of ungodly men, whether
out of the church or in the church.   " Behold the
Lord cometh with ten thousand of his saints, to
execute judgment upon all, and to convince all that
are ungodly, of all their ungodly deeds, which they
have ungodlily committed, and of all their hard
speeches, which ungodly sinners have spoken against
him," Jude 14, 15, whether his person or members.
Every sin, with all the circumstances and aggravations; yea, omissions shall then be reckoned to

those who thought themselves safe, because they were not gross and scandalous sinners, Matt. xxv. 42, 43 : men shall be judged for their *nots ;* yea, for defects and coming short in the manner of duties, as well as the matter, Mal. i. 14. Formality and hypocrisy shall then come into open view. In a word, all the world of ungodly men, that have sinned, and not repented of their sin, shall be judged at Christ's tribunal, and every man, according to the light and law under which he hath lived ; " As many as have sinned without law, shall perish without law," Rom. ii. 12. Heathens shall be judged by the light of nature ; and as many as have sinned in the law, shall be judged by the law ; and they that have sinned under the gospel, shall be judged by Jesus Christ according to the gospel. Yea, they that sin against the gospel, shall be judged by the light of nature, by the law of Moses, and by the gospel too, as having not only sinned against Moses' ink, but against Christ's blood. And all these trials will be severe, but especially the trial in the gospel-court ; so that whereas sinners flatter themselves with thoughts, that trial by the gospel will be the easiest trial, as if the gospel were all mercy ; the trial of the gospel will be found to be the most severe, and above all others intolerable. It was indeed a gospel of mercy, and a gospel of peace, in the tenders, and invitations, and expostulations, and wooings, and beseechings, that were used ; the tears of the ministers, and the blood of a crucified Redeemer, while once the long-suffering of God waited in the day of grace. But all these are now past and gone, having been rejected, despised, and laughed to scorn by wretched, proud sinners ; who, with the bloody Jews, preferred a **Barabbas** before a Jesus; a base lust before a precious Saviour: now is the time of recompense come, the day of vengeance from the presence of the Lord is come, and the sinner shall know it. The terror of which day will further appear in these following particulars.

(1.) There will be no denying of any matter, small or great, that shall be charged upon those guilty malefactors. By the mouth of those two witnesses, the book of God's remembrance, and the book of conscience, shall every branch of the indictment be established. The one of these books was kept before the face of the Lord continually, so that the great accuser himself, nor any of his malignant agents, could get in thither to alter or add to any thing upon record in that sacred register; and the other book, the book of conscience, was in the sinner's own keeping, and who could break in there to interline it? Indeed, the sinner wrote down many sins there with the juice of a lemon, but the fire of the day of judgment will make it legible; he wrote them with the point of an onion, but God wrote them with a pen of iron, and with the point of a diamond, in deep and durable characters, that should never be erased out of the conscience of a sinner. Now these two books will agree so exactly, like two tallies, one with another, that it will be impossible for the sinner to deny any particular, but he will be self-condemned.

(2.) As there will be no denying, so there will be no room for extenuation; this was one of the sinner's hiding-places while in the land of the living. Sinners now have their buts; it was but thus, and thus, it was but a little one, &c. Great sins were but small sins; and small sins were no sins. Now,

the sinner will have no such sanctuary to fly unto :
the account will now be inverted; those that were
no sins before, will be sins now; small sins will be
great sins, and great sins will be infinite. The last
judgment will give sin its just proportion. That
which the law could never do, though it were given
on purpose, the fire of the day of judgment will
effectually do—make sin appear exceeding sinful.
The carnal protestant will then find, to his cost,
there is no such thing as a small sin; because then
he will be convinced there is no small God, against
whom sin is committed; no small law, whereof sin
is the violation; no small Christ, whom sin hath
crucified; no small heaven, which sin hath forfeited;
no little hell, which sin hath merited, and by its
merit, hath now justly plunged him into for ever.

(3.) There will be no putting off of sin upon
others, as here below there was; the thief enticed
me, the drunkard seduced me, the harlot deceived
me, the serpent beguiled me, Gen. iii. 13: yea,
what bold sinners are not afraid to speak will not
then be heard amongst the malefactors at Christ's
bar; God tempted me, or God decreed it, Jas. i. 13.
No; these, and all other palliations and colours,
wherewith men do wash the face of sin, will melt
before the fire of the day of judgment. God will say
to the sinner, " Hast thou not procured these things
to thyself?" Jer. ii. 17. Yea, sinners shall then
own their own guilt, and confess that their destruction is of themselves: their heart shall cry out, as
Apollodore dreamed his heart cried to him in a caldron of boiling lead, O Apollodore, I am the cause
of this vengeance; how have I hated instruction, and
my heart despised reproof, and have not obeyed

the voice of my teachers, nor inclined mine ear to them that instructed me !

(4.) There will lie no appeal from this tribunal. Once, there lay an appeal from Moses to Christ, from the law to the gospel; but proud sinners scorned it, or securely presumed they had made the appeal by a loose verbal application of Jesus Christ; whilst yet they trusted in themselves and their own foolish presumptions, their serving of God, their good works, and their good meanings, and their good desires; and, why should not they be saved as well as others? But now, if they should appeal, their appeals, with themselves, will be cast out as reprobate silver. This is now the supreme and last judicatory; from hence is no appeal; once doomed here, the sentence is irreversible for ever.

(5.) Neither is there any pardon to be expected at this judgment-seat. Pardons were tendered in the gospel upon gracious terms, but ungracious sinners would have none of them, or would have them upon their own terms—sin and pardon too: their pardons were nothing unless they might have dispensations; but now the time of pardon is out; the day of grace is expired; no cries nor entreaties will prevail with the Judge: no, though the sinner would fall upon his knees, and weep as many seas of tears, as once the ministers wept tears of compassion over them; or as Christ himself shed drops of blood upon the cross. Christ was once upon his knees, in the person of his ministers, beseeching them to be reconciled, 2 Cor. v. 19, 20. Though the sinner was first in the transgression, yet God was first in the reconciliation; and followed the sinner, entreating him to accept of mercy, as if God had stood in as

much need of the sinner, as the sinner did of mercy;
but nothing would prevail, a deaf ear was still turned
to Christ's importunity, and now repentance is hid
from the eyes of the Judge, as once repentance was
hid from the eyes of the sinner. The things of their
peace are everlastingly hid, because they knew them
not in that the day of their visitation. As sinners
hardened their hearts against Christ's voice, so
Christ will harden his heart against the sinner's
cry, Prov. i. 24.

(6.) There shall be no mitigation of the punishment; not a farthing abated of the whole debt,
Matt. v. 26.   There was once mercy without judgment, before the sinner; now there shall be judgment without mercy: now sinners shall know that
God is not mocked, that the Lamb of God is also
the Lion of the tribe of Judah. His voice was once,
" Fury is not in me," Isa. xxvii. 4; now the voice will
be, Meekness is not in me, mercy is not in me.
Now must the sinner expect nothing but the utmost
severity of Divine justice, who once despised the
yearnings of Christ's bowels, the lowest condescen-
sions of Divine grace; the sinner in his day, knew
no moderation in sin, the Judge now in his day, will
know no mitigation of judgment; there will be a
sea of wrath, without a drop of mercy.

(7.) Not a word of any good that ever the wicked
did, shall now be mentioned to their honour or advantage: as none of the sins which ever the saints
committed, were mentioned to their shame in their
process; so none of the good that ungodly sinners
have done, shall be once named, unless it be by way
of aggravation of their sins.   The scripture tells us,
these woful wretches will be ready there, to plead
for themselves their duties and services which they

have done for Christ, as vile as they are, as they did
in the days of their flesh, " We have fasted, they
said, we have afflicted our souls," &c. Isa. lviii. 3 :
so now also in the day of judgment; false apostles,
and scandalous ministers will then be so bold as to
plead their preaching in Christ's name, and that,
possibly, not without success; " Lord, we have prophesied in thy name, and in thy name cast out
devils;" peradventure even to the work of conversion.
Judas might cast out the devil, and yet himself be a
devil, John vi. 70; he might convert others, and yet
be unconverted himself. They will plead their doing
of miracles, healing the sick, and raising the dead,
making the blind to see, and the deaf to hear, and
the lame to go, and in Christ's name have done
many mighty works, Matt. vii. 22. Likewise, loose
christians and formal professors, will then also plead
for themselves, their hearing sermons, and receiving
sacraments, &c.: take it in their own language,
" We have eaten and drunk in thy presence, and
thou hast taught in our streets," Luke xiii. 26;
their external familiarities with Christ in the assemblies of the saints, their common gifts and graces;
anything then that hath but the likeness of grace
upon it, Christ shall hear of it.   But all in vain;
the Judge, whose eyes are a flame of fire to search
the hearts and the reins, Rev. ii. 18. 23, will reprobate their persons and performances with an " I
know you not," Luke xiii. 25; and again, with
greater emphasis, " I tell you, I know you not,"
ver. 27; yea, once more with a more dreadful note
of abhorrence, " I never knew you," Matt. vii. 23;
I never approved of you, nor of any of your services,
which ever you performed from the first to the last;
but my soul hated both you and them.

(8.) There will be no begging further time of the Judge; no adjourning the trial to another assize-day. That court knows no reprieve; the sinner's trial, and sentence, and execution go all together: the day of patience was out in the other world; I gave her space to repent, and she repented not, and now the Judge swears in his wrath, that sinners shall never enter into his rest.

(9.) No days-man to intercede with the Judge. God will not; he "will laugh at their calamity and mock when their fear cometh," Prov. i. 26. Oh dreadful calamity, which God will stand and laugh at. Angels will not; and to which of the saints will those miserable sinners turn themselves? Job v. 1. They are upon thrones round about the Judge, but quite to other purposes than to become advocates to those guilty malefactors, as will soon appear.

(10.) Therefore, the Judge shall proceed to the last acts of judgment, which are two; first to pronounce them guilty of all the treasons and misdemeanours which those wretches have been indicted of. The Judge indeed, to vindicate the justice and equity of the court, will demand of the convicted sinner, whether he hath anything to say for himself, why he should not receive judgment to die, and sentence to be executed according to law? But now conscience shall speak impartially between the Judge and the sinner, justifying the Judge, and condemning the sinner; who having beforehand received in himself the sentence of death, shall now be without excuse, not able to make the least apology or defence on his own behalf, Rom. ii. 20, but shall confess before that formidable assembly; Lord, though thou judge me to everlasting flames, yet thou dost me no wrong, but art justified in what thou speakest, and clear when thou judgest, Psa. li. 4. And alas! what a miserable thing is this, that all the time that the sinner and his conscience dwelt together under one roof, and conscience would fain have spoken out, the vile wretch should stop the mouth of his own conscience, and never suffer it faithfully to do its office, till now, when it will do him no good, and tend to no other end but to justify God, and to aggravate his own condemnation! Oh that sinners would seriously consider this, and lay it to heart in time, and hearken to the secret whispers of conscience before it be too late; and deal kindly with conscience now, that conscience may deal kindly with them in that day, when one good word from conscience will be worth a thousand worlds. Oh if the sinner would have done that once willingly, which now he doth whether he will or no, if he would have judged himself in the day of the gospel; it might have prevented this fatal judgment now, he should not have been judged of the Lord, 1 Cor. xi. 31. Oh if the Judge would now speak such a word to the convicted multitude of reprobate cast-aways, as once he did to wretched sinners! Behold I make you this offer, that, if yet before I proceed to sentence, you will unfeignedly judge yourselves, I will not judge you, neither shall the sentence of condemnation pass upon you. Oh, what an uproar of joy would there be among those miserable sinners! how would they down on their knees, and judge themselves worthy of a thousand hells, and be content to suffer a thousand years torment, to expiate their guilt! But though they would do this, and (if it were possible) ten thousand times more, no such word shall ever be spoken to them by the Judge; their time of sinning is past, and their time of being judged is come; and, though they do now really judge themselves, yet the Judge will proceed to judge them also. The sinner having thus justified the Judge, the Judge shall now condemn the sinner out of his own mouth; and solemnly setting himself down in the judgment-seat, shall openly in the court proclaim the sinner guilty; guilty of the whole indictment preferred against him; and then proceed to pronounce sentence in some such words as these: Sinner, thou hast been indicted, arraigned, and convicted of high treason, against the Supreme Majesty of heaven, in the breach of his holy law, and in contempt of his blessed gospel, trampling the Son of God under foot, Heb. x. 29, and crucifying him over and over again, and putting him to an open shame, &c. ch. vi. 6. Hear now therefore thy sentence; thou art accursed for ever; the wrath of God abideth upon thee, thou shalt not see light; go, thou cursed into everlasting burnings, " prepared for the devil and his angels," Matt. xxv. 41. And what shall be said to one, shall be said to all, " Depart from me ye cursed, into everlasting fire, where the worm never dieth, and the fire is not quenched; into outer darkness, where is weeping, and wailing, and gnashing of teeth, there to be tormented with the devil and his angels for ever."

Now during all this tremendous transaction, the saints shall sit in judicature as assessors, or justices of the peace, with Christ upon the bench, seeing and hearing all that is done by the Judge; voting with him, approving and applauding him in his judicial proceedings, crying out with loud acclamations, " Thou art righteous, O Lord, which art, and wast, and shalt be, because thou hast judged thus:" and other saints shall echo to them, saying,

M

" Even so Lord God Almighty, true and righteous are
thy judgments!" Rev. xvi. 5. 7.   Thus the saints
shall judge the world, 1 Cor. vi. 2, yea, they shall
judge the angels, the reprobate angels.

5. I come now to the fifth end of the saints'
meeting with Christ, namely, to receive their complete and final benediction.   " Come ye blessed of
my Father, inherit the kingdom prepared for you
from the foundation of the world," Matt. xxv. 34.
A blessed sentence indeed, every word in it is heaven
before the saints come to heaven.

" Come," my love, my dove, my undefiled one,
stand no longer at a distance, come and follow me,
whither I go: I will that where I am, there you
may be also.

" Ye blessed;" blessed with all spiritual blessings
in heavenly places.   Your enemies on earth accounted you the filth of the world, and the offscouring of all things, 1 Cor. iv. 13.   Satan hath
desired to have you, that you might be accursed
with him for ever; but ye are blessed, and shall be
blessed for ever.

" Blessed of my Father," blessed in the eternal
electing love of the Father: blessed in the Son's
purchase; you have washed your garments white in
the blood of the Lamb: blessed by the laver of
regeneration, and renewing of the Holy Ghost,
Tit. iii. 5.

" Inherit;" ye are children, heirs, heirs of God,
joint-heirs with Christ; behold, I have adopted
you to be fellow-heirs with myself, and the Father
hath made you meet to be partakers of the inheritance of the saints in light.   O come now and take
possession of your inheritance, behold it is not less
than a

" Kingdom," for it is your Father's good pleasure to give you the kingdom, Luke xii. 32; the kingdom of heaven, the kingdom of glory. Behold it is " Prepared," in the Father's decree; God hath laid it out for you before the foundation of the world was laid; and it is prepared by my purchase, and by my taking possession of it long since in your name: I went before " to prepare a place for you," John xiv. 2.

" For you," whom I also prepared for it; and for every one of you personally, every one of you shall receive an entire kingdom to yourselves, and you shall live and reign with me for ever and ever. As heaven hath been kept for you, so you have been kept for it, by the power of God, through faith to salvation, 1 Pet. i. 5. O come now and take possession! Behold, this is the saints' full and final benediction!

I should have spoke to this before I spoke of the sentence passed upon the reprobate; for in our Lord's method it doth precede, Matt. xxv. 34, compared with ver. 41; yet because execution of the sentence begins with the wicked, and ends with the godly, as ver. 46, to the end that the saints may behold with their eyes the sentence executed, and seeing they may (as God himself doth) address them, saying, " Lo these are the men that made not God their strength, but trusted in the abundance of their riches, and strengthened themselves in their wickedness," Psa. lii. 7; I have, I say, therefore chosen to speak of the sentence of blessedness, which the Judge shall pass upon the saints, in this place, that from thence I might pass immediately to the happy execution thereof upon them, nothing intervening as to the persons of saints, which is the

6. Sixth and last end of the saints' meeting with Christ in the air; namely, their solemn and triumphant attendance on the Judge, to take possession of the kingdom. This last judicial process being thus solemnly finished, sentence on both sides pronounced by the Judge; the reprobate already dragged away by the executioners of Divine vengeance, to the place of execution, where they shall be tormented with the devil and his angels for ever and ever; immediately the bench will rise, the court shall be broken up, that great assembly shall be dissolved, and forthwith the Judge shall ascend, his majestic chariot waiting ready for him; and all the saints shall follow him in their wedding-garments, glittering as the sun in his meridian glory, upon their several chairs of state; all the holy angels of God attending round about them, with their ensigns of glory flying, trumpets sounding, angels singing, the saints themselves shouting, all the regions of the air resounding with their celestial harmony, the like whereunto never entered the ear of man, from the day wherein God laid the foundations of the heaven and earth, to this happy moment. In this triumphant posture shall they march, till they come to the walls of the New Jerusalem, where the gates of pearl—to whom it shall be proclaimed, " Lift up your heads O ye gates, and be ye lifted up ye everlasting doors, and the King of glory shall enter in,"—shall stand wide open to receive them; an entrance shall be administered unto them abundantly into the everlasting kingdom of our Lord and Saviour Jesus Christ; through the streets whereof, which are of pure gold, as it were transparent glass, they shall ride in triumph, till they come to the throne of his Majesty, where " the Ancient

of days sitteth, whose garment is as white as snow, and the hair of his head like pure wool; his throne is like the fiery flames, and his wheels as burning fire," &c. Dan. vii. 9, 13. Then shall the Son of God come to him, and taking his new bride in his hand, shall present her to his Father, and bespeak him in some such language as this : " These are they which come out of great tribulation, who have washed their robes white in my blood ; these are they which have kept the word of my patience; these are they that overcame by my blood, and by the word of their testimony.   Thou gavest them me out of the world, thine they were, and thou gavest them me ; and they have kept thy word.   While I was with them in the world, I kept them in thy name ; those that thou gavest me, I have kept, and none of them is lost but the son of perdition, that the scriptures might be fulfilled.   I have given them thy word ; and the world hath hated them, because they were not of the world, even as I was not of the world. O righteous Father, for these I opened my mouth, and for these I opened my sides and my heart; for these was I mocked and scourged, and blindfolded, and buffeted, and crucified ; for these I wept, and sweated, and bled, and died.   Father, I will that they whom thou hast given me, may be with me where I am, that they may behold my glory which thou hast given me; for thou hast loved me before the foundation of the world," &c. Rev. vii. 14 ; iii. 10 ; xii. 11 ; John xvii. 6, 12. 14. 24. &c.

Then shall the Father rise from his throne, and say unto them, Come near unto me, my sons and my daughters, that I may kiss you: see, the smell of my children is like the smell of a field, which the Lord hath blessed.   Then shall he call for crowns

to put upon their heads, and bracelets upon their
arms, rings upon their fingers, palms of victory
and sceptres of royalty into their hands, and appoint
them their several thrones; the mansions which their
Lord went before to prepare for them; upon which
they shall be placed, that they may sit, and live, and
reign with Christ, their heavenly Bridegroom, for
ever and ever; everlasting joy shall be upon their
heads, all tears shall be wiped from their eyes, and
sorrow and mourning shall flee away.   And so shall
they ever be with the Lord.

X. I come to the tenth and last word of comfort, the
saints' blessed cohabitation and fellowship with the
Lord; " so shall we ever be with the Lord."   This
consequence of Christ's coming is the perfection and
crown of all the rest; cohabitation, and fellowship
with the Lord, together with the extent and duration of it.

Now cohabitation, or being with the Lord, containeth four glorious privileges. I. Presence. II.
Vision. III. Fruition. IV. Conformity.

I. The first privilege which being with the
Lord implieth, is presence.   The saints, after their
triumphant reception by Christ into his glory, shall
ever be where he is.   The scriptures abound with
expressions of this nature; appearing in God's presence, Psa. xlii. 2; Col. iii. 4; standing before him,
Luke xxi. 36; abiding in his tabernacle, dwelling
in his holy hill, Psa. xv. 1; yea, dwelling in him, and
he in us, sitting upon his throne, and following
of him wherever he goes, John xvii. 24, and xiv. 3.
Rev. xiv. 4, and i. 5, 6.   A glorious privilege certainly; for it is the purchase of Christ's blood, the
fruit of his prayer, and one of the great ends of his
coming in person at the end of the world, that his

saints may be where he is; dwell in his family, be as near him, as rationally they can desire; ever stand before him, 1 Kings x. 8, and enjoy uninterrupted fellowship with him. If the queen of Sheba accounted it the happiness of Solomon's servants, that they might stand continually before him, and hear his wisdom; how much rather may we proclaim them happy, thrice happy, whose feet may stand within the gates of the New Jerusalem; for behold, a greater than Solomon is here, even he, of whom the psalmist sings, " In thy presence is fulness of joy, and at thy right hand are pleasures for evermore," Psa. xvi. 11,

II. Another privilege is vision. The saints shall not only be where Christ is, but they shall enjoy the beatifical vision; they shall see and behold that, which the seeing and beholding of will make them blessed for ever.

Now there are six beatifical objects in heaven; 1. The seat and mansions of blessed souls. 2. The glorified saints. 3. The elect angels. 4. The glorified body of the Lord Jesus. 5. God in the Divine essence. 6. All things in God.

1. The first vision which the saints shall see, is the seat or habitation of blessed souls, the mansions of glory, which our Lord hath purchased for his redeemed, and which he went before to prepare for them, John xiv. 2 ; the third heavens, 2 Cor. xii. 2, the palace of the great King. A glorious place certainly, for therefore it is called paradise, Luke xxiii. 43, 2 Cor. xii. 4, and Rev. ii. 7, to set forth the beauty and pleasantness of the situation ; that as the paradise wherein God put man in his innocency, was the beauty and delight of the whole nether world; so heaven, the place which God hath prepared for man

restored to perfection, is the beauty and glory of all the upper regions, the top and perfection of the whole creation. Behold, the outside of this stately palace is very glorious, beautified, and adorned with all those bright and glittering luminaries, the sun, moon, and stars; what think you is the inside? Consult that description which the Spirit of God hath made of it in the Revelation. Surely, heaven will as much exceed the description of it in glory, as the bodies of the saints in the resurrection shall exceed in beauty these vile bodies of ours, when they are resolved into dust and rottenness. What shall I need say more? Heaven is a place as beautiful and glorious as the wisdom and power of God could devise to make it, that it might be the royal palace of his own residence. That august and magnificent fabric which the proud Babylonian tyrant stood boasting over, " Is not this great Babylon that I have built, for the house of the kingdom by the might of my power, and for the honour of my majesty?" Dan. iv. 30, was but a prison or hovel in comparison of this building of God, " that house not made with hands, eternal in the heavens," 2 Cor. v. 1. Those words are proper only for the mouth of God; Is not this the New Jerusalem which I have built for the house of the kingdom and for the glory of my majesty? What David spake of the temple, that little type of heaven, " The house that is for the Lord must be exceeding magnifical of fame and of glory," &c. must be infinitely more august and magnificent in the antitype; this the glorified saints shall behold, and it will, beyond conception, be marvellous in their eyes.

2. They shall see the glorified saints, all the elect of God that ever were in the world, from Adam until the second coming of Jesus Christ. It is a

glorious sight to see the king, and all his peers and nobles in their parliament robes, with crowns and embellishments of honour, sitting in their state and order; this is a sight which every one covets and crowds to see. What then will it be to see the King of saints, with all the redeemed ones of God in their robes, washed white in the blood of the Lamb, and crowns of gold upon their heads, and palms of victory and triumph in their hands! a parliament all of kings and priests, every one of them shining forth " as the sun, in the kingdom of their heavenly Father," Matt. xiii. 43. The sun when it breaks forth out of a cloud, and displays its refulgent beams in full lustre and brightness, what a glorious creature is it! and with what a beauty doth it gild and adorn the world! O my soul! what a sight will that be when I shall see a heaven full of suns, scattering their rays of glory through all those celestial regions! There is another scripture which makes the glory of this vision yet more splendid and radiant, every one of the glorified bodies of the saints shall be made conformable to Christ's own glorious body, Phil. iii. 21. The glory of the Father shines forth in the Son, and the glory of the Son shall shine forth in the saints; he in his Father's glory and they in his Surely the luminaries of the first magnitude in the visible heavens, the sun and moon, will be turned into darkness before the glory of this vision. They shall shine as so many Christs in the kingdom of their Father, that will be a glorious vision indeed! And then too, the communion and converse with the saints in heaven will be as sweet to the taste as the vision of them will be glittering to the eye; there will be heaven in both. Behold! their fellowship and converse here was so sweet that David could say,

All my delight is in the saints that are in the earth, and in the excellent ones, Psa. xvi. 3. David could take no pleasure in the company of any in the world, but only in God's holy ones, who were beautified with his image. Oh what will their communion and fellowship, think you, be in heaven, when they shall be totally divested of all their sinful corruptions and natural infirmities; when there shall be such a perfect harmony amongst the saints, as if there were but one soul to act that whole assembly of the first born? When there will be nothing in them to converse with but pure grace; grace without mixture, grace and nothing else but grace? Yea, not pure grace only, but perfect grace; when every grace shall be in its perfect state, and have its perfect works. Now the saints are like an instrument out of tune, jarring and disharmonious; when one is alive, the other is dead; when this is hot, the other is cold; when one is ready to give, the other is not fit to receive the communications of grace. But oh, when all the instruments of glory are alike strung, and equally tuned, what sweet rapturous harmony, what heavenly music will they make.

And there too it will be no small security to the mutual love of the saints, that in heaven they shall be set beyond all possibility of being mistaken in one another's condition. Here below, how easily and how often are we deceived! Behold a Judas amongst the disciples, whom none of them could discover, but only their Lord; "Have I not chosen you twelve, and one of you is a devil," John vi. 70. Oh dreadful, Judas a follower of Christ, and yet a devil! a disciple, and yet a devil! a preacher, and yet a devil! fast and pray, and yet a devil! do miracles, and yet a devil! cast out devils, and yet a devil! Oh dreadful mistake! And such mistakes, when discovered, oh what a shame! what grief! what perplexity of spirit do they occasion amongst God's upright ones!

But now are the saints in heaven delivered from all danger and fear of such charitable errors. There shall be no hypocrite in heaven, upon whom the saints can lose their love. Hypocrites shall be all locked up in one infernal dungeon together, that they may never deceive any more, Matt xxiv. 51. What an access of joy will this be to the communion of saints in glory!

It may be asked, whether or no in this blessed vision the saints shall see one another with a distinguishing sight; that is, see them so as to know them under such relations and respects as once they stood in one to another in this imperfect state? Whether Abraham shall know Isaac as once his son, and Isaac know Abraham as sometime his father? Whether the husband shall know his wife, and the wife her husband, as once such that have drawn together in the same conjugal yoke? Whether kindred shall know their gracious kindred, and friend his friend? Whether the godly minister shall know his gracious people that were of his particular flock, and the flock know him as once standing in that ministerial relation to them.

This, I say, is a question which seems neither difficult nor fruitless to be resolved. Probability, without doubt, falls upon the affirmative, and that whether we consult reason or scripture.

Reason saith, It is very likely we shall know them. Behold here in this dark region, what quick and admirable recoveries of things past, do the senses of the body and faculties of the soul make sometimes. The eye can distinguish its wonted objects after many years' separation; the memory can presently recall the face, and voice, and gestures of an intimate friend, after sleep, which is death's image, yea, after twenty years' absence, or more.*   At the resurrection, the soul, I make no question, will know its own body at the first sight; proportionably, in the state of glory, must the mutual knowledge and remembrance of old relations be more quick, lively, and, if I may so say, intuitive, according to the admirable and glorious capacity which they shall then be invested with.   Make then but a just allowance for the vast disproportion between the regenerate state on earth, and the glorified state in heaven, and you may rationally conclude the affirmative.

And if we consult scripture, it votes no less for the affirmative than reason doth.   Did Peter, and James, and John, know Moses and Elias at our Lord's transfiguration, whom they had never seen? Matt. xvii. 4; and shall not the saints know one another at the first view, whom they knew and mutually conversed with, while they were here on earth? Surely the knowledge of the beatifical vision shall excel the knowledge of Peter and John, as far as the state of glory excels the state of grace? 1 Cor. xiii. 12. Did Peter and John know Elias on the mount, whom they had not seen, and shall not Peter know John, and John Peter, whom they had mutually seen.

Again, the scriptures tell us, that Dives in hell

* There shall no knowledge be wanting which now we have, but only that which implieth imperfection ; and what imperfection can this imply ? To know one another as well in the glorified estate, as we did in the state of mortality, and better. The good of this blessed state consisteth in the knowledge one of another, communion one with another, and mutual content in that knowledge and communion. *Baxter.*

knew Abraham and Lazarus in heaven, Luke xvi. 23; shall the reprobate have better eyes in hell, than the elect of God have in heaven? Shall Dives know Lazarus, and shall not Lazarus know Paul and Peter?

And again, the scriptures tell us, the poor saints on earth shall know their rich benefactors when they come to heaven, how else can they receive them, in what sense soever, into everlasting habitations? Shall the saints know one another upon the account of a temporal alms, and shall they not know one another upon the account of spiritual offices performed one for another?

And again, Paul dignifieth his Thessalonians with those glorious titles, " his hope, his joy, the crown of rejoicing," his glory and joy, and that " in the presence of the Lord Jesus Christ at his coming," 1 Thess. ii. 19, 20. Could they be all this to the apostle in the resurrection, and he not know them and be able to distinguish them from all other saints of God that shall stand on Christ's right hand at that day? It cannot be.

Ministers should so preach, so live; parents and governors so educate and govern their children and families; as that they may mutually rejoice one in another, and for another, in heaven. It cannot but add much to their blessedness and joy in heaven, and be matter of praise and glory to God to all eternity, especially over such as to whom God hath made us instrumental, either to their conversion or to their edification; while in this vale of tears, here we mourned and wept bitterly, when we kissed their pale lips and cold cheeks, when we followed the corpse to the grave, and laid them down in their cold beds of dust; but there will be joy and glory,

N

with infinite compensation, when we shall see and say, Oh, here is my spiritual father, who begot me to Christ, under whose ministry I drew my first spiritual breath; how sweet are such acknowledgments here! Certainly they are the richest rewards of God's despised and persecuted servants and ambassadors here on earth; oh what will it be in heaven, when grace shall have put on its royal apparel! Oh what a joy to parents, to see the dear child that got into heaven, as it were, before its time! and the child to embrace the parent, Oh this is my father, my mother, my grandfather, my grandmother, that travailed with me the second time, till they saw Christ form in my heart; oh blessed be God that ever I saw their faces on earth, and now shall see them for ever in heaven! And so for friends, Oh this was my soul friend, this was a brother, that a kinsman, who loved me with a spiritual love, a heavenly love, that loved me into Christ, to heaven, to this glory I now possess.

We may not presume to speak definitely in cases not clearly stated by the holy scriptures; but this we may with safety and modesty conclude, that if such a mutual knowledge of godly relations in heaven may contribute any glory to God, and any addition to the joy of the saints, the absolute perfection of the glorified estate will not permit any doubt about this matter; surely, if our natural affections of love, and delight, and joy, be not extinguished in heaven, but perfected, it cannot but add to the elect mother's joy, to see her elect infant now adult in glory; and so for other nearest relations, will it not be some accent to their hallelujahs to say, This was my precious yoke-fellow, this my holy parent, this my gracious brother, kinsman, friend, with whom I had sweet communion on earth in holy duties? We went to the house of God as friends, &c. Especially, when it may be added, whom God made instrumental to the pulling me out of the infernal lake, where the devil and his angels are tormented for ever, and for the bringing of me into this place of rest and glory! Thanks be to God for ever and ever.

If it be objected, doth not this distinct knowledge of our elect relation infer a distinct knowledge also of the saints' reprobate relations in hell? And may not that be a vision of as much terror as the other of rejoicing? I answer, No; and that upon a two-fold ground.

First. It stands with the analogy of faith, to be-lieve that all those affections which imply defect or imperfection shall be totally abolished in heaven, as inconsistent with the glorified estate: "God shall wipe all tears from their eyes," Rev. vii. 17; xxi. 4.

Secondly. We answer, that there shall be such a perfect conformity of will between God and the saints, that there will be no dissent in the least. It shall not be then, as it is now, to the no little em-bittering of their present estate, first by sin, and then by grief for sin, but what pleaseth God shall abundantly please them. This the saints pray for here, but there shall they be fully possessed of it; here it is their duty, but there it shall be their re-ward. The saints in glory would have nothing otherwise than God would have it; so that now, to the full and perpetual silencing of this objection, I answer, that the glory of God shall so perfectly swallow up all private personal considerations, that, I am confident, it is no breach of charity to say, that the believing husband shall fully admit the justice of the damnation of the unbelieving wife, the holy parent in the damnation of the stubborn and ungodly child, &c. God's will is the law, and his glory the triumph, of the heavenly inhabitants.

Oh let parents, and ministers, and governors, and tutors, and yoke-fellows, brethren, friends, &c., be but as good now as Dives was in hell; I mean, let them be but in as good earnest here as he was there, that their relations may never come into that place of torment; and if they do wilfully cast themselves headlong into that irrecoverable gulf, it will be no grief of heart to them when they come to heaven: but even as God himself, they being then swallowed up in God, they will even laugh at their calamity, and mock when they see their condemnation.

3. Another vision which the saints shall have in heaven, is, that of the angels; they shall see those glorious, ministering spirits, those flames of fire, the angels of God, by what names or titles soever they are dignified or distinguished in their hierarchical orders; and not so only, but have sweet and heavenly converse and communion with them.

In what way and manner this mutual converse and communion betwixt the saints and angels in glory shall be managed, is not determinable by us poor mortals, until this mortal shall put on immortality. But whatever the way or manner be, this we may be sure, that the communion and converse with the angels in heaven, will be no small augmentation of their happiness, and of their joy; if we consider their angelical perfections, especially those two of knowledge and zeal; therefore they are called in scripture flaming fire: flames, for brightness of illumination, and fire, for the ardency of their love and zeal.

Oh what rare notions and experiences will the

angels be able to communicate to the saints in heaven, having ministered about the throne of God from
the foundation of the world, and been sent forth
continually to manage the great affairs of the world,
but especially of the churches! The apostle tells us,
they are beholden to the lectures read in the assemblies of the saints, for some insight into the mystery
of Christ in the gospel, Eph. iii. 10.   Oh how
ready and able will they be to pay their debts, with
an abundant interest, out of the immense volumes
of knowledge which they have treasured up!   The
communications of their love, their holiness, their
zeal, their heavenliness, &c.; what united flames
will they make when they be joined in communion
and converse with the graces and perfections of the
saints!

If it be objected, Is there not enough in God to
fill the saints, to the vastest capacity?   What need
then of starlight when the sun shines?   Yea, may
not the saints conversing with angels and one another, be thought to be a diversion from the supreme
Object of light and love?   To this I answer, No;
and the reason is, because all the perfections and
excellences which are in the creature, are as so
many beams and emanations, leading the eye of the
beholder to the sun itself, the body and fountain
from which they do spring; or as learned and holy
men's commentaries and expositions are to the holy
scripture, which do neither detract from, nor add to
that immense volume of truth, but serve only to
illustrate it, and to render it more intelligible to the
dark and imperfect understanding of the creature.
Surely such an infinite full text as God is, will stand
in need of some marginal notes, as it were, to help
the reader.   As Christ is said, in the days of his

flesh, to be the Interpreter of the Father unto us,
John i. 18; so may the angels be to the saints in
heaven. And such is all the glory of heaven; yea,
so is the human nature of Christ himself, now in
glory, the great Expositor of the Divine essence; a
mirror or glass, wherein we come to see God more
clearly and fully.

4. Another object of the beatifical vision is, Christ
himself, or the glorified human nature of the Lord
Jesus; Christ, in his human nature, exalted to the
right hand of his Father, the highest seat in glory,
" Far above all principality, and power, and might,
and dominion, and every name that is named, not
only in this world, but also in that which is to come,"
Eph. i. 21. This is the highest beatifical object in
heaven—the sight of Christ as man. It was the great
design which the Lord Jesus had in redeeming them
with his blood; " Father, I will that they whom
thou hast given me, be with me where I am, that
they may behold my glory, which thou hast given
me," John xvii. 24. And surely this will be a glorious sight indeed; behold, of the glory of Christ
in his transfiguration, it is said, that his face did
shine as the sun, and his raiment was white as the
light! If the glory of his transfiguration were so
excellent, what will the glory be of his exaltation!
If the glory of his foot-stool were so excellent, how
will the glory of his throne excel in glory! If he
appeared so bright upon an earthly mountain, how
transplendent will he appear upon Mount Sion, the
mountain of God, that heavenly mountain! If such
were his lustre in his state of humiliation, before his
passion; what beams of majesty will shine from his
face, in his state of glorification, when he is to receive the reward of his passion! Behold, there

appeared then, with him, only Moses and Elias; but what will his glory be, when all the patriarchs and prophets, all the apostles and martyrs, the whole society of the saints, with the whole host of the mighty angels, shall begird his throne, with their hallelujahs and joyful acclamations. That vision of Christ on earth did fill Peter and the disciples with wonder and astonishment, even to an ecstasy, so that the text tells us, he knew not what he said, Mark ix. 6. Oh with what joy and rapture shall the sight of Christ in glory fill the glorified saints, when their faculties shall be so raised, that they shall understand what they see, and profess what they understand! Surely Peter and all his fellow-saints will then say, and know what they say, " Lord, it is good for us to be here !"

It were good sometimes in our thoughts to compare the abasement of Christ and his exaltation together; to set them, as it were, in columns one over against another. He was born in a stable, but now he reigns in his royal palace; then he had a manger for his cradle, but now he sits in a chair of state; then oxen and asses were his companions, now thousands of saints, and ten thousand thousands of angels minister round about his throne; then, in contempt, they called him the carpenter's son, now he obtains by inheritance a more excellent name than the angels; " for to which of the angels said he at any time, Thou art my Son, this day have I begotten thee ?" Then he was led away into the wilderness to be tempted of the devil, now it is proclaimed before him, " Let all the angels of God worship him ;" then he had not a place to lay his head on, now he is exalted to be the heir of all things ; in his state of humiliation he endured the contradiction of sinners, in his state of exaltation he is adored and admired of saints and angels; then he had " no form or comeliness, when we saw him, there was no beauty that we should desire him," now the beauty of his countenance shall send forth such glorious beams, that shall dazzle the eyes of all the celestial inhabitants round about him; once he was the shame of the world, now the glory of heaven, the delight of his Father, the joy of all the saints and angels; once he was the object of the reprobate's scorn and the devil's malice, now they shall be the objects of his most righteous vengeance; he shall speak unto them in his wrath, and vex them in his sore displeasure; he that was called the deceiver, shall now be adored as the Amen of the Father, the faithful and true Witness; a man of sorrows then, but now the mirror of glory, Prince of peace; then accounted a servant of servants, now he shall be called the Lord of lords, King of kings; then they put upon him a mock robe, but now he shall be " clothed with a royal garment down to the foot, girt about the paps with a golden girdle;" the feeble reed shall now be turned into a massive sceptre of gold; his cross of wood into a throne of glory, and the crown of thorns into a crown of stars. In the day of his abasement he was the butt and scorn of his enemies, spoken against by every profane fool, but now in the day of his exaltation, his enemies shall be made his foot-stool; yea, thrones and principalities being made subject unto him; surely the very prints of his hands and feet, and the holes that were bored in his sides, shall be so many signal marks and trophies of victory, and Thomas, set now above all doubting, may sing in triumph, " My Lord and my God." And lastly, the Lord Jesus himself, instead of his desertion, the lowest step of all his abasement, shall solace himself for ever in the vision and fruition of his Father and of the blessed Spirit, and instead of " My God, my God, why hast thou forsaken me ?" he shall triumph, " I and my Father are one; thou Father in me, and I in thee."

These are some crevices through which we may have a glimpse of the glory of our Lord's once crucified body; the full discovery of it you will never be able to make, until you come eye to eye, to see and enjoy it in the kingdom of heaven.

A second consideration, evidencing what a glorious beatifying object the glorified humanity of our Lord Jesus will be in heaven, is, the personal and hypostatical union which the human nature hath with the Divine nature of the Son of God; the fulness of the Godhead dwelleth in Christ bodily, Col. ii. 9; that is, in his body : the fulness of the Divine essence dwells in the human nature, and is, as it were, transparent through his flesh. Therefore he is called, " The brightness of the Father's glory," Heb. i. 3; the brightness or refulgency of God the Father's glory; not only in reference to his Divine essence, the second person in Trinity, but as he is the Word incarnate, as he is God-man; because all the beams of Divine majesty do shine forth with a most resplendent brightness in his flesh. The Divine nature and essence is the fountain and body of glory, from whence all brightness and splendour doth beam and issue. And as a glass or mirror receives into it the beams of the sun, such a mirror is the flesh of Christ to the Divine essence, wherein all the glorious beams of Divine wisdom, holiness, mercy, goodness, and truth, &c., do shine forth. This is the mystery St. Paul admireth ; God was

manifested in the flesh, 1 Tim. iii. 16, or, God made
visible in a body of flesh : Jesus Christ was nothing
else but visible Deity; and so he was even while he
was on earth; "The Word was made flesh, and dwelt
amongst us, and we beheld his glory, the glory as of
the only begotten of the Father," John i. 14. The
flesh of Christ was but, as it were, a veil, through
which men might look upon the Sun of righteousness; which, open and naked, would have been too
vehement and strong for mortal eyes. We saw his
glory; there did beam forth, at times, such rays of
glory through the body of Jesus Christ, that whoever
had not wilfully shut his eyes, might have discovered
him to be more than man, and been constrained,
with the centurion, to cry out, " Surely this was the
Son of God;" " We saw it," saith the apostle of himself and the rest that were Christ's witnesses. Now, if
by virtue of the personal union of the two natures
in Christ, so much of God was conspicuous in the
flesh of Christ while he was on earth, how much
more abundantly do the emanations of Divine glory
dart themselves forth through the human nature,
now that that human nature is glorified and exalted
to the right hand of the Father in heaven!

Go forth then, O ye daughters of Sion, behold
your heavenly Solomon, with the crown wherewith
his Father crowned him in the day of his solemn
nuptials, when he was married to his heavenly bride,
in the day of the gladness of his heart, Cant. iii.
11. Anticipate, O my soul, that beatifical vision, by
spiritual and fixed meditation; get into heaven before thy time; and so much the rather, not only
because of the eminency of the object, but because
of the saints' interest in this object,—Christ in glory
and Christ ours; as much of the eternal brightness

of the infinite God, as is possibly visible to an eye
of glorified sense, will be seen in the human nature
of Christ; that will be glorious: and as much of that
glory made ours, as the creature can be capable of;
this will be joyful.   To see all this glory that is put
upon the person of the Lord Jesus Christ, and to
appropriate it, to see it mine!   And how mine?
Why mine by purchase; he that is the object of this
vision was the purchaser of it; he bought it for me;
yea, he purchased both it and me by his blood : it
for me, and me for it. The sight of his glorified body
was the fruit of his crucified body; as once he gave
his crucified body to my faith, so now he gives his
glorified body to my sight, to be my portion and my
bliss for ever!   O blessed vision, wherein, indeed,
Purchaser, and purchase, and purchased, do all meet
together, to suffer no more separation for ever! This
surely will make the saints sing their hallelujahs,
" To him that loved us, and washed us from our sins
in his own blood, and hath made us kings and priests
unto God and his Father, to him be glory and dominion for ever and ever, Amen," Rev. i. 5, 6.

5. I come now to the fifth object in the beatifical
vision, which is the Divine essence. This is denied
by some, and well it may, if the assertion were so to
be understood, that the essence of God is to be discerned by the bodily eye, though in its glorified
capacity; for whatever the excellency be which God
will put upon the glorified bodies of the saints in
heaven, yet still they retain the nature of corporeal
beings; and God's essence is so infinitely pure and
spiritual, that the angelical nature compared with it,
would seem to be but of a material and corporeal
constitution ; so that to affirm God to be visible to
an organical eye, though glorified, would seem to

imply one of these two things,—either that the
Divine essence hath matter and corporeality in it,
or that the glorified sense were made altogether
immaterial and spiritual; either of which is repug-
nant to the analogy of faith.

But it will be asked, What profit is there then
of the beatifical vision? or, What advantage have
they who see God in heaven, above the saints who
see him in the evangelical vision? I answer,
much every way. Concerning which, not to say any
thing that exceeds sobriety, and yet to say somewhat that may help our understandings, I would
ascend to the highest pitch of what my weak, narrow apprehension can reach unto of this blessed
vision, by these several steps and gradations.

(1.) We shall know more of God than ever we
understood of him in this life either by faith or by
the highest revelation that ever God made of himself
to our souls; more than ever the best of the saints
discovered by faith or Divine manifestation; yea,
we shall know more of God than ever the most holy
of the patriarchs, the most illuminated prophet, the
most seraphic evangelist, the most inspired secre-
taries and amanuenses of the Holy Ghost, on this
side heaven did ever know. Yea, what Abraham, the
friend of God; Jacob, who at one time had God in
his arms, and at another time had his Peniel, the
facial vision of God, Gen. xxxii. 24—30; Moses, the
favourite of heaven, to whom God is said to talk as a
man speaketh to his friend, Exod. xxxiii. 11, and
to know face to face, Deut. xxxiv. 10; Elijah, who
wore, as it were, the keys of heaven at his girdle,
and could open and shut them as he pleased, James
v. 17, and at length ascended thither in a fiery
chariot; Daniel, who had the visions of God,

Dan. x. 5–8; John the Evangelist, whose Patmos was turned into a paradise, where he had and wrote the revelation of Jesus Christ; and finally, holy Paul, who was rapt up into the third heaven, and heard things ineffable, 2 Cor. xii. 4; what these, I say, or any of these knew of the most high God, was but as the primer learning of children, to the vast readings of the greatest masters of learning, in comparison of that of God which shall be known to blessed souls. The least of God's infants, going from their mother's womb to the grave, shall know more of God the first moment it entereth into glory, than the profoundest divine in the church of God could by study or revelation ever attain to in this world; this is much.

(2.) The glorified saints shall know more of God and the Divine nature, than Adam did in paradise. He was prevailed upon by the tempter, to affect a greater and higher degree of knowledge than he had, above what the Creator saw fit to bestow; more than belonged to his nature and state: he would have known as God knows; that is, to full satisfaction and complacency.

(3.) We shall know God as much as the angels in heaven do. They behold the face of God, Matt. xviii. 10. Glorified saints are with the angels, and are said to be like angels, and equal to the angels, as angels, angels incarnate. And what inconsistency is there to the analogy of faith, to conceive that the saints shall enjoy as full a prospect of God in heaven, as the angels themselves do? for though their bodies be united to their souls, yet shall not their bodies be any hinderance to their soul's vision of God; since the soul dependeth not now upon any corporeal organ of the body, inward or outward sense; and the body shall be refined, by the power of Christ in the resurrection, to such a spiritual perfection, that it is itself even of an angelical nature.

In a word, the saints shall know God to perfection, though not to infinitude; they shall see him so as to repose themselves in him with full complacency and delight, so that they shall say they have enough. In this life, some of the saints, at some times, have had such manifestations of God, as have made them weep as bitterly, as ever any under desertion, crying out, Lord, withdraw thy glory, else the vessel will split, and I shall dishonour God. And it may justly be our wonder, how it should be otherwise to the saints in the other world; a wonder that a created, finite faculty should be able to bear the weight of glory which filleth the infinite object, and not be destroyed by the immensity of it; especially since we read of the very angels themselves, who in a vision of somewhat an inferior nature to that facial vision in glory, for the exceeding brightness of it, are said to veil their faces and their feet: their faces, as having their eyes dazzled with the exceeding brightness of his glorious appearance; and their feet, as abashed in the apprehension of their own meanness and imperfection, in comparison with God's incomparable and incomprehensible perfections.

In order to a full reception of these Divine manifestations of God, which shall be furnished in heaven, we learn from the scriptures that the glorified understanding shall be adorned with a six-fold perfection. 1. Spirituality. 2. Clarity. 3. Capacity. 4. Sanctity. 5. Strength. 6. Fixedness.

[1.] The first perfection of the understanding shall be spirituality : it shall be spiritualized. Spiritual it is now; as spiritual is opposed to corporeal, though not as spiritual is opposed to natural. The soul is now forced to be a caterer for a body of flesh, to provide things that are necessary for the sustenance of the animal life; it busieth itself to satisfy the appetites of hunger and thirst, &c. If it can redeem a few hours for actions more proper and peculiar to it, it is so clogged, so pressed down with the body's infirmities, as that it soon drops down to the earth, and is drawn aside to attend the impertinencies of this present life. But when it shall be joined to an animate, spiritual body, and itself, in its glorified capacity, then it shall be wholly taken up with objects spiritual and heavenly, and made, as it were, connatural to them, elevated by the light of glory, to the vision of God.

[2.] By virtue of this supernatural influx of the Divine object, the faculty shall be brightened and cleared. There is now upon this mirror of the understanding many spots and stains, whereby the vessel is defiled; the breath of the world, and the steam of corruptions from within, do so sully this crystal glass, that it cannot receive into it the beams of light which shine upon it; the more impurity the dimmer the vision: " Blessed are the pure in heart, for they shall see God," Matt. v. 8. Why now in glory all these stains and spots shall be perfectly wiped off, and the vessel shall be made a clear, burning glass, to receive and contain the glorious rays of Divine excellency, which emit themselves into it. Hence this vision of God is called by divines, a clear, distinct, and perfect sight of God ; not as if the blessed did see all whatever is in the Divine essence, but as opposed to our present dim, obstructed vision, 1 Cor. xiii. 12 ; so that it perfectly takes in what the Divine will is pleased to reveal, without any the least obstruction or diminution.

[3.] The faculty in glory shall be widened and extended to a vast capacity. Now the understanding is large, there is no bounding or limiting of it, it is higher than the heavens, and deeper than the sea, and wider than the world. But in glory, the understanding shall be widened to a vaster capacity, to take in, not the little things of the creature only, but the infinite God; I do not say infinitely, but apprehensively. It is worth our notice to compare those two expressions of the beatifical vision, the one, where it is said, "The angels do always behold the face of God," Matt. xviii. 10; the other, where the angels and saints, the number of whom is said to be, ten thousand times ten thousand, and thousands of thousands, are described surrounding God's throne, Rev. v. 11, they are round about the throne. Compare them together; they always behold the face of God, and yet are round about; and it hints us this blessed notion, God hath no back parts in heaven : God to the blessed inhabitants there is all face, and they are always beholding it. How should not so transplendent an object confound the spiritual organ, with the immense splendour and glory thereof, but that the object itself doth sustain and nourish the faculty!

[4.] Another perfection is sanctity; the understanding shall be made perfect in holiness. In the state of separation, the spirits of just men are made perfect, Heb. xii. 23; and surely the soul loseth nothing of its sanctity, by being united to the body in glory. Now of all Divine qualities, none doth more capacitate the soul for the vision of God than holiness; witness that holiness is called the Divine nature, 2 Pet. i. 4. Holiness assimilateth unto God ; and the perfection and delight of vision is founded in conformity : it is so in the evangelical vision, " Blessed are the pure in heart, for they shall see God ;" according to the purity of the heart is the vision of God. What a glorious vision of God will that be, which the perfection of holiness shall advance the soul unto, when the glorious object shall both enlarge and purify the faculty.

[5.] Another perfection is strength. The vision of God doth fortify the understanding. In nature, the more vehement and intense the object, the more it hurts and crusheth the sense ; the vision of God, though but under a veil, did undo the prophet Isaiah. Holy Daniel's vision, though but a vision, did disspirit him, and left him without strength, Dan. x. 7, 8. St. John's vision, though but the darker side of the beatifical sight of God, slayeth him outright for a time, " I fell at his feet as dead," Rev. i. 17. The souls of the blessed in heaven, are set beyond all fear of such a surprise of glory; while God fills their faculty, he doth also sustain and perfect it, by means whereof the faculty shall never be weary of its object, but shall behold it with fresh vigour and delight.

[6.] Another perfection is fixedness. In the state of grace the mind is exceeding slippery, like that of little children, whom you cannot fix. We lie upon spiritual objects, as upon a bank of ice, where we slide, and slide, and never leave sliding, till we be in the dirt; and this comes to pass by reason of those mixtures of impurity which are in these natural minds of ours ; the objects are pure and simple, but the faculty is wofully clogged with " superfluity of naughtiness," James i. 21 ; hence the lubricity and floating that is in the understanding, like the sea itself. But now in glory all that mixture is abolished, so that there is nothing remaining to divert or distract the faculty; yea, the object itself shall unite the faculty to itself. Oh blessed and blessed-making vision! Glorious things are spoken of thee, O thou vision of God! Truly beatifical for ever! Eye truly hath not seen, &c.

Before we leave this vision, let us make some use of it.

Use 1. Study holiness. There are two visions of God mentioned in scripture. The vision of God in grace; the vision of God in glory.

But of both these visions, holiness is the indispensable qualification; without holiness there is no admission into heaven. " There shall in no wise enter into it any thing that defileth," Rev. xxi. 27. And when entered, without holiness there is no vision, for " without holiness no man can see the Lord," Heb. xii. 14. And holiness doth dispose the soul for this blessed vision three ways. By removing the distance between God and the creature; by assimilating the soul to God; by causing mutual delight and complacency between them.

Sin is that great gulf which separates between God and the creature; and surely sin sets a vaster distance between the holy God and a sinner, than there is between heaven and hell; yea, than there is between God and the devil; that is, between God as a Creator, and the devil as he is a creature.

Until this distance is removed, there is no possible access for the soul to God. This partition wall is broken down when holiness is set up; and according to the degree of purity is the degree of vision; as the soul passeth from one degree of holiness to

another, so it passeth from one state and degree of
vision to another; " We all beholding as in a glass,"
&c , 2 Cor. iii. 18. The purer the glass, the brighter
the vision.

Christians, as then ye love God's face, look to
your holiness. God loveth holiness more than he
loveth the creature; God's holiness is his glory,
" glorious in holiness," Exod. xv. 11. He accounts it
the most radiant jewel in his crown royal, the very
varnish and beauty of all his glorious attributes; for
the love he beareth to which, he loveth to see the
very image and likeness of it in the creature. Oh
love that, dear souls, which God loves so much, and
loveth to see in his saints, who are therefore called
saints from their holiness. There is nothing can
make you so beautiful in God's eye as holiness; because in your holiness he seeth the reflection of his
own beauty ; " Thou wast comely through the
comeliness which I put upon thee," Ezek. xvi. 14.
God cannot fail to love his own likeness wherever
he seeth it. O love the Lord all ye his saints, and
" give thanks at the remembrance of his holiness,"
Psa. xxx. 4. Let your hearts leap within you as
oft as you think what a holy God you have ; who, if
he can but see true holiness in your faces, will admit you to see that holiness which is in his face for
ever. Love holiness, I say, but be sure it be such a
holiness as God loves. There is a holiness in the
world, which is but a thing like holiness, but is not
so ; moral righteousness, a harmless innocence, a
sober retiredness from sensual excesses, a pretty in-
genuity, a readiness to do offices of love ; a negative
religion, concerning which you may better tell what
it is not, than what it is. And there is a supersti-
tious holiness, which to the evangelical holiness is

no better than what the ivy is to the oak, and hath
eaten out the very heart of it ; a brat which, as one
saith,the devil hath put to nurse to the romish church,
which hath taken a great deal of pains to bring it
up for him; and it hath brought in no small revenue,
as to herself, of worldly riches and treasure, so to
him of souls ; for such holiness is the very road to
hell ; the followers of antichrist fill up the greatest
part of it.   But hear our Lord plainly telling you,
" Except your righteousness exceed the best of these,
ye cannot enter," &c. O christians, get you a copy
of grace out of the scripture records, those court-rolls
of heaven, which may be seen and allowed by God,
and angels, and saints.

But as for such as are without holiness, to them the
apostle sends this word expressly, there is no room
for them in heaven.   And indeed what should such
do there ?   There is nothing in heaven but what is
holy; holy angels and holy saints, and above all a
thrice holy Trinity—Father, Son, and Holy Ghost;
Holy, holy, holy, Lord God Almighty, Rev. iv. 8;
the beauty of whose face is holiness : alas ! there is
nothing for them to see or hear, but what is an
abomination to their souls !   Holy words, yea, the
very word holiness, they now stop their ears at it ;
it is vinegar to their teeth.   Holy ordinances, they
cannot bear them ; the impurer the ordinance is,
the better they like it. A holy God, they say of him,
" Cause the Holy One of Israel to depart from before
us," Isa. xxx. 11.   Preach as much as you will of
the Merciful One of Israel, and of the Bountiful One
of Israel, &c., but tell us not so much of the Holy
One of Israel. Molest us no more with messages of
holiness, and the severities thereof; yea, they say
not only so of God, but they say as much to God to

his very face. They say to the Almighty, " Depart
from us, we desire not the knowledge of thy ways,"
Job xxi. 14 ; they say so by interpretation, if not in
words at length. He that can expound actions as
well as language tells us they say so ; yea, they are
not ashamed of the very language ; it is a piece of
their gallantry to profess to them that reprove them,
or but meekly admonish them, I say, to answer
with scorn enough, " We are none of your saints."
Proud scorner, what art thou then ? An unclean swine;
yea, an unclean spirit, incarnate devil, a profane
scorner, for thy speech betrayeth thee? What need
further proof ? Put such an herd of swine into heaven, and verily they would need no other damnation.
But God made heaven for better purposes than to
be a hell for the haters of holiness. Tophet is
prepared of old for them, Isa. xxx. 33 ; and thither
they must be cast, with the reprobate angels ; down
they came, when they had laid aside their holiness,
and shall such maligners of holiness and holy ones
ever come there ? Let them not fear, the company
of saints shall never molest them ; they would have
none of their society on earth, and they shall have
none of their society in heaven. Possibly, with their
elder brother Dives, they may have a prospect of
heaven, where they may see Lazarus in Abraham's
bosom, Luke xvi. 23 ; and, with others of the reprobate family, they may see Abraham, Isaac, and
Jacob, and all the prophets in the kingdom of God,
Luke xiii. 28 ; but that vision will be so far from
beatifical, as that it will be the aggravation of
their damnation ; for as it follows, " They themselves shall be thrust out :" cast out with as much
contempt and violence, as ever they themselves
cast the saints out of their societies. Certainly that

vision will be weeping, and wailing, and gnashing of teeth.   Then shall the backslider in heart be, indeed, filled with his own ways, Matt. xxv. 41. They banished God and his saints out of their company; and now they themselves shall be banished from the presence of the Lord, and his saints, " and from the glory of his power," 2 Thess. i. 9.

Use 2. Labour to see God on this side glory, to begin your vision on earth, which shall never cease in heaven.   Indeed, the vision in grace and the vision in glory are one and the same vision; the object is the same—God; and the faculty is the same—the eye of the soul: they differ only in two circumstances.

First. In the medium.   Here we see in glasses, the works of God, the creatures are a glass, "The heavens declare the glory of God;" and the providences of God are a glass, " Day unto day uttereth speech, and night unto night showeth knowledge," Psa. xix. 1, 2. Every day's experience, and every night's experience, is a glass wherein much of God is to be seen.   And the gospel is a glass, wherein we all, as in a mirror, behold the glory of the Lord, 2 Cor. iii. 18.   And lastly, the glass of ordinances, preaching, and prayer, and sacraments, all these are glasses; and meditation is a glass.   Faith is another way of vision; by faith Moses saw him who is invisible, Heb. xi. 27.   All these, I say, are glasses wherein we may see God. But, alas! the glass takes away from the object, and darkens our vision; it lets in some light, but keeps out more; but in heaven we shall see without glasses, face to face; the Lamb shall be the light in that temple.

Secondly. These visions differ in their degree of light and clearness; here we see in part, this is but a partial vision; that in glory is extensive, a full-eyed vision, as one calls it, a most ample perfect vision; we shall know as we are known. The understanding here is dark, dim, and narrow; there clear, and vastly capacious.

Now, that which this word of exhortation calls you to, is, to exercise yourselves much in the vision of God here, and to that end I would have you make much of your glasses; be thankful for them. How many churches of Jesus Christ have their glasses taken away or broken! Robbed and spoiled of all their precious things, and have not so much as a glass left, wherein they might have some glimpses of Divine light conveyed into their understanding! O christians, before it be so with you, make use of your mediums; "While you have the light, walk in the light," &c. Bless God that the sun is not totally gone down upon your prophets, Mic. iii. 6, nor the day dark over them; God hath done that for you in as much wonder, and more mercy, that once he did for Joshua, caused your sun to stand still in your Gibeon, &c. O bless God for it! make his praise glorious.

Make then good use of your mediums, attend reading, and hearing, and prayer, and sacraments, while you have them; take heed of that dangerous notion, of being above ordinances; it is a precipice upon which many have stumbled into darkness. Oh that it may not prove utter darkness, the blackness of darkness for ever!

While, however, you use ordinances, take heed of resting in, and of resting contented with ordinances: an ordinance of God, without the God of the ordinance, what an empty glass is it? Oh then, let your hearts echo with David's; " Thy face, Lord, will I seek." What he meaneth by the face of God, he expounds himself, " That I may see thy power and thy glory in the sanctuary;" namely, the powerful and glorious manifestations of God in his ordinances, the manifestation of all his Divine attributes and excellences. Oh when it pleaseth God, by the Spirit, to beam in gospel-truth from the very face of Christ, not into the head only, but into the heart, with such a glorious light, that it seems to be the same in the soul as it is in Jesus, the very glory of God, 2 Cor. iv. 6, so that the soul stands wondering at the light, when in his light we see light, Divine truth, by a Divine irradiation; not by borrowed mediums and natural representations, but only by its own native brightness and lustre, 1 Pet. ii. 9.

This, this, christians, is gospel-vision, which, as it doth necessarily tend to, so it will infallibly end in the beatifical, facial vision in glory. How rare are those christians that do experience this vision of God in the ordinances; yea, how rare are they that do thus breathe, and pant, and cry out for the living God, with the holy psalmist! Hence darkness, hence deadness, hence formality, a powerless profession hath wofully spread itself upon the face of christianity, yea, upon the very reformed parts of it. Let christians stir up themselves, and let their souls press hard after God, when they come to ordinances, or else this very thing will be worse to them than all the evil that befell them from their youth until now, it may provoke God to withdraw even the evangelical vision from them here, and, without great repentance, to deny them admission to the beatifical vision hereafter. They that will not seek God's face in grace, shall not see God's face in glory.

6. The last object of the beatifical vision is, all things in God. God is the universal library of all truth, whether Divine or natural; yea, all truth is Divine, and doth emanate from the God of truth, in whom it is; there to be read as in its original, and lieth open for all the whole university of those heavenly academics to peruse. There the saints may read to the full the mystery of the blessed Trinity, how three in one, and one in three, Father, Son, and Holy Ghost, God blessed for ever! That thrice-glorious, and, till we come to heaven, not to be fathomed mystery, the wonder and adoration of the believing world, that immense ocean, over which so many daring spirits have assayed to fly, have fallen in, and been drowned : that burning light, unto which so many presuming to approach too near, have scorched their wings, and lost both their eyes and themselves together; that sacred ark, into which too many presumptuous Bethshemites, having dared, over-boldly to look, have been smitten. What is essence. And what is person. And how they differ. How the Father begets, and the Son is begotten, and how the Holy Ghost proceeds from both; how they are distinguished by their order, their personal properties, and manner of working upon the creature; how the Father worketh from himself, the Son worketh from the Father, and the Holy Ghost worketh both from the Father and the Son. These will be lectures which shall be read in the Trinity itself in glory, and that in a most clear and intelligible notion.

Then shall the saints be able to understand the mystery of the incarnation of the second Person, the Son of God, that mystery of godliness, 1 Tim. iii. 10 ; of godliness, because it transforms sinners into

saints ; and mystery, because it containeth so many
deep and mysterious wonders in it. The blessed,
blessed-making mystery of the incarnation of the
Son of God, our Lord Jesus Christ. Why the second
Person in the Trinity, rather than the first or third,
should be incarnate. Why he should take the nature of man rather than the nature of angels, and
that when it was at the worst? How he could take
the nature of sinful man, and yet not take the sinfulness of his nature. The union between the Divine
and human natures in the Lord Jesus, in one person ? That mysterious union between the Lord
Christ, the Head, and all believers, the true members of his body; what it is, and how they are made
one with Christ, as the Father and the Son are one ;
this precious mystery, I say, shall then be made
manifest, " At that day you shall know " both what
it is, and how it is, " that I am in the Father, and
you in me, and I in you," John xiv. 20, &c.; then,
and not till then. How he that is every where,
filling heaven and earth with his presence, should
yet become a child. How he that made the law,
should be made under the law. How the Ancient
of days should become an infant of moments. How
he that was begot before all time, should be born in
the fulness of time? Eph. iii. 10. These, and a
thousand difficulties more, whereinto the very angels
desire to peep, 1 Pet. i. 12 ; and for some imperfect
discoveries, whereof they are glad to be beholden to
the lectures read in the churches by their earthly
angels, the ministers of the gospel, Eph. iii. 10;
these, I say, shall be clearly read and understood in
that original wisdom wherein they were first conceived.

That profound and dark mystery of election, why

God should choose one, and leave another? Why first the Jews should be a church, and the gentiles, aliens, should afterward be adopted into the covenant, and the Jews broken off and cast out? That God should break open the heart of one rebellious sinner by efficacious grace, and leave another to perish in his transgressions? These, with all the other dark and profound mysteries of God's decrees, shall then be made clear. And lastly, that mystery of wickedness and abominations, and why God hath suffered him so long to reign, and to usurp so great a part of Christ's purchased and promised possessions, with all his witchcrafts and sorceries, whereby he hath deceived the nations, they shall all be discovered and brought to light, to his eternal shame and confusion? That God should shine out only upon some few spots of ground, with the light of the gospel, and leave the rest in palpable darkness

The creation of the world shall then be more clearly understood in the cause, than now it is in the effect; how all things were made out of the first matter, and that out of nothing. Those hard mysteries of Providence, which do now try and exercise the faith and patience of the saints, Rev. xiii. 10; xiv. 12. Why they that are best should speed worst? " That there be just men, unto whom it happeneth according to the work of the wicked." And again, " That there be wicked men, unto whom it happeneth according to the work of the righteous," Eccl. viii. 14; insomuch that " now we call the proud happy, and they that work wickedness are set up, yea, they that tempt God are even delivered?" Mal. iii. 15. Why the worse cause should many times have the better success? Why God should suffer his dearest children to be abused and insulted over, when wickedness in the mean while triumphs securely. Why wickedness should be set up in high places, and innocence should be trod under foot. Somewhat of these riddles the word doth now interpret unto the saints, blessed be God, to command their silence and submission to God; but " then shall they return, and discern between the righteous and the wicked, between him that serveth God, and him that serveth him not :" all this will be then seen in God to infinite satisfaction.

The grand article of the faith, the resurrection of the dead, being then already past, shall be fully understood; how the body, after thousands of years, through unutterable varieties of mutations and vast dispersions into all the quarters and corners of the world, should be revolved back again, bone to bone, and skin to skin, and every dust to its own dust, shall then clearly be expounded in the mirror of the Divine understanding, and exemplified in the counterpart thereof, the bodies of the aints. Then it shall no longer " be thought a thing incredible, that God should raise the dead," Acts xxvi. 8. All the hard places of scripture, that vex the profoundest divines, and make the believer sigh out his " How can I understand, except some man should guide me ?" Acts viii. 31, shall then be expounded in the original text of eternal verity, without looking into any other commentary; and oh what joy will that be, to understand the whole Bible without study! Then the meanest understanding shall be able to confute all the depths and fallacies of jesuitical seducers, whereby they have darkened the truth, and led away the willingly ignorant into their pernicious errors, and doctrines of devils, 2 Pet. iii. 17.

In a word, all the arcana of nature, and all the

mysteries of philosophy, properly so called, with all
occult things under the sun, and the highest specu-
lations of this nether orb; in the painful and knotty
disquisition whereof the greatest masters of secular
learning have tired themselves almost to distraction,
and upon the gaining of some little supposed satisfaction, wherein they have so much gloried, and insulted over other men—shall now be made easy and
familiar to the saints, the very A B C of heaven,
and only need a cast of their eyes, either as such
knowledge came from God, or as it leads them unto
God again.

For the use of this last branch of the heavenly
vision, it may serve to moderate and restrain the
inordinate curiosity of our natures, to be looking
into dark and hidden mysteries. We inherit both
from our first father and mother, a desire after forbidden knowledge; they desired a knowledge above
the capacity of their natures; they would know as
God knoweth; but by such an ambition of knowing
more than they ought, they forfeited what they had.
And while they aspired to be as God who made
them, they became like the beasts that perish. It
was the presumption of the Bethshemites that they
would be prying into the ark, and they died for it,
1 Sam. vi. 19: and there is a pride and wantonness
in our nature, which sets us a prying into the hidden and secret counsels of God. Adam's children
are yet sick of his disease; they would fain be as
wise as God, and know all things. But the " secret
things belong unto the Lord our God; but those
things which are revealed belong unto us, and to
our children for ever, that we may do them." And
in these revealed things there is matter enough to
exercise our studies, had we Methuselah's lease of

life sealed to us. In the revealed things of God, there is so much yet unrevealed, that we might search and dig into them, Prov. ii. 3, 4, with the addition of a promise to encourage industry, " Then shall we know, if we follow on to know the Lord," Hosea vi. 3; so much, I say, that when we have travelled many years in the disquisition and search thereof, we may sit down and complain, our lives are too short for our work, and truly confess, that the greatest part of what we know is nothing to what we are ignorant of. Oh that upon those studies christians would lay out their time and spirits! " proving what is that good, and acceptable, and perfect will of God," Rom. xii. 2. And for your encouragement and satisfaction keep this consideration alive upon your hearts, we shall not always be ignorant; secret things shall not always be secret: the time is coming when mysteries shall be revelations, when we shall be able to read that in the original, which we cannot now so much as spell out in the translation, nor in any measure understand with the help of all our commentaries.

And so it may abundantly satisfy the insatiable desires of inquisitive spirits, into the deep mysteries both of creation and redemption ; that " when Christ shall appear, we shall also appear with him in glory." And then shall the veil be taken away, and they shall see God, and all things in God's face which their souls desire to see; the soul shall be filled with variety of all desirable knowledge, that may any way tend to its perfection. This may satisfy; save that it may set their souls a longing for that day, and cause them to cry out with the bride, " Even so come Lord Jesus, come quickly."

III. The third privilege contained in being with the Lord, is fruition.

A third privilege implied in the saints being with the Lord, is fruition: vision in glory is accompanied with fruition : and this is that which makes it truly beatifical; whatever glorified saints see, they do enjoy, else this vision would not differ much from report, nor that state of glory from a heaven in a well-drawn landscape. The very outcasts, it seemeth, have a prospect of heaven, but to their torment, they themselves being thrust out, Luke xiii. 28.

Now, fruition consists of a tenfold ingredient or property. 1. Proprietorship. 2. Possession. 3. Intimacy. 4. Suitableness. 5. Satiety, or fulness. 6. Freshness. 7. Present. 8. Fixedness. 9. Reflection. 10. Complacency.

1. Proprietorship. Whatsoever the saints see in heaven is their own. God saith to Abraham now in the heavenly Canaan, what he once said to him of the earthly; " Lift up thine eyes, and look from the place where thou art, northward, southward, eastward, and westward; for all the land which thou seest, to thee do I give it," Gen. xiii. 14, 15. Whatever is within that vast circumference of heaven it is Abraham's, and all his spiritual seed's for ever. Now David may tune his song of praise a key higher; and instead of, " Gilead is mine, and Manasseh is mine, Ephraim and Judah," &c., Psa. lx. 7, 8, he may now sing, God is mine, and Christ is mine, and the Spirit is mine; all the elect angels are mine, and all the whole congregation of the first-born mine, all the glory of heaven is mine : and so may the least of the saints in heaven triumph, all is mine; and what pleasures, or riches, or honours, or glory,

or joys, are in the presence of God, they are all mine. They did sing so while yet in the valley of tears; or they might have sung so, John i. 12; faith gave them a title, a right to heaven, but the blessed vision giveth them now real interest and right in heaven; and they need not now fear to call it theirs. They might have said, My God, my Christ, and my Comforter, here below, but one thing was to be done first; sound scripture evidence was to be cleared out, and sealed up to their souls, but some or other defect therein did not seldom check their confidence, and damp their joy for a time. But now in glory, all is theirs beyond all dispute; their evidences were seen and allowed at their first admission into heaven, and now mine, mine, is their song and triumph to all eternity; and God is not ashamed to be called their God. Truly he was not ashamed to be called so, even when they had but too much cause to be ashamed of themselves, and gave God too much cause to be ashamed of them. But now God is so far from being ashamed of owning them, that he rejoiceth in them, and glorieth over them.

The Lord Jesus Christ is not ashamed to call them brethren, Heb. ii. 11; to own them for subjects, friends, co-heirs with himself in glory, his bride. And they claim their proprietorship in him as such. The King of saints, Rev. xv. 3, with his Father's name written in their foreheads, chap. xiv. 1; they follow the Lamb whithersoever he goeth, chap. xiv. 4; owning themselves as his beloved, his redeemed, kings and priests unto God and his Father, chap. i. 6; yea, as the Lamb's wife, chap. xxi. 9. They have a title in all the elect angels of God: they be still their angels, Matt. xviii. 10, as ready to do them brotherly offices as ever, and take more complacency in their company and in them than ever, by how much more purified and angelified they are, than when they lay among the pots of the earth; now made like themselves, fellow-angels, as it were, as well as fellow-saints.

They have proprietorship in one another, although they may know some of the saints under the notion of natural relations; yet do these all cease there, as now being retired into the first and chief root and spring-head of Divine relation; children of one heavenly Father, in whose house they are altogether, embracing one another in purest communion and communications of love; each saint not more himself than his fellow-saints.

In a word, the place where the saints are met together, never to part, is their own; not a strange country, where they see one another as strangers and pilgrims do sometimes visit and comfort one another. Heaven is not a borrowed palace, where they are admitted by courtesy, to celebrate a festival for a few days or years; but the saints in heaven are at home now, in their own house and kingdom, 2 Cor. v. 2.

2. Possession. The saints have not only proprietorship in heaven, but possession of heaven. When their dearest and sweetest Lord left the world, and ascended to his Father, they took possession of heaven in him, as in their great Representative and Head, John xiv. 2. But when they ascend to him, they take possession of it in their own persons. They had livery and possession given them by the Father, upon the consummation of their marriage with his dear Son Jesus Christ, their royal Bridegroom. And it was done in the presence of the

eternal Spirit, the public notary of heaven, 1 John
v. 7. All the holy angels standing by as so many
witnesses; so that God himself could not make
heaven surer to them than he hath made it.

While the saints were upon earth, heaven was
theirs, but it was only in reversion, and they counted
themselves blessed in that, Matt. v. 3. But now
reversion is turned into possession; the saints hold
nothing in heaven by reversion, that title ceaseth
there. All the beatitudes in heaven are present
possession; God, and Christ, and the Holy Spirit;
angels, and saints, and all the glory of the upper
world, are so many possessions: the saints are possessed of God, and possessed of Christ, and possessed of the Holy Ghost, and possessed of glory:
as, on the contrary, the damned in hell are possessed
of the devil, they are possessed of hell, and of utter
darkness, and of the worm that shall never die, &c.
O dreadful possession!

Hope was once their tenure; " In hope of eternal
life, which God that cannot lie," &c. Titus i. 2;
Rom. v. 2; and this hope was very precious unto
them, a little heaven upon earth; save that now and
then some clouds of fear and doubts did interpose
between heaven and their dim eye, and so eclipsed
their vision. But faith and hope did set them
down at the gate of heaven, and then, with
Moses, died in the mount, and took leave of them
for ever.

And if faith was so precious to them then, what
is sight now? If hope made their hearts, not seldom,
leap for joy, how doth possession now fill them with
joy unspeakable and glorious, above all hyperbole
of expression. .

If any should be so critical as to object, In heaven

the saints live in the hope and faith of the continuance of heaven! We make use of the apostle's maxim for answer; " Hope seen is not hope," Rom. viii. 24. All the glory of heaven is seen, and all is present, there is no futurity in heaven; heaven is but one point of eternity; the saints have all beatitudes, and all at once in God; now abideth indeed faith and hope, but then possession, 1 Cor. xiii. 13. " They shall sit down with Abraham, Isaac, and Jacob, in the kingdom of heaven," Matt. viii. 11. The kingdom of heaven is theirs, and they shall sit in it. All the precious privileges of the gospel, which cost Christ so dear, are now perfected into full possession. Adoption is now perfect; now they are the sons of God, and they know what it is to be the sons of God. Justification is now complete: sanctification is now at perfect age. In a word, all their hopes are now their inheritance. This is fruition!

3. Another ingredient, of which fruition doth consist, is intimacy. Proprietorship and possession are not sufficient to constitute fruition. Mutual converse will not serve the turn, without intimate communion: communion, not with one another's persons only, but with one another's spirits; this is fruition, when friends are possessed of one another's hearts, and one another's spirits. This is the great beatitude of heaven, even vital vision, with all the beatifying objects thereof; mutual in-dwelling, and mutual in-being. God dwells in the saints, and the saints dwell in God: it was so here, " God is love; and he that dwelleth in love, dwelleth in God, and God in him," 1 John iv. 16. The saints' love to God is now made perfect, without a figure, and as their love is, so is their mutual in-being, perfect; " I in them,

and they in me, that they may be made perfect in
one," John xvii. 23 : perfect according to the
supreme Exemplar; " As thou, Father, art in me,
and I in thee, that they also may be one in us,"
ver. 21.

The angels and saints in light, behold they dwell
not with one another only, but in one another; they
inhabit, as it were, in one another's hearts. That
primitive congregation, Acts iv. 32, was a lively type
of this royal congregation of the first-born, they are
all with one accord in one place, Acts ii. 1; so
these, one place holds them all, and one soul ani-
mateth and acts them all. The whole multitude of
saints in heaven are all of one heart and of one
soul.

4. Another ingredient in fruition is fulness.
There is in heaven good, and there is enough of it :
fulness to satisfaction ; " They shall be abundantly
satisfied with the fatness of thy house, and thou shalt
make them drink of the river of thy pleasures,"
Psa. xxxvi. 8. The joys of heaven are compared to
a feast, consisting of all imaginable rarities, both of
meats and drinks; fatness expressing the delicacy of
food ; and the river of Eden, for so the word signifieth—of the river of thy Eden, the delightful sweetness of their drink, infinitely beyond all that is
fancied by the poets, of the nectar and ambrosia of
the gods ; which, indeed, was but an imperfect notion
of the joys of heaven, filched out of some fragments
of scripture by those blind naturalists. But of such
deliciousness doth this marriage supper consist of,
and there is plenty of them, plenty even to satiety,
they shall be satisfied with the fatness, and filled
with those wines upon the lees well refined. The
Master of the feast will say to his guests, then in the

feast, what he said here below in the figure. " Eat,
O friends, drink, yea, drink abundantly, O beloved," Cant. v. 1.

And it must needs be so; for every one of the
glorified inhabitants doth enjoy a whole heaven, with
all the felicities of it, as much as if heaven had been
made but for one individual person. For although
the church of the first born in heaven consists of ten
thousand times ten thousand, and thousands of
thousands, yet hath no one the less for what others
do enjoy. As in nature, every beholder hath a whole
sun, and the whole heavens to himself, with all their
splendour and influence, as much as if there were
but one man in the world. In terrestrials, indeed,
it is not so; there what one man hath, another hath
not; and where many share, every single man's portion is the less; whence it is that *Mine* and *Thine*
fills all the world with quarrels and confusions.
But there is no such thing in heaven; the multitude
of heirs do not divide or lessen the inheritance; the
reason is, because there are no particles in essentials;
every one hath all, and none the less for what another enjoyeth. Yea, the more, because the joy of
one is the joy of all; every heir of glory enjoyeth
not only what himself hath, but what his coheir
hath too; so that upon the point each saint enjoys
as many heavens as there be angels and saints in
heaven : a blessed mystery of multiplication.

The saints shall have as much glory as they are
able to stand under; hence we read of a weight of
glory, a weight that would utterly sink and crush
them into nothing, were there not an arm of omnipotence to sustain them, and to make them bear it,
as their crown, not as a burden, with ease and
delight.

Q

5. Suitableness is another ingredient in fruition, without which both the former would be a burden, and not a bliss; suffering rather than fruition.

Earth is a place of mixture and composition, somewhat suitable, and somewhat unsuitable; some pleasure, some vexation: hell and heaven are the extremes. Hell is a place of unmixed torment; nothing there but what is opposed to the will of the damned; nothing present but what the reprobate would not; nothing absent but what he wisheth for. Heaven is a place of unmixed joy; nothing wanting of all that blessed souls can rationally desire; nothing absent, the absence whereof can possibly give any check to their fullest delight.

All the beatitudes of that upper world, both in their nature and degree, shall be most agreeable to the constitution of the saints: in their nature, they being suitable to the nature of the saints, to the heavenly principles of purity and holiness communicated to them from the Divine nature; both the objects and subjects of glory are of one and the same constitution. This must needs produce inconceivable delight.

And as suitable are all the joys of heaven in their degrees and proportions to the heavenly capacities; neither too much, nor too little, nor too heavy, for the saints to bear; nor too light, neither too vehement, nor over-flat. The weight of that prepared glory shall not be heavier than those blessed souls shall be well able to sustain with exceeding pleasure, neither shall it be so light, that they shall be able to say, I could bear more. The light of glory shall not hurt the organ by an over-vehement brightness; neither yet shall there be the least dimness in it to abate the delight of the acutest sense.

The language of the New Jerusalem shall be one and the same throughout all the streets thereof, not a speech deeper than the meanest saint can perceive, Isa. xxxiii. 19, nor a barbarous tongue that they cannot understand, shall be heard there, but the mother-language, Gal. iv. 26, intelligible and easily to be understood and spoken by the meanest inhabitant, shall be the language of the upper Canaan, that all may hear, and all may understand, to their unspeakable satisfaction.

The music of heaven shall be sweetest melody to every ear; and though it consists of the rarest strains and most delicate airs that ever ear heard, yet it shall not transcend the skill of the lowest capacity; but the meanest chorister in the heavenly temple shall bear his part with the most seraphic angel, in the higher or lower praises of the most high God in most perfect symphony.

The infinite variety of the greatest delicacies wherewith the table shall be spread, where Abraham and all his spiritual seed shall be feasted, shall consist of relishes suitable to the palate of every guest there; what is fancied of the manna of the nether heavens, shall be fully verified of the manna of the third heaven; it shall give that taste to every palate which every palate likes best; yea, all the saints shall be but of one and the same taste, the delight of one is the delight of all.

And though, possibly, there may be several orbs of glory, " for as one star differeth from another in glory, so also is the resurrection of the dead," yet shall not the inferior orb envy the superior, nor think itself too low ; there shall be no such voices heard from the mouth of any the meanest inhabitant : Oh were I but in such a superior orb I should he happy; such a mansion would please me better. This would destroy fruition, and make heaven cease to be heaven; but no such whisper is to be heard, no such thought in that holy mountain; because the glory of one is the glory of all, and every saint is as happy in another's fulness as in his own; yea, it enjoyeth its own and the other's glory too: the narrowest capacity is widened by the other's fulness; the joy of one is the joy of all. In a word, the saints shall live in love, and have all in Him who is all, not so much as wishing their fellow-saints less; or themselves more, nor any thing in that whole world of felicities otherwise than it is. This is fruition!

Oh that all who have this hope in them would study to begin this life here below!

6. The next property of this fruition is fixedness. There is scarce a comfort which we possess in this movable world, that we can find the same at the year's end, or at the month's end, which we fancy them to be at the beginning; all our most beautiful objects, how quickly they change colour! "In the morning it flourisheth, and groweth up, in the evening it is cut down, and withereth," Psa. xc. 6.

The world is compared to a stage, where the scene is quickly changed, and another face of things doth suddenly appear, 1 Cor. vii. 31; 1 John ii. 17; but heaven is a place of fixed and immutable beatitudes. Heaven is still of one fashion, their work the same; "they rest not day and night, saying, Holy, holy, holy, Lord God Almighty, which was, and is, and is to come," Rev. iv. 8. And their joy the same; "They do always behold the face of their heavenly Father," Matt. xviii. 10. They are in God, like God, "Yesterday, and to-day, and the same for ever; with whom is no variableness, neither shadow of turning." The saints in heaven are so far from mutation, that there is no shadow of it. Here on earth our choicest delights meet with changes; created beings show their face awhile, then hide them again; their colour goes and comes. Godly acquaintance is sweet, but the farewell is bitter; we call at the door, and sip of the cup, but we cannot stay by it. The best of our time is but a seventh part of it, and how wofully full of diversions! Such is our heaven on earth; but our heaven in glory, or our glory in heaven, is not so. God is the only unchangeable object of the soul; there the soul stays, and sucks, and drinks immeasurably, and yet there is not a drop less in the object.

7. Another property is assurance. Assurance is one of the choicest ingredients in fruition : to enjoy heaven in all the beatitudes thereof, and to know I do enjoy it, this is the beatitude of all beatitudes.

It fareth with many a poor believer here in the wilderness of desertion, as it did with Hagar in hers, Gen. xxi. 16—18; they sit down to die, for want of water, when there is a well before them, yea, many a well of living water, the precious promises, out of which wells of salvation they might with joy draw water, Isa. xii. 3, and drink and forget their sorrows, but alas they see them not, until God open their eyes, and then they can go and fill their bottles, and drink, and cause others to drink also, Gen. xxi. 19. This is often the state of the way! Oh but now, in the country, the land of fruition, there the saints see, and they know they see ; they love, and they know they love ; yea, they are beloved, and they know they are beloved. They are bathing themselves in the rivers of pleasures, and they know where they are, and what they do. All tears are

Q 3

wiped from their eyes, and they know who wiped them off with the kisses of his mouth. They are safe, yea, and they are sure ; they are blessed, and they know they are blessed. The spouse is now got into the throne, the bosom of her beloved, the King of glory, and there she singeth, " Here I sit as a queen, and am no widow, and shall see sorrow no more for ever," Rev. xviii. 7.

In a word, all the acts of love, and joy, and delight, in heaven, are acts of highest assurance, without the least mixture of doubt and uncertainty. There is no fear in this love, because love being now perfected, hath cast out fear.

8. Freshness   The joys of the glorified saints are always fresh from the spring-head, that makes them so sweet: what we receive by the mediation of creature-conduits, loseth much of its native delicacy.

Adam and Eve were created in the prime ripeness and bravery of the human nature, in perfection of beauty and strength ; and such shall all the saints be restored, of what age and state of body soever they lay down in the grave; the children of the resurrection shall rise, in the morning, in the most sparkling beauty and vigour of youth, and in that posture shall be for ever.

We would fain espouse all our worldly beatitudes to ourselves, and write eternity upon them; but how brave and sprightly soever they appear in our first apprehension of them, they quickly grow old and fastidious, and signify no more than so many impotent grasshoppers. But now there is no such thing in heaven; there is eternity, but no old age; the joys of heaven are always young. The flowers of paradise, of which the saints' posy is made, do neither wither nor change colour; the drops of their morning dew standing thick upon them, like orient pearls, preserve them in their perpetual verdure and odoriferousness.

God himself, the fountain and spring of all those glorious beings, is not a moment older than he was from all eternity; and therefore all their fresh springs being in God, their roots feed their branches with continual and unchangeable moisture and influence. God, who is an object of infinite fulness, doth always feast the glorified saints and angels with fresh visions of delight and wonder. Yea, God himself, the fountain and spring-head of all those glorious beatitudes, doth wash their roots perpetually with fresh moisture and influence.

9. All the joys of heaven are present.

Glory borrows that immense title of the God of glory, (what the Jews say of the ten commandments,) " is, and was, and is to come," Rev. i. 4; a name that is not to be divided or taken asunder, but must be spoken all together in one word. So is, as that it was; so was, as that it shall be; so shall be, as that it is. Eternity is a single point, such are all the blessednesses of the saints, were, and are, and shall be: so past, as to come, and so to come, as present; this is a mystery, and it is marvellous in our eyes.

10. Out of these nine ingredients or properties, there ariseth a tenth, the very top of all, delight and complacency; and this makes heaven to be heaven indeed, the joy of the Lord, even the same joy which God himself possesseth; the same for kind, though not for degree.

Behold faith in the glorious Redeemer doth, at times, raise the soul of the poor believer to a marvellous high pitch of joy and rapture; " Whom having not seen ye love; in whom, though ye now see him not, yet believing, ye rejoice with joy unspeakable and full of glory," 1 Pet. i. 8.   The expression is very full; faith brings the soul in love with an unseen Christ, and fills the heart with joy; not ordinary joy, such as men do easily express upon all occasions, but unspeakable; the heart conceives such joy that the tongue cannot utter; yea, it is not to be uttered by the tongue of men or angels; it cannot be spoken, it is ineffable; and that is not all, it follows, it is glorious; and our translation gives it an addition very emphatical, full of glory. And yet that reacheth not the top of this joy, for the Greek signifieth not glorious only, but glorified: faith fills the heart with glorified joy, a joy that rivals, as it were, the joy of the glorified saints; a joy which sets the soul for the present above itself, and puts it into heaven before its time.   O christians, if faith, which must not enter in within the veil, can transport the soul into such ecstatical raptures, what can vision and fruition do?   Oh the mountings of mind, the rapturous joys of heart, the solace of soul, which glorified saints possess in the beatifical vision!

The soul shall live in joy, and be filled with delight in the mirror of all delights; love and joy shall run in a circle, and mutually empty themselves into one another; love shall dissolve into joy, and joy shall resolve into love, a river, an ocean of unmixed complacency, wherein the soul shall bathe itself for ever.

IV. The last privilege contained in being with the Lord is conformity.

Even in the evangelical state below, conformity is the fruit of vision; vision produceth assimilation. " We all with open face, beholding as in a glass the glory of the Lord, are changed into the same image from glory to glory, even as by the Spirit of the Lord," 2 Cor. iii. 18. Surely the heavenly vision will beget so much more full and perfect conformity, by how much the mirror is more vital and energetical. The apostle reacheth forth this blessed truth, and the reason of it together, as a known doctrine.

" Beloved, now are we the sons of God," 1 John iii. 2 ; that were dignity enough for a poor sinner, one would think, but that is not all ; it is well, and it shall be better. God hath laid out much upon us ; but how much glory he hath laid up for us we cannot conceive ; " it doth not yet appear what we shall be!" This only we know, " that when he shall appear, we shall be like him '" That is infinite honour indeed ! But how doth he prove it ? Why, he proves our conformity from our vision, " we shall be like him, for we shall see him." Even in the days of his flesh, 1 Tim. iii. 16, the flesh of Christ was a veil, through which the Deity of Christ did appear, God was conspicuous in the human nature ; if it were so, upon earth, how much more will it be verified in heaven! The glorified body of our Lord will be as transparent glass, through which the glorious beams of Divinity will display themselves to the eye of the blessed beholders : and in the beholding whereof, there will go forth a transforming virtue, which will change them into the same image.

" We shall be like him." Like him in our souls ; like him in all the faculties of our souls : our understandings shall be like the Divine understanding ; we shall know all things, past, present, and to come, so far as shall be for our good.

The will is made like unto God's will, not a

fountain indeed, but a large vessel full of goodness and holiness. The saints shall be holy as God is holy, pure as God is pure, perfect as he is perfect; they were so on earth, truly; now in heaven they are so, perfectly; the will shall be as holy as it would be, as holy as the holy God would have it be, so holy that there will be mutual joy and delight between God and the saints in the contemplation of their holiness. In heaven there is but one will between God and the saints, and that will is God's.

Moreover, the saints are like God in their affections. They love what God loveth, they hate what God hateth; their joy is God's joy; they rejoice in God and in his glory; they rejoice in Jesus Christ, their Bridegroom, and he rejoiceth in them. As the bridegroom rejoiceth over the bride, so shall thy God rejoice over thee, Isa. lxii. 5; that was but the word spoken to the church at her espousals, what must the joy be upon her wedding-day!

The saints are like God in their memories. They shall have holy memories; their memories shall be like the ark of the covenant, which was overlaid with gold, wherein, according to the apostle's inventory, were the golden pot that had manna, and Aaron's rod that budded, and the tables of the covenant. The ark of the memory now overlaid with glory, likewise shall contain the manna, that angelical food of word, sacraments, promises, ordinances, providences, experiences, wherewith God was wont to feed the soul, while in the wilderness of the world. Aaron's rod that budded; God's fatherly rod of correction, which though " for the present seemed not joyous but grievous, yet afterwards it yielded the peaceable fruits of righteousness, in them that were exercised thereby," **Heb.**

xii. 11. And the tables of the covenant: the two covenants, which God made with man; the one of works, the witness of God's holiness and perfection; the other of grace, the witness of God's goodness and commiseration.

In a word, the entire image of God, which was imprinted upon the soul in the first creation, and reprinted upon it, though in an imperfect character, in the new creation, shall now be perfected to the life in the regeneration; the saints shall be as like God as ever children were like their father; Eph. v. 1, so that there will be nothing but looking and liking the one upon the other.

Anticipate that holy gaze now, O ye children of the most high God; be often taken up in the beholding and contemplation of the face of your heavenly Father; behold, will it not quicken you to duty? comfort you in your droopings? cause you to overlook the contempt of the world with an holy pride, and even be the dawnings of glory upon your faces, whereby some line and lineaments of beauty shall be added daily to that blessed draught begun already against that day?

Once more, before we go off from this pleasing contemplation, we add, the very bodies of the saints shall share in this blessed conformity, as well as the soul. It had its degree in the first paradise; man had an evident superiority in the very make of his body, beautiful, upright, active, no such visible picture of God, in heaven or earth, as man was; not sun, moon, nor stars, not earth, and sea, or the visible heavens themselves, have so much of their Maker in them as the body of man; his very corporeal senses had much of God in them, one might easily have known who was their father

But now in glory, saith the apostle, " Our vile body shall be fashioned like unto his glorious body," Phil. iii. 21. The glorified body of Christ shall be the glory and the wonder of heaven ; and our body, saith the apostle, shall be like his, conformable unto his glorious body. What a mirror of glory will the saints be, in their souls conformed to the Divine nature, and their body conformed to the glory of the human nature of Jesus Christ, the Lord of glory ; Oh wonderful, astonishing transfiguration ! Well said the apostle, " It doth not yet appear what we shall be." Surely eye hath not seen, nor ear heard, neither can it enter into the heart of man, &c.

This will be an infinite compensation to the saints of God, for all their holy endeavours of being like to God ; that as obedient children they have been followers of their heavenly Father, Eph. v. 1 ; and for all the reproaches and abasements they sustained from a reprobate world, because of those endeavours.

Oh, how much better are the reproaches of Christ than all the grandeur and applause in the world ! Be of good cheer, all ye servants of God, the time is coming when you shall not repent of your conformity to God and Christ in holiness, but shall ever sing, I thank the Lord who gave me counsel, and taught me to choose the better part, which shall never be taken away from me.

I come now to the completion and perfection of this last fruit and consequence of Christ's coming, the saints' cohabitation and fellowship with the Lord, namely, the extent and duration of it in this particle, " ever." " We shall ever be with the Lord." Ever, a little word, but of immense signification ! a child may speak it, but neither man nor angel can understand it. Oh who can take the dimensions of eternity? The whole space between the creation of the world and the dissolution of it, would not make a day in eternity; yea, so many years as there be days in that space would not fill up an hour in eternity. Eternity is one entire circle, beginning and ending in itself. This present world, which is measured out by such divisions and distinctions of times, is therefore mortal, and will have end, 2 Cor. iv. 18.

If eternity did consist of finite times, though ever so large and vast, it would not be eternity, but a longer tract of time only; that which is made up of finite is finite. Eternity is but one immense, indivisible point, wherein there is neither first nor last, beginning nor ending, succession nor alteration, but is like God himself, one and the same for ever.

But why? What good have the saints done to merit such an everlasting of bliss.

Nay, christians, if we go that way to work, we shall be sure to fall short of this ever. A heaven proportionable to the saints' merit is not to be found; unless it be amongst their antipodes in the regions of darkness, if there be a heaven there: "The wages of sin is death, but the gift of God is eternal life through Jesus Christ our Lord," Rom. vi. 23. Hell is the wages of sin, pure and proper merit; but heaven is a free, gratuitous gift, a gift in regard of us, though merit in regard of Christ. Eternal life is the gift of God, through Jesus Christ our Lord.

So that if it be demanded, Why heaven must be for ever? The first and only account of merit is the blood of Jesus Christ; the saints were once a lost generation, that had sold themselves and their inheritance too, and had not wherewithal to redeem either. But they had a near kinsman, even their elder Brother by the mother's side, to whom the right of redemption did belong, who being a mighty man of wealth, the Heir of all things, undertook to be their *Goel*, and, out of his own proper substance, to redeem both them and their inheritance; them to be his own inheritance, Eph. i. 10, and heaven to be theirs, 1 Pet. i. 4. And therefore, had heaven been but a moment short of eternity, the Redeemer had over-bought it, for he laid out the infinite treasures of his blood upon the purchase, Acts xx. 28. Had not heaven been infinite also, as in value, so likewise in duration, it had not stood with the justice of God, or his love to his Son, to have taken so dear for it.

It is this " ever " in the text, which makes heaven to be but an even bargain : were there a period of time, though after the revolution of never so many ages, wherein the purchase were to expire; price, and inheritance, and heirs, were all lost for ever.

A second account may be in respect of the saints themselves. The saints have immortal souls, souls that have an " ever" stamped upon them; an ever, an enduring ever, though not a beginning ever, or rather an ever without beginning; of such an ever the saints were incapable : God himself, with holy reverence be it spoken, could not have bestowed such an ever upon the creatures, for then he must have made them so many gods; and this God could not do : but now an ever, an enduring ever, God by Divine covenant conferred upon their souls, and will invest their bodies also with at the resurrection, that so eternal beings might be capable of eternal rewards : the wicked of torments, the godly of bliss, both eternal; if there were not this ever upon the beatitudes, as well as upon the persons of the saints, they would be extremely losers by it, and outlive their own happiness

A third reason is, that such a cessation of the joys of heaven would be as inconsistent with the saints' graces, as it is with their beings. God hath beautified their immortal souls with immortal graces, their love abides for ever, 1 Cor. xiii. 13; their zeal is eternal, their holiness eternal, and all their qualifications for glory are eternal; and can their glory itself be mortal? It were in vain to contend for perseverance in grace, should we admit falling away from glory. Poor saints indeed, if neither grace here, nor glory hereafter, could secure their happiness! If grace, indeed, could be lost in this life, and glory in the future, the foundation of the Lord were not sure, and the saints of all men most miserable! Such a cessation is totally inconsistent with the orthodox faith.

But the main pillars upon which this blessed article of our faith, everlasting life, is built, are the glorious attributes of God: I shall therefore pursue the discovery of this delightful contemplation unto the spring-head.

1. The wisdom of God is the head corner stone, upon which we build the belief of this doctrine, heaven's eternity. Not to recur to any thing already spoken, I shall only take the hint of the psalmist's question, Psa. lxxxix. 47; " Wherefore hast thou made all men in vain?" For the better understanding whereof, we are to take notice, that the rise of the question is an affecting complaint of the prophet concerning the brevity and misery of the present life, in Job's phrase, (Heb.) " Short of days and full

of trouble:" in the former part of the verse, " Lord, remember how short my time is." And in this latter part of the verse he doth, as it were, expostulate the case with God, why God would have it so? " Wherefore hast thou made all men in vain?" In which words, although he seem to ask God the question, yet he giveth himself the answer, and the answer is negative—No; God made not men in vain: it is not possible that the wisdom of God should make such an excellent creature as man, the masterpiece of the whole nether world, to no purpose. It cannot be, that God should bring in such a creature only to take a turn or two in the world, and then to disappear, never to be heard of any more! What then? Why thence he doth rationally infer, that certainly in man's creation God had a design upon him, in order to a future estate. And what was that? but what the wise man discovers to us, " The Lord hath made all things for himself," Prov. xvi. 4, for his own glory: the wicked for the day of evil, to the manifestation of his justice, and the godly for the day of redemption, to the exaltation of his free grace.

But now after all this, should there be a period wherein the flames of hell should be extinguished, or the joys of heaven annihilated; if after the first creation suffered a miscarriage, the second also should prove an abortion; if man should outlive his heavenly paradise, as he did the earthly, though his lease should be made for ever so many lives, this would but aggravate the vanity of his creation. Surely such an improvidence is totally inconsistent with that immense understanding, whose most just title is, the only wise God.

2. Another attribute upon which this beatifical truth standeth is, the veracity and truth of God.

The Father of glory, who best knew what he had begotten, baptizeth the new and spiritual being of the saints, and all its high prerogatives, with the name of eternity, and of eternal glory, 2 Tim. ii. 10; 1 Pet. v. 10. Everlasting life; fourteen times so called in the New Testament, and once in the Old, Dan. xii. 2. Eternal life; thirty times so called by the evangelists and apostles. Everlasting kingdom, 2 Pet. i. 11. Enduring substance, Heb. x. 34. An incorruptible crown, 1 Cor. ix. 25. Pleasures for evermore, Psa. xvi. 11. A kingdom that cannot be moved, Heb. xii. 28. An eternal weight of glory, 2 Cor. iv. 17. Heaven is a weight of glory; both the Hebrew and Chaldee words signify both weight and glory; heaven is made all of massy glory; glory that would be too heavy even for the shoulders of glorified saints, were not underneath them the everlasting arms.

But as God puts forth omnipotence to cause the damned to subsist under their otherwise intolerable pains, for the glory of Divine justice; so, in heaven, he is pleased to exert the arm of his almighty power, to sustain the saints under their inconceivable weight of glory, for the more illustrious manifestation of his everlasting love.

But this is not all; as there is a weight of glory to make heaven as great as the saints can joyfully bear, so that weight must also be eternal, that so the glory may not be too short for them, but every way commensurate to all the dimensions of their souls.

This, this is the witness and testimony which God himself hath given to the saints' inheritance in light; and to show the infallibility of this testimony, the apostle gives that glorious character of God, " God that cannot lie," Tit. i. 2; and that in the very same scripture wherein he makes this glorious promise, " Eternal life, which God, that cannot lie, hath promised before the world began." Observe it, as if the apostle by the Spirit did foresee what atheism might object, or weakness of faith might call in question—the eternity of heaven. How can that be? Oh yes, saith the apostle, it must needs be so, God who cannot lie hath called it eternal life : cannot— he saith not will not, but cannot lie.

If heaven were but a moment shorter than the measure which the scripture giveth us, the apostle had ascribed to God a mistaken title, God that cannot lie. Upon such a testimony as this from the mouth of God, how securely may the saints lie down in their beds of dust, in confidence of enjoying an eternal rest, after the resurrection ?

3. Another attribute which mightily contributes assurance to the faith of heaven's eternity, is God's immutability. The unchangeableness of his counsel and purpose, will set the " ever" of the saints' vision and fruition of God beyond all dispute and hesitation. It was the very design and purpose of God upon the saints, in their regeneration and renewing by the Holy Ghost, which he shed upon them abundantly through Jesus Christ our Saviour, that being justified by his grace, they should be made heirs of eternal life. Did God manifest his eternal purpose to the world, of eternal life, and make such solemn provision for the carrying on that purpose upon the heirs of promise, by interesting the third person in the glorious Trinity, the Holy Ghost, in it, and after all this can heaven become but a peradventure, and the saints' everlasting communion with God prove a scepticism or ungrounded opinion only ?

4. Such a supposed cessation of heaven's glory is totally inconsistent with the mercy and goodness of God. That man of God, holy David, begins his psalm of thanksgiving, in this lower choir of saints, with this strain, " Oh give thanks unto the Lord, for he is good, for his mercy endureth for ever," Psa. cxxxvi. 1. And having begun in that strain, he can sing no other tune all the psalm over, it is the burden of the song, " For his mercy endureth for ever." And shall we imagine he is now tuning his hallelujahs to a lower key in that celestial choir, to him that sitteth upon the throne, and to the Lamb!

No; mercy in God is not a moral, or mortal, virtue, but an essential attribute, God himself eternal. Mercy in God hath been from eternity, and shall be to eternity; it can no more outlive its objects, " the vessels of mercy prepared unto glory," Rom. ix. 23, than it can cease to be mercy. God is the Father of mercies, and mercy can never go childless; God must exercise the infiniteness of his mercy exten- sive to all eternity, as well as intensive above all dimensions.

5. The omnipotence of God doth gratify his mercy in this design; for while mercy poureth in this strong cordial of the Lord's joy immeasurably into the vessels of glory, omnipotence doth support and strengthen those vessels, that they split not with their own fulness; it were not else imaginable how created vessels should hold uncreated glory; and if the vessel should run out, or fail, the liquor would be lost.

6. God is eternal, and therefore heaven must be eternal also. In heaven there are no second causes, which are obnoxious to contingency or alteration.

All causes there are resolve. into the first Being
and sovereign cause, where they remain fixed and
immutable as that immense Being himself; and because he liveth eternally, they shall so live also.
The eternity of God's being lays the foundation of
the eternity of the saints' glory.

"The Lord God Almighty, and the Lamb, are
the temple of it," Rev. xxi. 22 ; the sun that shineth
there by day, and the moon by night, are no part of
the first creation, which is to pass away, Matt. v. 18,
but "the glory of God doth lighten it, and the Lamb
is the light thereof," Rev. xxi. 23.   There shall not
be so much as a post of the old fabric in this new
building, to weaken or endanger it.   God alone is the
roof and foundation of heaven ; the very centre and
circumference is God.   All the arches and pillars of
heaven are made of the tree of life, in which no
worm can breed, which may corrode or consume the
saints' mansions.   No moth is there to fret and eat
out the long white robes wherewith the saints are
adorned ; nor thief to break into the palace of the
great King, to steal away their crown from them.
There is malice enough, indeed, in that Apollyon, the
angel of the bottomless pit, and all his cursed crew,
to act such hellish villanies, not upon the saints only,
but upon God himself, even to pull him out of his
throne if they could ; but thanks be to God, they
are made fast enough in the lowest dungeon, where
they are staked down by a perpetual decree, and
"reserved in chains of darkness for ever ;" so that
the saints need not fear that anti-christian brood
shall ever break loose to cast one fire-ball into the
walls of the New Jerusalem, or to break open the
gates thereof to disturb their peace.

In a word, the manna of those upper heavens,

which is the angelical food the saints live on, is not
subject to breed worms, which may corrupt their
constitution : behold ! the worm is only in the nether
place of darkness ; and yet neither can that eat out
any part of the subject on which it feedeth !   Oh
how sweet would that worm be to the lost, if but
once in a thousand years it might eat out but a piece
of them, till they were utterly consumed ! but, woe
and alas ! the worm knows only how to augment,
but not how to shorten the torments of the damned;
but as it is a never-dying worm itself, so is the
miserable subject also upon which it feedeth. There
is fire in hell, but it is such only as doth nourish its
fuel, not diminish it.   Whence should this be, but
because " the breath of the Lord like a stream of
brimstone doth kindle it?" Isa. xxx. 33.

And if the justice of God gives eternity both to
the torment of hell, and the tormented also to sustain it, how much easier and sweeter is it to conceive that the shining of God's face is both the eternity of the blessed in glory, and of their bliss also.

7. Another attribute is love.   Which way should
the glory of the saints come to be extinguished, or
so much as eclipsed ?   If such a thing could be, it
must arise from a cessation of Divine love, which
cannot be supposed.   Will God grow weary of their
company? Behold! he made them, when he brought
them into that state of glory, as perfect as he would
have them be ; I had well nigh said, as perfect as
he could make them, that they might be a meet
bride for his only begotten Son ; and now behold,
he that hated putting away in the fantastical
Jew, unless it were in case of adultery, will he
give the Lamb's wife a bill of divorce, and put
her out of doors, in whom, since her first reception,

there was never found the least disloyalty, no not in thought, but remaineth without spot, or wrinkle, or any such thing, as immaculate as the elect angels? or must they also fare no better than the angels that kept not their first estate? Must all be cast out for ever, and heaven stand as a house to be let, without a tenant? Were not this more than a " shadow of turning?" James i. 17. Of the Lord and Head of the saints in the days of his flesh it was said, " Having loved his own, he loved them to the end." And is his love less now in heaven than it was on earth? These are prodigious blasphemies, not once to be admitted into our thoughts. Nay, saith God, " The Lord hath appeared of old unto me, saying, Yea, I have loved thee with an everlasting love, therefore with loving kindness have I drawn thee," Jer. xxxi. 3.

8. Another attribute is justice. The cessation of heaven and hell would utterly destroy Divine justice, and make that cease also for ever. Take away those two tremendous patterns of rewards and punishments, by which the saints here below do justify God, and vindicate the truth of the christian religion against all other religions in the world, and you cut the very sinews of religion, and make the laws of God vain and insignificant; you starve the hope of the godly, and extinguish the fear of the wicked.

Christians, this is the measuring reed of the New Jerusalem, the cube of the heavenly temple, the breadth, and length, and height, whereof none but he that can lay his right hand on the one end of eternity, and his left hand on the other end, hath given unto us; the computation whereof infinitely exceeds our arithmetic, yea, the arithmetic of all the angels in heaven.

Those comparisons of the running out of an hour-glass by a single sand once in the revolution of a thousand years, by which computation there would be scarce six sands lessened in the glass since the creation of the world to this day; or, a little bird's carrying away a mountain of sand by one small dust once in a twelvemonth; the emptying of the sea by a drop once in an age, and whatever of the like nature, these are but like the span of an infant to measure the circle of the heavens, so many empty ciphers without a figure to calculate eternity by, though they may seem hyperboles to our childish capacities; oh who can describe eternity? It is an ocean without a bottom, it cannot be fathomed; a sea that can never be sailed over from shore to shore.

Ever is that which cannot be measured but by itself; ever is that out of which take ever so many ages, and worlds of time, there is not a moment less to come; ever is still to begin, never to end. Eternity is still entire, a spring which fills as fast as it empties; a vast circle, which begins where it ends, and ends where it begins.

And now christians, is this the duration of heaven? Is this, nothing less than this, the measuring line of the saints' abode with God? What! ever with the Lord? Oh the purchase of Christ! Oh the gift of God! Oh the love of the Spirit! How unsearchable are his counsels, and his thoughts past finding out! Thanks be to God for his unspeakable gift!

And here might fix a full point to mine own and the reader's labour; but because I find our apostle closing his words of comfort with a word of counsel, " Wherefore comfort one another," &c., give me leave to follow my guide, and before we dismiss this beatifical contemplation, let us inquire a little further what blessed improvement may be made of it, even on this side of eternity !

Use 1. Learn then in the first place, who is the truly blessed man, and wherein real blessedness consists. We see all the sons and daughters of Adam seeking for happiness, but few or none finding what they seek for ; all agree in the notion, but they differ in the object. People generally go for happiness to the world's trinity ; " The lust of the flesh, the lust of the eyes, the pride of life," 1 John ii. 16. But, alas ! these have it not to give ; men would fain squeeze that out of the world which God never put into it.

Such of the sons and daughters of Adam as have had the candle of the Lord, which was put out by the fall, lighted anew by the Sun of righteousness, are mightily enabled by the irradiation of the Holy Ghost, to discern the airiness and emptiness of all sublunary and elementary happiness ; and to make choice of more solid, supercelestial excellences for their chief good ; to sing with the sweet singer of Israel, " In thy presence is fulness of joy, and at thy right hand there are pleasures for evermore," Psa. xvi. 11.

Moses in the Old Testament, and Paul in the New, stand as two pillars of fire, to light men the way to true blessedness. Moses was courted by all the honours, pleasures, and treasures of Egypt, to espouse them as his ultimate and supreme beatitudes, but he shakes them off all, as once Paul the viper into the fire, not less full of poison than that venomous beast was, Acts xxviii. 3, 4. The honour and grandeur of Pharaoh's court came to do him homage; every one in the king's court, for there he was brought up, bowed the knee, and saluted Moses by the prince-like title of the son of Pharaoh's daughter; it is generally thought that he was no less than heir-apparent to the crown of Egypt, Pharaoh having no child but that daughter, and she, having adopted him to be her son from the cradle of bulrushes; yet all this glory did Moses, when he came to years, and able to make his own choice, refuse, by faith seeing what a hollow, insignificant advancement this was. It was not the Egyptian monarchy which could make Moses happy, especially in the terms he must take it; namely, to turn Egyptian, and forsake the society of God's people. No, said Moses, I will have none of it; to suffer with God's people here, and to reign with God hereafter, is a felicity infinitely to be preferred before all the empires in the world.

This temptation failing, next succeeded pleasure, called by the apostle " the lust of the flesh," and impudently solicits Moses. All the beauties of the king's court, delicious fare, ravishing music, beautiful gardens, stately walks, fruitful orchards, pools of water, princely sports and pastimes; in a word, all the delights of the sons of men, the sensual fruitions of an Egyptian paradise; if these can make Moses happy they are at his service, he may be where he will, and do what he please : oh dangerous temptation! Did it not take? What is the reason? Why, faith here also stepped in to Moses' rescue; Moses by his piercing eye of faith did quickly discern a sad blemish in the face of pleasure, though it was ever so artificially painted.

This offer also thus despised, the mammon of Egypt presents itself to Moses; money may tempt him that is not taken with beauty. What say you, Moses; all the treasures of Egypt attend your highness, ready to make you one of the richest monarchs in the world, for so at that time Egypt was for jewels, gold, silver, precious stones, all the peculiar treasure of kings; the most opulent of all kingdoms round about, the very magazine of the world; Moses need never to fear being poor any more; is not this enough to make a man happy? No, not a Moses; a covetous mammonist might have taken it down with a grateful swallow, such a one as Felix was, that insatiable gulf of riches, as the historian calls him; but Moses, as the papists once said of Luther, could not be caught with money. The reproach of Christ was a mountain of infinitely more valuable, invaluable treasure; esteeming the reproach of Christ, that is, Christ in the promise, or the reproach of the church, which is Christ mystical, 1 Cor xii. 12. Oh, saith Moses, let me be counted worthy to suffer reproach for Christ and his people's sake, and I desire no more riches in the world. How so? Moses' faith did clearly outbid all the proffers of Egypt, he looks within the veil, fixing his eye upon the "recompense of reward," Heb. xi. 26, and there he discovered such honours, pleasures, treasures, as eye never saw, ear never heard, nor can enter into the heart of man, 1 Cor. ii. 9, in comparison whereof all the preferments, delights, and riches of Egypt were but as so many gilded crowns, painted banquets, insignificant ciphers, ten thousand of which in the sum total make just nothing.

Thus Moses turns his back upon the world and all her glittering elements, protesting, as it were, as it is said of Luther, that God should not turn him off with these things; he had weighed them in the balance of faith, and found them too light to make a chief good of, there wanted something within.

Such an account doth the apostle Paul, that evangelical Moses, bring in concerning the whole visible world, when it was, as it were, set forth to sale in all its splendour and gallantry, to what merchants would bid for it. Paul would offer nothing, but passeth by in a holy scorn, and will not so much as cast an eye upon it. "We look not at the things which are seen, but at the things which are not seen," 2 Cor. iv. 18.

How much doth the judgment of saints differ from the judgment of the men of the world; the things which fall under sight and sense were Paul's nothings, but they are the men of the world's only solid substances and realities; on the other hand, invisible things of eternity, they were in the holy apostle's estimation, the only entities and real beings, but in the judgment of the men of the world, they are the only chimeras and shadows, which have no more being than what they have in the fancy : so far were the things of the world from being able to make up a happiness for a rational creature, that the apostle accounts them not worth a look, unless it be of contempt and derision. Mark the most proper title which the wisdom of God can give these seen things is, a nonentity; the world in all its gaiety and bravery is nothing else but an apparition, a great, goodly, gilded nothing; and why so, but upon the account of their lubricity and fickleness, there is no more staying of them than of the running stream, or wind, or bird in the air, for riches verily make themselves wings; riches, that is, whatever it is which men make their confidence, they make themselves wings ; a metaphor from a bird in the nest, it

s 2

is hatched naked, yet feathers out of the very nature
of the bird, if no hand take it out of the nest, yet in
short time it will take wings and fly away ; just so
it is with riches, of what species soever, if the plun-
derer or oppressor, the thief, fire, inundations, &c.
give them no wings, they will quickly give themselves wings, and take their flight towards heaven,
from whence they came.

And are these the things which are proper to
make up to a man a standing, holding felicity ?
No, saith the apostle, the " things which are not
seen are eternal." God, and Christ, and the Holy
Ghost, and angels, and the spirits of just men made
perfect, and heaven, and glory, &c. these are the
only beatifying objects, as being only of a pure, spiritual, fixed, immutable nature; the " things that are
not seen are eternal," and upon that account only
able to constitute an adequate blessedness for an
immense and an immortal soul, an intellectual
being.

Corporeal delights, like so many sparks, may
make a crack and vanish ; nothing can seem great
and excellent to him that knows the infinite vast-
ness of eternity. " Ever with the Lord," here is a
chief good for a heaven-born soul : this Moses kept
his eye upon, and therefore all terrestrial felicities
were but as sounding brass and a tinkling cymbal,
much noise, but no harmony. He saw Him that is
invisible; an elegant contradiction : he saw him that
could not be seen ; he saw him by an eye of faith,
whom he could not see by an eye of sense, and so
did saint Paul, and so did all his fellow-apostles and
saints, " We look on the things which are not seen,"
that is, we look on them, and them alone, as our
ultimate, unmixed, and supreme good.

Be wise now, therefore, O ye kings, and be instructed, O ye people of the earth, spend not your strength in vain, and your labour for that which satisfieth not, strive not to force that out of the creature which God never put in; you may as well extract fire out of the ocean, mollify rocks into syrup, wash the Ethiopian white, as squeeze happiness out of mortality.

Behold! vast sums are required to make up a chief good, as goodness, fulness, suitableness, and immutability.

Find me such a creature under the moon, and do with it what you please : but saith the church, " Lord, thou shalt choose our inheritance for us," Psa. xlvii. 4 ; yea, " The Lord is my portion, saith my soul," Lam. iii. 24. It is impossible to churn happiness out of a chest of gold, it will never come; you can never make unfading crowns of fading flowers.

Or, I will tell you when pleasures, profits, honours, will make you blessed; when you can sow your fields with grace, and fill your barns with sheaves of saffron; when the Lord Jesus is your wine, the word of God your bread, the bosom of Christ your bed of love, the honour of Christ your trade, the graces of the Spirit your gold, then, and not till then, you may write happiness upon these things. These are the pleasures which are for evermore, this is the enduring substance, these the crowns that wither not, here you may find that which your soul seeketh for; here is the mine, here is the vein, here the spring of happiness, " ever with the Lord."

The devil offers you the glory of the world, God offers eternal glory; put not a scorn upon God's

s 3

offers, nor a cheat upon your own souls. The devil's offers are not only inconsiderable, but fraudulent, he offers that which is none of his own to give, the world; or if it were, it would be infinitely too short of the price he will have for it, your precious and immortal souls : " What shall a man give in exchange for his soul?" And suppose thou shouldst repent of thy bargain, the devil will not repent of his, nor will he sell as he buyeth, shouldst thou say to him, Here, devil, take the world, and give me my soul again, I repent; he would but laugh at thee, and say as the priests said to Judas, " See thou to that, what is that to me ?" thou hadst what thou agreedst for, I have done thee no wrong.

The sinner's feast is soon served in, but the messengers of Divine justice are preparing the reckoning, and then are ready to take away. And how sad will the catastrophe of that pleasure be, when the sting of the payment must survive in the conscience of the sinner to all eternity ! Glorified saints are entertained upon free cost; no affrighting thoughts need discompose them, so as to break any one draught of those pleasures wherewith their cup runs over, or to hinder the pleasing swallow of those delicate morsels wherewith their table is full fraught; no army of evils or of devils can break in upon them, to make them forsake their nuptial feast.

Oh what a prodigious forfeiture of reason is this, for the momentary satisfaction of a sordid lust, to lose an eternal dwelling with God, this transcendant beatitude, "ever with the Lord!" Yea, to plunge oneself into that opposite gulf of misery, never with the Lord, but to " be punished with everlasting destruction from the presence of the Lord, and from the glory of his power," 2 Thess. i. 9.

Use 2. It may serve, in the next place, not only to inform the erroneous judgment, but also to awaken the sleepy conscience. Is this heaven? Is this the chief good of immortal souls? Then oh how much is every one of us concerned to secure our interest in this glory! What a folly is it for men to take such indefatigable pains to make sure an earthly inheritance, to run from lawyer to lawyer, to attend early in the morning, and late at night, to give fee upon fee, to spend half a patrimony or an estate to secure the rest, and as if heaven and the beatifical vision were the only trivial, worthless thing, a mere accident that might be present or absent without the least prejudice at all to a man's happiness; I say, to take up that upon trust, and to leave this " ever with the Lord," upon a peradventure! Oh unspeakable folly and madness!

Oh that men would consider seriously, what avail will it be at death and judgment, to have had assurance of many large earthly possessions while they lived, and then to have neither scrip nor scroll, as we say, to show for heaven, that blessed inheritance of the saints in light, when they come to die! to be able to say now, My house and my land, and my silver, and my crown, and my kingdom, but not then, My Lord and my God, my heaven and my inheritance! I have bestowed all my time and strength to assure my earthly possessions, but now I can keep these no longer, and can call nothing mine own but the dungeon of darkness, there to be staked down to easeless and endless torments ; or at best to cry out with Adrianus, I know not whither thou art going, O my precious darling, my never-dying soul!

Confident and presumptuous suppositions may quiet

and satisfy the sleepy and slothful conscience in fair weather; but in the hour of temptation, when the rain shall descend, and the floods come, and the winds blow, then these foolish confidences will fall, because they were built upon the sand, and great will be the fall thereof, Matt. vii. 27

Then, when in hell, the miserable soul, made now as sensible as formerly it was secure, shall from thence lift up its eyes, and see Abraham, and Isaac, and Jacob, and all the prophets in the kingdom of God, and itself thrust out, what furious and fiery reflections will then rend and vex the conscience, and the sinner cry out with horror, " O wretch that I am, I might have had pardon and glory as well as others; I had as many means and motives, I had as much need as they, it was as much my concern as any others, but I trifled and took up all upon trust, and would not give diligence to the full assurance of hope to the end ; oh now a thousand worlds, if I had them, for a may be, which once I had ; oh for one of those days of grace which I then sinned away, and idled out in the pursuit of vanity ; for one of those tenders and offers of salvation, which then pursued me, and I would not hearken, but thought I might have had heaven time enough when I had done with the world ; but now I see how miserably I have mocked God, and deceived myself; the day of grace is now gone, and the time of peace is at its full stop and period, and instead of ever with the Lord, here I must lie in these flames with the devil and reprobate spirits for ever."

Oh that sinners would therefore in this their day be wise, and know the things which belong unto their peace, before they be hid from their eyes

I knew a rich mammonist, near the place where

I was born, that would once a day take all his bags
of silver and gold out of his trunks, and laying them
in several heaps (for he was exceeding rich) upon a
large table, would go to the utmost end of the room,
and there having glutted his eyes with so delightful
an object for a good while, would all on a sudden
take his run to the table, and with stretched out
arms, gathering all into one vast heap, as a man
overcome and distracted with joy, cry out, All is
mine, all is mine! Why may not the children of
the kingdom rejoice in hope of the glory of God?
and collecting those treasures of glory into several
heaps, and embracing them with the arms of faith,
cry out in an holy ecstasy, All is mine, all is mine!
Shall the adult heir of a fair lordship, or principality, be often inquiring into his patrimony, search
into his writings, and even grow great with the
thoughts and contemplations of what he is born to?
And shall not the heirs of the inheritance of the
saints in light, much rather delight themselves with
the fore contemplation of their incorruptible, undefiled inheritance, that fadeth not away, reserved in
heaven for them? 1 Pet. i 4.

Yes, so we would, if we were sure it were ours.
And is that the cause of your apathy and flatness
of spirits to these heavenly fruitions? Truly, this
very uncertainty should even startle and affright us
into an earnest contention to make heaven sure; so
infinite a weight of glory, and we not ascertained of
our interest upon some good scripture evidence, is
enough to make us to forget to eat our meat, enough
to break our sleep, and to keep our eyes waking all
the night long, and to make us take little comfort in
the present comforts we possess.

You will surely ask, then, what are the evidences ?

Evidence 1. Why, truly this one thing would amount to an evidence, (and not the least evidence,) namely, active endeavour to assure ourselves of a share in this inheritance of the saints ; this would argue an high estimate of this estate in the practical judgment, as most incomparably and absolutely eligible ; this is the very language of an heaven-born soul, What have I to count upon but my treasure which is in heaven ? What business have I on earth comparable to this, to ensure my portion in heaven ? for this cause I was born, and for this end I came into the world; the whole earth, in comparison of heaven, is but a dunghill.

Evidence 2. Especially if the holiness of heaven do kindle those desires in us more than the happiness ; when a poor soul can truly say, I should not account it an heaven, were it not that it is a land of holiness, a land flowing with milk and honey, of pure and immaculate joys ; that there the beauty of holiness shines forth with inconceivable lustre and glory ; and there, saith the soul, I shall be in some degree like my God, glorious in holiness ; this is not only an evidence of heaven, but heaven itself.

Evidence 3. Again, an universal hatred of sin is a good token that heaven is designed for thee ; for hatred of sin is the negative part of holiness, and heaven is a place provided by God on purpose, that there the saints may be as holy as they will without disturbance or reproach. Fear not to think much and often of heaven ; if sin be an offence to thee, if sin be a hell on earth to thee, heaven is designed for thee to be thy paradise. Fear not to be often solacing thyself in the contemplation of that place where sin never entered, or if it did, it was cast out as soon as ever it was conceived.   Indeed it is but a fancy men have taken up, that they love happiness, while they continue to love sin ; a chaste love of heaven can never consist with the love of impure lusts.   Sin is the devil's image, holiness is God's ; he loves not the beauty of holiness that would have the devil advanced thither.   If men would not have it so, why else do they give sin such free entertainment in their own bosoms, and will by no means give it a bill of divorce ?

Evidence 4. A superlative love to Him that hath purchased this state for us, and us for it, is an infallible evidence of our right to it, and interest in it, that is, the Lord Jesus Christ; and a strong motive upon which gracious souls are so often in heaven by their contemplations, is, that thereby an eye of faith they may behold, not the purchase only, but the Purchaser, whom having not seen we love, and whom loving, we would fain see; and this is the glory of every one that is so affected ; so it is expressly said, " The things which God hath prepared for them that love him," 1 Cor. ii. 9. Dost thou love the Lord Jesus ? Ascend often in the chariot of love, that thou mayest see his face, and in his face the glory and beauty of heaven.   Surely such as love not Christ, and yet think they love heaven, are miserably mistaken, they know neither heaven nor Christ, and may well cry out, " Is there not a lie in my right hand ?" Isa. xliv. 20.

Well, christians, you that would gladly have your portion in this glory, shut your eyes downward. I may invert the angel's question to the men of Galilee, Acts i. 11, and say, Why stand ye poring upon the earth ? Yea, why crawl ye with your bellies upon tne ground, as if you had inherited the serpent's curse as well as your own ? Lift up your hearts, let your souls often withdraw and bid the body farewell for a time, that you may, with Paul, be rapt up to the third heaven, and then see things which may even transport your souls out of your bodies ; seek the things above, set your affections on things above, where Christ sitteth at the right hand of God. Pre-enjoyment by faith is a kind of prepossession, an entrance beforehand into the glorious joys of our Lord and Master ; an ascent into the mount of transfiguration, when the soul may truly say, " Master, it is good for us to be here ;" and the oftener ye come, the more welcome Christ will make you. They that know the Divine relishes of such contemplation, would not exchange them for the most delicious fruitions of the whole inferior creation. Oh strive to antedate glory, and to get into heaven before your time !

Strive above all things to obtain full assurance of future bliss. To this end take heed of neglecting your communion with God in holy duties ; take heed of bitterness, wrath, anger, by all these the Spirit is grieved. It is a tender thing, and you may quickly grieve it ; and if you grieve your Comforter, who shall comfort you ? And if you grieve the Holy Spirit, who shall sanctify you ? And if you grieve the sealing Spirit, who shall seal you to the day of redemption ? Never expect a pre-enjoyment of heaven as long as you are not afraid of grieving the Spirit, which is the earnest of the inheritance. Carnal men's question is, May I do this, and not be damned ? But a godly man's question is, Can I do this, and not grieve the Spirit of God ? Will not Jesus Christ take this unkindly ?

Take heed too of any thing that may darken your evidences; a small drop of ink or dirt falling upon an evidence, may make it illegible, or darken it: people make nothing of small sins, but small sins do not the least hurt to the soul; the least hair casts its shadow; and a barley-corn laid upon the light of the eye, will hinder the sight of the sun as well as a mountain. "Abstain from all appearance of evil," if you desire God should be a "God of peace" to you, 1 Thess. v. 22, 23. Abstain from all appearance of evil, if you expect a pre-enjoyment of heaven.

Make much of the least intimations of love and favour from God, in prayer, hearing, or reading, meditation, at Christ's table, or any other of your holy converses with God; the least beam or ray of God's face upon thy soul, let it be as life from the dead; do as Benhadad's servants did to the king of Israel, "Diligently observe whether any thing will come from him," 1 Kings xx. 33; any smile from Christ's face, any wink of his eye, any sweet breath, any whisper of peace from his lips, such as, possibly, "Son be of good cheer, thy sins be forgiven thee," or the like, and hastily catch at it; Thy son, Lord! I am most unworthy to be called so, not worthy to be a hired servant; but, Lord, since thou pleasest to deign me so infinite an honour, "Behold the servant of the Lord, and be it unto me according to thy word," Luke i. 38. Come in, thou blessed Lord, and take possession of my soul, and rule in me according to all the desire of thine heart, making me meet for that heaven thou hast prepared for me.

Be much in duties of mortification: lie often in sackcloth and ashes before the Lord; exercise thyself in frequent acts of self-denial; little dost thou know how soon God may put a new song into thy

T

mouth : "Lord, thou hast turned for me my mourning into dancing, thou hast put off my sackcloth, and girded me with gladness, to the end my glory may sing praise unto thee and not be silent," &c., Psa. xxx. 11, 12.

Be careful to mortify corruptions, " and to crucify the flesh with the affections and lusts," Gal. v. 24. A mortified christian is the fittest vessel to contain the precious liquor of assurance : mortification first purifieth, and then dilates the heart, and makes it capacious to Divine consolations. " I keep under my body and bring it into subjection," 1 Cor. ix. 27, was his voice that could say, " We know that if our earthly house of this tabernacle were dissolved, we have a building of God," &c. 2 Cor. v. 1. "He filleth the hungry with good things."

Set others to pray for thee : yet not every one, who, it may be, can pray; assurance of future glory is not an errand to send every common christian to the throne of grace about : special favourites are employed to princes for special favours; thou canst not pray thyself, nor set any of the household of faith at work for a higher boon than for assurance. Oh get some special favourite, under the great Mediator, some Noah, some Job, some Daniel, &c., men or women of great acquaintance and much communion with God, christians of large experience and eminent holiness, to such God usually denieth nothing. " The secret of the Lord is with them that fear him, and he will show them his covenant," Psa. xxv. 14.

Speak to others as men and women ordinarily bespeak prayers; Pray, pray for me, and the like; and, truly for the most part, it passeth for a common, if not a vain compliment, and there is an end of it.

Speak to some, not heathen, and they will laugh at thee, they know not what thou sayest; speak to others, and they will forget thee: he that makes not assurance his own concernment, how can he make it thine? Speak to serious, solid, broken-hearted christians, who know what assurance is, and what it is worth, earnestly beg of them, " If there be any consolation in Christ, if any comfort of love, if any fellowship of the Spirit, if any bowels and mercies?" that they would plead hard for that, in the interest of our Lord Jesus, if God would remember your poor thirsty soul for one draught of this wine of consolation, assurance of heavenly bliss; and they cannot, yea, they dare not forget thee : they know whose prayers have prevailed for themselves in the like petitions, and they dare not but pay their debts.

But whilst thou settest others to pray for thee, forget not to pray for thyself : if thou settest others to pray for thee, and prayest not thyself, thou art a hypocrite, and God will account thee as one that mocketh, and thou wilt get a curse, and not a blessing. Wherefore pray, pray constantly, and pray instantly; knock hard at the gate of heaven for this grand mercy, and if God open not the first, or second, or twentieth, or the hundredth time, yet, with Peter, continue knocking; let God know, as it were, that thou art resolved to take no denial to thy petition for assurance. This was the greatness of the poor woman of Canaan's faith, she would not be denied, Matt. xv. 27.

Be constant and conscientious in your attendance upon Christ's table ; behold it is the sealing ordinance, his banqueting-house, his presence-chamber, his marriage-feast, his bed of love, where he doth use to give out to his spouse his loves, Cant. vi. 12. Behold, the spirits run in the blood, and the sealing Spirit of Christ is not seldom conveyed in the precious streams of Christ's blood, in that mysterious ordinance. The holy supper was the pledge of his dying love, a seal of his last coming to receive home his spouse to himself. " This cup is the new testament in my blood ; this do ye, as oft as ye drink it, in remembrance of me. For as often as ye eat," &c. 1 Cor. xi. 25, 26. Christ would have his spouse perpetuate the remembrance of his dying love, that thereby they might look for a hastening of his coming, 2 Pet. iii. 12.

Oh let not thy place be empty at such a glorious festivity, who can tell whether the Lord may come in the very hour of this solemn ordinance, which he hath appointed to be the very sanction and pledge of his glorious and triumphant coming, and say concerning thee, " Where is the son of Jesse to-day ?" 1 Sam. xx. 27. Oh, at such a time for the Bridegroom to find thee absent, how unkindly may he take it ! Who that he might be sure not to miss thy company at this love-feast, hath said, " As often as ye eat," &c.

Use 3. It may serve as a spur to diligence and activity in the ways of God. On the other side of the resurrection, God hath prepared an eternity of glory for you, and therefore bestir yourselves in good earnest; do somewhat for God on this side the grave, that may, if possible, bear some proportion with your future expectation. Thou hast but a moment to work in, but an eternity to rest in; be industrious now, and anon thou shalt be glorious. Enter now into thy Lord's vineyard, and soon thou shalt enter into thy Lord's joy. Take pains here, there remains a rest, an eternal rest; not an eternity of being only, but an eternity of well-being; ever be with the Lord.

Ply the oar of duty, christians, a blessed haven is at hand; you look for more than others, what do you do more than others? Never did servants expect such a recompense of reward, " The gift of God is eternal life," Rom. vi. 23. Oh let the fear of missing this glory urge you to the greater diligence; let it stir you up to the most devoted acts of holiness and obedience.

There is no inducement to take pains comparable to this, " Ever with the Lord;" ever in the presence-chamber of the greatest Monarch in the world. Nay, ever upon the throne, giving laws to kingdoms; ever increasing treasures of gold, and silver, and precious stones; ever bathing in the full streams of sublunary pleasures, is no ways comparable to one moment's enjoyment of the presence of the Lord in heaven. Let that man's money perish with him, said that noble marquis Galeacius Caracciolus, who esteemeth all the gold in the world worth one day's society with Jesus Christ and his holy Spirit, &c.

I have often thought with myself, that if heaven were capable of grief, those very rivers of pleasures would swell with the tears of glorified souls, to think that they have served God no more, served him no better, did no more for that God who hath prepared such a heaven full of glory for such an unprofitable servant as I have been. Oh how coldly did I pray for this inestimable blessedness! With how little affection did I hear the report of this great salvation! And what little pains did I take for this exceeding and eternal weight of glory, which exceeds all hyperbole; while the slightest expressions are too big for my diligence! What! all this joy, and so little pains to obtain it! All this glory, and so little zeal for the glory of God! So great a harvest, and so little seed sown! So great a reward, and so little service! Surely there would be a day of humiliation kept in heaven, and it might well take up half eternity, to bewail the saints' remissness in the work of the Lord, were heaven capable of it, or did not the reflection of glorified souls upon the former iniquities of their holy things, issue only unto the admiration of the riches of that grace which hath brought them to glory

But though heaven will not admit of grief, thy present estate will: mourn, therefore, that thou hast been so dead and so dull in the service of God, who hath set before thee no less a reward than the enjoying of himself to all eternity; and let the sense thereof quicken thy dead heart to work after another rate for the little remnant of mortality yet behind. say not, Yet there is too much sand left in the glass for God and eternity; say rather, Oh that, were it not to keep me so much the longer from my Father's presence, oh that every hour yet behind were a day, every day a month, every month a year, every year a life! it were all too little for that hope which is laid up for me in heaven! Oh had I a hundred pair of hands, they were too little to employ in my heavenly Father's work! a hundred pair of feet, they would not carry me fast enough in the way of his commandments! a hundred pair of eyes were not enough to behold God in every creature round about me! a thousand tongues were not sufficient to trumpet forth his praises, "who hath made me meet to be a partaker of the inheritance of the saints in light!" Col. i. 12. Oh, what shall I do? If I cannot love God more, serve him better, bring him more glory, than hitherto I have done, I am undone, I am undone. Oh redeem your time, Eph. v. 16.

Christians, the eternal jubilee is at hand, the trumpet is ready to sound, and the glorious eternal liberty of the saints and servants of God ready to be proclaimed; up and be doing now, as ye would be found, when Christ shall come with his mighty angels, and his reward with him, that you may hear the blessed welcome, " Well done, good and faithful servant, enter into the joy of thy Lord," Matt. xxv. 21.

Use 4. This may serve as a preservative to the people of God to keep them from fainting and falling away in time of sufferings, and persecution for righteousness' sake.

" Ever with the Lord;" here is a short fight, but an eternal triumph; a short race, but an imperishable crown of glory; a short storm, but an eternal harbour, who would not almost be covetous and ambitious of suffering upon such gainful terms? One day with the Lord will more than pay for all the saints' sufferings, how much more this " ever with the Lord?" There is no proportion between a christian's cross and his crown, if the apostle have brought us in a true account, " I reckon that the sufferings of this present time are not worthy to be compared with the glory which shall be revealed in us," Rom. viii. 18. Compare a mole-hill with a mountain, a glow-worm with a sun, a drop with the ocean, and more disproportionable are a saint's sufferings unto his glory : here he lets drop a few tears, there he swims in a river of pleasures for

evermore.   To convince us of the odds, the apostle
puts both into scales, and the scales into the hand
even of reason itself, See, saith he, how infinitely
the reward preponderates the sufferings, 2 Cor. iv.
17. Affliction light, glory heavy; a weight of glory,
yea, an exceeding weight, yea, a far more exceeding
weight, hyperbole upon hyperbole.   Affliction but
for a moment, glory eternal ; let sense and reason
give sentence, what equality or proportion !   A
heavy burden may be borne a moment ; how much
more easily a light one, especially if ye add this
consideration, that after that little, little moment
past, burden shall never be laid upon the back any
more for ever ! We are apt to think that our sufferings are not only heavy, but intolerable, the only
unparalleled affliction in the world ; never sorrow
like our sorrow ! But they will appear as they are,
poor and inconsiderable, when we come to heaven ;
then our mountains will appear mole-hills.   How
will a prison look then, when for a few days' con-
finement we shall have the glorious liberty of the
sons of God, in the highest heavens days without
end ?   How will then the reproach of Christ appear
to be greater riches than the treasures of Egypt,
when for a little shame and ignominy, thou shalt
shine as the sun in the firmament for ever ?   How
will thy former poverty for Christ look then, when
thou shalt be possessed of the inheritance of the
saints in light ; " incorruptible, and undefiled, and
that fadeth not away, reserved in heaven for you ?"
1 Pet. i. 4. Nay, if thou shalt lose thy life for Christ,
it shall seem but a poor stake, when thou shalt be
crowned with all the beatitudes of life eternal.

If there could be grief in heaven about sufferings,
it would grieve the saint, who is now led by his suf-

ferings into so much glory, that he had suffered no more for Christ, or suffered with no more patience, courage, and holy triumph over the persecutors. Pore not then upon thy sufferings, but look up to the crown that is prepared to be set upon thy head after thy sufferings; behold martyrdom itself shall be but as Elijah's chariot, to carry thee up to heaven in triumph: "If we suffer with him, we shall also reign with him;" if we wear his crown of thorns, we shall wear his crown of glory; if we die with him, we shall also rise with him, and reign with him for ever. Think much of the kingdom to expel base fears in sufferings. Heaven in our eye will make us heroic in our persecutions; we glory not only in God, but "we glory in tribulation," Rom. v. 3. Hold out then, faith and patience, but one stile more, said Dr. Taylor, when he went to the stake, and I am at my Father's house. Oh this word, at my Father's house, at home, ever with the Lord! this made the holy man to leap over the stile, as if he had been a young man going to be married to his bride.

Use 5. It may serve as a sovereign cordial against the fear of death. Man having an immortal soul, naturally desireth and breatheth after eternity; but man in his corrupt estate, being ignorant and mindless of a blessed eternity with God, is not willing to die, to leave the shore of this life, and to venture upon the unknown, immense ocean of eternity; none but a Paul, who is ballasted with the hope of an everlasting habitation with the Lord, can desire to loose from the shore, to hoist up sail, and make for the heavenly Canaan.

Come hither then, O you trembling souls, who through the fear of death have all your life-time been subject to bondage, come hither, I say, and set your feet upon the neck of this king of terrois, and fear not to make that triumphant challenge of the apostle, " O death! where is thy sting? O grave! where is thy victory?" 1 Cor. xv. 55.   Death is swallowed up in victory, and, being conquered, serves to that high and honourable end—to be the saints' usher of state, to bring them into the presence of the King of glory, to behold his face, and to hear his wisdom ; from thenceforth to be, for ever to be, with the Lord.   Death serves the saints now for no use, but to kill mortality, and to extinguish corruption ; " This corruptible must put on incorruption, and this mortal must put on immortality," ver. 53   We shall ever be with the Lord in a perfect, incorruptible state of glory ; and this must be effected by means of death. Oh, what were ten thousand deaths, ushering in the soul into so much glory !

The glimmering presence of God with a believer here below, may conquer the fear of death ; " Though I walk through the valley of the shadow of death, I will fear no evil, for thou art with me," Psa. xxiii. 3. How much more may the hope of a full fruition of God in glory, deliver the saints from the bondage of fear.

" Ever with the Lord :" this puts lilies and roses into the ghastly face of death, and makes the king of terrors to outshine Solomon in all his glory. " Ever with the Lord," this makes death not only tolerable, but amiable, desirable ; for in this we groan, in this tabernacle, for this is earthly, earnestly desiring to be clothed upon with our house, which is from heaven ; the reason is, because that house is eternal in the heavens.   A saint looks out of the windows of this earthly tabernacle, and crieth out, as the mother of Sisera, " Why stay the wheels of his chariot thus long?" When shall I be carried to those eternal mansions, where I shall ever be with my Lord and Bridegroom?

Then tremble thou not, believer, at the approach of death, but go forth and meet him with this friendly salutation, Come in, thou blessed of the Lord; art thou come to fetch me to my Father? Welcome death! thou art my best friend next to Jesus Christ: death is only my passage into a blessed eternity. Death is Joseph's chariot, not to carry the saints down into Egypt, but up into Canaan; and how quickly doth he carry a believer thither! It is but winking, and he is at home; as soon as the eye of the body is closed here, the eye of the soul is open there! O blessed vision! to behold at once all the glories of eternity! Say then, with Jacob, Jesus, my Lord and Redeemer, is yet alive, and seated on the throne at the right hand of the Majesty on high, there proclaiming in the ears of all his trembling followers, " I am he that liveth and was dead: and behold I live for evermore. Amen, and have the keys of hell and death," Rev. i. 18. Fear not, O thou believer, to say with Jacob, " I will go and see him," not before I die, but I will die, that I may go and see him. Death is but the flame that must singe asunder the cords of thy mortality; the hand that shall open the cage, that thy soul may get loose, and take her flight for the mountain of spices, the glorious immortality and liberty of the sons of God.

Use 6. Lastly, it may teach us how to prize Christ, Love is a triumphant grace, a grace that hath eternity stamped upon it; it out-lives faith, for faith gives way to vision; and it doth out-last hope, for hope is swallowed up in fruition; what a man seeth,

why doth he yet hope for? "Whether there be pro
phesies, they shall fail; whether there be tongues,
they shall cease; whether there be knowledge, it
shall vanish away," 1 Cor. xiii. 8; but charity never
fails, but as long as God lives it lives; for God is love,
and they that love, dwell in God, and God in them.

I have finished, I cannot say perfected, the main
work intended, namely, the opening of the ten
words, or arguments of comfort, here laid down in
this model or platform by the Holy Ghost, as so
many sovereign cordials to revive disconsolate and
fainting christians over the death of their hopeful
relations, with the several improvements which
each word by itself may afford unto us.   But
before I do dismiss this discourse, I do observe
divers useful instructions lie couched in the general
improvement of these words, "comfort one another,"
which will serve as so many branches of information, which I cannot omit, and they are ten.

1. Sorrow not as men without hope, but comfort one another.   There is a sorrow for departed
friends which God condemns not.   Hopeless sorrow
is forbidden, ver. 13, but simply to mourn for the
loss of our gracious relations is not.   He that hath
wrapt up natural affections in our hearts, doth not
prohibit the due and moderate exercise of them.
Those persons without natural affections are in the
black roll amongst the most abominable part of
mankind : to be without natural affections is to do
violence against nature herself, and to violate the
law of humanity.   Covenant breakers without natural affection are monsters, not men.   Christ himself, who knew no sin, yet being acquainted with all
our griefs, even had this kind of sorrow for the dead;
" Jesus wept," John xi. 35, and his tears do here

instruct us in our duty. Holy Paul blots his epistle
to the Philippians with his tears for Epaphroditus,
"Lest," saith he, "I should have sorrow upon sorrow;"
he was sorrowful for his sickness, had he died there
would have been another flood of tears, sorrow upon
sorrow.   Where mention is made of the death of
public persons, there public lamentations for them
is mentioned also : the Spirit of God doth nowhere
reprove those tears, but rather puts a value upon
them as so many pearls.   As in the mourning for
Jacob, Gen. l. 11, for Josiah, 2 Chron. xxxv. 24, for
Samuel, 1 Sam. xxv. 1, for Stephen, Acts viii. 2. It is
reckoned amongst God's thunderbolts, their widows
made no lamentation, Psa. lxxviii. 64. The removal of
God's peace from a people, and prohibition to mourn
for their dead, are twin-judgments, or one the birth of
another . " Enter not into the house of mourning,
neither go to lament nor bemoan them, for I have
taken away my peace from this people," Jer. xvi. 5.
Tears are like wine, you may pour them out, but
take heed of excess ; you may weep, but as those
that weep not; you may mourn, but not as others,
which have no hope, 1 Cor. vii. 30.

2. Hence we learn, there is another work or duty
incumbent on christians, under the loss of gracious
relations, than only to mourn for them, namely, to
inquire, yea, with Benhadad's servants, diligently
to observe what words of comfort do fall from the
lips of scripture, and hastily to catch at them,
1 Kings xx. 33.   Comfort one another with these
words : yea, Lord, with these words do thou comfort thy servant !

We are usually either senseless under, or swallowed
up, with great losses ; either our affections are made
of iron, or they melt like wax, and we faint away.

u

Vehement sorrow is like raging fire, that turns every
thing into its own nature. It is thy work therefore to
study consolation, as well as to pore upon thy losses ;
to ballast thy soul with Divine comforts : " If I go
not away the Comforter will not come." Many times
the best of our earthly enjoyments stand between us
and our heavenly consolations : " But if I depart I
will send him unto you," John xvi. 7.   It is good
to resolve with ourselves, be my loss in this world
ever so great, it is capable of a reparation. For certainly, if the loss of Christ in his bodily presence
were to be repaired, there is nothing under the
whole heaven, the loss whereof we can sustain, but
may much more easily be made up with advantage ;
to be sure the presence of the Comforter is able to
do it with an infinite overplus.   It is thy wisdom,
therefore, to balance thy soul with Divine comforts ;
as afflictions abound, run to thy cordial, these words,
that thy consolations may abound also. If the affliction scale be heavier than the consolation scale,
thou wilt certainly sink in thy spirit, and then thy
burden will break thy back : The spirit of a man
is able to sustain his infirmity, Prov. xviii. 14.
Thou mayest mourn, but that is not all thou hast to
do, it concerns thee to get a cordial to keep thy
heart from fainting : " For this cause we faint not,"
2 Cor. iv. 16.   Mark, the apostle had always his
cordial about him ; so do thou, be equally just to
thyself, as to thy deceased friends   Thou owest
them a debt of tears, hast thou paid it ?   Now be
just to thyself ; thou owest a care to thy soul, that
thou sin not, to thy spirit, that it sink not ; must
thou needs die, because thy husband, thy child, thy
friend is dead ?   Look after Divine consolation ; let
it not be a small thing to thee, neither say thou, by

interpretation, Nay, if God will have this comfort from me, let him take all. Take heed of weeping thyself blind, as to the consolations of God, as Hagar did ; there was a well-spring of water close by her, but she had cried out her eyes, and could not see it, Gen. xxi 16, until God opened her eyes, ver. 19. There is too much of the pride and sullenness of the Babylonish favourite in us, who, when he had made a large and boasting recital of his court favours, could throw away all in a pet for want of a complement, " Yet all this availeth me nothing, so long as I see Mordecai the Jew sitting at the king's gate," Esther v. 13.

3. Observe, further, the goodness and condescension of God, who hath laid in comfort beforehand against a time of sorrow and mourning.

God dealeth in this case with his people, just as he dealt with our first parents, providing a plaster beforehand to clap on the wound of conviction of sin, in the promise of the seed of the woman " that should break the serpent's head," Gen. iii. 15. Lest the wound should take cold, fester, and, by delay, prove incurable, all the promises in scripture are but so many receipts written down beforehand in the book of the great Physician of souls for the use of all God's family, the saints of God from the beginning of the world; there are given unto us " exceeding great and precious promises," 2 Pet. i. 4. Thither, therefore, let all God's patients go, and search, and read, and take whatever receipt suiteth best with their malady ; and they shall, rightly applied, find present ease, and infallible cure, in the constant and believing use thereof: " For whatsoever was written aforetime, was written for our

learning, that we through patience and comfort of
the scriptures might have hope," Rom. xv. 4.

4. Here you may see the absolute and indispensable necessity of faith; without which, all the
choicest consolations, and richest cordials the word
can afford, are but so much water of life in a dead
man's mouth, or as Elisha's staff upon the face of
the dead child, 2 Kings iv. 31, which causeth neither
voice nor motion.   " The just shall live by faith,"
Heb. x. 38 ; an unbelieving man is but a dead man ;
for as faith is the first principle of spiritual life, so
it is the constant medium, whereby the spiritual
fuel and restoratives of that life are brought in, and
made vital to the soul.   The word of God is the
" power of God to salvation," Rom. i. 16 ; but it is
to them only who believe.   God hath provided a
cup of consolation for his fainting people in their
swooning fits, but it is the hand of faith that must
take it, and the mouth of faith only that can drink
it.   There is an inexhaustible fulness of comfort in
Christ, and in the promises, but not one drop to be
drawn forth without faith.   A man may as well
live and laugh without a soul, as have true evangelical comfort without faith ; which is the bond of
union between Christ and the soul, and so being
united to the fountain, " Believing, ye rejoice with
joy unspeakable, and full of glory," 1 Pet. i. 8. This
is that golden pipe, through which all the golden
oil of grace and comfort, Zech. iv. 12, is derived
into the heart.   The men of the world may have
vast proportions of knowledge, both natural and
divine, but mere knowledge is light without heat ;
but faith warms the heart, as they said one to another, " Did not our hearts burn within us, while he

talked unto us?" Luke xxiv. 32. If I assent and consent to the glorious doctrine of the resurrection, knowing, with Job, that my Redeemer liveth, &c., I can triumph over all evils that occur, over the grave itself, though it swallow up my dearest relations : if I believe not, I am like a thirsty man at a well without a bucket, where I may sooner drown myself than quench my thirst. Oh get the bucket of faith, and then with joy may ye draw water out of these wells of salvation.

5. Hence we are informed, that it is a special duty of christians, to administer words of comfort to their mourning friends, according to their various temptations and trials. It is the very law of those consolations, wherewith the Holy Ghost doth comfort us in our afflictions, that we may be able to comfort them, which are in any trouble, by the comfort wherewith we ourselves are comforted of God. A lesson, it seemeth, Job's friends had learned, and came to put in practice, when by mutual consent they met together at Job's house, Job ii. 11 ; this was their end, though unhappily they mistook their work, by spicing their cup of consolation with too many bitter ingredients : let their error be our caution. Thus also we read in the gospel of many friends, who came to comfort Martha and Mary concerning their brother.

Christians, your eyes are not your own; we are commanded to rejoice with them that rejoice, and to weep with those that weep. In point of affection, we should be like the primitive christians, have all things in common ; we should joy in our brethren's joys, mourn their sorrows, lament their sufferings, and seek after their comfort as our own, else we turn engrossers ; yea, we become guilty of sacrilege

in robbing one another of Divine treasure; our
comforts are not given us for ourselves only, but for
the afflicted. Saints have a common right one to
another's graces, comforts, and experiences; and
Christ's word should always sound in our ears,
" Strengthen thy brethren." How ornamental were
those christians in the once famous Roman church,
of whom the apostle presumeth, " I myself also am
persuaded of you, my brethren, that ye also are full
of goodness, filled with all knowledge, able also to
admonish one another," Rom. xv. 14. Oh that as
many as do abound in abilities, would pray for wisdom to parcel out those abilities into all the christian offices commended to them by the Holy Ghost
in their several seasons : to warn the unruly, comfort the feeble-minded, support the weak, &c. Oh
how beautiful are the feet of those christians, who
are " ready to every good work," Tit. iii. 1, as the
hand in joint, ready to turn every way for the use
and service of the body! A christian should never
be unfurnished with a reproof for sinners, a word of
comfort for distressed saints. Let none have cause
from thee in their sorrows to complain, as the weeping church in the Lamentations, saying, " There is
none to comfort me." Be not of the sect of the
stony-hearted Levite, who had not one drop of pity
to pour into the wounded traveller, lest thy wounds
another day, as so many mouths, plead for pity to
deaf ears. Hast thou not thyself been comforted in
thy troubles? Hath not Christ made good that
great promise, " I will not leave thee comfortless,
I will come unto thee?" John xiv. 18. How often
have the everlasting arms kept thy soul from sinking! How frequently have the messengers of Christ
refreshed thy weary soul! And hast thou so forgot

those arms of mercy, as not to help thy brother
with thy little finger? Hath God conferred on thee
such treasures of comfort, and hast thou not one
mite to bestow upon thy disconsolate brother?

6. God's words of comfort are the only words of
comfort: God is the God of consolation; "the Father
of mercies, and the God of all comfort," 2 Cor. i. 3:
all comfort doth emanate from God as water out of
the fountain; nothing can be in the stream, but
what was first in the fountain. He is the Father
of mercies; there are no mercies pure and legitimate
but what are from him; no waters are pure and
vital, but those that are fetched out of the fountain:
and therefore those pronouns are very sweet, and
carry the greatest emphasis with them, "Thy comforts delight my soul," Psa. xciv. 19. "My peace
I leave with you," John xiv. 27. It was not all the
honours and pleasures of David's dominions, it was
not all the victories and spoils of his enemies, yea,
it was not all his prayers and tears, though every
night he made his couch swim with them, Psa. vi.,
that could whisper a syllable of comfort to his sin-
scorched conscience, until God himself spake them.
That is the specialty of comfort, which the apostle
begs for his Thessalonians, "Now the Lord of peace
himself, give you peace," 2 Thess. iii. 16. "Now
our Lord Jesus Christ himself, and God even our Father, himself, comfort you," ch. ii. 16. That is right
peace which God himself giveth, and that is true
comfort which Christ himself speaks: therefore
prayeth the holy man, Make me to hear joy and gladness; which denotes, Lord, speak so loud, that I may
hear the voice, and speak so distinctly, that I may
know whose voice it is; that I may know it is thou

thyself that speakest to my soul, that I may say, It is the voice of my Beloved, &c.

It is true, the devil and the world have their counterfeit cordials, their gilded pills and plasters, which make quick cures, but they never really heal; they may for a time stupify the sense, but they do not mortify sensuality; ease the smart, but not cleanse the wound. Saul, when the evil spirit was upon him, calls for a harp; and when God hath forsaken him, he goes to the witch, as if, because God would not answer him, the devil should. Most people have learned a way of their own, some to drink down their sorrow, and sleep out the sense of those breaches, which God hath made upon their relations, or in a crowd of worldly business can lose their sorrows; but, alas, all these are but lying vanities, and will stand men in least stead when they stand in most need of comfort. Oh that men had faith to believe, that all these are physicians of no value. Christ's words are the only words of comfort, Then shall we be ever with the Lord. So our Lord again, " Let not your heart be troubled, ye believe in God, believe also in me; in my Father's house are many mansions," John xiv. 1, 2 : " With thee is the fountain of life, and in thy light we shall see light," Psa. xxxvi. 9. These, these indeed, are apples of gold, which, when they meet with pictures of silver, Prov. xxv. 11, hearts truly capable of such consolation, are very beautiful. " Comfort one another with these words."

7. Hence be we instructed, if it be the duty of christians to administer words of comfort to mourners, then it is also the duty of mourners to open their ears and hearts to receive those words. If God

should send an angel, or any messenger of peace to comfort you in your trouble, what a sin would it be to make him go away ashamed, with an Who hath believed our report? Or, Lord, I have delivered thy message, and all thy precious cordials were of no value. I know there are few or none of God's mourners, who dare do this in express language; but what and if a deaf ear, and a dejected countenance, and a dead heart, and uncheerful conversation, after all the words of comfort which God sends thee by his messengers, be so with God, by interpretation? May not this provoke God to afflict thee more, and to increase thy sorrows, until the pride of thy heart be abated? May I not say unto thee, as Joab to David, when he grew sullen upon the death of Absalom, Thou hast shamed the face of God's messengers, and hast declared, that the consolations of God are small in thine eyes? 2 Sam. xix. 5. Now therefore arise, and thankfully embrace their message of peace, or else it may be worse unto thee, than all the evil that befell thee from thy youth, until now. Surely it is as great an indignity to slight God's comforts, as it is to scorn God's counsels: this spurns against God's authority, that tramples upon his compassion; this man doth resist the Spirit, that man doth grieve the Spirit, and if thou grieve away the Comforter, who shall comfort thee at length? If David took the affront, which Hanun put on his messengers sent to comfort him over his father's death, so heinously, that he armeth Joab, and all his men of war against him, to avenge the indignity, how justly may God send forth armies of afflictions against thee, for thy sullen refusal of his tender-hearted consolations?

Poor disconsolate soul, know thou that every

crumb of comfort, which falls from Christ, is more precious than a ruby ; and who art thou, that thou shouldst refuse cordials from heaven? Jewels taken out of God's own cabinet. Away, away, christian, with Rachel's peevishness, and Jonah's passion, which serve for nothing, but to turn sorrow into sin. I do well to be angry, doth ill become the meekness of Christ's spouse ; say rather, " I will bear the indignation of the Lord, because I have sinned against him," Mic. vii. 9. What if God hath given thee a bitter potion, he comes now to comfort thee, he offers thee a sovereign cordial. Oh, spill it not upon the ground, as a vile thing, nor say in thy passion, Let God keep his cordials to himself, and so, as it were, take revenge on God for afflicting thee. Oh, lay thine hand upon thy mouth, yea, put thy mouth in the dust, that it may not cause thy flesh to sin.

8. In the next place, hence we gather this sad truth, that there is not a word of comfort belonging to wicked men when they die, nor while they live in sin. Comfort one another ; none other but one another: not the ungodly ; they and their parasites may flatter themselves and one another ; but there is not one word of comfort belonging to them : of all those rivers of pleasures that are at God's right hand not one drop for a Dives. Of all those treasures of glory not one mite for an Esau. Indeed pity belongs to wicked men, and reproof belongs to them, " Reprove them rather," Eph. v. 11, and counsel belongs to them, Let the wicked forsake his wickedness : and expostulation belongs to them, Why will ye die ? &c. And prayer belongs to them, Father, forgive them, &c. But comfort doth not belong to them. Consolation is none of their portion in the state wherein they are. As there is no peace to the

wicked, so consequently no comfort for them. In-deed a wicked man hath his portion, but it is a dreadful one; " Upon the wicked shall the Lord rain snares, fire and brimstone, (alluding to the de-struction of Sodom,) this shall be the portion of their cup," Psa. xi. 6 ; these fiery ingredients shall be put into their cup, after the delicious draughts of sinful pleasures : this was the rich man's case, Luke xvi. 23, 24, &c. ; after his delicate fare, flaming fire was his portion for ever ; and this is all the comfort that is to be administered to them. Say thou to the wicked it shall be ill with him, Isa. iii. 11 ; they shall be cast into utter darkness with the devil and his angels for ever, &c. These are their words of comfort ; they are ministers of hell, who have any better words of comfort for wicked men, while wicked : for the devil would have them dance about the snare till their foot be taken in his gin. They that can cry, Peace, peace, when there is no peace, are the devil's factors, who bring him in the greatest revenues to his kingdom.

But alas ! how shall a wicked man be comforted? His death is not a sleep, but death indeed ; death armed with all its horrors, Rev. vi. 8 ; death with its sting, which is sin ; death with hell at the heels of it, death with the wrath of God, and death with the loss of eternal life. Indeed, a wicked man shall rise again, but it is that he may have the more solemn trial, and more tremendous sentence from the Judge, in the face of heaven and earth ; and who can com-fort him, that doth truly represent his condition to him ?

9. How much then are we concerned to labour to be such as may have comforters in our own death, and leave matter of comfort to our surviving friends.

It is a duty incumbent on us, to make our death as comfortable to ourselves and our godly friends, as may be. And how is that done, but, in a word, to get an interest in Christ, scripture evidence of that interest, and the seal of the Spirit to those evidences ?

The death of some persons is exceedingly dreadful, not only to themselves, but to standers by; this is the supposed reason of that lamentable cry of David, O my son Absalom, my son, my son Absalom. Absalom died in his rebellion, I fear he is fallen into a worse hand than Joab's : O that my death might have prevented so dreadful a miscarriage ; O Absalom ! would God I had died for thee !

But alas, my brethren, it is not freedom from such parricidal villanies ; no, nor all the moral innocence in the world, nor civil righteousness in the altitude of it, that can fill a dying saint with joy, or the surviving godly mourners with comfort : whatever blaze unregenerate persons make in the world, they go out like a stinking snuff; but a saint leaves a perfume behind him, he embalms his own death, he leaves every one of his weeping friends a legacy of hope concerning his eternal state ; he sets up a lustre in the house of mourning, brighter than those were with which great men's hearses are watched, and in an instant turneth it into a house of rejoicing ; he is entered into glory, and hath left behind him the prints of his feet to guide us thither; and being dead yet speaks to us, as Christ to Mary Magdalene, Why weepest thou ? " The wicked is driven away in his wickedness, but the righteous hath hope in his death," Prov. xiv. 32. Study therefore, I say, an interest in Christ, that while you are enraptured with the joys of heaven, you may leave comfort on earth for your godly relations.

Carnal friends are satisfied with a negative holiness for themselves, or for their relations that die before them; to be better than the worst is evidence enough to them of a blessed state; or, whatever their life hath been, put but in a little dead repentance into the premises, they will put heaven into the conclusion; Oh, say they, he is happy, he is in heaven sure enough.

But christians, whose eyes have been opened to look into the horror of the bottomless pit, out of which free grace hath redeemed the saints, the purity of the gospel rule, and the glory that shall be revealed at the appearance of the Lord Jesus; they cannot take up with such miserable comforts as men usually die with. And it must needs be an addition to the torments of hell, to leave godly relations mourning under the dreadful apprehensions of a relation miscarrying to all eternity. And to be regardless of our friends' anxiety of spirit even in this respect, is somewhat less charity than they have in hell. Dives in hell was solicitous to prevent his brethren's coming thither.

Graceless relations dying, with the marks of their unregeneracy upon them, do even scorch the hearts of their gracious surviving friends, with the sense of those flames which they suffer.

Therefore, impartially and accurately examine your own estates, make your consciences faithfully to answer this question, Can I give myself or friends comfort in this present state, should I die this very moment? If conscience, assisted with scripture light, say No, this is a lost estate, this is a damnable condition I am now in; oh poor wretch! how highly doth it concern thee this very hour to look about thee! for thou knowest not how near thou art to the last point and period of thine appointed time. It is a vain thing for thee to comfort thyself without some scripture grounds of interest in Christ, who is the resurrection and the life. Paul sends Tychicus to comfort the Colossians, but he must know their state first, that he may comfort their hearts, Col. iv. 8.

We have a generation that comfort others, without knowing their spiritual estate; which is to clap on a plaster without searching the wound; a way to lead men to hell hoodwinked; the spiritual estate must be known before comfort can be well applied. Examine, therefore, and suffer others to examine and search how it is with your souls in relation to Christ and grace; what knowledge, what repentance, what faith, what mortification, what contempt of the world, what love to Christ, what thoughts of the world to come.   If these things be in you and abound, then comfort your hearts; for so an entrance shall be ministered unto you abundantly, into the everlasting kingdom of our Lord and Saviour Jesus Christ.

10. In the last place: hence we are informed how much it concerns every man and woman, that would comfortably observe this blessed command, of administering comfort to himself, or others who are in tribulation; I say, how much it concerns them to search the scriptures. Oh study the scriptures, that magazine and storehouse of all Divine comfort! Especially in the reading of the scriptures, to make a collection of the promises, which are the nests and boxes of Christ's cordials and antidotes against the fainting fits to which believers themselves are subject: there are the soul-refreshing water-brooks, the wells of salvation, ever sending forth streams of

consolation, to make glad the city of God.   Here is
Christ's wine-cellar and banqueting-house, to
which he doth invite his disconsolate spouse, and
where he doth revive her fainting soul, according to
her longing desire; " Stay me with apples, and
comfort me with flagons, for I am sick of love,"
Cant. ii. 5.

What though the scriptures and the promises do
abound with consolation, if we be ignorant and un-
acquainted with the variety, nature, and use of these
heavenly ingredients ; they signify no more to us,
than for a man to be in an apothecary's shop,
fraught with the richest drugs, but he knows not the
boxes where they are laid, nor the virtue of them ;
he and his friends may die in a fit, and miscarry in
the midst of all those preservatives ; or if he venture on them, he may, peradventure, take poison
instead of cordials.   Wherefore study the promises,
and in studying of them, be careful to refer them to
their distinct heads : make yourselves catalogues of
promises, that refer to several soul distresses and
exigencies ; and do as apothecaries, write their titles
over their heads :—promises for pardon, promises
for power against corruption, promises for comfort,
prison promises, sick-bed promises, promises relating to the loss of gracious relations, &c.   I say, be
careful skilfully to sort your promises, that you may
know whither to go when you repair to the scriptures, and may not administer mistaken ingredients,
corrosives instead of cordials, as Job's friends did ;
nor cordials instead of corrosives, as the generality
of ignorant christians do.

Labour to know to which of the offices of Christ
every promise doth relate ; which to his kingly office,
as the promises of grace, and increase of grace, and

power against temptation, the conquering of death, and the fear of death : which belong to his prophetical office, as promises of knowing God, and Christ, and the Spirit; promises of being taught of God ; inward, powerful, experimental knowledge ; what promises belong to his priestly office, as promises of reconciliation to God, peace with God, acceptance of the person and performances, peace of conscience, joy in the Holy Ghost, comfort in the loss of sweetest relations : and this will be of great use to enable you in prayer to plead the promises, and to put them in suit in the proper office ; a great honour to Christ, and a mighty help and encouragement to faith.

Pray for the Spirit, whose office is to make good the promises to the children of promise, and upon that account called the Comforter; the promises are never comfort until the Spirit apply them to the conscience, and then they are cordials indeed, whether to ourselves or others ; then they are full of life and power, and can with one taste comfort more than all the arguments of philosophy in the world.

And verily, christians, as all the cordials in scripture are no cordials, until they are applied to the conscience by a powerful hand, and breathed into the soul by the warm vital animation of the Spirit of God to know it ; you are physicians of no value in this great work of comforting one another, until you learn to join the words of prayer with the words of comfort ; until by prayer you call in the presence and power of the Comforter, who only is able to make these words to be so many real consolations. Amen.

London : Printed by W. CLOWES, Duke-street, Lambeth.